ANNUAL EDI

World Politics 09/10
Thirtieth Edition

EDITOR

Helen E. Purkitt
United States Naval Academy

Dr. Helen E. Purkitt obtained her PhD in International Relations from the University of Southern
California. She is Professor of Political Science at the U.S. Naval Academy. Her research and
teaching interests include political psychology, African politics, and emerging national security
issues. Currently, she is coordinating a study of transnational illicit networks operating in or through
Africa. Last year she completed a study of ways to enhance African security through eco-tourism
and co-directed a project that constructed a semantic wiki data base of geographical areas or 'black
holes' worldwide where Jihadist terrorism may be operating. Past research findings about emerging
security threats tied to dual use technology are summarized in an article she wrote with V.G. Wells
entitled, "Evolving Bioweapon Threats Require New Counter-measures. The article, published in
the October 6, 2006 edition of *The Chronicle of Higher Education,* is reprinted in this volume of
Annual Editions: World Politics 09/10. Another well-known work is a co-authored book entitled,
South Africa's Weapons of Mass Destruction, which is available from Indiana University Press. She
has published dozens of peer-review monographs and articles, along with serving as an expert for
60 Minutes and other media forums.

 **Higher Education**

Boston   Burr Ridge, IL   Dubuque, IA   New York   San Francisco   St. Louis
Bangkok   Bogotá   Caracas   Kuala Lumpur   Lisbon   London   Madrid   Mexico City
Milan   Montreal   New Delhi   Santiago   Seoul   Singapore   Sydney   Taipei   Toronto

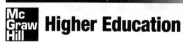

The McGraw·Hill Companies

Higher Education

ANNUAL EDITIONS: WORLD POLITICS, THIRTIETH EDITION

Annual Editions® is a registered trademark of the McGraw-Hill Companies, Inc.

Annual Editions is published by the **Contemporary Learning Series** group within the McGraw-Hill Higher Education division.

1 2 3 4 5 6 7 8 9 0 QPD/QPD 0 9

ISBN 978–0–07–812760–1
MHID 0–07–812760–2
ISSN 1098–0300

Managing Editor: *Larry Loeppke*
Senior Managing Editor: *Faye Schilling*
Developmental Editor: *Dave Welsh*
Editorial Coordinator: *Mary Foust*
Editorial Assistant: *Nancy Meissner*
Production Service Assistant: *Rita Hingtgen*
Permissions Coordinator: *DeAnna Dausener*
Senior Marketing Manager: *Julie Keck*
Marketing Communications Specialist: *Mary Klein*
Marketing Coordinator: *Alice Link*
Project Manager: *Sandy Wille*
Senior Production Supervisor: *Laura Fuller*
Cover Graphics: *Kristine Jubeck*

Compositor: Laserwords Private Limited
Cover Image: Department of Defense photo by Lt. Cmdr. John Gay (inset), Department of Defense (background)

Library in Congress Cataloging-in-Publication Data
Main entry under title: Annual Editions: World Politics. 2009/2010.
 1. World Politics—Periodicals. I. Purkitt, Helen, *comp.* II. Title: World Politics.
658'.05

www.mhhe.com

Editors/Advisory Board

Members of the Advisory Board are instrumental in the final selection of articles for each edition of ANNUAL EDITIONS. Their review of articles for content, level, currentness, and appropriateness provides critical direction to the editor and staff. We think that you will find their careful consideration well reflected in this volume.

Preface

In publishing ANNUAL EDITIONS we recognize the enormous role played by the magazines, newspapers, and journals of the public press in providing current, first-rate educational information in a broad spectrum of interest areas. Many of these articles are appropriate for students, researchers, and professionals seeking accurate, current material to help bridge the gap between principles and theories and the real world. These articles, however, become more useful for study when those of lasting value are carefully collected, organized, indexed, and reproduced in a low-cost format, which provides easy and permanent access when the material is needed. That is the role played by ANNUAL EDITIONS.

*A*nnual Editions: World Politics 09/10 is aimed at filling a void in materials for learning about world politics and foreign policy. The articles are chosen for those who are new to the study of world politics. The goal is to help students learn more about international issues that often seem remote but may have profound consequences for a nation's well-being, security, and survival.

International relations can be viewed as a complex and dynamic system of actions and reactions by a diverse set of actors. The articles in this volume convey just how dynamic, interdependent, and complex the relations among different types of international actors are in contemporary international relations. Once, the international system was dominated by nation-states. Today's system looks more like a cobweb of nation-states, international governmental, non-governmental organizations (NGOs), and a host of legal and illicit transnational networks (e.g., terrorist and criminal groups) that span continents and are highly adaptive in terms of their base of operations and modus operandi.

Increased globalization means that events in places as far away as Latin America, Asia, the Middle East, and Africa may effect the United States, just as America's actions—and inaction—have significant repercussions for other states. Interdependence also refers to the increased role of non-state actors such as multinational corporations, the United Nations, and a rich array of non-governmental actors such as the Cable News Network (CNN) and terrorist networks affiliated with or inspired by al Qaeda.

The September 11, 2001 terrorist attack on the World Trade Towers and the Pentagon tragically underscored the reality that non-state actors increasingly influence the scope, nature, and pace of events worldwide. However, the U.S.-led military interventions in Afghanistan in 2002, the U.S. military invasion of Iraq in 2003, the continuing fight between U.S. troops and insurgents in Iraq, the escalation of tensions between the United States and Iran, and ongoing conflicts among countries throughout the world confirm that inter-state conflicts will also continue as a key feature of international relations. At the same time, the rapid spread of the SARS epidemic in 2004, the continuing spread of new HIV/AIDS infections worldwide, the large number of deaths and devastation caused by the South Asia Tsunami tidal wave in 2005, and the continuing threat of a future global pandemic caused by a mutated flu virus remind us that natural disasters can also have wide ranging effects on world politics as well. A report by eleven retired senior military officials to the Center for Naval Analysis (CNA) think tank in 2007 warning that climate change will effect all aspects of the United States' national security defense readiness was another indicator that global warming is continuing. The CNA report was also a timely reminder that there are global security threats that may increasingly threaten the security and well-being of citizens living in nation-states in both the developing and developed world.

The rapidity with which the current financial crisis developed and quickly spread worldwide to become the worse economic slowdown since the 1930 depression surprised many foreign policy and economic experts. The economic crises that continue to adversely impact countries worldwide remind us of just how interdependent countries and citizens are in different parts of the world in a globalized system. The growing awareness of the implications of climate change and the impact of the contemporary international economic crises has also heightened awareness of just how tightly coupled national security, human security, and collective security concerns have become in the 21st Century.

Since international events proceed at such a rapid pace that what is said about international affairs today may be outdated by tomorrow, it is important for readers to develop a mental framework or theory of the international system. The collection of articles in this volume about international events provides up-to-date information, commentaries about the current set of issues on the world agenda, and analyses of the significance of the issues and emerging trends for the structure and functioning of the post—Cold War international system.

The thirtieth edition of *Annual Editions: World Politics* is divided into 11 units. While the United States remains the dominant military, political, and economic power in the post-Cold War system, indicators of an emerging multipolar system are everywhere. Complex trends in the current structure of the international system mean that we can no longer view international relations through a prism where the United States is considered the one lone superpower across all issue areas. Instead, subnational, national, regional, and transnational issues and actors are increasingly important aspects of international relations in a multidimensional world system.

I would like to thank Larry Loeppke, David Welsh, and their associates at McGraw-Hill Contemporary Learning Series for their help in putting this volume together. Many users of *Annual Editions: World Politics* took the time to contribute articles and comments on this collection of readings. I greatly appreciate these suggestions and the article evaluations. Please continue to provide feedback to guide the annual revision of this anthology by filling out the postage-paid *article rating form* on the last page of this book.

Helen Purkitt

Helen E. Purkitt
Editor

Contents

UNIT 1
The International System and Changing World Order of the Twenty-First Century

The concepts in bold italics are developed in the article. For further expansion, please refer to the Topic Guide.

UNIT 2
Managing Interstate Conflicts and the Proliferation of Weapons

The concepts in bold italics are developed in the article. For further expansion, please refer to the Topic Guide.

UNIT 3
Foreign Policy Decision Making

UNIT 4
Great Power Interstate Conflicts and Rivalries

The concepts in bold italics are developed in the article. For further expansion, please refer to the Topic Guide.

UNIT 5
North-South Interstate Conflicts and Rivalries

UNIT 6
Conflicts among Nation-States in the Global South, Sub-National Conflicts, and the Role of Non-State Actors in an Interdependent World

The concepts in bold italics are developed in the article. For further expansion, please refer to the Topic Guide.

UNIT 7
Asymmetric Conflicts: Trends in Terrorism and Counterterrorism

The concepts in bold italics are developed in the article. For further expansion, please refer to the Topic Guide.

UNIT 8
Contemporary Foreign Policy Debates

UNIT 9
International Organizations, International Law, and Global Governance

The concepts in bold italics are developed in the article. For further expansion, please refer to the Topic Guide.

UNIT 10
The International Economic System

UNIT 11
Globalizing Issues

The concepts in bold italics are developed in the article. For further expansion, please refer to the Topic Guide.

Correlation Guide

The *Annual Editions* series provides students with convenient, inexpensive access to current, carefully selected articles from the public press. **Annual Editions: World Politics 09/10** is an easy-to-use reader that presents articles on important topics such as *interstate conflicts and weapons proliferation, foreign policy, great power rivalries, terrorism,* and many more. For more information on *Annual Editions* and other *McGraw-Hill Contemporary Learning Series* titles, visit www.mhcls.com.

This convenient guide matches the units in **Annual Editions: World Politics 09/10** with the corresponding chapters in two of our best-selling McGraw-Hill Political Science textbooks by Rourke and Rourke/Boyer.

Annual Editions: World Politics 09/10	International Politics on the World Stage, 12/e by Rourke	International Politics on the World Stage, Brief, 8/e by Rourke/Boyer
Unit 1: The International System and Changing World Order of the Twenty-First Century	**Chapter 2:** The Evolution of World Politics **Chapter 5:** Globalism: The Alternative Orientation **Chapter 15:** Preserving and Enhancing the Biosphere	**Chapter 2:** The Evolution of World Politics **Chapter 5:** Globalization: The Alternative Orientation **Chapter 12:** Preserving and Enhancing the Biosphere
Unit 2: Managing Interstate Conflicts and the Proliferation of Weapons	**Chapter 8:** National Power and Statecraft: The Traditional Approach **Chapter 9:** International Law and Justice: An Alternative Approach **Chapter 10:** National Security: The Traditional Road **Chapter 11:** International Security: The Alternative Road	**Chapter 8:** International Law and Human Rights **Chapter 9:** Pursuing Security
Unit 3: Foreign Policy Decision Making	**Chapter 3:** Levels of Analysis and Foreign Policy **Chapter 9:** International Law and Justice: An Alternative Approach **Chapter 10:** National Security: The Traditional Road **Chapter 11:** International Security: The Alternative Road	**Chapter 3:** Levels of Analysis and Foreign Policy **Chapter 5:** Globalization: The Alternative Orientation **Chapter 8:** International Law and Human Rights **Chapter 9:** Pursuing Security **Chapter 11:** International Economics: The Alternative Road
Unit 4: Great Power Interstate Conflicts and Rivalries	**Chapter 9:** International Law and Justice: An Alternative Approach **Chapter 11:** International Security: The Alternative Road	**Chapter 9:** Pursuing Security **Chapter 11:** International Economics: The Alternative Road
Unit 5: North-South Interstate Conflicts and Rivalries	**Chapter 9:** International Law and Justice: An Alternative Approach **Chapter 11:** International Security: The Alternative Road **Chapter 12:** National Economic Competition: The Traditional Road **Chapter 13:** International Economic Cooperation: The Alternative Road	**Chapter 2:** The Evolution of World Politics **Chapter 8:** International Law and Human Rights **Chapter 9:** Pursuing Security **Chapter 11:** International Economics: The Alternative Road
Unit 6: Conflicts among Nation-States in the Global South, Sub-National Conflicts, and the Role of Non-State Actors in an Interdependent World	**Chapter 8:** National Power and Statecraft: The Traditional Approach **Chapter 9:** International Law and Justice: An Alternative Approach **Chapter 11:** International Security: The Alternative Road **Chapter 13:** International Economic Cooperation: The Alternative Road	**Chapter 2:** The Evolution of World Politics **Chapter 8:** International Law and Human Rights **Chapter 9:** Pursuing Security **Chapter 11:** International Economics: The Alternative Road
Unit 7: Asymmetric Conflicts: Trends in Terrorism and Counterterrorism	**Chapter 10:** National Security: The Traditional Road **Chapter 11:** International Security: The Alternative Road	**Chapter 8:** International Law and Human Rights **Chapter 9:** Pursuing Security
Unit 8: Contemporary Foreign Policy Debates	**Chapter 1:** Thinking and Caring about World Politics **Chapter 2:** The Evolution of World Politics **Chapter 3:** Levels of Analysis and Foreign Policy	**Chapter 1:** Thinking and Caring about World Politics **Chapter 2:** The Evolution of World Politics **Chapter 3:** Levels of Analysis and Foreign Policy
Unit 9: International Organizations, International Law, and Global Governance	**Chapter 2:** The Evolution of World Politics **Chapter 5:** Globalism: The Alternative Orientation **Chapter 7:** Intergovernmental Organizations: Alternative Governance **Chapter 9:** International Law and Justice: An Alternative Approach **Chapter 11:** International Security: The Alternative Road **Chapter 14:** Preserving and Enhancing Human Rights and Dignity	**Chapter 7:** Intergovernmental Organizations: Alternative Governance **Chapter 8:** International Law and Human Rights **Chapter 11:** International Economics: The Alternative Road
Unit 10: The International Economic System	**Chapter 13:** International Economic Cooperation: The Alternative Road	**Chapter 11:** International Economics: The Alternative Road
Unit 11: Globalizing Issues	**Chapter 5:** Globalism: The Alternative Orientation **Chapter 7:** Intergovernmental Organizations: Alternative Governance **Chapter 9:** International Law and Justice: An Alternative Approach **Chapter 14:** Preserving and Enhancing Human Rights and Dignity **Chapter 15:** Preserving and Enhancing the Biosphere	**Chapter 5:** Globalization: The Alternative Orientation **Chapter 7:** Intergovernmental Organizations: Alternative Governance **Chapter 8:** International Law and Human Rights **Chapter 11:** International Economics: The Alternative Road **Chapter 12:** Preserving and Enhancing the Biosphere

Topic Guide

This topic guide suggests how the selections in this book relate to the subjects covered in your course. You may want to use the topics listed on these pages to search the Web more easily.

On the following pages a number of Web sites have been gathered specifically for this book. They are arranged to reflect the units of this Annual Editions reader. You can link to these sites by going to *http://www.mhcls.com.*

All the articles that relate to each topic are listed below the bold-faced term.

Internet References

The following Internet sites have been selected to support the articles found in this reader. These sites were available at the time of publication. However, because Web sites often change their structure and content, the information listed may no longer be available. We invite you to visit http://www.mhcls.com for easy access to these sites.

Annual Editions: World Politics 09/10

General Sources

Central Intelligence Agency
http://www.odci.gov

Use this official home page to learn about many facets of the CIA and to get connections to other sites and resources, such as *The CIA Factbook,* which provides extensive statistical information about every country in the world.

CIA Factbook
https://www.cia.gov/cia/publications/factbook/index.html

This site provides information on various countries.

Country Indicators for Foreign Policy
http://www.carleton.ca/cifp/

Statistical data on nation-states compiled by Carlton University, Canada.

Ilike2learn.com
http://www.ilike2learn.com/ilike2learn/geography.asp

Interactive geography quizzes to help learn the locations of the countries and capitals of the world, along with important bodies of water and mountain ranges in the world.

Social Science Information Gateway
http://sosig.esrc.bris.ac.uk

A project of the Economic and Social Research Council (ESRC), this is an online catalog of thousands of Internet resources relevant to political education and research.

World Wide Web Virtual Library: International Affairs Resources
http://www.etown.edu/vl/

Surf this site and its links to learn about specific countries and regions, to research think tanks and organizations, and to study such vital topics as international law, development, the international economy, human rights, and peacekeeping.

Crisisweb: The International Crisis Group (ICG)
http://www.crisisweb.org/home/index.cfm

ICG is an organization "committed to strengthening the capacity of the international community to anticipate, understand, and act to prevent and contain conflict." Go to this site to view the latest reports and research concerning conflicts around the world.

IIMCR Institute for International Mediation and Conflict Resolution
http://www.iimcr.org

Programs, including training to become international mediators, publications, online resources related to conflicts, terrorism, and counter-terrorism.

UNIT 1: The International System and Changing World Order of the Twenty-First Century

The Globalization Website
http://www.emory.edu/SOC/globalization/

This site discusses globalization and is a guide to available sources on globalization.

Images of the social and political world
http://www-personal.umich.edu/~mejn/cartograms/

Cartograms showing different aspects of world Nation-states on basis of population, GNP, HIV-AIDS, greenhouse gases, and more. Created by Mark Newman, Department of Physics and the Center for the Study of Complex Systems, University of Michigan.

National Security and the Threat of Climate Change
http://www.npr.org/documents/2007/apr/security_climate.pdf

Report issued by eleven retired senior military officials in 2007 to the Center for Naval Analysis warning that climate change will effect all aspects of the United States' defense readiness.

Population Reference Bureau
http://www.prb.org

This site provides data on the world population and census information.

Women in International Politics
http://www.guide2womenleaders.com

This site contains data on women who have served as political leaders.

Avalon Project at Yale Law School
http://www.yale.edu/lawweb/avalon/terrorism/terror.htm

The Avalon Project Web site features documents in the fields of law, history, economics, diplomacy, politics, government, and terrorism.

UNIT 2: Managing Interstate Conflicts and the Proliferation of Weapons

U.S. Department of State
http://www.state.gov/index.cfm

The site provides information organized by categories as well as "background notes" on specific countries and regions.

Belfer Center for Science and International Affairs (BCSIA)
http://www.ksg.harvard.edu/bcsia/

BCSIA is a center for research, teaching, and training in international affairs.

FACTs
http://www.ploughshares.ca

Useful site for research on inter-state conflicts.

U.S.- Russia Developments
http://www.acronym.org.uk/start

This is a site maintained by Acronym Institute for Disarmament Diplomacy which provides information on U.S. and Russian disarmament activity.

The Bulletin of the Atomic Scientists
http://www.bullatomsci.org

This site allows you to read more about the Doomsday Clock and other issues as well as topics related to nuclear weaponry, arms control, and disarmament.

Internet References

Federation of American Scientists
http://www.fas.org

This site provides useful information about and links to a variety of topics related to chemical and biological warfare, missiles, conventional arms, and terrorism.

UNIT 3: Foreign Policy Decision Making

Carnegie Endowment for International Peace
http://www.ceip.org

One of the goals of this organization is to stimulate discussion and learning among experts and the public on a wide range of international issues. The site provides links to the journal *Foreign Policy* and to the Moscow Center.

The Heritage Foundation
http://www.heritage.org

This page offers discussion about and links to many sites of the Heritage Foundation and other organizations having to do with foreign policy and foreign affairs.

UNIT 4: Great Power Interstate Conflicts and Rivalries

Archive of European Integration
http://aei.pitt.edu/

The Archive of European Integration (AEI) is an electronic repository and archive for research materials on the topic of European integration and unification. The site contains official European Community/European Union documents and certain independently-produced research materials.

ISN International Relations and Security Network
http://www.isn.ethz.ch

This site, maintained by the Center for Security Studies and Conflict Research, is a clearinghouse for extensive information on international relations and security policy.

The Henry L. Stimson Center—Peace Operations and Europe
http://www.stimson.org/fopo/?SN=FP20020610372

The Future of Peace Operations has begun to address specific areas concerning Europe and operations. The site links to useful UN, NATO, and EU documents, research pieces, and news sites.

Central Europe Online
http://www.centraleurope.com

This site contains daily updated information under headings such as news on the Web today, economics, trade, and currency.

Europa: European Union
http://europa.eu.int

This server site of the European Union will lead you to the history of the EU (and its predecessors), descriptions of EU policies, institutions, and goals, and documentation of treaties and other materials.

NATO Integrated Data Service
http://www.nato.int/structur/nids/nids.htm

Check out this Web site to review North Atlantic Treaty Organization documentation, to read *NATO Review,* and to explore key issues in the field of European security and transatlantic cooperation.

Russia Today
http://www.russiatoday.com

This site includes headline news, resources, government, politics, election results, and pressing issues.

Russian and East European Network Information Center, University of Texas at Austin
http://reenic.utexas.edu/reenic/index.html

This is *the* Web site for information on the former Soviet Union.

Inside China Today
http://www.insidechina.com

Part of the European Internet Network, this site leads you to information on all of China, including recent news, government, and related sites.

Japan Ministry of Foreign Affairs
http://www.mofa.go.jp

Visit this official site for Japanese foreign policy statements and press releases, archives, and discussions of regional and global relations.

UNIT 5: North-South Interstate Conflicts and Rivalries

National Defense University Website
http://www.ndu.edu

This contains information on current studies. This site also provides a look at the school where many senior marine, naval officers, and senior civilians attend prior to assuming top-level positions.

The North American Institute
http://www.northamericaninstitute.org

NAMI, a trinational public-affairs organization, is concerned with the emerging "regional space" of Canada, the United States, and Mexico and the development of a North American community. It provides links for study of trade, the environment, and institutional developments.

Inter-American Dialogue
http://www.iadialog.org

This is the Web site for IAD, a premier U.S. center for policy analysis, communication, and exchange in Western Hemisphere affairs. The 100-member organization has helped to shape the agenda of issues and choices in hemispheric relations.

African Center for Strategic Studies (ACSS)
http://www.africacenter.org/Dev2Go.web?Anchor=acss_home_currentheadlines

The ACSS is a U.S. Dept. of Defense Initiative and component of the National Defense University established to promote security cooperation between the United States and African states. The Africa Center includes headlines drawn from media outlets around the globe that include the most important news affecting Africa today.

Observatory of Cultural Policies in Africa (OCPA)
http://ocpa.irmo.hr/resources/index-en.html

The OCPA Secretariat web page, Maputo, Mozambique contains links to African cultural politics and other relevant documentations, such as working papers, reports, and recommendations.

Internet References

United States Africa Command (AFRICOM)
http://www.africom.mil/

Official site of AFRICOM, led by General William E. Ward. The site includes transcripts and documents, news articles, Africa-Related links and frequency asked questions, including about employment with AFRICOM.

UNIT 6: Conflicts among Nation-States in the Global South, Sub-National Conflicts and the Role of Non-State Actors in an Interdependent World

Pajhwok Afghan News
http://www.pajhwak.com/

This site is Afghanistan's premier news agency offering the best on-the-ground coverage of economics, politics, and security by local reporters.

ei: Electronic Intifada
http://electronicintifada.net/new.shtml

EI is a major Palestinian portal for information about the Palestinian-Israeli conflict from a Palestinian perspective.

IslamiCity
http://islamicity.com

This is one of the largest Islamic sites on the Web, reaching 50 million people a month. Based in California, it includes public opinion polls, links to television and radio broadcasts, and religious guidance.

Palestine-Israel—American Task Force on Palestine
http://www.americantaskforce.org

The American Task Force on Palestine (ATFP) is a non-partisan organization dedicated to bringing peace to the Middle East.

Private Military Companies (Mercenaries)
http://www.bicc.de/pmc/links.php

Web site developed by the Bonn International Center for Conversion (BICC) Bonn, Germany to facilitate search for the most important (online) articles dealing with PMCs classified into a few key issues. It provides a wide range of information on all sectors concerning PMCs as well as a list of PMC-Websites. The list is arranged by the names of the articles, not the authors, because most of the contributions were found by the title.

Kubatana.net
http://www.kubatana.net

A vitual community of Zimbabwean activities who have formed the NGO Network Alliance Project. The project aims to improve the accessibility of human rights and civic information in Zimbabwe.

African News Services

AllAfrica.com
http://allafrica.com/

News 24
http://news.24.com/

Afrrican Resources

Columbia University Library Africa Studies Resources
http://www.cc.columbia.edu/cu/libraries/indiv/area/Africa/

Indiana University African Studies Center
http://www.indiana.edu/~afrist/

Northwestern University Program of African Studies
http://nuinfo.nwu.edu/african-studies/

Stanford University Guide to Internet Resoures for Africa South of the Sahara
http://www-sul.stanford.edu/depts/ssrg/africa/guide.html

University of Illinois, Urbana-Champaign, African Studies Center
http://www.afrst.uiuc.edu/

University of Pennsylvania African Studies Center
http://www.sas.upenn.edu/African_Studies/AS

University of Wisconsin, Madison, African Studies Center
http://www.wisc.edu/afr/

UNIT 7: Asymmetric Conflicts: Trends in Terrorism and Counter-Terrorism

Columbia International Affairs Online
http://www.ciaonet.org/cbr/cbr00/video/cbr_v/cbr_v.html

At this site find excerpts from al Qaeda's 2-hour videotape used to recruit young Muslims to fight in a holy war. The tape demonstates al Qaeda's use of the Internet and media outlets for propaganda and persuasion purposes.

Combating Terrorism Center at West Point
http://ctc.usma.edu/

Offers original analyses, translations of al Qaeda documents, and gateway to other terrorism research and government sites (http://ctc.usma.edu/gateway.asp)

SITE: The Search for International Terrorist Entities
http://www.siteinstitute.org/index.html

This is a site that includes background, current events, and web sites about or sponsored by terrorist groups.

Terrorism Research Center
http://www.terrorism.com

The Terrorism Research Center features definitions and research on terrorism, counterterrorism documents, a comprehensive list of Web links, and profiles of terrorist and counterterrorist groups.

United States Government Counterinsurgency Initiative
http://www.usgcoin.org/

Describes activities and papers from recent conference on U.S. Counterinsurgency activities.

UNIT 8: Contemporary Foreign Policy Debates

Iraq Web Links
http://www.usip.org/library/regions/iraq.html

This is a special web page of the United States Institute of Peace which includes general resources, NBC weapons, government agencies and international organizations, maps and guides, and other resources.

Iraq Dispatches
http://dahrjamailiraq.com

Dahr Jamail, an "unembedded journalist," accounts of conditions in Iraq and provides an alternative view to reports by reporters who are embedded with U.S. troops in Iraq. Jamail's dispatches are distributed through Alternet, a web-based independent media organization.

Internet References

ArabNet
http://www.arab.net

This page of ArabNet, the online resource for the Arab world in the Middle East and North Africa, presents links to 22 Arab countries. Each country page classfies information using a standardized system.

UNIT 9: International Organizations, International Law, and Global Governance

The Digital Library in International Conflict Management
http://www.usip.org/library/diglib.html

This link contains peace agreements and truth commissions from around the world.

InterAction
http://www.interaction.org

InterAction encourages grassroots action, engages policy makers on advocacy issues, and uses this site to inform people on its initiatives to expand international humanitarian relief and development assistance programs.

IRIN
http://www.irinnews.org

The UN Office for the Coordination of Humanitarian Affairs provides free analytical reports, fact sheets, interviews, daily country updates, and weekly summaries through this site and e-mail distribution service. The site is a good source of news for crisis situations as they occur.

International Court of Justice (ICJ)
http://www.icj-cij.org/

Seeks to resolve matters of international law disputed by state governments. General information, World Court decisions, and other resources.

United Nations
http://untreaty.un.org

This site contains text on over 30,000 UN treaties.

United Nations Home Page
http://www.un.org

Here is the gateway to information about the United Nations. Also see http://www.undp.org/missions/usa/usna/htm for the U.S. Mission at the UN.

Human Rights Web
http://www.hrweb.org

This useful site offers ideas on how individuals can get involved in helping to protect human rights around the world.

United Nations Peacekeeping Home Page
http://www.un.org/Depts/dpko/dpko/

Summaries past and current UN peacekeeping operations.

"A More Secure World: Our Shared Responsibility"
http://www.un.org/secureworld

Report delivered to Secretary General Kofi Annan in December, 2004 that contains 101 recommendations regarding how to change the United Nations.

Global Policy Forum
http://www.globalpolicy.org/

Monitors several different United Nation policy initiatives and programs to evalue the effectiveness of such programs and to promote "accountability of global decisions." Visitors who know what types of material they are looking for will want to search through the headings which include such themes as globalization, international justice, and UN reform. Each one of these sections contains a brief essay on their work, along with a smattering of reports, tables, and charts that highlight their analyses, past and present.

Amnesty International
http://www.amnesty.org/

A non-governmental organization that is working to promote human rights and individual liberties worldwide.

UNIT 10: The International Economic System

Kiva
http://www.kiva.org/

Kiva lets indiviuals make small loans for as little as $25 to a specific entrepreneur in the developing world so they can try to lift themselves out of poverty.

PeaceParkFoundation
http://www.peaceparks.org/

A private foundation to promote transfrontier conservation areas in southern Africa, including training Africans to become wildlife rangers. The organization works closely with the Southern African Development Organization (SADO) to help implement additional or plan new cross-border parks.

Transparency International
http://www.transparency.org/

Transparency International is the global civil society organisation leading the fight against corruption. TI publishes an annual International Corruption and International Bribery that ranks nation-states in terms of the extent of corruption and bribery occurring in each country.

The Earth Institute at Columbia University
http://www.earth.columbia.edu/

The Earth Institute at Columbia University, led by Professor Jeffrey D. Sachs, is dedicated to addressing a number of complex issues related to sustainable development and the needs of the world's poor.

International Monetary Fund
http://www.imf.org

This link brings you to the homepage for the International Monetary Fund.

Graphs Comparing Countries
http://humandevelopment.bu.edu/use_exsisting_index/start_comp_graph.cfm

This site allows you to compare various countries and nation-states with statistics using a visual tool.

Internet References

World Bank
http://www.worldbank.org

News (press releases, summaries of new projects, speeches) and coverage of numerous topics regarding development, countries, and regions are provided at this site. Go to the research and growth section of this site to access specific research and data regarding the world economy.

World Trade Organization
http://www.wto.org/

World Mapper Project
http://www.sasi.group.shef.ac.uk/worldmapper/

This page offers a collection of world maps, where territories are sized to reflect basic data from as recently as 2006.

UNIT 11: Globalizing Issues

CIA Report of the National Intelligence Council's 2020 Project
http://www.cia.gov/nic/NIC_globaltrend2020.html

This link contains the full text of the most recent CIA-sponsored 2020 Project Report on future global trends.

Commonwealth Forum on Globalization and Health
http://www.ukglobalhealth.org

This web site is sponsored by the Commonwealth Secretariat. Launched in April 2004, the Commonwealth Forum consists of a number of articles and excerpts on various facets of globablization and health.

The 11thHOURACTION.COM
http://www.11thhouraction.com/

Web resource page based on the same topics as are covered in the movie. Page includes recent articles, information, blog, and action meetups based on a map, and forums focused on various environmental issues related to climate change.

Greenpeace International
http://www.greenpeace.org/international/

"Greenpeace exists because this fragle Earth deserves a voice. It needs solutions. It needs change. It needs actions. Web site details recent environmental news related to climate changes and "greenpeace victories."

Commission on Global Governance
http://www.sovereignty.net/p/gov/gganalysis.htm

This site provides access to *The Report of the Commission on Global Governance,* produced by an international group of leaders who want to find ways in which the global community can better manage its affairs.

Global Trends 2005 Project
http://www.csis.org/gt2005/sumreport.html

The Center for Strategic and International Studies explores the coming global trends and challenges of the new millenium. Read their summary report at this web site. Also access Enterprises for the Environment, Global Information Infrastructure Commission, and Americas at this site.

HIV/AIDS
http://www.unaids.org

This is a site giving information on the rising toll of HIV/AIDS.

RealClimate
http://www.realclimate.org/

Site contains reports by climate scientists and recent events related to global warming and information about recent severe climate events.

UNIT 1

The International System and Changing World Order of the Twenty-First Century

Unit Selections

Key Points to Consider

- Which countries are likely to be the most dominant in a multi-polar world?

- Are independent nation-states likely to remain the most important factor in international relations or will national sovereignty be subverted or even replaced by other factors?

- Explain why you agree or disagree with the conclusion that China and India are both rising national powers who must be incorporated into the international system

- Which country, China or India, do you believe will become the dominant economic power in Asia?

- Will increased pollution and environmental degradation force China to become more or less democratic in the future?

- Why do you agree or disagree with Friedman's thesis that the United States can regain its international stature by taking the lead role in developing alternative energy production and implementing green policies designed to protect the environment?

Student Web Site
www.mhcls.com

Internet References

The Globalization Website
   http://www.emory.edu/SOC/globalization/
Images of the social and political world
   http://www-personal.umich.edu/~mejn/cartograms/
National Security and the Threat of Climate Change
   http://www.npr.org/documents/2007/apr/security_climate.pdf
Population Reference Bureau
   http://www.prb.org
Women in International Politics
   http://www.guide2womenleaders.com
Avalon Project at Yale Law School
   http://www.yale.edu/lawweb/avalon/terrorism/terror.htm

After the demise of the Cold War, the International System was often characterized as a unipolar system dominated by the United States. However, notions that a Pax Americana meant that Americans could take their national security for granted were quickly dashed by the September 11, 2001 terrorist attacks. The United States' retaliatory attack on Taliban forces in Afghanistan, the U.S. military invasion of Iraq, and the quick initial military victories by U.S. forces, led many observers to predict that U.S. military strength would be the determining factor in the outcome of armed conflicts for years.

However, as sectarian fighting in Iraq degenerated into civil war and the Taliban regrouped and increased their attacks against NATO forces in Southern Afghanistan, more analysts reluctantly concluded that earlier generations of counterinsurgency writers were correct in emphasizing that guerrilla wars were brutal, nasty, and long affairs. Over time, there was an acceptance on the part of the U.S. administration that it is impossible to win a guerrilla war without simultaneously implementing programs designed to win the hearts and minds of the populous.

By mid-2007, the United States had deployed additional troops as part of a military surge and started new civil affairs projects in Iraq. These programs succeeded in restoring more security and stability to many areas. U.S. progress resulted from efforts on the part of U.S. military commanders to forge alliances with local leaders, to support and pay local militias who helped drive out al Qaeda cells from several communities in Iraq, and to allow local militias to play a greater role in maintaining order in certain areas. During the same period, the frequency and seriousness of threats posed by Taliban and al Qaeda-led forces increased in many parts of Afghanistan. Most observers expect U.S. forces deployed in Afghanistan to increase in coming years.

The historic election of the first African-American to the American Presidency, Barak Obama, in November of 2008, was widely watched and celebrated throughout the world. President-elect Obama, a liberal, junior senator from Illinois, campaigned on a platform that included a promise to withdraw U.S. military troops in Iraq, close the Guantanamo prison in Cuba, rely more on multilateral diplomacy, and focus more on the welfare of average Americans by reversing many of the Bush Administration's policies at home and abroad and initiating new changes. However, no one knows yet, in the face of continuing instability in Iraq, rising violence in Afghanistan, unprecedented problems in the domestic and international economy, and a growing federal deficit, which of his campaign promises the incoming President will be able to translate into new polices.

The growing global financial crisis leads many International Relations experts to now speculate that the high costs that the United States is paying to fund financial bailouts and to pay for two wars, may accelerate the rise of an Asian-centered international system with China as an increasingly powerful actor. Others cite

© Don Bishop/Getty Images

the interdependence of China with other developed economies, particularly the U.S. economy, and predict that the future world will be one of "nonpolarity," where several nation-states play key roles across certain issues. What role rising powers, such as China or India, or emerging powers such as Brazil, will play in the future is even more uncertain than before the onset of the global economic crisis. This uncertainty is due largely to the fact that no one really knows what impact the current economic crisis will have on the existing distribution of economic and political power or whether governments will be able to work together to quickly resolve the intertwined and growing global crises.

What is clear from recent trends is that major status quo powers, such as the United States, will have to undertake bold new initiatives in order to turn their countries' economies around. Current problems are deep-seated political conflicts and structural economic problems that will take years, if not decades to solve. The need for major initiatives in such areas as the economy and energy alternatives are important reasons why some economists, businessmen and politicians, including Barak Obama, are calling for a massive new 'green initiative, similar to Eisenhower's interstate highway or FDR's new deal, as part of a strategy to help the United States regain its international stature as the leader in developing alternative energy and environmental initiatives.

The resurgence of fighting in Afghanistan and persistence of low-intensity conflicts throughout the world suggests that the United States and other international actors will have to continue to maintain some troops abroad to deal with ongoing asymmetric conflicts. These continuing demands for costly foreign deployments will increasingly come in competition for new calls to purchase new generation weapons in order to be prepared for traditional conventional security threats. While recent trends suggests to some analysts that asymmetric conflicts are likely to be an important, if not the dominant, mode of conflict in the International System for the foreseeable future, others argue that nation-states must continue to prepare for conventional threats at the same time.

The above trends also suggest that U.S. foreign policy will continue to rely more on diplomatic tools, including the judicious use of both political and economic carrots and sticks, while also attempting to coordinate U.S. policies with those of allies and other nation-states who shared common interests to achieve mutually desired outcomes. Shifting power relationships and the rise of new actors suggest that the foreign policy behaviors of many other nation-states are likely to change in future years.

The articles in this section reflect the diversity of viewpoints evident among experts about the relative importance of specific nation-states, the likelihood that new nation-state powers or empires will arise, and even whether traditional rules of statescraft, national security, and power politics will prevail or be overtaken by human security needs, or even collective security issues, such a global warming.

The Age of Nonpolarity
What Will Follow U.S. Dominance?

Richard N. Haass

The principal characteristic of twenty-first-century international relations is turning out to be nonpolarity: a world dominated not by one or two or even several states but rather by dozens of actors possessing and exercising various kinds of power. This represents a tectonic shift from the past.

The twentieth century started out distinctly multipolar. But after almost 50 years, two world wars, and many smaller conflicts, a bipolar system emerged. Then, with the end of the Cold War and the demise of the Soviet Union, bipolarity gave way to unipolarity—an international system dominated by one power, in this case the United States. But today power is diffuse, and the onset of nonpolarity raises a number of important questions. How does nonpolarity differ from other forms of international order? How and why did it materialize? What are its likely consequences? And how should the United States respond?

Newer World Order

In contrast to multipolarity—which involves several distinct poles or concentrations of power—a nonpolar international system is characterized by numerous centers with meaningful power.

In a multipolar system, no power dominates, or the system will become unipolar. Nor do concentrations of power revolve around two positions, or the system will become bipolar. Multipolar systems can be cooperative, even assuming the form of a concert of powers, in which a few major powers work together on setting the rules of the game and disciplining those who violate them. They can also be more competitive, revolving around a balance of power, or conflictual, when the balance breaks down.

At first glance, the world today may appear to be multipolar. The major powers—China, the European Union (EU), India, Japan, Russia, and the United States—contain just over half the world's people and account for 75 percent of global GDP and 80 percent of global defense spending. Appearances, however, can be deceiving. Today's world differs in a fundamental way from one of classic multipolarity: there are many more power centers, and quite a few of these poles are not nation-states. Indeed, one of the cardinal features of the contemporary international system is that nation-states have lost their monopoly on power and in some domains their preeminence as well. States are being challenged from above, by regional and global organizations; from below, by militias; and from the side, by a variety of nongovernmental organizations (NGOs) and corporations. Power is now found in many hands and in many places.

In addition to the six major world powers, there are numerous regional powers: Brazil and, arguably, Argentina, Chile, Mexico, and Venezuela in Latin America; Nigeria and South Africa in Africa; Egypt,

Iran, Israel, and Saudi Arabia in the Middle East; Pakistan in South Asia; Australia, Indonesia, and South Korea in East Asia and Oceania. A good many organizations would be on the list of power centers, including those that are global (the International Monetary Fund, the United Nations, the World Bank), those that are regional (the African Union, the Arab League, the Association of Southeast Asian Nations, the EU, the Organization of American States, the South Asian Association for Regional Cooperation), and those that are functional (the International Energy Agency, OPEC, the Shanghai Cooperation Organization, the World Health Organization). So, too, would states within nation-states, such as California and India's Uttar Pradesh, and cities, such as New York, São Paulo, and Shanghai. Then there are the large global companies, including those that dominate the worlds of energy, finance, and manufacturing. Other entities deserving inclusion would be global media outlets (al Jazeera, the BBC, CNN), militias (Hamas, Hezbollah, the Mahdi Army, the Taliban), political parties, religious institutions and movements, terrorist organizations (al Qaeda), drug cartels, and NGOs of a more benign sort (the Bill and Melinda Gates Foundation, Doctors Without Borders, Greenpeace). Today's world is increasingly one of distributed, rather than concentrated, power.

Today's world is increasingly one of distributed, rather than concentrated, power.

In this world, the United States is and will long remain the largest single aggregation of power. It spends more than $500 billion annually on its military—and more than $700 billion if the operations in Afghanistan and Iraq are included—and boasts land, air, and naval forces that are the world's most capable. Its economy, with a GDP of some $14 trillion, is the world's largest. The United States is also a major source of culture (through films and television), information, and innovation. But the reality of American strength should not mask the relative decline of the United States' position in the world—and with this relative decline in power an absolute decline in influence and independence. The U.S. share of global imports is already down to 15 percent. Although U.S. GDP accounts for over 25 percent of the world's total, this percentage is sure to decline over time given the actual and projected differential between the United States' growth rate and those of the Asian giants and many other countries, a large number of which are growing at more than two or three times the rate of the United States.

GDP growth is hardly the only indication of a move away from U.S. economic dominance. The rise of sovereign wealth funds—in countries such as China, Kuwait, Russia, Saudi Arabia, and the United Arab Emirates—is another. These government-controlled pools of wealth, mostly the result of oil and gas exports, now total some $3 trillion. They are growing at a projected rate of $1 trillion a year and are an increasingly important source of liquidity for U.S. firms. High energy prices, fueled mostly by the surge in Chinese and Indian demand, are here to stay for some time, meaning that the size and significance of these funds will continue to grow. Alternative stock exchanges are springing up and drawing away companies from the U.S. exchanges and even launching initial public offerings (IPOs). London, in particular, is competing with New York as the world's financial center and has already surpassed it in terms of the number of IPOs it hosts. The dollar has weakened against the euro and the British pound, and it is likely to decline in value relative to Asian currencies as well. A majority of the world's foreign exchange holdings are now in currencies other than the dollar, and a move to denominate oil in euros or a basket of currencies is possible, a step that would only leave the U.S. economy more vulnerable to inflation as well as currency crises.

U.S. primacy is also being challenged in other realms, such as military effectiveness and diplomacy. Measures of military spending are not the same as measures of military capacity. September 11 showed how a small investment by terrorists could cause extraordinary levels of human and physical damage. Many of the most costly pieces of modern weaponry are not particularly useful in modern conflicts in which traditional battlefields are replaced by urban combat zones. In such environments, large numbers of lightly armed soldiers can prove to be more than a match for smaller numbers of highly trained and better-armed U.S. troops.

Power and influence are less and less linked in an era of nonpolarity. U.S. calls for others to reform will tend to fall on deaf ears, U.S. assistance programs will buy less, and U.S.-led sanctions will accomplish less. After all, China proved to be the country best able to influence North Korea's nuclear program. Washington's ability to pressure Tehran has been strengthened by the participation of several western European countries—and weakened by the reluctance of China and Russia to sanction Iran. Both Beijing and Moscow have diluted international efforts to pressure the government in Sudan to end its war in Darfur. Pakistan, meanwhile, has repeatedly demonstrated an ability to resist U.S. entreaties, as have Iran, North Korea, Venezuela, and Zimbabwe.

The trend also extends to the worlds of culture and information. Bollywood produces more films every year than Hollywood. Alternatives to U.S.-produced and disseminated television are multiplying. Web sites and blogs from other countries provide further competition for U.S.-produced news and commentary. The proliferation of information is as much a cause of nonpolarity as is the proliferation of weaponry.

Farewell to Unipolarity

Charles Krauthammer was more correct than he realized when he wrote in these pages nearly two decades ago about what he termed "the unipolar moment." At the time, U.S. dominance was real. But it lasted for only 15 or 20 years. In historical terms, it was a moment. Traditional realist theory would have predicted the end of unipolarity and the dawn of a multipolar world. According to this line of reasoning, great powers, when they act as great powers are wont to do, stimulate competition from others that fear or resent them. Krauthammer, subscribing to just this theory, wrote, "No doubt, multipolarity will come in time. In perhaps another generation or so there will be great powers coequal with the United States, and the world will, in structure, resemble the pre-World War I era."

But this has not happened. Although anti-Americanism is widespread, no great-power rival or set of rivals has emerged to challenge the United States. In part, this is because the disparity between the power of the United States and that of any potential rivals is too great. Over time, countries such as China may come to possess GDPs comparable to that of the United States. But in the case of China, much of that wealth will necessarily be absorbed by providing for the country's enormous population (much of which remains poor) and will not be available to fund military development or external undertakings. Maintaining political stability during a period of such dynamic but uneven growth will be no easy feat. India faces many of the same demographic challenges and is further hampered by too much bureaucracy and too little infrastructure. The EU's GDP is now greater than that of the United States, but the EU does not act in the unified fashion of a nation-state, nor is it able or inclined to act in the assertive fashion of historic great powers. Japan, for its part, has a shrinking and aging population and lacks the political culture to play the role of a great power. Russia may be more inclined, but it still has a largely cash-crop economy and is saddled by a declining population and internal challenges to its cohesion.

The fact that classic great-power rivalry has not come to pass and is unlikely to arise anytime soon is also partly a result of the United States' behavior, which has not stimulated such a response. This is not to say that the United States under the leadership of George W. Bush has not alienated other nations; it surely has. But it has not, for the most part, acted in a manner that has led other states to conclude that the United States constitutes a threat to their vital national interests. Doubts about the wisdom and legitimacy of U.S. foreign policy are pervasive, but this has tended to lead more to denunciations (and an absence of cooperation) than outright resistance.

The transition to a nonpolar world will have mostly negative consequences for the United States.

A further constraint on the emergence of great-power rivals is that many of the other major powers are dependent on the international system for their economic welfare and political stability. They do not, accordingly, want to disrupt an order that serves their national interests. Those interests are closely tied to cross-border flows of goods, services, people, energy, investment, and technology—flows in which the United States plays a critical role. Integration into the modern world dampens great-power competition and conflict.

But even if great-power rivals have not emerged, unipolarity has ended. Three explanations for its demise stand out. The first is historical. States develop; they get better at generating and piecing together the human, financial, and technological resources that lead to productivity and prosperity. The same holds for corporations and other organizations. The rise of these new powers cannot be stopped. The result is an ever larger number of actors able to exert influence regionally or globally.

A second cause is U.S. policy. To paraphrase Walt Kelly's Pogo, the post-World War II comic hero, we have met the explanation and it is us. By both what it has done and what it has failed to do, the United States has accelerated the emergence of alternative power centers in the world and has weakened its own position relative to them. U.S. energy policy (or the lack thereof) is a driving force behind the end of unipolarity. Since the first oil shocks of the 1970s, U.S. consumption of oil has grown by approximately 20 percent, and, more important, U.S. imports of petroleum products have more than doubled in volume and nearly doubled as a percentage of consumption. This growth in demand for foreign oil has helped drive up the world price of oil from just over $20 a barrel to over $100 a barrel in less than a decade. The result is an enormous transfer of wealth and leverage to those states with energy reserves. In short, U.S. energy policy has helped bring about the emergence of oil and gas producers as major power centers.

U.S. economic policy has played a role as well. President Lyndon Johnson was widely criticized for simultaneously fighting a war in Vietnam and increasing domestic spending. President Bush has fought costly wars in Afghanistan and Iraq, allowed discretionary spending to increase by an annual rate of eight percent, and cut taxes. As a result, the United States' fiscal position declined from a surplus of over $100 billion in 2001 to an estimated deficit of approximately $250 billion in 2007. Perhaps more relevant is the ballooning current account deficit, which is now more than six percent of GDP. This places downward pressure on the dollar, stimulates inflation, and contributes to the accumulation of wealth and power elsewhere in the world. Poor regulation of the U.S. mortgage market and and the credit crisis it has spawned have exacerbated these problems.

The war in Iraq has also contributed to the dilution of the United States' position in the world. The war in Iraq has proved to be an expensive war of choice—militarily, economically, and diplomatically as well as in human terms. Years ago, the historian Paul Kennedy outlined his thesis about "imperial overstretch," which posited that the United States would eventually decline by overreaching, just as other great powers had in the past. Kennedy's theory turned out to apply most immediately to the Soviet Union, but the United States—for all its corrective mechanisms and dynamism—has not proved to be immune. It is not simply that the U.S. military will take a generation to recover from Iraq; it is also that the United States lacks sufficient military assets to continue doing what it is doing in Iraq, much less assume new burdens of any scale elsewhere.

Finally, today's nonpolar world is not simply a result of the rise of other states and organizations or of the failures and follies of U.S. policy. It is also an inevitable consequence of globalization. Globalization has increased the volume, velocity, and importance of cross-border flows of just about everything, from drugs, e-mails, greenhouse gases, manufactured goods, and people to television and radio signals, viruses (virtual and real), and weapons.

Globalization reinforces nonpolarity in two fundamental ways. First, many cross-border flows take place outside the control of governments and without their knowledge. As a result, globalization dilutes the influence of the major powers. Second, these same flows often strengthen the capacities of nonstate actors, such as energy exporters (who are experiencing a dramatic increase in wealth owing to transfers from importers), terrorists (who use the Internet to recruit and train, the international banking system to move resources, and the global transport system to move people), rogue states (who can exploit black and gray markets), and Fortune 500 firms (who quickly move personnel and investments). It is increasingly apparent that being the strongest state no longer means having a near monopoly on power. It is easier than ever before for individuals and groups to accumulate and project substantial power.

Nonpolar Disorder

The increasingly nonpolar world will have mostly negative consequences for the United States—and for much of the rest of the world as well. It will make it more difficult for Washington to lead on those occasions when it seeks to promote collective responses to regional and global challenges. One reason has to do with simple arithmetic. With so many more actors possessing meaningful power and trying to assert influence, it will be more difficult to build collective responses and make institutions work. Herding dozens is harder than herding a few. The inability to reach agreement in the Doha Round of global trade talks is a telling example.

Nonpolarity will also increase the number of threats and vulnerabilities facing a country such as the United States. These threats can take the form of rogue states, terrorist groups, energy producers that choose to reduce their output, or central banks whose action or inaction can create conditions that affect the role and strength of the U.S. dollar. The Federal Reserve might want to think twice before continuing to lower interest rates, lest it precipitate a further move away from the dollar. There can be worse things than a recession.

Iran is a case in point. Its effort to become a nuclear power is a result of nonpolarity. Thanks more than anything to the surge in oil prices, it has become another meaningful concentration of power, one able to exert influence in Iraq, Lebanon, Syria, the Palestinian territories, and beyond, as well as within OPEC. It has many sources of technology and finance and numerous markets for its energy exports. And due to nonpolarity, the United States cannot manage Iran alone. Rather, Washington is dependent on others to support political and economic sanctions or block Tehran's access to nuclear technology and materials. Nonpolarity begets nonpolarity.

Still, even if nonpolarity was inevitable, its character is not. To paraphrase the international relations theorist Hedley Bull, global politics at any point is a mixture of anarchy and society. The question is the balance and the trend. A great deal can and should be done to shape a nonpolar world. Order will not just emerge. To the contrary, left to its own devices, a nonpolar world will become messier over time. Entropy dictates that systems consisting of a large number of actors tend toward greater randomness and disorder in the absence of external intervention.

The United States can and should take steps to reduce the chances that a nonpolar world will become a cauldron of instability. This is not a call for unilateralism; it is a call for the United States to get its own house in order. Unipolarity is a thing of the past, but the United States still retains more capacity than any other actor to improve the quality of the international system. The question is whether it will continue to possess such capacity.

The United States no longer has the luxury of a "You're either with us or against us" foreign policy.

Energy is the most important issue. Current levels of U.S. consumption and imports (in addition to their adverse impact on the global climate) fuel nonpolarity by funneling vast financial resources to oil and gas producers. Reducing consumption would lessen the pressure on world prices, decrease U.S. vulnerability to market manipulation by oil suppliers, and slow the pace of climate change. The good news is that this can be done without hurting the U.S. economy.

Strengthening homeland security is also crucial. Terrorism, like disease, cannot be eradicated. There will always be people who cannot be integrated into societies and who pursue goals that cannot be realized through traditional politics. And sometimes, despite the best efforts of those entrusted with homeland security, terrorists will succeed. What is needed, then, are steps to make society more resilient, something that requires adequate funding and training of emergency responders and more flexible and durable infrastructure. The goal should be to reduce the impact of even successful attacks.

Resisting the further spread of nuclear weapons and unguarded nuclear materials, given their destructive potential, may be as important as any other set of undertakings. By establishing internationally managed enriched-uranium or spent-fuel banks that give countries access to sensitive nuclear materials, the international community could help countries use nuclear power to produce electricity rather than bombs. Security assurances and defensive systems can be provided to states that might otherwise feel compelled to develop nuclear programs of their own to counter those of their neighbors. Robust sanctions—on occasion backed by armed force—can also be introduced to influence the behavior of would-be nuclear states.

Even so, the question of using military force to destroy nuclear or biological weapons capabilities remains. Preemptive strikes—attacks that aim to stop an imminent threat—are widely accepted as a form of self-defense. Preventive strikes—attacks on capabilities when there is no indication of imminent use—are something else altogether. They should not be ruled out as a matter of principle, but nor should they be depended on. Beyond questions of feasibility, preventive strikes run the risk of making a nonpolar world less stable, both because they might actually encourage proliferation (governments could see developing or acquiring nuclear weapons as a deterrent) and because they would weaken the long-standing norm against the use of force for purposes other than self-defense.

Combating terrorism is also essential if the nonpolar era is not to turn into a modern Dark Ages. There are many ways to weaken existing terrorist organizations by using intelligence and law enforcement resources and military capabilities. But this is a loser's game unless something can be done to reduce recruitment. Parents, religious figures, and political leaders must delegitimize terrorism by shaming those who choose to embrace it. And more important, governments must find ways of integrating alienated young men and women into their societies, something that cannot occur in the absence of political and economic opportunity.

Trade can be a powerful tool of integration. It gives states a stake in avoiding conflict because instability interrupts beneficial commercial arrangements that provide greater wealth and strengthen the foundations of domestic political order. Trade also facilitates development, thereby decreasing the chance of state failure and alienation among citizens. The scope of the World Trade Organization must be extended through the negotiation of future global arrangements that further reduce subsidies and both tariff and nontariff barriers. Building domestic political support for such negotiations in developed countries will likely require the expansion of various safety nets, including portable health care and retirement accounts, education and training assistance, and wage insurance. These social policy reforms are costly and in some cases unwarranted (the cause of job loss is far more likely to be technological innovation than foreign competition), but they are worth providing nonetheless given the overall economic and political value of expanding the global trade regime.

A similar level of effort might be needed to ensure the continued flow of investment. The goal should be to create a World Investment Organization that would encourage capital flows across borders so as to minimize the chances that "investment protectionism" gets in the way of activities that, like trade, are economically beneficial and build political bulwarks against instability. A WIO could encourage transparency on the part of investors, determine when national security is a legitimate reason for prohibiting or limiting foreign investment, and establish a mechanism for resolving disputes.

Finally, the United States needs to enhance its capacity to prevent state failure and deal with its consequences. This will require building and maintaining a larger military, one with greater capacity to deal with the sort of threats faced in Afghanistan and Iraq. In addition, it will mean establishing a civilian counterpart to the military reserves that would provide a pool of human talent to assist with basic nation-building tasks. Continuing economic and military assistance will be vital in helping weak states meet their responsibilities to their citizens and their neighbors.

The Not-So-Lonely Superpower

Multilateralism will be essential in dealing with a nonpolar world. To succeed, though, it must be recast to include actors other than the great powers. The UN Security Council and the G-8 (the group of highly industrialized states) need to be reconstituted to reflect the world of today and not the post–World War II era. A recent meeting at the United Nations on how best to coordinate global responses to public health challenges provided a model. Representatives of governments, UN agencies, NGOs, pharmaceutical companies, foundations, think tanks, and universities were all in attendance. A similar range of participants attended the December 2007 Bali meeting on climate change. Multilateralism may have to be less formal and less comprehensive, at least in its initial phases. Networks will be needed alongside organizations. Getting everyone to agree on everything will be increasingly difficult; instead, the United States should consider signing accords with fewer parties and narrower goals. Trade is something of a model here, in that bilateral and regional accords are filling the vacuum created by a failure to conclude a global trade round. The same approach could work for climate change, where agreement on aspects of the problem (say, deforestation) or arrangements involving only some countries (the major carbon emitters, for example) may prove feasible, whereas an accord that involves every country and tries to resolve every issue may not. Multilateralism à la carte is likely to be the order of the day.

Nonpolarity complicates diplomacy. A nonpolar world not only involves more actors but also lacks the more predictable fixed structures and relationships that tend to define worlds of unipolarity, bipolarity, or multipolarity. Alliances, in particular, will lose much of their importance, if only because alliances require predictable threats, outlooks, and obligations, all of which are likely to be in short supply in a nonpolar world. Relationships will instead become more selective and situational. It will become harder to classify other countries as either allies or adversaries; they will cooperate on some issues and resist on others. There will be a premium on consultation and coalition building and on a diplomacy that encourages cooperation when possible and shields such cooperation from the fallout of inevitable disagreements. The United States will no longer have the luxury of a "You're either with us or against us" foreign policy.

Nonpolarity will be difficult and dangerous. But encouraging a greater degree of global integration will help promote stability. Establishing a core group of governments and others committed to cooperative multilateralism would be a great step forward. Call it "concerted nonpolarity." It would not eliminate nonpolarity, but it would help manage it and increase the odds that the international system will not deteriorate or disintegrate.

RICHARD N. HAASS is President of the Council on Foreign Relations.

China Views Globalization: Toward a New Great-Power Politics?

YONG DENG AND THOMAS G. MOORE

China is rising in the age of globalization. Although China initially accepted greater interdependence largely out of economic necessity early in the reform era, Beijing has since come to embrace interdependence and globalization with increasing enthusiasm. Yet, the country's political elites recognize that economic globalization is a double-edged sword for China. Although undoubtedly an engine of national economic growth, if mishandled, this transformative force could very well derail China's quest for great-power status. Globalization introduces powerful new sources of economic vulnerability. Similarly, the growth of nontraditional threats, such as terrorism and the spread of infectious disease, presents serious global challenges to China's security. Thus, although Beijing has embraced globalization overall, the Chinese government has also sought to manage the process by reconfiguring its thinking about security and taking bold steps such as domestic banking reforms and active trade diplomacy to defend the country's economic interests. The fact that Chinese political elites today perceive issues as diverse as capital flows, weapons proliferation, epidemics, terrorism, and cybercrime in terms of globalization suggests that the country's views on globalization have evolved in tandem with its tumultuous quest for development, security, and status during the past decade.

To the extent that globalization is perceived to be the distinguishing feature of contemporary U.S. hegemony, China's views on globalization reflect its evaluation of the world order and shape its strategic outlook as an aspiring great power. U.S. hegemony in its liberal and democratic forms benefits China in important ways, but through the lens of power politics it also disadvantages certain Chinese interests. Accordingly, efforts to restrain the United States characterize Beijing's latest and likely future response to globalization. In fact, mainstream Chinese strategic thinkers now believe that globalization, as manifested in transnational forces, international institutions, and a greater need for multilateralism, can be used to "democratize" the U.S. hegemonic order to minimize unilateralist power politics.

Even more broadly, China's strategic choices are increasingly designed to exploit globalization as a way of making China rich and strong and simultaneously reducing international fears of fast-growing Chinese material power. Under President Hu Jintao and Premier Wen Jiabao, the new Chinese leadership, sensitive to foreign reactions to China's growing power, has actively pursued cooperative security, win-win economic cooperation, and an increasingly multilateral approach to foreign policy in general, to an even greater extent and with greater success than their predecessors. China's new foreign policy choice highlights the potential role of globalization in transforming great-power politics from the unmitigated struggle for supremacy of earlier eras to a more cooperative form of interstate competition that increases prospects for China's peaceful rise.

The Changing Colors of Globalization

Although the term "globalization" did not enter official discourse in China until 1996, its leaders acknowledged throughout the 1990s that economic affairs were playing a growing role in post–Cold War international relations.[1] Some references to globalization appeared in academic writings in the early 1990s, but the dominant concepts in scholarly and policymaking circles were interdependence, integration, and internationalization. When globalization first entered Beijing's diplomatic lexicon, officials described it as a trend driven by advances in science and technology that were producing increased cross-national flows of capital, goods, and know-how. The emphasis on the technological drivers underlying this process conceptually restricted globalization to the economic realm in official Chinese analysis although the term was soon understood elsewhere in the world to include social, cultural, political, and security dimensions. Similarly, early attention to this emerging trend emphasized the opportunities for economic development and ignored concerns about U.S. hegemony, Westernization, national sovereignty, and other politically controversial issues.

Long before the term "globalization" became popularized worldwide in the 1990s, the benefits of China's growing participation in the world economy were undeniable. After Deng Xiaoping formally assumed power in 1978, transnational flows of capital, goods, information, and technology increased steadily throughout the 1980s, accelerating further during the 1990s as the contours of an emerging manufacturing juggernaut took shape. By the mid-1990s, economic ties to the outside world were widely seen as critical to the robust economic growth that made China the envy of industrializing countries everywhere. For example, by 1992 China stood as the world's leading recipient of foreign direct investment (FDI) among developing countries. Indeed, FDI accounted for sizable (and growing) percentages of China's domestic investment, industrial output, exports, tax revenues, and job growth before globalization became a catchphrase.

A series of events in the late 1990s tested China's initial, somewhat romantic, notions of globalization quickly and severely. The Asian financial crisis of 1997–1998 revealed the double-edged sword of globalization, that is, the challenges it presents as well as the opportunities. Although China escaped much of the turmoil, the travails of its neighbors highlighted the threats that global economic forces posed to national economic security. The crisis also reinforced suspicion that the United States and Japan seek every opportunity for strategic gain, even in ostensibly economic matters. Coupled with Washington's hard line in its ongoing negotiations over China's accession to the World Trade Organization (WTO), U.S. policy during the Asian financial crisis, namely the perceived U.S. indifference to the spreading chaos and its subsequent failure to support measures that many in East Asia sought as necessary for a quick recovery, underscored the significant economic, social, political, and even strategic risks that deeper participation in a globalizing world economy would entail for China. The economic dislocation and political upheaval in developing Thailand and Indonesia, not to mention industrialized South Korea, presented a sobering vision of the challenges to national sovereignty and well-being that can accompany greater integration into world markets.

Political elites recognize that economic globalization is a double-edged sword for China.

In Beijing's view, its experience with the Asian financial crisis and the WTO revealed not only that further reform and opening would be necessary to create a modern economy capable of competing effectively in a globalizing world economy but also that severe imbalances and inequities continued to persist in the international system. Even though China's strategic position compared favorably to most developing countries, Beijing did not see itself as immune to the vagaries and injustices associated with contemporary international economic relations. Strikingly, Chinese officials publicly explained this deleterious side as the result of an improper handling (political mismanagement at the international level) of the globalization process rather than as a danger inherent in deeper and more extensive ties among national economies. Indeed, Beijing's rhetoric and behavior in the late 1990s sought to maintain a distinction

between globalization (understood in terms of scientific and technological advances, the expansion of market forces, and the arrival of a new industrial revolution) and the international economic system (shorthand for Western-dominated, multilateral economic institutions and U.S. hegemony generally). Problems associated elsewhere in the world with globalization, such as widening disparities in North-South wealth, asymmetries in vulnerabilities to financial shocks between industrialized and developing countries, and unequal access to technology, were attributed to defects in the international economic system rather than to globalization per se.

The term 'globalization' did not enter official discourse in China until 1996.

By the late 1990s, even though China's official rhetoric continued to view globalization as an economic phenomenon, this belied a growing recognition in scholarly and elite discourse that globalization was also affecting great-power politics. Given the United States' advantage in technological innovation, revolution in military affairs, and cultural domination, globalization seemed to confer relative gains on the United States, enabling it to pursue its foreign policy virtually unchallenged. This belief has been reinforced by what Beijing has perceived as a series of unilateral U.S. actions threatening to Chinese interests, such as Washington's closer relationship with Taipei since the 1995–1996 Taiwan Strait crisis; the 1996–1997 strengthening of the U.S.-Japanese defense guidelines; the 1999 U.S.-led NATO intervention in Kosovo (and resulting bombing of the Chinese embassy in Belgrade); the intensification of U.S. plans for missile defense under President George W. Bush; the April 2001 EP-3 surveillance plane incident; and, most recently, the 2003 war in Iraq. The result has been a more realistic Chinese assessment of globalization's economic and security implications as well as a new recognition that globalization is not merely an economic trend but rather a process that must be actively managed politically as well.

The heightened profile of international terrorism, the spread of weapons of mass destruction, the growing problem of infectious diseases such as AIDS and the Severe Acute Respiratory Syndrome (SARS), transnational drug trafficking, and cybercrime have also influenced the evolution of China's views on globalization. Chinese officials have repeatedly acknowledged that, as security threats become increasingly globalized, the pursuit of security becomes more and more cooperative and multidimensional and, in an age of increasingly transnational threats, China's security is dependent on the security of others in unprecedented ways. Such new ideas have made "common security" and "globalized cooperation" regular features of China's foreign policy discourse in the new millennium, including then-President Jiang Zemin's analysis in 2002: "As countries increase their interdependency and common ground on security, it has become difficult for any single country to realize its security objective by itself alone. Only by strengthening international cooperation can we effectively deal with the security challenge worldwide and realize universal and sustained security."[2]

Just as globalization has prompted new thinking about security issues in China, nontraditional security threats have also significantly transformed China's understanding of globalization itself. Once restricted to economics, the discourse on globalization now extends to an expanding range of political and security matters. Such reconceptualization underscores the importance of globalization both as a real-world phenomenon and as a lens through which Beijing's grand strategy is filtered. It has facilitated China's satisfaction with, and boosted China's confidence in peaceful status mobility within, the international system.

The fact that China's support for globalization has never wavered, even in the wake of the Asian financial crisis and through a variety of subsequent foreign policy tests, reflects a strategic choice by China's leaders to deepen the country's participation in the world economy as the best means available to pursue economic modernization, cope with U.S. hegemony, and fulfill Beijing's great-power aspirations. Chinese leaders characterize globalization as an irreversible tide that no country can or should resist while emphasizing the need to manage the process proactively to maximize benefits and minimize harms. Most significantly, perhaps, Chinese policymakers and academic analysts alike have intently explored ways in which globalization can restrain U.S. power, reduce fears of a China threat, and ultimately make international relations defined more by the democratic exercise of legitimate authority and dictated less by coercive use of power.

'Democratizing' U.S. Hegemony through Multipolarization and Economic Globalization

China's official advocacy of multipolarity in world politics predated Beijing's explicit embrace of globalization by almost a decade. During much of the 1990s, political discussion treated multipolarization and globalization as two separate issues, demonstrating little concern with the implications of the combined trends for Chinese foreign policy. Having initially struggled to define the post–Cold War world, Beijing has in the new millennium propounded a new official formulation—"multipolarization and economic globalization"—that reinterprets the dual trends and their interconnectedness as the strategic context for Chinese foreign relations.[3]

Instead of predicting the imminent emergence of a dispersed power configuration, as was the case previously, China now views the trend toward multipolarization as a tortuous process of unspecified duration. Today, Chinese official media and mainstream analysts explicitly reject equating multipolarity with a hostile balancing drive against the predominant power of the United States. Notably, one Chinese scholar openly voiced his criticism of the official "multipolarity" notion for its anti-U.S. tone and implications of confrontational power politics.[4]

Beginning in the second half of 2003, the government in Beijing even toned down its explicit advocacy of multipolarity, for example, preferring to pledge to promote "multilateralism" in the Sino-French Joint Statement signed in late January 2004.[5] Rhetorical deployments aside, the new interpretation of multipolarization reflects a preference for a more democratic world order that emphasizes proper management of state-to-state relations over the redistribution of power. In other words, China is less concerned with U.S. power per se and more concerned with the way that power is exercised.

Globalization has become a lens through which Beijing's grand strategy is filtered.

As explained by the vice minister of foreign affairs, Wang Yi, the Chinese view of multipolarization differs from the traditional Western interpretation in that China seeks the "harmonious coexistence of all forces," including developing countries, rather than a confrontational great-power struggle.[6] According to this perspective, multipolarization is antithetical to the self-help, unilateralist approach to security and development associated with the traditional great-power game.

Chinese analysts and political elites clearly recognize that the United States enjoys great advantages in utilizing globalization across the military, technological, economic, political, and even cultural arenas to consolidate Washington's predominant position in the world further. These observers also recognize, however, that China's own national rejuvenation requires its active participation in such a world. The latest mainstream view recognizes that the force of interdependence and globalization is essential to convince the United States of what Joseph Nye Jr. calls "the paradox of American power," whereby U.S. power is simultaneously strengthened and restrained in the globalized world. To cope with the wide array of global challenges, cooperative and legitimate use of power is not only a virtual necessity but also strengthens the U.S. global leadership role.[7]

For example, Shen Jiru, director of strategic studies at the Institute of World Economics and Politics at the Chinese Academy of Social Sciences (CASS), argues that the United States did not retaliate against France, Germany, and Russia for their opposition to the U.S. war in Iraq because "the advance of economic globalization means that the interests of different countries are interwoven ever more closely, and this has become a powerful material force constraining U.S. hegemonism."[8] Elsewhere, Shen posits that diplomatic activism by Japan, Korea, China, Russia, and the United States on the North Korean nuclear issue is best explained by common concern over the devastating impact that a militarized conflict would have on the highly interdependent Northeast Asian regional economies.[9] Along the same lines, CASS scholar Zheng Yu argues:

> [T]he rising trend of economic globalization has led to an unprecedented level of economic interdependence, thereby effectively containing the possible escalation of

regional conflicts to great-power war. And it has become increasingly difficult to resort to economic coercion as a means to control the economic development of another country. As such, economic globalization has provided opportunities and favorable conditions for overall peace and development in the international community.[10]

These observations reflect the emerging Chinese interest in exploring how economic globalization can actually change the parameters of great-power politics from a traditional zero-sum game to win-win competition. "Under conditions of globalization there are no absolute winners or absolute losers," contends Luo Zhaohong, a CASS research fellow. Consequently, "the globalization age requires increased cooperation between all countries and regions, and we must apply the concept of 'both are winners' or 'all are winners' in place of the outdated 'zero-sum game' mentality."[11] Such a new concept presumably precludes Cold War–style antagonism between two great powers or two blocs. The win-win idea has been widely espoused in mainstream Chinese analyses, as it is considered a hallmark of China's new foreign strategy.

Chinese analysts and policymakers believe that economic globalization creates the open economic system necessary for China's growth. Although pressuring China to live up to international commitments, the globalized world also offers China opportunities to express its discontent, to take measures to defend its economic interests, and even to assert a leadership role in global governance, all without triggering fear that Beijing harbors revisionist intentions. China's diplomacy in the WTO provides a case in point.

Although China's leaders pursued WTO entry primarily to improve the country's own participation in the world economy, they also saw membership as a means to influence the shape of the international economic system. China's subsequent WTO participation has reiterated its new attitude toward leadership in a globalized world. In his speech at the 2001 ministerial conference in Doha, Qatar, China's trade minister, Shi Guangsheng, argued that equal attention should be paid to the "development of the world economy" and "trade and investment facilitation." In the speech, which marked the occasion of China's WTO accession, Shi referred to the "obvious defects of the existing multilateral trading system," namely its failure "to reflect the interests and demands of developing countries in a more adequate fashion."[12] In addition, in a declaration issued at the time of the Doha meeting, China insisted that the "developmental dimension" be fully incorporated into the multilateral trading system.

Beijing actively seeks to manage the course of globalization.

Similarly, at the September 2003 WTO ministerial meeting in Cancun, Mexico, Commerce Minister Lu Fuyuan assessed the positions of developed against developing countries, concluding that "their obligations are not balanced and their gains are not equal." Signaling Beijing's concern about fairness, Lu emphasized the "enormous commitment" to trade liberalization that China had made by joining the WTO. Indeed, he also noted that Beijing's accession protocol requires China to reduce trade barriers "well below the level of other developing countries."[13] By laying these rhetorical markers, Lu indicated his country's determination to prevent the Doha talks from resulting in further substantial obligations for Chinese liberalization.

Consistent with this stance, Beijing acted as a member of the Group of 22 (G-22) developing countries in Cancun to bargain collectively for a reduction in the use of agricultural subsidies by developed countries such as the United States, members of the European Union, and Japan. At first glance, Beijing's participation in the G-22 could be interpreted as evidence that China wanted to undermine the liberal international economic regime by blocking progress toward a new WTO agreement. In truth, however, China was much less strident in its criticism than were Brazil, India, and many other developing countries. Despite U.S. trade negotiators' clear disappointment that China had allied itself with the G-22 in Cancun, they praised Beijing afterward for working hard to broker a deal. Indeed, China displayed its customary pragmatism in trying to navigate the treacherous waters of agricultural policy and the so-called Singapore issues (trade facilitation, government procurement, investment rules, and competition policy). Presumably, this is why WTO Director General Supachai Panitchpakdi called on Beijing to "use its influence to be a bridge between developed and developing countries" in the wake of the collapse of the Cancun meeting.[14] This direct appeal to Chinese leaders, in which Supachai acknowledged that China is both a "developing nation" and an "emerging superpower," reflects the growing influence of Beijing in shaping the economic order from which it already benefits handsomely.

Like many developing countries, China believes that the WTO has failed to live up to the promises not only of the Doha "Development Round" launched in 2001 but also of the Uruguay Round concluded in 1994. In the latter case, developing countries were promised liberalization in agricultural and textile trade (which has been slow to materialize) in exchange for the adoption of rules advocated by developed countries on issues such as services and intellectual property rights (which have progressed further). Although there is no evidence that Beijing wishes to weaken the WTO, China does insist that any new agreement must be negotiated more inclusively and must deliver a more equitable outcome. To that end, China has recently expressed a willingness to play a more active and constructive role in reinvigorating the WTO talks that had stalled in Cancun in 2003.

By using an increasingly wide variety of economic platforms, including the WTO, the Asia-Pacific Economic Cooperation (APEC) forum, and various UN agencies, Beijing actively seeks to manage the course of globalization. Even though Beijing has attempted to assert a Chinese voice, its positions hardly constitute a confrontational, revisionist agenda vis-à-vis the existing international order. China has resisted the norms and principles of the liberal international economic system no more than most developing countries.[15]

Beijing's increased emphasis on the democratization of international relations beyond the economic arena can be seen in its promotion of the so-called new security concept. This notion was first introduced by the Chinese leadership in the context of managing relations with Russia and newly independent Central Asian states in the mid-1990s and has subsequently been applied elsewhere. This policy advocates an economic and political order in which mutual trust, benefit, equality, and cooperation characterize bilateral relations and multilateral institutions to reduce "insecurity and safeguard global strategic equilibrium and stability."[16] Also significant, and not all that surprising, the policy reflects Beijing's desire to circumvent Washington's well-established alliance networks by associating such structures with a Cold War mentality that is ill suited to an era of globalization in which security and development are positive-sum games requiring mutual cooperation, rather than the bloc politics of the past.

In this new spirit, Beijing has sought to infuse a sense of shared growth and security community into China's relations with its neighbors. The Shanghai Cooperation Organization (SCO), established in June 2001 to capitalize on earlier joint confidence-building efforts among China, Russia, Kazakhstan, Tajikistan, Kyrgyzstan, and Uzbekistan, is designed to achieve a more institutionalized form of cooperation on issues ranging from antiterrorism to trade. Chinese leaders now hail the SCO as a model of regional cooperation that enhances collective security for the participants while not threatening any outside party.

Similar motivations were behind Beijing's October 2003 signing of the Treaty of Amity and Cooperation, the non-aggression pact of the Association of Southeast Asian Nations (ASEAN). China simultaneously issued a joint declaration with ASEAN, the "Strategic Partnership for Peace and Prosperity," which included a call to establish a security dialogue between the 10 member countries of ASEAN and China. These initiatives built upon Beijing's ongoing efforts to forge a China-ASEAN free-trade agreement. China has also become an enthusiastic participant in the network of currency-swap arrangements launched by China, Japan, South Korea, and ASEAN in 2000 under the so-called Chiang Mai Initiative. Such initiatives to promote trade and monetary regionalism in East Asia reflect a comprehensive and multilateral approach to security.

Beijing now seeks to use interdependence as a de facto strategy to restrain the U.S.

Whereas interdependence served mainly as a means for advancing Chinese economic interests in the past, it now appears that China is coming to value interdependence partially for its own sake. More specifically, although China remains wary of the implications of interdependence for national autonomy, as are all nations to varying degrees, Beijing's grand strategy now shows signs of relying on formal and informal mechanisms (strengthened multilateral institutions and strong economic ties, respectively) of interdependence as a de facto strategy for restraining the United States.

For example, Beijing has deepened its involvement in the UN system in recent years, including its participation in the Security Council, where China had been extremely passive in the past. Since the 1999 NATO war in Kosovo, China has been more determined than ever to defend the relevance and authority of the UN. Elsewhere, China has actively promoted security initiatives in venues such as the ASEAN Regional Forum (ARF), in which its dialogue partners include the United States, Japan, the EU, and Russia as well as ASEAN members. At the 2003 annual ARF meeting, Beijing proposed that a security policy conference be established within ARF in which military as well as civilian personnel would participate. Only a few years earlier, because of China's victim complex originating from its century-long experience as a semicolony after the Opium War (1839–1842) and rigid notion of sovereignty, China's advocacy of such a position would have been unthinkable.

To the extent that globalization can create constraints on U.S. power—power that might otherwise be used to pursue unmitigated unilateralism—China believes it can pluralize and democratize the hegemonic order and strengthen incentives for Washington to engage Beijing rather than contain it.[17] As such, Chinese mainstream observers see globalization and multipolarization reinforcing each other to create common interests that can replace the China threat theory with the China opportunity theory. Such a world is most conducive to China's quest for economic prosperity and great-power status.

Global Threats and China's New Thinking on Security

China's concern about transnational threats such as terrorism, unregulated capital flows, weapons proliferation, epidemics, and cross-border criminal activities preceded the terrorist attacks of September 11, 2001. For example, the Asian financial crisis dramatically sensitized China to its own banking and economic vulnerabilities, given the broad similarities (such as high levels of nonperforming loans) to the conditions that contributed to weakness in neighboring countries such as Thailand, Indonesia, and South Korea. Similarly, one of the original missions of the SCO was to combat what member states call the three evil forces of terrorism, separatism, and extremism. The September 11 attacks and the SARS crisis undoubtedly raised Chinese awareness about what China's latest White Paper on National Defense specifically refers to as "diversifying and globalizing" security threats.[18]

Today, China no longer faces any imminent threat of military invasion by any foreign power. According to Chu Shulong, director of the Institute of Strategic Studies at Tsinghua University, Taiwan may be the only prominent traditional security issue currently facing China. Consequently, he argues, China should brace itself mainly against nontraditional threats that would endanger its social stability, economic vitality, and "human security."[19] Moreover, official Chinese views now also hold that effectively combating these global threats requires cooperative security rather than traditional competitive politics.

For China, no nontraditional threat hit home as abruptly as the outbreak of SARS in the first half of 2003. Originating in southern China in late 2002 (or earlier by some accounts), the epidemic quickly infected more than 8,000 people in 30-plus countries, causing nearly 800 deaths within six months. By the time the disease was finally brought under control, Beijing's initial mishandling of the crisis, as well as the SARS scourge itself, had taken a serious toll on China's economy and its international reputation. The silver lining of the tragedy, however, was the subsequent call by Chinese analysts for a comprehensive rethinking of national security with more attention to nontraditional threats to social stability and the rights and well being of the Chinese people.[20]

When China's top leadership finally acknowledged the SARS crisis and started to mobilize the "people's war" against the epidemic in April 2003, Chinese commentators emphatically characterized SARS as a global disease posing a common threat to the international community. They even compared the outbreak to the September 11 terrorist attacks on the United States: both came from new threats facing humanity and both required joint international efforts to eradicate them.

In response, foreign leaders generally echoed Beijing's characterization of SARS as a global challenge. Whereas the foreign media were more critical of Beijing's initial cover-up, world leaders, including Bush, refrained from openly casting blame on Beijing and offered support instead for the embattled Beijing leadership, which had been newly inaugurated in March. Foreign governments and international institutions provided a financial package worth $38 million in support of Beijing's fight against SARS. This support led a prominent Chinese international relations scholar, Yan Xuetong, to declare that SARS "not only tested our country's foreign relations, but to some extent strengthened China's cooperative relationship with the international society. Moreover, SARS has provided China with experience in international cooperation and a new environment for China's further integration into the international society."[21] Of particular note, he specifically attributed the enhanced international cooperation to the nontraditional nature of the SARS threat.

Taiwan may be the only prominent traditional security issue currently facing China.

The devastation of the Asian financial crisis, the fallout of the terrorist attacks, and the North Korean nuclear standoff further underscored the intertwined nature of traditional and nontraditional security threats. Chinese commentators have learned that nontraditional threats can imperil China's security environment and strike China's vital interests in social stability, national unity, and economic development. While calling for greater attention from their government to such threats, Chinese analysts also emphasize the inadequacy of an outdated, militarized, self-help approach to security. This emerging recognition among the political and intellectual elites of the need for a comprehensive, multilateralist, and cooperative model for security has resulted not only from the practical necessities in dealing with these new threats but also from China's greater interest in transforming great-power politics in ways that would improve the country's security environment.[22]

Indeed, cooperation between China and the United States on transnational threats such as terrorism and North Korean nuclear proliferation has significantly stabilized the bilateral relationship. Despite pervasive concerns about the offensive nature of Washington's hegemonic policies, the consensus within the Chinese policy community is that the global war on terrorism has defused, at least in part, U.S. strategic concerns about China becoming a peer competitor. In this way, the dark side of globalization, namely nontraditional threats, may serve to restrain U.S. power and reduce U.S. hostilities toward China. The six-party talks in Beijing on the North Korean crisis are a case in point. They have strengthened Sino-U.S. cooperation and diminished the U.S. unilateral impulse to settle the crisis through force.

Strategic Choice in a Globalized World

Despite Beijing's rhetoric bemoaning inequities in the international economic system, criticizing international military intervention, and denouncing U.S. unilateralism, Chinese foreign policy in recent years can in fact be best characterized as dynamic "system maintenance."[23] At the outset of the new millennium, China's international behavior is increasingly motivated by a desire to maintain the status quo by seeking stable relations with the United States as the world's sole current superpower and by promoting China's gradual rise in the international system.[24]

In the past decade, China has stepped up its great-power diplomacy. It has significantly improved relations with Russia, Germany, France, and the EU. As an exception, political relations with Japan have most recently stalled largely due to disputes over issues concerning Japanese wartime responsibility and a severe lack of confidence in each other's strategic intentions. President Hu Jintao's attendance of a North-South conference sponsored by the 2003 Group of Eight summit in France represented a breakthrough in China's view, which had long perceived the great-power club as Western-dominated and discriminatory. This turnabout underscores China's desire to participate in great-power forums. Individually, China has cultivated strategic partnerships with Russia, Germany, and France, not as a hostile alliance to the United States but to enhance its own international standing.

Within this broader foreign policy framework, the Chinese perception of and policy toward the United States are more nuanced and strategic than straightforward or clear-cut. Beijing prefers an enduring, robust relationship with the United States but resents the many ways in which U.S. hegemony disadvantages China's interests. To the extent that the United States remains the champion of economic liberalism, China benefits from U.S. leadership. Although Chinese elites often find U.S. hegemony objectionable, China also owes U.S. leadership for the largely tranquil and open international environment essential for its economic growth during the past three decades or so. At the regional level, Chinese officials in the past couple of years have openly accepted the U.S. role in Asia as long as that presence does not threaten China's interests.

Generally frustrated by the uncertainty and ambiguity of U.S. policy toward their government, Chinese leaders' discontent has focused specifically on what they perceive to be the United States' distrust of, and zero-sum power politics mindset toward, China. To avoid the prohibitive costs of confrontation and dispel any impressions of China's pursuit of old-style power politics, Chinese foreign policy has disavowed both all-out internal military mobilization and vigorous external military alliances. Neither China's military modernization nor its strategic partnership with Russia amounts to a classical balancing strategy. In the minds of most Chinese observers, the persistence (and even strengthening) of U.S. primacy after the end of the Cold War has rendered balancing a relatively impractical alternative.[25] Coupled with China's strategic self-restraint, the enduring power gap between China and the United States has dissuaded Beijing from trying to engage directly in peer competition with Washington.[26]

Thus, Chinese analysts have focused their attention on defining a position for their country within a global system of U.S. hegemony. It is in this context that the Chinese leadership has conceptualized the impact of globalization on China's economic agenda and security environment. By transforming the geo-economic context of interstate competition, globalization has created powerful incentives for China's participation in transnational economic structures and multilateral institutions. Pursuit of a balancing strategy, on the other hand, would require China to divert huge sums of scarce resources to a concerted arms buildup, to establish military alliances against Washington, and to withdraw from (and perhaps even actively undermine) the U.S.-led liberal international economic system—all to China's disadvantage. Such confrontational policies are likely to prove futile and self-defeating. Rather, a Chinese foreign policy that accommodates economic globalization and works toward active participation in international institutions is essential to maintaining the robust economic growth critical both to social stability and the political legitimacy of the Chinese Communist Party, let alone China's rising status and influence in international politics.

Throughout the series of foreign policy crises encountered in recent years, particularly as manifested in tensions between the United States and China, the leadership in Beijing has consistently concluded that China has no alternative but to continue and even to increase China's participation in the globalizing world economy. Nothing illustrates this commitment better

than the timing and circumstances of Beijing's November 1999 agreement with Washington on China's WTO accession, when President Jiang Zemin and Prime Minister Zhu Rongji delivered politically on a deal whose terms were strenuously opposed by significant bureaucratic interests at home. Even more striking, China's top leaders had to overcome an embarrassing negotiating rebuff by the Clinton administration during Zhu's April 1999 visit to Washington as well as the bombing of China's embassy in Belgrade the following month. The latter, in particular, made it difficult domestically for Jiang and Zhu to appear as if they were making concessions to gain U.S. blessing for China's WTO membership.

For China, no nontraditional threat hit home as abruptly as the outbreak of SARS.

In their public statements, China's leaders routinely acknowledge that globalization—economic globalization, initially, but now including its more fundamental implications—encourages broad participation in multilateral institutions both at the regional and global levels.[27] More specifically, across an increasingly wide range of trade issues, including disputes over steel tariffs, textile quotas, and antidumping duties, WTO mechanisms are proving an important means by which China can defend its interests against U.S. unilateralism. For example, China was one of the complainants who appealed to the WTO over the controversial imposition of U.S. tariffs on imported steel in March 2002. Indeed, China prepared retaliatory tariffs against U.S. imports, as allowed under WTO rules, in case the Bush administration had refused to lift the duties.

Similarly, global and regional institutions have provided a measure of support as Beijing has resisted pressure from Washington to revalue the renminbi on U.S. terms. In November 2003, for example, a majority of the International Monetary Fund's (IMF) directors found that China's currency was not substantially undervalued, noting in part the sharp decline in China's overall trade surplus.[28] This marked the third time in as many months that the Bush administration failed to secure multilateral pressure on China on this issue. In September, members of ASEAN with additional support from Australia undermined Washington's drive to have a statement issued on Beijing's currency policy at a meeting of APEC finance ministers. In October, Bush himself failed to make the U.S. case successfully at the annual APEC leaders' summit. At the October meeting, Japan went on the record in opposition to Washington's position. For their part, Chinese officials said that Beijing would consider changing its currency policy "if there was consensus in the region."[29] Any statement by the IMF or APEC would not have obliged China to take action, and Chinese officials undoubtedly expressed their willingness to consider the consensus view knowing what the outcome would be. These rejections of U.S. policy were important symbolically, however, in validating Beijing's determination to manage currency rates and undertake foreign exchange reform at its own pace.

The steady rise in China's status has vindicated its cooperative diplomacy.

Whereas recent emphasis has been on China's growing participation in multilateral institutions, similar arguments can be made about how informal mechanisms of interdependence, such as China's burgeoning commercial ties, have anchored its relations with other great powers. For all of China's oft-cited dependence on the United States as an export market, Washington's penchant for foreign borrowing contributes to leveling the playing field. By virtually any measure, Chinese holdings of U.S. debt, such as Treasury securities, dwarfs U.S. investment in Chinese factories. The result is a historically unusual relationship in which the rising power, developing China, provides both exports (second-leading supplier) and loans (second-leading foreign holder of government debt) to the superpower, the industrialized United States.

In this and other ways, China's economic ties with the United States are seen as weakening any impulse the United States may have to view China as a rival that needs to be contained. By many accounts, Beijing long ago adopted a conscious strategy of developing constituencies in the United States, particularly in the business community, who will support engagement policies toward China even if the noneconomic aspects of the bilateral relationship sour. Given the de facto constraints on using a balancing strategy to check the exercise of U.S. power, interdependence presents the most viable alternative currently available to China to restrain U.S. hegemony. Although deepening economic ties may produce their own tensions in the relationship, as the ongoing controversies over the proper valuation of the renminbi and the broader sources of the U.S.-Chinese trade imbalance illustrate, they still create mutual dependencies that most Chinese observers view as limiting hostilities.

Certainly, China continues to resort to power politics calculations as all states do in the still anarchic, albeit highly globalized world—for example, relying on coercive measures as an essential tool to prevent Taiwan's de jure independence—and is determined to strengthen its material power. Even in Taiwan, however, China's nicer, gentler image has made its threat of force less credible. Military confrontation over a democratic Taiwan would contradict Beijing's attempt to differentiate its own strategic choice of responsibility and peace from traditional great-power politics, characterized by the prominent role of violence and territorial conquest. In this sense, globalization and interdependence might have undercut the efficacy of China's coercive diplomacy in the short term and has no doubt drastically increased the cost of a military solution. Yet, decision-makers in Beijing still believe that the same process has deepened cross-strait interdependence, increased international support for stability in the region, and overall held the prospect of decisively turning the tide in mainland China's favor.

Beijing still finds certain aspects of U.S. hegemony detrimental to its interests, but the bottom line is that mainstream Chinese strategic thinkers believe that attempts to change the status quo radically carry substantial risks of international instability that, particularly in terms of geo-economic fragmentation, are anathema to China's pressing developmental needs. As such, China's strategic calculus is characterized by a dynamic status quo orientation that seeks what Robert Gilpin terms "changes in an international system" rather than "change of an international system."[30] The past decade has proven China's determination to advance its interests within the globalized world.

Toward a New Great-Power Politics?

Great-power politics has traditionally been viewed in terms of an unmitigated struggle for power among nation-states. Specifically, some mainstream international relations theories attribute inevitable great-power conflict to the supreme value that states attach to superior relative power. It is from this perspective that China's economic growth and rise in power are viewed as detrimental by many observers outside China. This line of reasoning overlooks the potential role globalization can play in transforming Chinese foreign policy choice and the corresponding responses to China's rise by other great powers.

In the preceding sections, we have outlined the mainstream views among top Chinese leaders and prominent strategic researchers within leading Chinese civilian think tanks and academic institutions. To be sure, these views are contested by more traditional security thinking, particularly among military analysts.[31] Yet, the prevailing views and the strategic choices that Beijing has made in recent years raise the question of whether China has, in fact, already begun to pursue a different approach to great-power politics, one that seeks to overcome the security dilemma fueled by great-power transitions. Skillful management of the Taiwan issue in particular remains critical to entrenching such an emerging Chinese view. Assuming that is successfully navigated, such an approach emphasizes positive state-to-state relations at the expense of narrower concerns about undercutting other states in the interest of enhancing China's own relative power.

Globalization by no means negates competition, but in today's increasingly globalized world, rules and institutions may moderate competitive politics. Chinese experience with and perceptions of globalization show that globalization has facilitated its status quo orientation despite U.S. hegemony. The same process has in turn led to international responses to China's rise that are, overall, characterized by a much more constrained balance-of-power logic than was evident in traditional great-power politics. The steady rise in China's international and regional status has vindicated its cooperative diplomacy.

It is by no means certain that China will not retreat from cooperative security thinking, nor is a new great-power system solely a Chinese choice. China's strategy and the constraints imposed by both the bright and dark sides of globalization on the unilateral exercise of coercive power, however, may provide other states the kind of mutual reassurance of each other's intentions and mutually beneficial outcomes that have been largely absent in traditional great-power relations. Countries thus may increasingly engage in multifaceted, dynamic, win-win competition rather than maintain a single-minded, zero-sum power struggle. As such, beyond the changes globalization appears to be bringing to China's foreign policy in particular, mainstream Chinese global thinking suggests the possible emergence of a new kind of great-power politics where peacefully contested change may replace the worst manifestations of hostile competition.

Notes

1. The term "globalization" was introduced by then-Foreign Minister Qian Qichen during the General Debate of the United Nations General Assembly on September 25, 1996, UN document A/51/ PV.8.

2. Jiang Zemin, "Together Create a New Century of Peace and Prosperity," Xinhua, April 10, 2002, in FBIS, CPP2002–0410000101. On common security, see Wu Bangguo, "Create a Hundred Years of Peace in Asia, Jointly Build Sustained Development of Asia," September 1, 2003, in FBIS, CPP2003–0901000066. On globalized cooperation, see Li Zhaoxing, speech to UN General Assembly, New York, September 24, 2003, www.un.org/webcast/ga/58/statements/chinaeng030924.htm (accessed October 9, 2003).

3. See Jiang Zemin, report to the Sixteenth Congress of the Chinese Communist Party, Beijing, November 8, 2002, in "Building a Well-off Society in an All-Out Effort, Creating a New Situation for the Cause of Chinese-Style Socialism," *Renmin Ribao* (overseas edition), November 18, 2002, pp. 1–3.

4. Ye Zicheng, "Transcend the 'Polarity' Mentality: Thoughts on China's Diplomatic Strategy," *Southern Weekend*, www.irchina.org/news/view.asp?id5297 (accessed January 20, 2004).

5. *Renmin Ribao*, (overseas edition), January 28, 2004, pp. 1, 4.

6. Wang Yi, "Safeguard Peace, Promote Development, Create a New Situation For Diplomatic Work," *Shijie Zhishi*, January 16, 2003, pp. 8–10, in FBIS, CPP2003–0204000110.

7. Joseph S. Nye Jr., *The Paradox of American Power: Why the World's Only Superpower Can't Go It Alone* (London and New York: Oxford University Press, 2002).

8. Shen Jiru, "Will the World Pattern Change?" *Renmin Ribao*, April 3, 2003, p. 13, in FBIS, CPP2003–0403000067.

9. Liao Lei, "PRC Expert Shen Jiru on Role of Economic Factors for Improving DPRK–U.S. Relations," Xinhua, August 26, 2003, in FBIS, CPP2003–0826000123.

10. Zheng Yu, "The Primary Goals of Chinese Diplomacy at the Beginning of the Century," *Huangiu Shibao*, September 5, 2003.

11. Luo Zhaohong, "Grasping Changes in the Environment from an Economic Perspective," *Xiandai Guoji Guanxi*, no. 11, November 20, 2002, in FBIS, CCP2002–1211000217, p. 2.

12. "Statement by Foreign Trade Minister Shi Guangsheng to the Fourth Ministerial Conference of the WTO Following the Adoption of the Decision on China's Accession to the WTO," November 10, 2001, http://english.mofcom.gov.cn/article/200211/20021100050101_1.xml (accessed April 4, 2004).

13. "Statement by H.E. Mr. Lu Fuyuan, Minister of Commerce," WT/MIN/(03)/ST/12, September 11, 2003, http://docsonline.wto.org/DDFDocuments/t/WT/Min03/ST12.doc (accessed April 4, 2004) (from the Fifth Session of the Ministerial Conference, Cancun, September 10–14, 2003).

14. Rebecca Buckman, "WTO Head Asks China to Help Revive Talks," *Asian Wall Street Journal*, November 11, 2003, p. A3.

15. Margaret M. Pearson, "The Major Multilateral Economic Institutions Engage China," in *Engaging China: The Management of an Emerging Power*, eds. Alastair Iain Johnston and Robert S. Ross (London: Routledge and Kegan Paul, 1999), p. 207.

16. Jiang Zemin, "Together Create a New Century of Peace and Prosperity."

17. Wu Xinbo, "Globalization and the Restructuring of the Strategic Foundation of Sino-U.S. Relations," *Shijie Zhengzhi Yu Jingji*, September 14, 2002, pp. 55–60, in FBIS, CPP2002–1011000334.

18. China State Council, Information Office, "China's National Defense, 2002," *Renmin Ribao* (overseas edition), December 10, 2002, pp. 1–4.

19. Chu Shulong, "China's Diplomatic Strategy During the Period of Comprehensively Building a Well-Off Society," *Shijie Zhengzhi Yu Jingji*, August 2003, p. 5, www.iwep.org.cn/wep/200308/chushulong.pdf (accessed April 21, 2004).

20. See Xue Lan and Zhang Qiang, "Confronting the Crisis—SARS Predicament and the Transformation of China's Governance," *Renmin Wang*, May 19, 2003.

21. Yan Xuetong, "SARS Tests China's Foreign Relations," *Global Times*, May 23, 2003.

22. Qian Qichen, "Adjustments of the U.S. National Security Strategy and International Relations in the Early New Century," *Renmin Ribao* (domestic edition), January 19, 2004, p.4, www.people.com.cn/GB/guoji/14549/2303998.html (accessed January 18, 2004).

23. Samuel S. Kim, "China and the United Nations," in *China Joins the World: Progress and Prospects*, eds. Elizabeth Economy and Michel Oksenberg (New York: Council on Foreign Relations, 1999), p. 46. See Alastair Iain Johnston, "Is China a Status Quo Power?" *International Security* 27, no. 4 (spring 2003): 5–56.

24. See Zhang Yunling, "How to Understand the International Environment China Faces in the Asia-Pacific Region," *Dangdai Yatai*, no. 6, June 15, 2003, pp. 3–14, in FBIS, CPP2003–0717000218, p. 3.

25. For a related discussion, see Banning Garrett, "China Faces, Debates the Contradictions of Globalization," *Asian Survey* 41, no. 3 (May–June 2001): 409–427.

26. This specific analysis on China is consistent with the general argument made in William C. Wohlforth, "The Stability of a Unipolar World," *International Security* 24, no. 1 (summer 1999): 5–41.

27. On economic affairs, one example is Jiang Zemin's speech at the Eighth APEC Informal Leadership Meeting, Brunei, November 16, 2000, www.fmprc.gov/cn/eng/6004.html (accessed March 11, 2003). On security affairs, see Tang

Jiaxuan's speech at the Ninth ASEAN Regional Forum Foreign Ministers' Meeting, Brunei, July 31, 2002, http://fmprc.gov.cn/eng/33228.html (accessed March 11, 2003). Portions of this and the following three paragraphs draw in part from Thomas G. Moore, "Chinese Foreign Policy in the Age of Globalization," in *China Rising: Power and Motivation in Chinese Foreign Policy*? eds. Yong Deng and Fei-Ling Wang (Lanham, Md.: Rowman and Littlefield, forthcoming).

28. "Risk of Divorce—Strains Grow in the U.S.-China Marriage of Convenience," *Financial Times*, November 20, 2003, p. 20.

29. "Asia Leaves U.S. to Fight Alone Over Yuan Policy," *Asian Wall Street Journal*, October 21, 2003, p. A1.

30. Robert Gilpin, *War and Change in World Politics* (Cambridge and New York: Cambridge University Press, 1981), p. 208 (emphasis in original).

31. For a representative military view, see Lt. Gen. Li Jijun, "China's National Security in the Globalization Era," *Outlook Weekly*, http://news.xinhuanet.com/2004-03/27/content_1387461.htm (accessed March 27, 2004) (reprint).

YONG DENG is an associate professor of political science at the United States Naval Academy. Thomas G. Moore is an associated professor of political science at the University of Cincinnati.

India's Path to Greatness

After decades of dormancy, India has blossomed into one of Asia's two emerging powers and an important strategic partner of the United States. How—and whether—it navigates its rise could well determine the future of the whole region.

MARTIN WALKER

When the U.S. Air Force sent its proud F-15 fighter pilots against the Indian Air Force in the Cope India war games two years ago, it received a shock. The American pilots found themselves technologically outmatched by nimbler warplanes; tactically outsmarted by the Indian mix of high, low, and converging attack waves; and outfought by the Indians, whose highly trained pilots average more than 180 flying hours a year—roughly the same as their U.S. and Israeli counterparts and slightly more than those of NATO allies such as France and Germany. U.S. general Hal Homburg said that the results of the exercise, against Indian pilots flying Russian-built Sukhoi Su-30 and French Mirage 2000 fighters, were "a wake-up call." According to testimony in a House Appropriations Defense Subcommittee hearing, the U.S. F-15s were defeated more than 90 percent of the time in direct combat exercises against the Indians.

But beyond the evidence of India's military expertise and its possession of state-of-the-art fighter aircraft, the real significance of the Cope India war games is that they demonstrated the extent of the cooperation between the Indian and U.S. militaries. Their mountain troops now train together in the Himalayas and Alaska, and their special forces mount joint exercises in jungle and underwater warfare. Their aircraft carrier task forces have conducted exercises in the Indian Ocean, and joint antipiracy and antisubmarine drills are routine. Indian and U.S. forces are working together with an intimacy once reserved for the closest NATO allies. The goal—that the militaries of the two countries be able to operate in lockstep—would have been inconceivable in the Cold War era, when India, with its Soviet-supplied military, was seen as a virtual client of Moscow.

The foundation of this new relationship was laid before George W. Bush took office in the White House. In the spring of 1999, Bush, then governor of Texas, was briefed for the first time by the team of foreign-policy advisers that became known as the Vulcans, after the Roman god of fire and iron. Bush began with the frank admission that he knew little about foreign policy. The Vulcans, led by Condoleezza Rice—later to be his national security adviser and then secretary of state—delivered a broad-brash survey of the world, its problems, and its prospects, and recommended muscular American leadership in cool-headed pursuit of American interests. When the group finished, Bush had one question: What about India? Another Vulcan team member who was present, future ambassador to India Robert Blackwill, recalled asking Bush why he was so interested in India: "He immediately responded, 'A billion people in a functioning democracy. Isn't that something? Isn't that something?'"

Bush's curiosity had been stirred by a number of Indian supporters living and prospering in Texas, including some businessmen who helped build the state's high-tech corridor, dubbed Silicon Canyon. One of those businessmen was Durga Agrawal, born in Lakhanpur, a central Indian village without water or electricity, who had earned a master's degree at the University of Houston and stayed on to found a highly successful company called Piping Technology & Products and to raise more than $100,000 for the Bush presidential campaign in the local Indian community. After Bush became president, Agrawal was invited to the White House as a guest at the banquet for visiting Indian prime minister Manmohan Singh, where Bush introduced him as "my good friend from Texas."

Bush's question to his Vulcans prompted Rice to include a highly significant paragraph in her January 2000 *Foreign Affairs* essay "Promoting the National Interest," which was widely studied as the blueprint for a Bush administration foreign policy. She contended that China should be regarded as "a strategic competitor, not the 'strategic partner' the Clinton administration once called it," and suggested that America should redirect its focus. The United States "should pay closer attention to India's role in the regional balance. There is a strong tendency conceptually to connect India with Pakistan and to think only of Kashmir or the nuclear competition between the two states. But India is an element in China's calculation, and it should be in America's, too. India is not a great power yet, but it has the potential to emerge as one."

The intervening September 11 terrorist attacks and the Iraq war perhaps explain why it took five years for the Bush administration to act formally on that calculus. But on a March 2005 visit to India, Rice told Prime Minister Singh that part of the United States' foreign policy was to "help India become a major world power in the 21st century" At a later briefing, U.S. ambassador to India David Mulford described the vision behind a broader strategic relationship with India that would foster cooperation on a number of fronts. "The U.S.-India relationship is based on our shared common values. We are multiethnic democracies committed to the rule of law and freedom of speech and religion" Mulford said, adding that "there is no fundamental conflict or disagreement between the United States and India on any important regional or global issue."

A July 2005 visit by Prime Minister Singh to Washington, and President Bush's trip this year to New Delhi, along with detailed negotiations for nuclear, military, economic, and technological cooperation, have institutionalized that relationship. But, as former deputy secretary of state Strobe Talbott said of his own earlier path-breaking negotiations with foreign minister Jaswant Singh, "What took us so long?"

The short answer is the Cold War. American officials were uncomprehending and resentful of India's determination to stay neutral as a founder and pillar of the Non-Aligned Movement. By contrast, Pakistan swiftly decided to become an American ally and to buy American weapons. In response, India bought Soviet weapons. Pakistan, with whom India has fought three wars since the two countries simultaneously became independent from Britain in 1947, was also a close ally of China, so the Sino-Soviet split gave Soviet diplomats a strong incentive to cement their ties with India, deepening American suspicions.

India's explosion of a nuclear device (not a weapon, Indira Gandhi's government insisted) in 1974 exposed India to various restrictions in obtaining nuclear supplies under the Nuclear Non-Proliferation Treaty, and to some other mildly punitive but symbolic U.S. legislation. After India's full-scale nuclear weapons tests in 1998 (swiftly followed by rather less impressive tests by Pakistan), the Clinton administration sought engagement through the Talbott-Singh talks and Bill Clinton's own highly successful visit to India. When Pakistan-backed militants crossed Kashmir's mountains into the Indian-controlled area of Kargil, Clinton's intervention prevented the incursion from escalating into a full-scale war. The Bush administration had to launch another panicked round of diplomacy in early 2002, after an attack on the Indian parliament by Kashmiri terrorists with apparent Pakistani connections. At one critical point, then-U.S. deputy secretary of state Richard Armitage asked his staff, "Who thinks they're heading for nuclear war?" and everyone except for Armitage reportedly raised a hand. One senior British official who was involved recalls it as the nearest thing to nuclear war since the 1962 Cuban Missile Crisis.

Perhaps these brushes with disaster served as an awful warning to India. Or perhaps its successful market-style economic reforms in the 1990s, along with the palpable weakness of its old friends in Moscow, gave the country's leaders the spur and the self-confidence to rethink India's foreign policy. But there was a further goad: India's nervousness at the rapid growth of its Asian neighbor, China, by whom it had been humiliated in a brief border war in 1962. In May 1998, at the time of India's nuclear tests, Indian defense minister George Fernandes claimed that China was exploiting Pakistan, Burma, and Tibet in order to "encircle" India. "China has provided Pakistan with both missile as well as nuclear know-how," Fernandes said, adding, "China has its nuclear weapons stockpiled in Tibet right along our borders." He concluded that China was India's most severe threat, and that while India had pledged "no first use" of nuclear weapons, the Indian nuclear arsenal would be targeted appropriately.

With Pakistan to the west and China to the north and east, India has long feared encirclement. Despite soothing diplomatic statements, China has sharpened these fears with an assertive new presence in the Indian Ocean, beginning in the late 1990s with an electronic listening post in Myanmar's Coco Islands. In 2001, China agreed to help Pakistan build a new port and naval base at Gwadar, close to the Iranian border and the Persian Gulf. China has also pitched in to build a road network from the new port to the Karakoram Highway, a feat of engineering that connects China and Pakistan through the Himalayas. The Gwadar naval base planned to India's west is matched by another to the east, where Chinese engineers are building a similar facility on Myanmar's Arakan coast, connected by a new road and rail link through Myanmar to China's Yunnan Province. China is also helping Cambodia build a rail link to the sea, and in Thailand, it is proposing to help fund a $20 billion canal across the Kra Isthmus, which would allow ships to bypass the Strait of Malacca. A recent Pentagon report described these new bases as China's "string of pearls" to secure the sea routes to the vital oil fields of the Persian Gulf.

The tension between India and China, both rising powers, is underscored by their rivalry for essential energy sources.

In a number of off-the-record conversations in New Delhi on the eve of Bush's visit earlier this year, including extremely rare meetings with senior officials of the secretive Research and Analysis Wing, Indian security and military figures stressed their profound concern at these developments. The degree of alarm is evident in India's recent flurry of arms purchases, including a $3.5 billion deal to buy six Scorpene "stealth" submarines from France along with the technology to build more. The Scorpene will augment India's existing submarine fleet of 16 vessels, mainly Soviet-built Kilo and Foxtrot attack submarines. India was the world's biggest customer for arms last year, and more deals for advanced aircraft are in the works, which seem likely to include U.S.-made F-16 and F-18 warplanes, even as India builds its own family of nuclear-capable Agni missiles, the latest version of which is designed to reach Shanghai. With almost 1.4 million troops, India's armed forces are already roughly the same size as those of the United States, and they are increasingly well trained and well armed. India is so far the only Asian country with an aircraft carrier, which can deploy British-built Sea Harrier fighters, vertical-takeoff jets like those used by the U.S. Marines.

The alarm over China's rise is plain in India's military and policy debates. An article last year by the Indian Defense Ministry's Bhartendu Kumar Singh in the journal *Peace and Conflict*, published by the New Delhi-based Institute of Peace and Conflict Studies, is typical. Singh speculated that China's military buildup might be explained in part by Taiwan, but that its long-term goal could be to ensure Chinese dominance of the Asia-Pacific region. While Singh doubted that this challenge would result in an all-out war between China and India, India was bound "to feel the effects of Chinese military confidence. . . . Is India prepared? It can wage and win a war against Pakistan under every circumstance, but it is not sure about holding out against China."

The irony and the danger is that China has similar reasons to feel encircled. The United States has established new military bases in Central Asia since 9/11, adding to existing outposts in Japan and South Korea, and it is expanding its existing facilities at Guam to include a base for submarines and long-range stealth bombers. Now Beijing nervously watches the warming strategic partnership between Washington and New Delhi. Moreover, China's construction of the "string of pearls" reflects its own deep concern about the security of its oil supplies. Its tankers must pass through the Indian Ocean, and China's new pipeline from the Kazakh oil and gas fields of Central Asia will lie within easy cruise missile or air strike distance of India.

The tension between these two rising powers is underscored by their rivalry for essential energy resources. "India, panicked over future oil supply, went after international oil assets competing directly with China," *India Daily* reported last year when Subir Raha, chairman of India's Oil and Natural Gas Corporation, announced that the company was buying a fifth of Iran's giant Yadavaran oil field and was in the market to buy assets of Yukos, the Russian energy giant. The Indian company had already invested nearly $2 billion to buy a share of the Sakhalin-1 field in Siberia, run by ExxonMobil. India, which imports more than two-thirds of its oil, has since signed a $40 billion deal with Iran to import liquefied natural gas and join in developing three Iranian oil fields.

Energy geopolitics can promote harmony as well as rivalry. Pakistan and Turkmenistan have signed a memorandum of understanding on a multibillion-dollar gas pipeline through Afghanistan that could eventually end as a "Peace Pipeline" in India, in what would be a major breakthrough in Indo-Pakistani relations. Former Indian petroleum minister Mani Shankar Aiyar, a strong advocate for the pipeline, says, "Almost everywhere in the world where an Indian goes in quest of energy, chances are that he will run into a Chinese engaged in the same hunt." Aiyar proposed that India, China, Japan, and South Korea establish a system of cooperative access to energy supplies. His subsequent demotion to minister for youth and sport was widely perceived in India as reflecting U.S. pressure against the Iran oil deal.

Indian security officials already see themselves fated to play central roles in what Aaron Friedberg, a Princeton scholar now on the White House national security staff, has called "the struggle for mastery in Asia." That phrase was the title of an essay he published in the neoconservative monthly *Commentary* when Bush was first elected. Friedberg's central message was that over the next several decades the United States would likely find itself engaged in an "open and intense geopolitical rivalry" with China. "The combination of growing Chinese power, China's effort to expand its influence, and the unwillingness of the United States to entirely give way before it are the necessary preconditions of a 'struggle for mastery,' " he wrote, adding that hostilities or a military confrontation could be slow to develop or could occur as a result of a "single catalytic event, such as a showdown over Taiwan."

India is now playing tortoise to China's hare, not only in its rate of growth but also because the Indian and Chinese economies are two very different creatures.

The strategic and energy concerns of the United States, China, and India will be difficult to manage. But Pakistan, Russia, Japan, and North and South Korea all factor into the extraordinarily complex equation of Asian security. (India maintains that Pakistan's missile technology came from China and North Korea.) And through Pakistan and the terrorist attacks from militants in Kashmir, India also feels itself threatened by Islamic extremism, a matter of grave concern for a country whose population of just over one billion includes 145 million Muslims.

It is in this context that the nuclear dimension of the Bush administration's embrace of India has aroused so much controversy. The administration seeks to steer India into "compliance" with the Non-Proliferation Treaty and the International Atomic Energy Agency (IAEA) system while leaving India's nuclear weapons reactors out of the international control regime. This stance has been challenged by critics in the United States for driving a coach and horses through the Non-Proliferation Treaty just as international support for diplomatic pressure on Iran depends on strict compliance with it.

Under the deal, India will separate its civilian from its military nuclear programs, but it has until 2014 to complete this division. New Delhi will declare 14 of an expected total of 22 nuclear reactors to be for civilian use and place them under IAEA controls. But India has managed to keep its new fast-breeder reactors out of the control system, which means that there will be no nuclear fuel shortages to constrain the future manufacture and development of nuclear weapons. Moreover, because India will reserve the right to determine which parts of its nuclear program will be subject to IAEA controls and which will not, it will be able to shield its own nuclear research labs from the IAEA system. New Delhi has also reinterpreted the U.S. insistence that the deal be made "in perpetuity" by making this conditional on continued supplies of enriched uranium, of which India is desperately short, to fuel its reactors.

The main concession India made was cosmetic. It agreed not to be formally included, in the eyes of the United States and the IAEA, in the category of the five recognized nuclear weapons states (the United States, Russia, Britain, France, and China). The deal is still the subject of hard bargaining in the U.S. Congress, where it has yet to be ratified, despite intense pressure from the Bush administration. But if, as expected, the agreement succeeds, India will become a special case, with a free hand to augment its nuclear weapons systems, and to develop its nuclear power stations with full access to the fuel and technology monopolized by the 45-nation Nuclear Suppliers Group. And India will secure all this with the blessing of the IAEA, thus negating the efforts of the international community since the 1970s to constrain India's nuclear ambitions by putting sanctions on its access to nuclear fuel and technology.

In India, the agreement has come in for criticism for wedding the country to U.S. strategic interests, to the detriment of India's relations with China and Iran. The policy is also viewed by some Indians as a lever to steadily increase international control over India's nuclear assets, and to make it more dependent on the United States as the prime supplier of nuclear fuel.

India long saw itself as neutral and nonaligned, endowed by Gandhi's nonviolent legacy with a singular innocence of such geopolitical games. It has been thrust with remarkable speed into a prominent strategic role that matches its new economic robustness. But its ability to sustain military power and buy advanced weaponry will dearly depend on its economic growth, which began in earnest 15 years after China launched its own economic reforms. While India 30 years ago enjoyed a slightly higher per capita income than China, today it has an annual per capita income (at purchasing power parity) of $3,300, not quite half of China's level of $6,800, and less than one-tenth of the $41,800 level of the United States.

India is now playing the tortoise to China's hare, not only in its rate of growth but also because the Indian and Chinese economies are two very different creatures. China has become the world's low-cost manufacturing center, making and assembling components that are often designed or developed elsewhere, and relying heavily on foreign investment. India's boom, by contrast, has so far been largely based on services and software, and it has been self-financing, with about a tenth of China's level of foreign direct investment. Still, it has produced an Indian middle class—usually defined by the ability to buy a private car—of some 300 million people, a number greater than the entire population of the United States.

One central reason why India has not enjoyed a Chinese-style boom led by manufacturing is the dismal state of so much of the country's infrastructure. Its ports, railroads, highways, electricity supplies, and grid systems are aged and ramshackle, and traffic jams and power outages are routine, reinforcing each other when the traffic lights blink out. Critical segments of the economy—such as the container transport system, which allows easy shipping of freight by land, sea, and air—have been state monopolies, subject to the usual debilitating problems of the breed. Arriving foreigners receive a startling introduction to the bustle and backwardness of India before they ever reach a hotel. On my most recent trip to New Delhi and Jaipur, the maddening endemic traffic jams included bicycles,

flimsy three-wheeled rickshaws, and somnolent cows, whose excrement was swiftly scooped up by hordes of small children and patted into flat, plate-shaped discs, which are dried in the sun and sold for fuel. So to the usual tourist dangers of stomach upsets from eating local foods is added the prospect of respiratory infection from breathing air suffused with fecal matter.

Yet there is no denying the furious commercial energy of a country that is currently signing up five million new mobile phone subscribers each month. Competition has come to the container industry, the airports are being privatized despite labor union opposition, and new highways are being built. The gas and electricity grids are slated for reform next. India has its high-tech centers of Bangalore and Hyderabad, as well as a few new towns such as Gurgaon, just outside Delhi, with a modern automaking plant, high-rise shopping malls, and telemarketing centers. But it can boast nothing like the jaw-dropping array of new skyscrapers that zigzag the skylines of modern Shanghai and Guangdong.

Still, some of the smart money is on the tortoise. The global consultancy firm PwC (still better known by its old name, Price Waterhouse Coopers) produced a report this year forecasting that India would have the fastest growth among all the major economies over the next 50 years, averaging 7.6 percent annually in dollar terms. In 50 years' time, the Indian and U.S. economies would be roughly equivalent in size. The report also suggested that by 2050 the existing economies of the G-7 group of advanced industrial nations (the United States, Britain, France, Germany, Italy, Japan, and Canada) would be overtaken by the E-7 emergent economies of China, India, Brazil, Russia, Indonesia, Mexico, and Turkey.

There is no denying the furious commercial energy of a country that is currently signing up five million new mobile phone subscribers each month.

The most significant difference between India and China, however, may be how their respective demographic trends and political systems shape their futures. The Chinese leadership is already coming to regret its nearly 30-year-old policy of permitting most couples to have only one child. Now China is rapidly aging and heading for a pensions crisis, as an entire generation of only children grapples with the problem of helping to support two parents and four grandparents. A recent DeutscheBank survey on Chinas pension challenge predicted, "China is going to get old before it gets rich." The policy has also created a serious gender disparity. The ability to predict the sex of a fetus in a country limited to one child per family has led to a situation in which 120 boys are born for every 100 girls, and President Hu Jintao last year asked a task force of scientists and officials to address the tricky problems posed by an excess of single men. India has a similar sex disparity problem in certain regions, notably those where Sikhs are numerous, but overall, with half of its population below the age of 25, it boasts a far healthier demographic profile.

The contest between the Indian tortoise and the Chinese hare has a political dimension as well. India is a democracy, without an equivalent of China's ruling Communist Party. Its elections, provincial governments, and free news media give the country great social resilience. China's breakneck economic growth and social disruption seem likely to have potent consequences as its new middle class finds a political voice.

The Chinese Communist Party is becoming less ideological and far more technocratic in its orientation, but it still can manipulate the most authoritarian levers of state power in aggressive pursuit of economic and strategic goals. Indians are stuck with their messy but comfortable democracy. Montek Singh Ahluwalia, an Oxford-educated economist who is deputy chairman of the national planning commission, says, "The biggest thing about India is that it's a very participative, very pluralistic, open democracy where even if the top 1,000 people technocratically came to the conclusion something is good, it has to be mediated into a political consensus. And I'm being realistic. I don't think it's going to be that easy to put in place everything that from a technocratic point of view everybody knows needs to be done."

In short, India's pluralism could be to China's advantage, although given the track record of bureaucratic technocrats from Moscow to Japan in wasting massive resources to pursue the wrong goals, it may not be that simple. But India has its own special asset, recognized by the American presidential candidate George W. Bush and suggested by the celebrated prediction a century ago by Otto von Bismarck that "the most important fact of the 20th century will be that the English and the Americans speak the same language." The most important factor in the 21st century may well be that Americans and Indians (and perhaps Britons and Australians and Microsoft employees and global businesspeople) all speak English. This is not simply a matter of a shared language, although that is important; it also encompasses those other aspects of the common heritage that include free speech and free press, trial by jury and an independent judiciary, private property, and individual as well as human rights. While retaining its rich and historic cultures, India is thoroughly familiar with these core values and determinants of the American civic system. And as a religiously tolerant, multi-ethnic democracy with commercial, legal, and educational systems developed during the British Raj, India is—like the English language itself—familiar and reassuring to Americans.

A decisive factor in the short term may be India's importance to the United States in the strategic and cultural campaign now being waged against Islamic extremism. This will be a struggle much deeper and longer than the mainly military effort the Bush administration calls GWOT (Global War on Terrorism), as currently being fought in Afghanistan and Iraq. India, itself a regular target, has been from the beginning a firm partner in the war on terrorism, instantly offering flyover and landing rights to U.S. aircraft engaged in the war against the Taliban. But with its 145 million Muslims, India risks becoming embroiled in the tumult now shaking so much of the Islamic world as the faithful try simultaneously to grapple with the cultural, theological, economic, and social revolutions now under way.

Facing the additional problem of militant Hindu nationalism, India has no choice but to stand in the front line against Islamic extremism. India is the great geographic obstruction to an Islamic arc that would stretch from Morocco across Africa and the Middle East all the way to Malaysia, Indonesia, and into the Philippines. Pakistan and Bangladesh are deeply uncomfortable neighbors for India, being Muslim, poor, the scenes of concerted jihadist campaigns, and worrisomely close to becoming failed states. But there is another arc, which stretches from Japan and South Korea through China and the increasingly prosperous countries of the Association of Southeast Asian Nations to India. This swath of rising prosperity and economic growth now includes three billion people—half the world's population. It is easy to foresee wretched outliers such as North Korea, Myanmar, Bangladesh, and Pakistan being swept up in the wake of this boom, should it continue, but for that to happen, Asia needs stability, peace, and a cessation of arms races.

It is an open question whether the burgeoning new strategic friendship of India and the United States will help this process or derail it. It could do both, deterring China from adventurism or bullying its neighbors, and stabilizing the strategic environment while India and China manage a joint and peaceful rise to wealth and status. But at the same time, the new U.S.-Indian accord could help spur a new nuclear arms race in Asia, where Russia, China, India, Pakistan, and probably North Korea already have the bomb, and Japan, South Korea, and Taiwan have the technological capability to build it quickly. One wild card is already being played that could bring this about: the prospect of Japan and India sharing in American antimissile technology. If India gains the ability to shoot down incoming missiles, this threatens to negate the deterrent that Pakistan and China thought they possessed against India, with potentially destabilizing results.

Even though India's prospects now look brighter than they have for a generation, the country faces some sobering challenges, including the accelerating pace of expectations among its own people and their understandable demand that the new wealth be shared quickly, that the poorest villages get schools and electricity. Almost half the population still lives in rural hamlets, and only 44 percent of these rural residents have electricity. Enemies of globalization populate the Indian Left and sit in the current coalition government. India must grapple with the familiar difficulties of Hindu nationalism, inadequate infrastructure, and a large Muslim population, as well as environmental crisis, deep rural poverty, and the caste system.

India finds itself in a delicate position. It must manage and maintain its relationship with China while accommodating American strategists who are relying on its support to keep Asia on the rails of democratic globalization. Americans also regard India as insurance against China's domination of Asia to the exclusion of the United States. India, on the other hand, wants freedom of action and does not want to serve merely as a tool of American influence.

"We want the United States to remain as the main stabilizer in Asia and the balance against China until such time as India can manage the job on its own" an influential security adviser to the Indian government said recently, very much on background. What will happen once India believes it can do this alone? I asked. "Well, then we shall see," he replied. "By then it will be a different Asia, probably a different China, and possibly a different America. It will certainly be a different world, dominated by the Indian, Chinese, and American superpowers."

MARTIN WALKER is the editor of United Press International and a senior scholar at the Wilson Center. His most recent books are *America Reborn: A Twentieth-Century Narrative in Twenty-Six Lives* (2000) and the novel *The Caves of Périgord* (2002).

Lula's Brazil: A Rising Power, but Going Where?

One of the most interesting features of the Lula years has been a pessimistic view of the international system combined with a belief that there is scope for an activist and assertive foreign policy.

ANDREW HURRELL

As the world enters a period of increasing challenges to US hegemony, attention shifts naturally to rising powers, emerging nations, threshold states, and regional powers. Such states obviously will be central to the dynamics of the balance of power in the twenty-first century, as well as to the possible emergence of new concert-style groupings of major powers. But these states will also be crucial to the development of international institutions and global governance. Indeed, the current detachment from—or outright opposition to—existing international organizations on the part of many of these nations represents one of the most important weaknesses in the global institutional order.

Think of the major emerging economies' distancing themselves from the World Bank and International Monetary Fund, or the opposition (led by Brazil and India) to developed countries' preferences in the World Trade Organization (WTO), or the effective breakdown of the global aid regime in the face of the emergence of new aid donors such as China and India. These countries are substantively critical to the management of major global challenges such as climate change and nuclear proliferation. And they are procedurally critical if international institutions are to reestablish legitimacy and a degree of representativeness.

Ranking just after China and India, Brazil figures prominently in almost all lists of emerging states and regional powers. As US Secretary of State Condoleezza Rice put it: "In the twenty-first century, emerging nations like India, China, Brazil, Egypt, Indonesia, and South Africa are increasingly shaping the course of history. . . ." But there are other reasons to focus on Brazilian foreign policy. For many on the left (especially in Europe), for many inside Brazil, and for many in the developing world, the assertive foreign policy of the government of President Luiz Inácio Lula da Silva (Lula) is seen as a progressive force in global affairs.

Lula and the Workers Party government may well have been tainted at home by corruption and an association with old-style Brazilian machine politics. They may have followed an orthodox domestic macroeconomic policy and made little progress on structural reforms in areas such as taxation, land redistribution, or tackling violent crime. Nonetheless, Brazil's foreign policy (along with its conditional cash-transfer program to reduce poverty) is widely regarded as a great success story, as well as a potential bellwether for the global strategies of other emerging powers.

A Nationalist Worldview

The Lula government that came to power in January 2002 sought to differentiate its own more assertively nationalist foreign policy from that of its predecessor, which it portrayed as insufficiently resolute in the defense of Brazilian interests and too closely tied to the acceptance of the liberalizing and globalizing agenda of the 1990s. The incoming administration brought with it a view of foreign policy that stressed both the instability of the international environment and the growing concentration of political and military power, wealth, and ideological sway on the part of the United States and its developed-country allies.

Reflecting a deep-rooted strand of nationalist thought in Brazil (on both right and left), this approach to foreign affairs regards the global economy as containing more constraints and snares than opportunities. It views globalization as a force working to reinforce the power of the developed world while creating new sources of instability (especially in relation to recurrent financial crises) and promoting politically dangerous and morally unacceptable inequality (both within and across countries).

Political power, according to this view, was used throughout the post-cold war period to incorporate developing economies

23

into the globalized system. Developed nations and the international institutions that they control have exploited developing countries' external financial vulnerability, created new forms of coercion and conditionalities, and imposed new economic norms that have generally reflected and reinforced their own political power and the interests of the core economies.

Even before the presidency of George W. Bush, many in Brazil and in particular many who later were associated with the Lula government suspected that the liberal norms of the 1990s concerning human rights, democracy, and free markets had been used in selective ways to reflect narrow national interests. Since the terrorist attacks of September 11, 2001, many have suspected Washington of exploiting new security threats to mobilize support at home and abroad for the projection and expansion of US power.

Within this harsh and conflict-oriented view of the international system, Brazil is seen as vulnerable—on one hand because of its internal inequalities, social cleavages, and incomplete development and, on the other, because of its continued external weaknesses and its absence from international decision-making structures. Yet the country is not without options. Indeed, one of the most interesting features of the Lula years has been a pessimistic view of the international system combined with a belief that there is scope for an activist and assertive foreign policy. Foreign policy discussions repeatedly invoke the idea that Brazil is not small or insignificant and that it has room to maneuver in a world where, despite all the challenges, unipolarity is more apparent than real.

Facing "hegemonic structures of power," Brazil needs to reassert its national autonomy, according to the currently prevalent line of thinking. It needs to form coalitions with other developing states in order to reduce its external vulnerability and increase its bargaining power, and to work, however modestly, toward a more balanced world order. Brazil should seek "to increase, if only by a margin, the degree of multipolarity in the world," as the foreign minister, Celso Amorim, put it.

Building up technological capacity also matters, as can be seen in Brazil's determination to continue protecting its industrial base. Because the proposed Free Trade Area of the Americas is seen as a threat in this regard, the Lula administration has downplayed and significantly diluted the negotiations. Likewise, the government has placed renewed emphasis on the long-term goal of developing the country's nuclear technological capacity (seeking to preserve industrial secrets while maintaining good relations with the global inspection regime).

The Multilateral Route

The cornerstones of Brazilian foreign policy have followed from this general outlook. The Lula years have witnessed efforts to increase Brazil's presence in international institutions—including a (so far unsuccessful) campaign for permanent membership in the UN Security Council, and a (successful) drive to join the core group of states negotiating in the World Trade Organization's Doha Round of talks. Brazil has sought to expand relations with other major developing countries—especially India, China, and South Africa—while launching a more activist policy toward Africa and, to a lesser extent, the Middle East.

Brazil has sought to expand relations with other major developing countries— especially India, China, and South Africa.

The Lula administration has also intensified relations within South America. It has attempted to deepen and broaden Mercosur, the common market that, in addition to Brazil, includes Argentina, Paraguay, Uruguay, and now Venezuela. Lula's apparent aim is to shift Mercosur's focus from purely economic relations toward the development of a political bloc. And Brazil has launched the Union of South American nations, a fledgling intergovernmental organization that will unite Mercosur with the region's other major free-trade bloc, the Andean Community, as part of a continuing process of South American integration.

Brazilian officials have sought to portray foreign policy as the external face of the Lula government's domestic social commitment. As Lula put it: "Alongside the theme of security, the international agenda should also privilege those issues which aim at the eradication of asymmetries and injustices, such as the struggle against social and cultural exclusion, the genuine opening of the markets of the rich countries, the construction of a new financial architecture, and the imperative of combating hunger, disease, and poverty."

In keeping with both its perceived identity and its power-related interests, Brazil continues to for-swear a hard-power strategy in favor of a heavy emphasis on multilateralism. The Lula administration is attempting to exploit what one observer has called Brazil's diplomatic GNP: its capacity for effective coalition-building and insider activism within international institutions, as well as its ability to frame its own interests in terms of arguments for greater justice. Thus, mobilizing claims for greater representational fairness (as with membership in the Security Council) and distributional justice (as with the promotion of a global hunger fund) has been a central tool of Brazil's recent foreign policy.

Notwithstanding this concentration on soft power, however, it is worth noting that the past five years have seen the first glimmering of a more focused discussion of links between foreign policy and military strategy. This has few concrete implications for current policy, but it represents a new development that could have a significant impact in the future, especially if security relations in the region deteriorate.

A Return to History?

Where does Lula's foreign policy fit within the broader historical picture? How much does it represent a sharp discontinuity with the past? In fact, assertions that Brazil is destined to play a more influential role in world affairs have a long history inside the country. The intensity of these predictions has varied across time. At times ideas about national greatness have been little more than vague aspirations—hardly tied to practical political action or concrete foreign policies and commonly engendering a good deal of cynicism. At other times they have assumed a much more direct role in the shaping of foreign policy, as in the 1970s when high growth rates seemed to establish Brazil as an upwardly mobile middle power, if not one moving ineluctably toward eventual great power status. In this respect, the claim that Brazil should be seen as a major player speaks to a long tradition of thought, and some critics have interpreted the Lula foreign policy in terms of "nostalgia" for the idea of *Brasil-potência* (Brazil as a power).

The third-worldism *(terceiro-mundismo)* of the Lula years also feeds into another debate with deep historical roots that reflects the complex origins of Brazil's international identity. On one hand, Brazil was formed as part of the process of European colonial settlement, a process that involved subjugation of indigenous peoples. Brazil's elites have seen themselves as part of the West in cultural and religious terms and the country harbors a strong tradition of liberalism, including Western ideas about international law and society. On the other hand, Brazilian society has been shaped by the legacies of colonialism and poverty, the imperatives of economic development, and longstanding connections to Africa, the Middle East, and Asia—connections created most powerfully by the slave trade but also by other waves of immigration.

This duality has remained an important element of Brazilian discussions about where the country "fits in." The cold war years witnessed a persistent and often highly politically charged debate as to whether Brazil was part of the West in its battle against communism and the Soviet Union or a member of the third world in its struggle for development and a greater role in international affairs.

Embracing the Third World

In general terms, the developmentalist line won out. Brazil came to place great emphasis on the pursuit of national autonomy, the politicization of international economic relations, and complaints against the freezing of the international power structure by the powers that be. By the end of the 1960s the close alignment with the United States that followed a coup in 1964 had given way to a broader and more pragmatic approach. Relations with Washington varied between cool and distant, and Brazil sought to diversify its foreign and economic relations, expanding ties with Western Europe, Japan, the socialist countries, and, increasingly, the third world.

Thus, Brazil played a prominent role in such third world forums as the Group of 77 (a United Nations coalition of developing countries) and was heavily engaged in debates during the 1970s regarding a "New International Economic Order." Brazil's embrace of the third world was not as thoroughgoing as India's—and it certainly did not include calls for global revolution, as China's did before 1978—but it did figure prominently in the country's sense of itself and its place in the world.

The developmentalist-nationalist stance was closely tied to economic policy. Brazil's economic policies for much of the post-1945 period relied on a strategy of import substitution, subsidies to strategic sectors, large-scale direct investment in state-owned enterprises, technological nationalism, and a deeply rooted belief in the imperative of continued growth even at the cost of high inflation. The project of national economic development came to be institutionally embedded within and around the Brazilian state and was backed by a wide array of powerful interest groups and a relatively high degree of elite consensus.

It also gave rise to a set of unspoken assumptions whose influence continues to be apparent in Brazilian foreign policy: the importance of defending economic and political sovereignty; the imperative of developing a more prominent international role for the nation; and the suspicion that the United States is more likely to be a hindrance than a help in securing the country's upward progress.

This pattern of foreign policy was not significantly affected by the return to civilian rule in 1985. It began to change, however, by the early 1990s, as the established economic model came under increasing strain, as Brazil along with other countries in the region moved toward economic liberalization, and as the end of the Cold War seemed to force acceptance of the reality of both a unipolar world and economic globalization.

The Cardoso Legacy

How far Brazil actually abandoned its foreign policy traditions and embraced "neoliberal globalization"—especially under the government of Fernando Henrique Cardoso from 1994 to 2002—is a subject bitterly contested inside the country. (One important trend in recent years has been a politicization of foreign policy, both within the foreign ministry and in Brazilian politics more generally.)

It is certainly true that the central preoccupation of the Cardoso administration was with economic stabilization and economic reform rather than foreign policy. It is also the case that the Cardoso government tended to stress the need for Brazil to accommodate itself to US power and to liberal globalization. Brazil showed a greater willingness to accept many of the dominant norms of the post-Cold War period. For example, the country moved during the 1990s toward increased acceptance of international norms controlling missile technology, arms exports, and nuclear proliferation.

Similarly, in relation to the environment, Brazil moved sharply away from its defensiveness of the 1980s toward an acknowledgement of the legitimacy of international concerns about environmental matters. Brazil came to accept the activities of nongovernmental organizations, which before had often been denounced as subversive, and it engaged more positively in international negotiations, especially in the process leading to the 1992 Earth Summit in Rio. A parallel move could be seen in relation to international human rights.

It is true, as well, that Brazilian foreign policy during the 1990s frequently demonstrated national reticence, as captured by Cardoso's view that "to provoke friction with the United States is to lose," or by a comment in his memoirs that Brazil's capacity to influence the region politically remained limited. Thus, while action to help maintain democracy in Paraguay was viable, thoughts of involvement in Colombia were resisted as something Brazil was not "yet" able to contemplate.

Nevertheless, Cardoso's own view of the international system and of Brazilian development was never that of a straightforward neoliberal. And over the course of the decade his foreign policy shifted in a more critical and nationalist direction. Even if his approach had achieved its important initial purpose of reestablishing Brazil's international political and economic credibility, by the late 1990s the Cardoso foreign policy of "autonomy via participation" had come to face increasingly serious challenges. The relative optimism with which policy makers had viewed the post-Cold War international environment was giving way to a greater emphasis on Brazil's international economic vulnerability and the difficulty of translating into concrete results the country's adaptation to global liberal norms.

There are important differences between Cardoso and Lula, but they cannot be simplified in terms of a contrast between "pro-Western liberalizer" and "progressive third-worldist." Cardoso believed the changing structures of global capitalism meant that there was little alternative but to adapt to globalization and that the potential political opportunities for successful foreign policy activism were limited. But he combined this pragmatic view of the world with a significant degree of optimism that structural reform at home was both possible and necessary and that democracy had become an overriding value.

The Lula government, by contrast, has been rather modest in its domestic policy ambitions, stressing economic orthodoxy and large-scale targeted social programs. But it has combined this domestic accommodation with a high degree of optimism as to what can be achieved abroad.

Regional Destiny?

How is Lula's foreign policy working out? Let us look first at South America. The Latin-Americanization of Brazil's foreign policy in fact goes back to the late 1970s. By the end of the 1990s it was already common to talk of Mercosur as part of Brazil's "destiny" (as opposed to the Free Trade Area of the Americas, which was seen as an option). Nevertheless, it is clear that the Lula government has worked hard to develop a more prominent role in Latin America. Especially during the first Lula administration, the body language (if you will) of assertive regional leadership was highly visible, however much it was couched in the rhetoric of "non-hegemonic leadership."

The Lula government has committed considerable rhetorical energy and high-level political effort in particular to relaunching Mercosur; to restoring with neighboring states economic ties that had frayed during the Argentinian economic crisis at the start of the millennium; to seeking new areas for cooperation, such as with anti-poverty initiatives; and to indicating in a variety of ways a greater willingness to bear costs and make some concessions in order to help sustain the regionalist project.

Brasilia has also been prepared to assume a more assertive political role in the region—in the sense of an expansion of party-to-party relations and greater involvement in politically contested areas, such as Brazil's leadership of the UN peace mission to Haiti (where it has 1,200 troops on the ground) and its recent expressions of willingness to mediate in Colombia.

Yet it is in relation to the region that the limits of Brazil's foreign policy appear in sharpest light. Mercosur itself is now far more divided than at any time in its history. Its already weak institutional structures have not been strengthened, and it is difficult to believe that Venezuela's 2005 accession will do anything other than weaken them still further. The early activism of the Lula years was too personalist and too voluntarist to have much of an institutional impact, and there has been a yawning gap between the rhetoric of leadership and the concrete political, military, and economic resources made available to sustain substantive achievements.

Lula's foreign policy overestimates the willingness of the region to fall into line behind Brazilian pretensions to a global role as the region's leader.

Lula's foreign policy overestimates the willingness of the region to fall into line behind Brazilian pretensions to a global role as the region's leader. In fact, there have been across Latin America numerous instances of resistance to Brazil's role—in opposition, for example, to its campaign for UN Security Council membership and to Brazilian candidates in international organizations. Brazil's foreign policy has also underestimated the readiness of many in the region to find an accommodation with Washington (a readiness likely to become more noticeable in a post-Bush world). And perhaps most difficult, Brazil's pretensions to regional leadership have encountered Venezuela's Hugo Chávez—both as a leader with his own ideas about hemispheric integration and as a symptom of deep-rooted discontent within Latin America.

If the measure of success for Brazil's regional strategy is the creation of a regional bloc with a significant degree of internal cohesion and a capacity to increase the region's power in the world, then there can be little doubt that the strategy has failed. It is crucial, however, to note the structural factors both shaping Brazil's regional policy and constraining its actions.

Compared to 20 years ago, Brazil is now much more firmly enmeshed in the region, and it has to live with the spillovers and externalities that go with ever greater social, economic, and energy interdependence. In this respect Brazil is living with the consequences of a sustained period of successful regional integration. Not only have economic, infrastructural, and energy ties increased, but the protracted violence and the narco-economy of the Andean region have had profound effects on patterns of violence in Brazil's cities.

Equally important, the political complexion of the region has changed dramatically in ways that make it very difficult for Brazil to steer regional developments or to project its own model. The *chavismo* emanating from Venezuela may not establish itself as a stable counter-narrative to political and economic liberalism, but it is more than a purely local or transitory phenomenon, and it reflects the widely perceived failures of economic liberalism, the narrowness of many accounts of electoral democracy, and a powerful resurgence of economic nationalism.

Brazil has thus become ever more entangled in an unstable and crisis-prone area without its being clear that the country has the economic or military resources to play a leadership role. The regional story of the past five years is in some ways better understood in terms of damage limitation under difficult conditions than in terms of the projection of regional leadership.

Relations with Washington

There is a common but mistaken view that relations between Brazil and the United States have historically been harmonious. It is true that there have been periods of close relations, such as the years following Brazil's entry into the Second World War and following the coup in 1964. Still, for much of the Cold War era the relationship was not especially close; on the contrary, it was characterized by real clashes of interest (especially over economic and trade issues), by deep divergences in the two countries' views of the international system, and by a recurrent sense of mutual frustration. More recent policy making in Brazil has aimed at prudent coexistence with the United States, possible collaboration, and minimal collision, but it has shied away from any kind of special relationship. Many Brazilians share the traditional nationalist perception that Washington is a potential obstacle to Brazil's progress.

There is also strong and widespread opposition to US policy in Colombia, which is seen as dangerously militarizing conflicts in the Andean region. US policy has also revived in some quarters the old fear that the United States poses a threat to the sovereignty of the Amazon. (The other element of this fear is that viewing tropical forests as part of the common heritage of humanity will lead to calls for the international administration of the region.) And, of course, the unilateralism and interventionism of the Bush years have fueled anti-Americanism even in a country in which such sentiments have traditionally been weak (compared to, say, Mexico or Argentina).

On the other hand, recent relations with Washington have actually been rather cordial. There has, after all, not been much to quarrel about. US foreign policy has obviously been focused elsewhere. And the integrating impulses of the 1990s had already faded by the end of that decade, as is evident in the absence within the United States of either the foreign policy will or the domestic political support to negotiate a Free Trade Area of the Americas.

Much is made of the unique position of the United States, the degree to which (unlike all other modern great powers) it faces no geopolitical challenge from within its region, and how it has been able to prevent, or more accurately to contain, the influence of extra-regional powers. But the other important regional aspect of US power is that country's ability to avoid deep entanglements and mostly to escape from lower-level conflicts within its backyard that could ensnare and divert it. Washington has been able to take the region for granted and, for long periods, to avoid having a regional policy at all—as has arguably been the case since 2001.

And there has been space for some shared interests with Brazil. New issues such as biofuels have provided a basis for cooperation. After the brief and absurd portrayal of Lula in some neoconservative quarters as part of a South American axis of evil, Brazil has been viewed in Washington as a potentially moderating force in the region, especially in relation to Chávez in Venezuela and Evo Morales in Bolivia. While Brazil's economy has not been growing as fast as China's or India's, foreign investment has been rising fast and economic stability has been maintained. Brazilian diplomats, though formally rejecting any role as "bridge-builders," have sometimes stressed the country's moderating influence and fire-fighting role.

Brazil has been viewed in Washington as a potentially moderating force in the region, especially in relation to Chávez in Venezuela and Morales in Bolivia.

Still, limits to an active or close relationship with Washington remain. Brazil has to maintain a very delicate balancing act that would be upset, both within the region and inside Brazil, by any attempt to act as a provider of regional order on behalf of the United States. Serious differences persist over the two countries' preferred models of regional economic integration: Brazil rejects the US notion of integration along the lines of the North American Free Trade Agreement.

There has been considerable frustration in Washington, as well, over Brazil's determination in trade talks to press for deeper agricultural liberalization in the United States and the European Union while resisting further trade and investment openings in Brazil. And on the issue of climate change, Brazil has firmly maintained its position that the internationally accepted formula of "common but differentiated responsibilities" means that the United States and the developed world have a duty to take the lead in reducing greenhouse gas emissions (including accepting binding targets) and to provide funds and technology to help developing countries reduce their emissions.

Above all, the US-Brazilian relationship features none of the sorts of concrete political, security, or economic interests that have underpinned the strategic realignment that has taken place in the case of US-Indian relations. Brazil is not closely linked to major American geopolitical interests, as India is with China, Pakistan, and the issue of nuclear proliferation. The economic relationship with Brazil is nothing like America's with India. Nor is there a large Brazilian diaspora in the United States pushing for improved ties.

Southern Strategy

If Brazil's aspirations for regional leadership and its relations with the United States have so far produced limited gains, the same might be said of the Lula administration's vaunted South-South diplomacy. Critics of Brazil's attempted solidarity with emerging economies say the policy has generated more rhetoric than concrete achievement.

In 2003, Brazil, along with India and South Africa, formed within the World Trade Organization a coalition of developing countries—the Group of 20—that decided to block the Doha round of trade talks until their demands were met. For many orthodox economists, the G-20 coalition shackles Brazil's true interests as a major agricultural exporter with powerful stakes in trade liberalization. Although South-South trade has increased, the core of Brazil's external economic relations remains with the developed world.

The critics of South-South diplomacy, both in Brazil and elsewhere, argue that economic engagement with the developed world should be given far higher priority—especially since China appears to be emerging more as a competitor to Brazil than an ally. According to this view, China's failure to support Brazil's bid for a seat on the UN Security Council demonstrates that Brazilian talk of "strategic partnerships" with India and China is radically out of line with Brazil's actual status in the foreign policies of those countries. Some observers have also noted that Brazil's efforts to gather support for its Security Council membership and its broader attempts at southern solidarity have at times led the country to compromise on its commitment to human rights.

And yet, although there has indeed been a gap between some of the rhetoric and the concrete achievements in South-South diplomacy, the critics' arguments underestimate the way in which Brazilian foreign policy has contributed to perceptions that global power is more diffuse than had appeared to be the case even five years ago. Brazil's weight as a player in international trade, for example, is limited, but its activism and assertiveness have worked to convince many that Brazil has to be part of any stable global trade regime for reasons of political legitimacy as much as narrow economic logic. In relation to climate change, Brazil has helped to shift the focus of negotiations back toward recognition of global warming as a shared and common problem, and has advanced the notion that the responsibilities and burdens of the developed and developing world need to be differentiated.

In general, Lula's Southern strategy forms a clear contrast to the nearly total disappearance of third world self-identification on the part of China, as well as, in Indian foreign policy, the displacement of nonalignment and the relative downgrading of multilateralism. In part, Brazil's approach reflects its relative power position. Brazil is a threshold state that seeks entry into the ranks of the powerful, but for whom coalitions with other developing countries continue to make political sense.

But Brazil's foreign policy under Lula has also reflected a powerful set of ideas about nationalism, development, and globalization that resonate both in the country and across Latin America. As Brazil seeks to carve out a regional and global position for itself as an emerging power, its foreign policy is likely to continue to be marked by tensions among the different facets of the nation's strategy and identity—as a leader of the South, as a potential bridge between North and South, and as a rising power that uses the rhetoric of South-South solidarity and claims for global justice for its own instrumental purposes.

ANDREW HURRELL is director of the Center for International Studies at Oxford University and a faculty fellow of Nuffield College, Oxford. He is the author of *On Global Order: Power, Values, and the Constitution of International Society* (Oxford University Press, 2007).

From *Current History*, February, 2008, pp. 51–58. Copyright © 2008 by Current History, Inc. Reprinted by permission.

The Power of Green

**What does America need to regain its global stature?
Environmental leadership.**

THOMAS L. FRIEDMAN

I.

One day Iraq, our post-9/11 trauma and the divisiveness of the Bush years will all be behind us—and America will need, and want, to get its groove back. We will need to find a way to reknit America at home, reconnect America abroad and restore America to its natural place in the global order—as the beacon of progress, hope and inspiration. I have an idea how. It's called "green."

In the world of ideas, to name something is to own it. If you can name an issue, you can own the issue. One thing that always struck me about the term "green" was the degree to which, for so many years, it was defined by its opponents—by the people who wanted to disparage it. And they defined it as "liberal," "tree-hugging," "sissy," "girlie-man," "unpatriotic," "vaguely French."

Well, I want to rename "green." I want to rename it geostrategic, geoeconomic, capitalistic and patriotic. I want to do that because I think that living, working, designing, manufacturing and projecting America in a green way can be the basis of a new unifying political movement for the 21st century. A redefined, broader and more muscular green ideology is not meant to trump the traditional Republican and Democratic agendas but rather to bridge them when it comes to addressing the three major issues facing every American today: jobs, temperature and terrorism.

How do our kids compete in a flatter world? How do they thrive in a warmer world? How do they survive in a more dangerous world? Those are, in a nutshell, the big questions facing America at the dawn of the 21st century. But these problems are so large in scale that they can only be effectively addressed by an America with 50 green states—not an America divided between red and blue states.

Because a new green ideology, properly defined, has the power to mobilize liberals and conservatives, evangelicals and atheists, big business and environmentalists around an agenda that can both pull us together and propel us forward. That's why I say: We don't just need the first black president. We need the first green president. We don't just need the first woman president. We need the first environmental president. We don't just need a president who has been toughened by years as a prisoner of war but a president who is tough enough to level with the American people about the profound economic, geopolitical and climate threats posed by our addiction to oil—and to offer a real plan to reduce our dependence on fossil fuels.

After World War II, President Eisenhower responded to the threat of Communism and the "red menace" with massive spending on an interstate highway system to tie America together, in large part so that we could better move weapons in the event of a war with the Soviets. That highway system, though, helped to enshrine America's car culture (atrophying our railroads) and to lock in suburban sprawl and low-density housing, which all combined to get America addicted to cheap fossil fuels, particularly oil. Many in the world followed our model.

Today, we are paying the accumulated economic, geopolitical and climate prices for that kind of America. I am not proposing that we radically alter our lifestyles. We are who we are—including a car culture. But if we want to continue to be who we are, enjoy the benefits and be able to pass them on to our children, we do need to fuel our future in a cleaner, greener way. Eisenhower rallied us with the red menace. The next president will have to rally us with a green patriotism. Hence my motto: "Green is the new red, white and blue."

The good news is that after traveling around America this past year, looking at how we use energy and the emerging alternatives, I can report that green really has gone Main Street—thanks to the perfect storm created by 9/11, Hurricane Katrina and the Internet revolution. The first flattened the twin towers, the second flattened New Orleans and the third flattened the global economic playing field. The convergence of all three has turned many of our previous assumptions about "green" upside down in a very short period of time, making it much more compelling to many more Americans.

But here's the bad news: While green has hit Main Street—more Americans than ever now identify themselves as greens, or what I call "Geo-Greens" to differentiate their more muscular and strategic green ideology—green has not gone very far down Main Street. It certainly has not gone anywhere near the distance required to preserve our lifestyle. The dirty little secret is that we're fooling ourselves. We in America talk like we're already "the greenest generation," as the business writer Dan Pink once called it. But here's the really inconvenient truth: We have not even begun to be serious about the costs, the effort and the scale of change that will be required to shift our country, and eventually the world, to a largely emissions-free energy infrastructure over the next 50 years.

II.

A few weeks after American forces invaded Afghanistan, I visited the Pakistani frontier town of Peshawar, a hotbed of Islamic radicalism. On the way, I stopped at the famous Darul Uloom Haqqania, the biggest madrasa, or Islamic school, in Pakistan, with 2,800 live-in students. The Taliban leader Mullah Muhammad Omar attended this madrasa as a younger man. My Pakistani friend and I were allowed to observe a class of young boys who sat on the floor, practicing their rote learning of the Koran from texts perched on wooden holders. The air in the Koran class was so thick and stale it felt as if you could have cut it into blocks. The teacher asked an 8-year-old boy to chant a Koranic verse for us, which he did with the elegance of an experienced muezzin. I asked another student, an Afghan refugee, Rahim Kunduz, age 12, what his reaction was to the Sept. 11 attacks, and he said: "Most likely the attack came from Americans inside America. I am pleased that America has had to face pain, because the rest of the world has tasted its pain." A framed sign on the wall said this room was "A gift of the Kingdom of Saudi Arabia."

Sometime after 9/11—an unprovoked mass murder perpetrated by 19 men, 15 of whom were Saudis—green went geostrategic, as Americans started to realize we were financing both sides in the war on terrorism. We were financing the U.S. military with our tax dollars; and we were financing a transformation of Islam, in favor of its most intolerant strand, with our gasoline purchases. How stupid is that?

Islam has always been practiced in different forms. Some are more embracing of modernity, reinterpretation of the Koran and tolerance of other faiths, like Sufi Islam or the populist Islam of Egypt, Ottoman Turkey and Indonesia. Some strands, like Salafi Islam—followed by the Wahhabis of Saudi Arabia and by Al Qaeda—believe Islam should be returned to an austere form practiced in the time of the Prophet Muhammad, a form hostile to modernity, science, "infidels" and women's rights. By enriching the Saudi and Iranian treasuries via our gasoline purchases, we are financing the export of the Saudi puritanical brand of Sunni Islam and the Iranian fundamentalist brand of Shiite Islam, tilting the Muslim world in a more intolerant direction. At the Muslim fringe, this creates more recruits for the Taliban, Al Qaeda, Hamas, Hezbollah and the Sunni suicide bomb squads of Iraq; at the Muslim center, it creates a much bigger constituency of people who applaud suicide bombers as martyrs.

The Saudi Islamic export drive first went into high gear after extreme fundamentalists challenged the Muslim credentials of the Saudi ruling family by taking over the Grand Mosque of Mecca in 1979—a year that coincided with the Iranian revolution and a huge rise in oil prices. The attack on the Grand Mosque by these Koran-and-rifle-wielding Islamic militants shook the Saudi ruling family to its core. The al-Sauds responded to this

challenge to their religious bona fides by becoming outwardly more religious. They gave their official Wahhabi religious establishment even more power to impose Islam on public life. Awash in cash thanks to the spike in oil prices, the Saudi government and charities also spent hundreds of millions of dollars endowing mosques, youth clubs and Muslim schools all over the world, ensuring that Wahhabi imams, teachers and textbooks would preach Saudi-style Islam. Eventually, notes Lawrence Wright in "The Looming Tower," his history of Al Qaeda, "Saudi Arabia, which constitutes only 1 percent of the world Muslim population, would support 90 percent of the expenses of the entire faith, overriding other traditions of Islam."

Saudi mosques and wealthy donors have also funneled cash to the Sunni insurgents in Iraq. The Associated Press reported from Cairo in December: "Several drivers interviewed by the A.P. in Middle East capitals said Saudis have been using religious events, like the hajj pilgrimage to Mecca and a smaller pilgrimage, as cover for illicit money transfers. Some money, they said, is carried into Iraq on buses with returning pilgrims. 'They sent boxes full of dollars and asked me to deliver them to certain addresses in Iraq,' said one driver. . . . 'I know it is being sent to the resistance, and if I don't take it with me, they will kill me.' "

No wonder more Americans have concluded that conserving oil to put less money in the hands of hostile forces is now a geostrategic imperative. President Bush's refusal to do anything meaningful after 9/11 to reduce our gasoline usage really amounts to a policy of "No Mullah Left Behind." James Woolsey, the former C.I.A. director, minces no words: "We are funding the rope for the hanging of ourselves."

No, I don't want to bankrupt Saudi Arabia or trigger an Islamist revolt there. Its leadership is more moderate and pro-Western than its people. But the way the Saudi ruling family has bought off its religious establishment, in order to stay in power, is not healthy. Cutting the price of oil in half would help change that. In the 1990s, dwindling oil income sparked a Saudi debate about less Koran and more science in Saudi schools, even experimentation with local elections. But the recent oil windfall has stilled all talk of reform.

That is because of what I call the First Law of Petropolitics: The price of oil and the pace of freedom always move in opposite directions in states that are highly dependent on oil exports for their income and have weak institutions or outright authoritarian governments. And this is another reason that green has become geostrategic. Soaring oil prices are poisoning the international system by strengthening antidemocratic regimes around the globe.

Look what's happened: We thought the fall of the Berlin Wall was going to unleash an unstoppable tide of free markets and free people, and for about a decade it did just that. But those years coincided with oil in the $10-to-$30-a-barrel range. As the price of oil surged into the $30-to-$70 range in the early 2000s, it triggered a countertide—a tide of petroauthoritarianism—manifested in Russia, Iran, Nigeria, Venezuela, Saudi Arabia, Syria, Sudan, Egypt, Chad, Angola, Azerbaijan and Turkmenistan. The elected or self-appointed elites running these states have used their oil windfalls to ensconce themselves in power, buy off opponents and counter the fall-of-the-Berlin-Wall tide. If we continue to finance them with our oil purchases, they will reshape the world in their image, around Putin-like values.

You can illustrate the First Law of Petropolitics with a simple graph. On one line chart the price of oil from 1979 to the present; on another line chart the Freedom House or Fraser Institute freedom indexes for Russia, Nigeria, Iran and Venezuela for the same years. When you put these two lines on the same graph you see something striking: the price of oil and the pace of freedom are inversely correlated. As oil prices went down in the early 1990s, competition, transparency, political participation and accountability of those in office all tended to go up in these countries—as measured by free elections held, newspapers opened, reformers elected, economic reform projects started and companies privatized. That's because their petroauthoritarian regimes had to open themselves to foreign investment and educate and empower their people more in order to earn income. But as oil prices went up around 2000, free speech, free press, fair elections and freedom to form political parties and NGOs all eroded in these countries.

The motto of the American Revolution was "no taxation without representation." The motto of the petroauthoritarians is "no representation without taxation": If I don't have to tax you, because I can get all the money I need from oil wells, I don't have to listen to you.

It is no accident that when oil prices were low in the 1990s, Iran elected a reformist Parliament and a president who called for a "dialogue of civilizations." And when oil prices soared to $70 a barrel, Iran's conservatives pushed out the reformers and ensconced a president who says the Holocaust is a myth. (I promise you, if oil prices drop to $25 a barrel, the Holocaust won't be a myth anymore.) And it is no accident that the first Arab Gulf state to start running out of oil, Bahrain, is also the first Arab Gulf state to have held a free and fair election in which women could run and vote, the first Arab Gulf state to overhaul its labor laws to make more of its own people employable and the first Arab Gulf state to sign a free-trade agreement with America.

People change when they have to—not when we tell them to—and falling oil prices make them have to. That is why if we are looking for a Plan B for Iraq—a way of pressing for political reform in the Middle East without going to war again—there is no better tool than bringing down the price of oil. When it comes to fostering democracy among petroauthoritarians, it doesn't matter whether you're a neocon or a radical lib. If you're not also a Geo-Green, you won't succeed.

The notion that conserving energy is a geostrategic imperative has also moved into the Pentagon, for slightly different reasons. Generals are realizing that the more energy they save in the heat of battle, the more power they can project. The Pentagon has been looking to improve its energy efficiency for several years now to save money. But the Iraq war has given birth to a new movement in the U.S. military: the "Green Hawks."

As Amory Lovins of the Rocky Mountain Institute, who has been working with the Pentagon, put it to me: The Iraq war forced the U.S. military to think much more seriously about how to "eat its tail"—to shorten its energy supply lines by becoming more energy efficient. According to Dan Nolan, who oversees energy projects for the U.S. Army's Rapid Equipping Force, it started last year when a Marine major general in Anbar Province told the Pentagon he wanted alternative energy sources that would reduce fuel consumption in the Iraqi desert. Why? His air-conditioners were being run off mobile generators, and the generators ran on diesel, and the diesel had to be trucked in, and the insurgents were blowing up the trucks.

"When we began the analysis of his request, it was really about the fact that his soldiers were being attacked on the roads bringing fuel and water," Nolan said. So eating their tail meant "taking those things that are brought into the unit and trying to generate them on-site." To that end Nolan's team is now experimenting with everything from new kinds of tents that need 40 percent less air-conditioning to new kinds of fuel cells that produce water as a byproduct.

Pay attention: When the U.S. Army desegregated, the country really desegregated; when the Army goes green, the country could really go green.

"Energy independence is a national security issue," Nolan said. "It's the right business for us to be in. . . . We are not trying to change the whole Army. Our job is to focus on that battalion out there and give those commanders the technological innovations they need to deal with today's mission. But when they start coming home, they are going to bring those things with them."

III.

The second big reason green has gone Main Street is because global warming has. A decade ago, it was mostly experts who worried that climate change was real, largely brought about by humans and likely to lead to species loss and environmental crises. Now Main Street is starting to worry because people are seeing things they've never seen before in their own front yards and reading things they've never read before in their papers—like the recent draft report by the United Nations's 2,000-expert Intergovernmental Panel on Climate Change, which concluded that "changes in climate are now affecting physical and biological systems on every continent."

I went to Montana in January and Gov. Brian Schweitzer told me: "We don't get as much snow in the high country as we used to, and the runoff starts sooner in the spring. The river I've been fishing over the last 50 years is now warmer in July by five degrees than 50 years ago, and it is hard on our trout population." I went to Moscow in February, and my friends told me they just celebrated the first Moscow Christmas in their memory with no snow. I stopped in London on the way home, and I didn't need an overcoat. In 2006, the average temperature in central England was the highest ever recorded since the Central England Temperature (C.E.T.) series began in 1659.

Yes, no one knows exactly what will happen. But ever fewer people want to do nothing. Gov. Arnold Schwarzenegger of California summed up the new climate around climate when he said to me recently: "If 98 doctors say my son is ill and needs medication and two say 'No, he doesn't, he is fine,' I will go with the 98. It's common sense—the same with global warming. We go with the majority, the large majority. . . . The

31

key thing now is that since we know this industrial age has created it, let's get our act together and do everything we can to roll it back."

But how? Now we arrive at the first big roadblock to green going down Main Street. Most people have no clue—no clue—how huge an industrial project is required to blunt climate change. Here are two people who do: Robert Socolow, an engineering professor, and Stephen Pacala, an ecology professor, who together lead the Carbon Mitigation Initiative at Princeton, a consortium designing scalable solutions for the climate issue.

> **People change when they have to, and falling oil prices make them have to. That is why if we are looking for a Plan B for Iraq there is no better tool than briging down the price of oil.**

They first argued in a paper published by the journal *Science* in August 2004 that human beings can emit only so much carbon into the atmosphere before the buildup of carbon dioxide (CO_2) reaches a level unknown in recent geologic history and the earth's climate system starts to go "haywire." The scientific consensus, they note, is that the risk of things going haywire—weather patterns getting violently unstable, glaciers melting, prolonged droughts—grows rapidly as CO_2 levels "approach a doubling" of the concentration of CO_2 that was in the atmosphere before the Industrial Revolution.

"Think of the climate change issue as a closet, and behind the door are lurking all kinds of monsters—and there's a long list of them," Pacala said. "All of our scientific work says the most damaging monsters start to come out from behind that door when you hit the doubling of CO_2 levels." As Bill Collins, who led the development of a model used worldwide for simulating climate change, put it to me: "We're running an uncontrolled experiment on the only home we have."

So here is our challenge, according to Pacala: If we basically do nothing, and global CO_2 emissions continue to grow at the pace of the last 30 years for the next 50 years, we will pass the doubling level—an atmospheric concentration of carbon dioxide of 560 parts per million—around midcentury. To avoid that—and still leave room for developed countries to grow, using less carbon, and for countries like India and China to grow, emitting double or triple their current carbon levels, until they climb out of poverty and are able to become more energy efficient—will require a huge global industrial energy project.

To convey the scale involved, Socolow and Pacala have created a pie chart with 15 different wedges. Some wedges represent carbon-free or carbon-diminishing power-generating technologies; other wedges represent efficiency programs that could conserve large amounts of energy and prevent CO_2 emissions. They argue that the world needs to deploy any 7 of these 15 wedges, or sufficient amounts of all 15, to have enough conservation, and enough carbon-free energy, to increase the world economy and still avoid the doubling of CO_2 in the atmosphere.

Each wedge, when phased in over 50 years, would avoid the release of 25 billion tons of carbon, for a total of 175 billion tons of carbon avoided between now and 2056.

Here are seven wedges we could chose from: "Replace 1,400 large coal-fired plants with gas-fired plants; increase the fuel economy of two billion cars from 30 to 60 miles per gallon; add twice today's nuclear output to displace coal; drive two billion cars on ethanol, using one-sixth of the world's cropland; increase solar power 700-fold to displace coal; cut electricity use in homes, offices and stores by 25 percent; install carbon capture and sequestration capacity at 800 large coal-fired plants." And the other eight aren't any easier. They include halting all cutting and burning of forests, since deforestation causes about 20 percent of the world's annual CO_2 emissions.

"There has never been a deliberate industrial project in history as big as this," Pacala said. Through a combination of clean power technology and conservation, "we have to get rid of 175 billion tons of carbon over the next 50 years—and still keep growing. It is possible to accomplish this if we start today. But every year that we delay, the job becomes more difficult—and if we delay a decade or two, avoiding the doubling or more may well become impossible."

IV.

In November, I flew from Shanghai to Beijing on Air China. As we landed in Beijing and taxied to the terminal, the Chinese air hostess came on the P.A. and said: "We've just landed in Beijing. The temperature is 8 degrees Celsius, 46 degrees Fahrenheit and the sky is clear."

I almost burst out laughing. Outside my window the smog was so thick you could not see the end of the terminal building. When I got into Beijing, though, friends told me the air was better than usual. Why? China had been host of a summit meeting of 48 African leaders. *Time* magazine reported that Beijing officials had "ordered half a million official cars off the roads and said another 400,000 drivers had 'volunteered' to refrain from using their vehicles" in order to clean up the air for their African guests. As soon as they left, the cars returned, and Beijing's air went back to "unhealthy."

Green has also gone Main Street because the end of Communism, the rise of the personal computer and the diffusion of the Internet have opened the global economic playing field to so many more people, all coming with their own versions of the American dream—a house, a car, a toaster, a microwave and a refrigerator. It is a blessing to see so many people growing out of poverty. But when three billion people move from "low-impact" to "high-impact" lifestyles, Jared Diamond wrote in "Collapse," it makes it urgent that we find cleaner ways to fuel their dreams. According to Lester Brown, the founder of the Earth Policy Institute, if China keeps growing at 8 percent a year, by 2031 the per-capita income of 1.45 billion Chinese will be the same as America's in 2004. China currently has only one car for every 100 people, but Brown projects that as it reaches American income levels, if it copies American consumption, it will have three cars for every four people, or 1.1 billion vehicles. The total world fleet today is 800 million vehicles!

That's why McKinsey Global Institute forecasts that developing countries will generate nearly 80 percent of the growth in world energy demand between now and 2020, with China representing 32 percent and the Middle East 10 percent. So if Red China doesn't become Green China there is no chance we will keep the climate monsters behind the door. On some days, says the U.S. Environmental Protection Agency, almost 25 percent of the polluting matter in the air above Los Angeles comes from China's coal-fired power plants and factories, as well as fumes from China's cars and dust kicked up by droughts and deforestation around Asia.

The good news is that China knows it has to grow green—or it won't grow at all. On Sept. 8, 2006, a Chinese newspaper reported that China's E.P.A. and its National Bureau of Statistics had re-examined China's 2004 G.D.P. number. They concluded that the health problems, environmental degradation and lost workdays from pollution had actually cost China $64 billion, or 3.05 percent of its total economic output for 2004. Some experts believe the real number is closer to 10 percent.

Thus China has a strong motivation to clean up the worst pollutants in its air. Those are the nitrogen oxides, sulfur oxides and mercury that produce acid rain, smog and haze—much of which come from burning coal. But cleaning up is easier said than done. The Communist Party's legitimacy and the stability of the whole country depend heavily on Beijing's ability to provide rising living standards for more and more Chinese.

So, if you're a Chinese mayor and have to choose between growing jobs and cutting pollution, you will invariably choose jobs: coughing workers are much less politically dangerous than unemployed workers. That's a key reason why China's 10th five-year plan, which began in 2000, called for a 10 percent reduction in sulfur dioxide in China's air—and when that plan concluded in 2005, sulfur dioxide pollution in China had increased by 27 percent.

But if China is having a hard time cleaning up its nitrogen and sulfur oxides—which can be done relatively cheaply by adding scrubbers to the smokestacks of coal-fired power plants—imagine what will happen when it comes to asking China to curb its CO_2, of which China is now the world's second-largest emitter, after America. To build a coal-fired power plant that captures, separates and safely sequesters the CO_2 into the ground before it goes up the smokestack requires either an expensive retrofit or a whole new system. That new system would cost about 40 percent more to build and operate—and would produce 20 percent less electricity, according to a recent M.I.T. study, "The Future of Coal."

China—which is constructing the equivalent of two 500-megawatt coal-fired power plants every week—is not going to pay that now. Remember: CO_2 is an invisible, odorless, tasteless gas. Yes, it causes global warming—but it doesn't hurt anyone in China today, and getting rid of it is costly and has no economic payoff. China's strategy right now is to say that CO_2 is the West's problem. "It must be pointed out that climate change has been caused by the long-term historic emissions of developed countries and their high per-capita emissions," Jiang Yu, a spokeswoman for China's Foreign Ministry, declared in February. "Developed countries bear an unshirkable responsibility."

So now we come to the nub of the issue: Green will not go down Main Street America unless it also goes down Main Street China, India and Brazil. And for green to go Main Street in these big developing countries, the prices of clean power alternatives—wind, biofuels, nuclear, solar or coal sequestration—have to fall to the "China price." The China price is basically the price China pays for coal-fired electricity today because China is not prepared to pay a premium now, and sacrifice growth and stability, just to get rid of the CO_2 that comes from burning coal.

"The 'China price' is the fundamental benchmark that everyone is looking to satisfy," said Curtis Carlson, C.E.O. of SRI International, which is developing alternative energy technologies. "Because if the Chinese have to pay 10 percent more for energy, when they have tens of millions of people living under $1,000 a year, it is not going to happen." Carlson went on to say: "We have an enormous amount of new innovation we must put in place before we can get to a price that China and India will be able to pay. But this is also an opportunity."

V.

The only way we are going to get innovations that drive energy costs down to the China price—innovations in energy-saving appliances, lights and building materials and in non-CO_2-emitting power plants and fuels—is by mobilizing free-market capitalism. The only thing as powerful as Mother Nature is Father Greed. To a degree, the market is already at work on this project—because some venture capitalists and companies understand that clean-tech is going to be the next great global industry. Take Wal-Mart. The world's biggest retailer woke up several years ago, its C.E.O. Lee Scott told me, and realized that with regard to the environment its customers "had higher expectations for us than we had for ourselves." So Scott hired a sustainability expert, Jib Ellison, to tutor the company. The first lesson Ellison preached was that going green was a whole new way for Wal-Mart to cut costs and drive its profits. As Scott recalled it, Ellison said to him, "Lee, the thing you have to think of is all this stuff that people don't want you to put into the environment is waste—and you're paying for it!"

So Scott initiated a program to work with Wal-Mart's suppliers to reduce the sizes and materials used for all its packaging by five percent by 2013. The reductions they have made are already paying off in savings to the company. "We created teams to work across the organization," Scott said. "It was voluntary—then you had the first person who eliminated some packaging, and someone else started showing how we could recycle more plastic, and all of a sudden it's $1 million a quarter." Wal-Mart operates 7,000 huge Class 8 trucks that get about 6 miles per gallon. It has told its truck makers that by 2015, it wants to double the efficiency of the fleet. Wal-Mart is the China of companies, so, explained Scott, "if we place one order we can create a market" for energy innovation.

For instance, Wal-Mart has used its shelves to create a huge, low-cost market for compact fluorescent bulbs, which use about a quarter of the energy of incandescent bulbs to produce the same light and last 10 times as long. "Just by doing what it does best—saving customers money and cutting costs," said Glenn Prickett of Conservation International, a Wal-Mart adviser, "Wal-Mart can have a revolutionary impact on the market for green technologies. If every one of their 100 million customers in the U.S. bought just one energy-saving compact fluorescent lamp, instead of a traditional incandescent bulb, they could cut CO_2 emissions by 45 billion pounds and save more than $3 billion."

Those savings highlight something that often gets lost: The quickest way to get to the China price for clean power is by becoming more energy efficient. The cheapest, cleanest, non-emitting power plant in the world is the one you don't build. Helping China adopt some of the breakthrough efficiency programs that California has adopted, for instance—like rewarding electrical utilities for how much energy they get their customers to save rather than to use—could have a huge impact. Some experts estimate that China could cut its need for new power plants in half with aggressive investments in efficiency.

Yet another force driving us to the China price is Chinese entrepreneurs, who understand that while Beijing may not be ready to impose CO_2 restraints, developed countries are, so this is going to be a global business—and they want a slice. Let me introduce the man identified last year by Forbes Magazine as the seventh-richest man in China, with a fortune now estimated at $2.2 billion. His name is Shi Zhengrong and he is China's leading manufacturer of silicon solar panels, which convert sunlight into electricity.

Clean-tech plays to America's strength, because making things like locomotives lighter and smarter takes a lot of knowledge—not cheap labor. Embedding clean-tech into everything we design can revive America as a manufacturing power.

"People at all levels in China have become more aware of this environment issue and alternative energy," said Shi, whose company, Suntech Power Holdings, is listed on the New York Stock Exchange. "Five years ago, when I started the company, people said: 'Why do we need solar? We have a surplus of coal-powered electricity.' Now it is different; now people realize that solar has a bright future. But it is still too expensive. . . . We have to reduce the cost as quickly as possible—our real competitors are coal and nuclear power."

Shi does most of his manufacturing in China, but sells roughly 90 percent of his products outside China, because today they are too expensive for his domestic market. But the more he can get the price down, and start to grow his business inside China, the more he can use that to become a dominant global player. Thanks to Suntech's success, in China "there is a rush of business people entering this sector, even though we still don't have a market here," Shi added. "Many government people now say, 'This is an industry!' " And if it takes off, China could do for solar panels what it did for tennis shoes—bring the price down so far that everyone can afford a pair.

VI.

All that sounds great—but remember those seven wedges? To reach the necessary scale of emissions-free energy will require big clean coal or nuclear power stations, wind farms and solar farms, all connected to a national transmission grid, not to mention clean fuels for our cars and trucks. And the market alone, as presently constructed in the U.S., will not get us those alternatives at the scale we need—at the China price—fast enough.

Prof. Nate Lewis, Caltech's noted chemist and energy expert, explained why with an analogy. "Let's say you invented the first cellphone," he said. "You could charge people $1,000 for each one because lots of people would be ready to pay lots of money to have a phone they could carry in their pocket." With those profits, you, the inventor, could pay back your shareholders and plow more into research, so you keep selling better and cheaper cellphones.

But energy is different, Lewis explained: "If I come to you and say, 'Today your house lights are being powered by dirty coal, but tomorrow, if you pay me $100 more a month, I will power your house lights with solar,' you are most likely to say: 'Sorry, Nate, but I don't really care how my lights go on, I just care that they go on. I won't pay an extra $100 a month for sun power. A new cellphone improves my life. A different way to power my lights does nothing.'

"So building an emissions-free energy infrastructure is not like sending a man to the moon," Lewis went on. "With the moon shot, money was no object—and all we had to do was get there. But today, we already have cheap energy from coal, gas and oil. So getting people to pay more to shift to clean fuels is like trying to get funding for NASA to build a spaceship to the moon—when Southwest Airlines already flies there and gives away free peanuts! I already have a cheap ride to the moon, and a ride is a ride. For most people, electricity is electricity, no matter how it is generated."

If we were running out of coal or oil, the market would steadily push the prices up, which would stimulate innovation in alternatives. Eventually there would be a crossover, and the alternatives would kick in, start to scale and come down in price. But what has happened in energy over the last 35 years is that the oil price goes up, stimulating government subsidies and some investments in alternatives, and then the price goes down, the government loses interest, the subsidies expire and the investors in alternatives get wiped out.

The only way to stimulate the scale of sustained investment in research and development of non-CO_2 emitting power at the China price is if the developed countries, who can afford to do so, force their people to pay the full climate, economic and geopolitical costs of using gasoline and dirty coal. Those countries that have signed the Kyoto Protocol are starting to do that. But America is not.

Up to now, said Lester Brown, president of the Earth Policy Institute, we as a society "have been behaving just like Enron the company at the height of its folly." We rack up stunning profits and G.D.P. numbers every year, and they look great on paper "because we've been hiding some of the costs off the books." If we don't put a price on the CO_2 we're building up or on our addiction to oil, we'll never nurture the innovation we need.

Jeffrey Immelt, the chairman of General Electric, has worked for G.E. for 25 years. In that time, he told me, he has seen seven generations of innovation in G.E.'s medical equipment business—in devices like M.R.I.s or CT scans—because health care market incentives drove the innovation. In power, it's just the opposite. "Today, on the power side," he said, "we're still selling the same basic coal-fired power plants we had when I arrived. They're a little cleaner and more efficient now, but basically the same."

The one clean power area where G.E. is now into a third generation is wind turbines, "thanks to the European Union," Immelt said. Countries like Denmark, Spain and Germany imposed standards for wind power on their utilities and offered sustained subsidies, creating a big market for wind-turbine manufacturers in Europe in the 1980s, when America abandoned wind because the price of oil fell. "We grew our wind business in Europe," Immelt said.

As things stand now in America, Immelt said, "the market does not work in energy." The multibillion-dollar scale of investment that a company like G.E. is being asked to make in order to develop new clean-power technologies or that a utility is being asked to make in order to build coal sequestration facilities or nuclear plants is not going to happen at scale—unless they know that coal and oil are going to be priced high enough for long enough that new investments will not be undercut in a few years by falling fossil fuel prices. "Carbon has to have a value," Immelt emphasized. "Today in the U.S. and China it has no value."

I recently visited the infamous Three Mile Island nuclear plant with Christopher Crane, president of Exelon Nuclear, which owns the facility. He said that if Exelon wanted to start a nuclear plant today, the licensing, design, planning and building requirements are so extensive it would not open until 2015 at the earliest. But even if Exelon got all the approvals, it could not start building "because the cost of capital for a nuclear plant today is prohibitive."

That's because the interest rate that any commercial bank would charge on a loan for a nuclear facility would be so high— because of all the risks of lawsuits or cost overruns—that it would be impossible for Exelon to proceed. A standard nuclear plant today costs about $3 billion per unit. The only way to stimulate more nuclear power innovation, Crane said, would be federal loan guarantees that would lower the cost of capital for anyone willing to build a new nuclear plant.

The 2005 energy bill created such loan guarantees, but the details still have not been worked out. "We would need a robust loan guarantee program to jump-start the nuclear industry," Crane said—an industry that has basically been frozen since the 1979 Three Mile Island accident. With cheaper money, added Crane, CO_2-free nuclear power could be "very competitive" with CO_2-emitting pulverized coal.

Think about the implications. Three Mile Island had two reactors, TMI-2, which shut down because of the 1979 accident, and TMI-1, which is still operating today, providing clean electricity with virtually no CO_2 emissions for 800,000 homes. Had the TMI-2 accident not happened, it too would have been providing clean electricity for 800,000 homes for the last 28 years.

Instead, that energy came from CO_2-emitting coal, which, by the way, still generates 50 percent of America's electricity.

Similar calculations apply to ethanol production. "We have about 100 scientists working on cellulosic ethanol," Chad Holliday, the C.E.O. of DuPont, told me. "My guess is that we could double the number and add another 50 to start working on how to commercialize it. It would probably cost us less than $100 million to scale up. But I am not ready to do that. I can guess what it will cost me to make it and what the price will be, but is the market going to be there? What are the regulations going to be? Is the ethanol subsidy going to be reduced? Will we put a tax on oil to keep ethanol competitive? If I know that, it gives me a price target to go after. Without that, I don't know what the market is and my shareholders don't know how to value what I am doing. . . . You need some certainty on the incentives side and on the market side, because we are talking about multiyear investments, billions of dollars, that will take a long time to take off, and we won't hit on everything."

Summing up the problem, Immelt of G.E. said the big energy players are being asked "to take a 15-minute market signal and make a 40-year decision and that just doesn't work. . . . The U.S. government should decide: What do we want to have happen? How much clean coal, how much nuclear and what is the most efficient way to incentivize people to get there?"

He's dead right. The market alone won't work. Government's job is to set high standards, let the market reach them and then raise the standards more. That's how you get scale innovation at the China price. Government can do this by imposing steadily rising efficiency standards for buildings and appliances and by stipulating that utilities generate a certain amount of electricity from renewables—like wind or solar. Or it can impose steadily rising mileage standards for cars or a steadily tightening cap-and-trade system for the amount of CO_2 any factory or power plant can emit. Or it can offer loan guarantees and fast-track licensing for anyone who wants to build a nuclear plant. Or—my preference and the simplest option—it can impose a carbon tax that will stimulate the market to move away from fuels that emit high levels of CO_2 and invest in those that don't. Ideally, it will do all of these things. But whichever options we choose, they will only work if they are transparent, simple and long-term— with zero fudging allowed and with regulatory oversight and stiff financial penalties for violators.

The politician who actually proved just how effective this can be was a guy named George W. Bush, when he was governor of Texas. He pushed for and signed a renewable energy portfolio mandate in 1999. The mandate stipulated that Texas power companies had to produce 2,000 new megawatts of electricity from renewables, mostly wind, by 2009. What happened? A dozen new companies jumped into the Texas market and built wind turbines to meet the mandate, so many that the 2,000-megawatt goal was reached in 2005. So the Texas Legislature has upped the mandate to 5,000 megawatts by 2015, and everyone knows they will beat that too because of how quickly wind in Texas is becoming competitive with coal. Today, thanks to Governor Bush's market intervention, Texas is the biggest wind state in America.

President Bush, though, is no Governor Bush. (The Dick Cheney effect?) President Bush claims he's protecting

American companies by not imposing tough mileage, conservation or clean power standards, but he's actually helping them lose the race for the next great global industry. Japan has some of the world's highest gasoline taxes and stringent energy efficiency standards for vehicles—and it has the world's most profitable and innovative car company, Toyota. That's no accident.

The politicians who best understand this are America's governors, some of whom have started to just ignore Washington, set their own energy standards and reap the benefits for their states. As Schwarzenegger told me, "We have seen in California so many companies that have been created that work just on things that have do with clean environment." California's state-imposed efficiency standards have resulted in per-capita energy consumption in California remaining almost flat for the last 30 years, while in the rest of the country it has gone up 50 percent. "There are a lot of industries that are exploding right now because of setting these new standards," he said.

VII.

John Dineen runs G.E. Transportation, which makes locomotives. His factory is in Erie, Pa., and employs 4,500 people. When it comes to the challenges from cheap labor markets, Dineen likes to say, "Our little town has trade surpluses with China and Mexico."

Now how could that be? China makes locomotives that are 30 percent cheaper than G.E.'s, but it turns out that G.E.'s are the most energy efficient in the world, with the lowest emissions and best mileage per ton pulled—"and they don't stop on the tracks," Dineen added. So China is also buying from Erie—and so are Brazil, Mexico and Kazakhstan. What's the secret? The China price.

"We made it very easy for them," said Dineen. "By producing engines with lower emissions in the classic sense (NOx [nitrogen oxides]) and lower emissions in the future sense (CO_2) and then coupling it with better fuel efficiency and reliability, we lowered the total life-cycle cost."

The West can't impose its climate or pollution standards on China, Dineen explained, but when a company like G.E. makes an engine that gets great mileage, cuts pollution and, by the way, emits less CO_2, China will be a buyer. "If we were just trying to export lower-emission units, and they did not have the fuel benefits, we would lose," Dineen said. "But when green is made green—improved fuel economies coupled with emissions reductions—we see very quick adoption rates."

One reason G.E. Transportation got so efficient was the old U.S. standard it had to meet on NOx pollution, Dineen said. It did that through technological innovation. And as oil prices went up, it leveraged more technology to get better mileage. The result was a cleaner, more efficient, more exportable locomotive. Dineen describes his factory as a "technology campus" because, he explains, "it looks like a 100-year-old industrial site, but inside those 100-year-old buildings are world-class engineers working on the next generation's technologies." He also notes that workers in his factory make nearly twice the average in Erie—by selling to China!

The bottom line is this: Clean-tech plays to America's strength because making things like locomotives lighter and smarter takes a lot of knowledge—not cheap labor. That's why embedding clean-tech into everything we design and manufacture is a way to revive America as a manufacturing power.

"Whatever you are making, if you can add a green dimension to it—making it more efficient, healthier and more sustainable for future generations—you have a product that can't just be made cheaper in India or China," said Andrew Shapiro, founder of GreenOrder, an environmental business-strategy group. "If you just create a green ghetto in your company, you miss it. You have to figure out how to integrate green into the DNA of your whole business."

Ditto for our country, which is why we need a Green New Deal—one in which government's role is not funding projects, as in the original New Deal, but seeding basic research, providing loan guarantees where needed and setting standards, taxes and incentives that will spawn 1,000 G.E. Transportations for all kinds of clean power.

Bush won't lead a Green New Deal, but his successor must if America is going to maintain its leadership and living standard. Unfortunately, today's presidential hopefuls are largely full of hot air on the climate-energy issue. Not one of them is proposing anything hard, like a carbon or gasoline tax, and if you think we can deal with these huge problems without asking the American people to do anything hard, you're a fool or a fraud.

Being serious starts with reframing the whole issue—helping Americans understand, as the Carnegie Fellow David Rothkopf puts it, "that we're not 'post-Cold War' anymore—we're pre-something totally new." I'd say we're in the "pre-climate war era." Unless we create a more carbon-free world, we will not preserve the free world. Intensifying climate change, energy wars and petroauthoritarianism will curtail our life choices and our children's opportunities every bit as much as Communism once did for half the planet.

Equally important, presidential candidates need to help Americans understand that green is not about cutting back. It's about creating a new cornucopia of abundance for the next generation by inventing a whole new industry. It's about getting our best brains out of hedge funds and into innovations that will not only give us the clean-power industrial assets to preserve our American dream but also give us the technologies that billions of others need to realize their own dreams without destroying the planet. It's about making America safer by breaking our addiction to a fuel that is powering regimes deeply hostile to our values. And, finally, it's about making America the global environmental leader, instead of laggard, which as Schwarzenegger argues would "create a very powerful side product." Those who dislike America because of Iraq, he explained, would at least be able to say, "Well, I don't like them for the war, but I do like them because they show such unbelievable leadership—not just with their blue jeans and hamburgers but with the environment. People will love us for that. That's not existing right now."

In sum, as John Hennessy, the president of Stanford, taught me: Confronting this climate-energy issue is the epitome of what John Gardner, the founder of Common Cause, once described as "a series of great opportunities disguised as insoluble problems."

Am I optimistic? I want to be. But I am also old-fashioned. I don't believe the world will effectively address the climate-energy challenge without America, its president, its government, its industry, its markets and its people all leading the parade. Green has to become part of America's DNA. We're getting there. Green has hit Main Street—it's now more than a hobby—but it's still less than a new way of life.

Why? Because big transformations—women's suffrage, for instance—usually happen when a lot of aggrieved people take to the streets, the politicians react and laws get changed. But the climate-energy debate is more muted and slow-moving. Why? Because the people who will be most harmed by the climate-energy crisis haven't been born yet.

"This issue doesn't pit haves versus have-nots," notes the Johns Hopkins foreign policy expert Michael Mandelbaum,

"but the present versus the future—today's generation versus its kids and unborn grandchildren." Once the Geo-Green interest group comes of age, especially if it is after another 9/11 or Katrina, Mandelbaum said, "it will be the biggest interest group in history—but by then it could be too late."

An unusual situation like this calls for the ethic of stewardship. Stewardship is what parents do for their kids: think about the long term, so they can have a better future. It is much easier to get families to do that than whole societies, but that is our challenge. In many ways, our parents rose to such a challenge in World War II—when an entire generation mobilized to preserve our way of life. That is why they were called the Greatest Generation. Our kids will only call us the Greatest Generation if we rise to our challenge and become the Greenest Generation.

THOMAS L. FRIEDMAN is a columnist for *The New York Times* specializing in foreign affairs.

UNIT 2

Managing Interstate Conflicts and the Proliferation of Weapons

Unit Selections

Key Points to Consider

- Will NATO be able to expand both its membership and missions in the future given Russia's recent policy stances and actions?

- When will China be able to rival the United States in terms of its military capabilities and economic power?

- Why is Iran more assertive in recent years and why does Israel feel increasingly threatened by Iran's strategic goals?

- Is Israel likely to launch a preemptive strike against Iran in the future? What about the United States?

- How many of the nearly 50 countries who know how to build nuclear bombs might forego their development if the Nunn-Lugar Cooperative Threat Reduction (CRT) process was extended to new partners?

- What can be done to prevent future A.Q. Kahn-type networks from selling the knowledge and components needed to produce sophisticated nuclear weapons?

- Are biological weapons a real security threat?

- What additional homeland defense measures should be taken to prepare for a future nuclear, biological, chemical or radiation (NBCR) attack in the United States?

Student Web Site

www.mhcls.com

Internet References

U.S. Department of State
  http://www.state.gov/index.cfm

Belfer Center for Science and International Affairs (BCSIA)
  http://www.ksg.harvard.edu/bcsia/

FACTs
  http://www.ploughshares.ca

U.S.- Russia Developments
  http://www.acronym.org.uk/start

The Bulletin of the Atomic Scientists
  http://www.bullatomsci.org

Federation of American Scientists
  http://www.fas.org

As economic, political, and military power diffuses throughout the International Systems, an increased number of nation-states are using the traditional forms of statecraft used by major nation-state powers to obtain their national-interests. The world was reminded of the enduring nature of power politics during August of 2008. While millions worldwide watched the historic opening ceremonies of the Olympics in Beijing on televisions, millions more turned in to news stations to view clips of Russian tanks rolling into South Ossetia, a rebel province of Georgia. The military intervention into two disputed areas inside Georgia was the former super power's first major military operation outside of Russia's national borders since the invasion of Afghanistan in 1979. The invasion came as a surprise to many observers. However, experienced realists claimed that the incursions were part of a long-term goal of Russia that had only temporarily been suspended in the years immediately following the collapse of the Soviet Union. Others, who noted that Russia may have been responding to provocations by the Georgian government, were largely ignored as most analysts called for renewed efforts to form an alliance among Baltic Central Europe, and Ukraine within EU and NATO without regard to how threatening such an alliance might appear to Russia.

At the same time that realpolik approaches were playing out in Europe, China's national government continued to display the country's remarkable economic progress and rising international status in several ways throughout the 2008 Olympics. The People's Liberation Army (PLA) figured prominently in some of China's public ceremonies during the games. The salient PLA role was no accident as the increasing capabilities and effectiveness of the PLA is an important aspect of the government's foreign and domestic power. The importance that China's leaders place on building up the PLA is reflected in sustained increases in the military budget for years. Despite a steady increase in the sophistication and reach of China's military capabilities, most analysts predict that it will be several years before China's military muscle matches its economic power, and several more years before China will rival the military might of the United States.

Nearly 50 nation-states may know how to make nuclear arms. As nuclear proliferation research and development continues unabated, analysts are now primarily concerned about what members of the nuclear club, especially the United States and Israel, will do as Iran moves closer to having operational nuclear weapons capabilities. An Israeli air attack on a Syrian facility believed to have been a clandestine nuclear reactor in 2007 was similar in intent to an earlier air attack in 1981 on an Iraqi facility, Osiraq. In both cases, the Israeli government decided to launch a preventive security attack. Israeli's past actions are designed to provide credibility to verbal warnings that Israel will not hesitate to destroy suspected WMD facilities in neighboring countries. In "Israeli Military Calculations towards Iran," the authors describe the strategic reality that three-quarter of Israel's population is

© Digital Vision/Getty Images

extremely vulnerable to a nuclear attack since they live "on a narrow strip of coastline from Ashkelon to Haifa." This demographic fact is one reason why Israel has relied on preemptive strikes of suspected nuclear facilities, such as the raid on an alleged covert weapons facility in Syria during the fall of 2007. Many analysts are now taking bets on when Israel or the United States will attempt to disrupt Iran's alleged nuclear weapons program as well.

As nation-states redouble their reliance on nuclear fuels, many proposals have been made to stop nuclear materials from proliferating further. Richard G. Lugar, one of the architects of the Cooperative Threat Reduction (CRT) process developed to prevent nuclear weapons proliferation from the former Soviet Union, argues that extension of the CRT process to new partners is one way to prevent the spread of nuclear, biological, and chemical weapons worldwide. Proposals to expand the CRT process or expand the mandate of the International Atomic Energy Agency to include multinational fuel banks where countries pursuing nuclear energy research could draw on nuclear fuel are designed to slow down the number of dual-use nuclear facilities being built that could secretly be used for weapons research. Such proposals require nation-states to band together, cooperate and watch over one another to make sure no former weapons scientists are hired to work on covert WMD programs and no nuclear fuel is diverted for bomb production.

Unfortunately, such programs will not stop committed deviants such as A.Q. Khan, the former head of Pakistan's nuclear weapons program, from selling his WMD expertise and components upon retirement. While the extent of proliferation damage caused by the A.Q. Kahn network remains unknown, it is clear that several nation-states, including North Korea and Libya, could not have progressed so fast towards developing sophisticated nuclear weapons without the expertise and components supplied by A..Q. Kahn's network. Such amorphous, highly adaptive, and underground transnational criminal networks may increasingly pose the greatest dangers to nation-state and the collective security of citizens in several countries

Scholars and practitioners tend to disagree whether nation-states, terrorists, or lone deviants are most likely to use chemical or biological agents as weapons of terror against civilians in the future. There is even less agreement now than in past years about whether it is possible to deter or counter the use of chemical or biological weapons. It took seven years for the FBI to announce that the former U.S. Army microbiologist Bruce Ivins, was implicated in the U.S. anthrax letter attacks in 2001. The resulting skepticism that Ivins, was the sole perpetrator of the attacks, even though he killed himself prior to being arrested, illustrates just how difficult it can be to determine who is the attacker in a single or series of biological incidents.

The difficulties determining the extent of sophistication of several past covert chem-bio weapons programs in such varied countries as South Africa, Iraq, and Libya further illustrate why it is probably impossible to apply the same type of control strategies to deny would-be nuclear proliferators access to nuclear energy or to control the proliferation of equipment, supplies, or expertise needed to build chemical or biological weapons. These difficulties are compounded by the fact many countries throughout the developing and developed world are attempting to develop high tech biotechnology, nanotechnology, and information technologies economic sectors which can mask covert chem-bio weapons research and development, especially if the goal is mass disruption rather than mass destruction. In "Evolving Bioweapon Threats Require New Countermeasures," Helen Purkitt and Virgen Wells discuss why it is impossible to control the equipment, supplies, and knowledge needed to develop sophisticated or naturally occurring biological agents as weapons. Instead of instituting control strategies, Purkitt and Wells advocate designing public policies that will promote new transparency norms among nation-states and citizens throughout the world.

War in Georgia, Jitters All Around

Moscow's ambitions . . . directly undermine the entire European project of peace, freedom, and prosperity.

Svante E. Cornell

Near midnight on August 8, a column of several hundred Russian tanks rolled through the Roki Tunnel, which connects Russia to Georgia's breakaway province of South Ossetia. This action represented Russia's first military attack on another state since the Soviet invasion of Afghanistan in 1979—hence, it was an event whose significance extended far beyond the South Caucasus. Indeed, while the humanitarian consequences of the war that ensued in Georgia do not compare with what transpired in Chechnya (or Bosnia) in the 1990s, the conflict arguably marked the most significant challenge to Europe's security architecture since the end of the cold war.

Within 10 days, Russian troops had taken control of South Ossetia and started a second front in Georgia's other separatist region, Abkhazia. And they had also intruded deep into non-contested Georgia, moving on the towns of Gori, Poti, Zugdidi, and Senaki. Military and civilian infrastructure had been bombed across Georgia, as had the railway connecting the eastern and western parts of the country. Even the prized Borjomi-Kharagauli National Park was in flames on account of Russian firebombing.

Russia's invasion was a surprise—but only in terms of its scope and brutality. For months if not years, Russia had been pressuring Georgia in various ways, singling it out among countries in the region for particularly aggressive treatment. This spring, several analysts predicted a war would take place, some even timing it to August. Yet Western leaders were caught unaware, and appeared unable or unwilling to respond meaningfully to Russia's attack. Why did this small war in the Caucasus happen, and who started it? What implications will it have for the South Caucasus, for the former Soviet Union more broadly, and for Europe as a whole?

Caucasian Empowerment

In recent years, the nations of the South Caucasus have made some of the most remarkable progress that has been seen anywhere in the post-Soviet space. This comes in stark contrast to these countries' first decade of independence, during the 1990s, when debilitating ethnic wars, political instability, and economic collapse made a shambles of the region. In that era Armenia and Azerbaijan fought a vicious war, and Georgia was torn apart as the two northern autonomous regions effectively seceded with Russian help. Afterwards, these conflicts remained unresolved, and the West ignored them despite the peril in doing so.

The war and destruction of the 1990s make the progress of recent years all the more remarkable. The region's states have hardly become model democracies. They remain afflicted by widespread corruption and by a constant tug-of-war between authoritarian and democratic forces that are fighting for influence both in government and in opposition groups. But the region's three countries— Georgia, Armenia, and Azerbaijan—have, in fact, become real states.

Of the three, Georgia has achieved the most impressive transformation. At the start of the current decade the central government— controlled by aging former Soviet Foreign Minister Eduard Shevardnadze—had failed to gain real control over territories outside the capital's immediate vicinity, let alone the breakaway regions. Georgia was known as a failing state. But in 2003, the "young reformers" whom Shevardnadze had cultivated turned into an opposition and carried out the peaceful "Rose Revolution." With a reformist zeal previously seen nowhere in the former Soviet Union except the Baltic States, a government led by President Mikheil Saakashvili turned Georgia around. Petty corruption was effectively eliminated; Soviet-era practices were thrown out and institutions revamped; and the tax system was rebuilt. Georgia's budget quadrupled and the country became solvent again.

But the state's newfound successes ruffled feathers in Georgia. The flamboyant Saakashvili's government sometimes appeared arrogant, and lacked sensitivity regarding the adverse effects of its policies. In November 2007, street protests organized by opposition groups funded by a shady oligarch, along with a subsequent crackdown, harmed the government's legitimacy. But the government survived this crisis. Most of the legitimacy was restored, moreover, when early elections were held, and were judged by international observers mostly free and fair. Saakashvili was reelected with 52 percent of the vote, more than double the share of his closest opponent, and in parliamentary elections the ruling party maintained control. While Georgia still has much work ahead of it in terms of building institutions, the rule of law, and a fully democratic political culture, one struggles to identify a country anywhere that has experienced as rapid a turnaround as Georgia has in the past decade.

Azerbaijan and Armenia have also experienced some success, though it has occurred along different trajectories from Georgia's. In Azerbaijan, the astute diplomacy of Heydar Aliyev, the country's returned Soviet-era leader, brought billions of dollars of investment in the country's rich Caspian oilfields in the 1990s, along with stability. Aliyev also succeeded in securing a Western export route for the country's oil—the US- supported Baku-Tbilisi-Ceyhan pipeline, which was completed in 2005.

In 2003, Aliyev handed power to his son, Ilham. The latter, a progressive man with an acute understanding of market economics, presides over a stable and rapidly growing country. But he has had to deal with the first signs of "Dutch disease" (a decline in other economic sectors corresponding with the dominance of energy exports) and a government run to a large extent by the oligarchs of his father's tenure. They, whose positions in power are entrenched enough to bring to mind feudal barons, limit his scope of action and his ability to reform the country.

Armenia, which lacks Azerbaijan's oil fields and has not experienced a revolution like Georgia's, lost almost half its population to emigration in the 1990s. Moreover, most regional infrastructural projects bypassed Armenia because of its war with Azerbaijan, which lasted from 1988 to 1994. Thanks to serious reforms, Armenia has managed to make its economy a success story, with double-digit growth rates characterizing the past decade. Yet the country's political system has remained sclerotic. It is dominated by a crop of politicians whose fortunes were linked to the war over the ethnic enclave of Nagorno-Karabakh in southwestern Azerbaijan, from which Armenia's current leaders hail.

All three countries, in short, have their problems, the largest of which are unresolved territorial conflicts. But the past decade has seen the nations evolve into functioning states with a capacity to formulate and implement policies. Paradoxically, this strengthening of statehood is what has caused the region's unresolved conflicts to reemerge on the world agenda. The leaders of Azerbaijan and Georgia, with their renewed strength and capacities, resolved to reverse the humiliating defeats and losses of territory that their countries suffered in the 1990s, thus rejecting a status quo to which the international community had grown accustomed.

Status Quo No Longer

Indeed, Baku and Tbilisi became anti–status quo powers, calling into question weak international mechanisms for conflict resolution and investing a substantial share of their growing national wealth in their military budgets. This explains some of the recent bewilderment of European powers that were suddenly asked, despite their having to juggle dozens of other concerns, to address conflicts in a distant neighborhood that they understood poorly. But most of all, it explains Russia's increasingly assertive interference in the conflicts—especially those in Georgia.

When Saakashvili came to power in Georgia in early 2004, he immediately raised the Council of Europe's flag beside Georgia's in front of the national parliament. Of course, the Council of Europe's flag is identical to that of the European Union—12 stars on a deep blue background—so flying it was a powerful statement of Georgia's European aspirations. Not long afterwards, Saakashvili declared Georgia's intention to seek NATO membership. Shevardnadze before him had expressed such desires; but because of Saakashvili's furious pace of reform, this was a bid for membership that could not simply be laughed away. Saakashvili saw his country following in the footsteps of Central and Eastern European countries that were, just as he gained power, being admitted to NATO and the EU.

Europe, however, was developing a serious case of enlargement fatigue—and with EU efforts to reform an ungovernable union of 27 members already foundering, it was developing internal difficulties as well. More ominously than this, the Russia of 2005 was not the Russia of 1995. No longer dependent on Western loans, Russia was now buoyed by an oil windfall and was in the midst of a self-aggrandizing effort to restore its great power status.

The country's president, Vladimir Putin, was determined to roll back the "color revolutions" that had brought pro-Western leaders to power in Tbilisi and Kiev, and which had put Georgia and Ukraine on a trajectory toward NATO membership. Putin saw these trends as a direct result of Moscow's weakness in the 1990s, and he thought displays of Russian strength were needed. Nowhere has Moscow's readiness to flex its muscles been clearer than in Georgia.

Initially, Moscow was put on the defensive by Georgia's increasingly assertive steps to achieve progress regarding its unresolved territorial conflicts. Georgia's efforts in 2004 to curtail widespread smuggling of drugs, untaxed cigarettes, and other contraband across South Ossetia led to a serious skirmish with the separatists. In 2006, Georgia took control of the mountainous Kodori Gorge in upper Abkhazia, which had been dominated by a local warlord.

These measures were seen as militaristic, but Tbilisi also made a series of political and economic proposals to the separatist leaderships, and sought greater international participation in the processes of conflict resolution. Georgia reversed its earlier policies of isolating the unrecognized republics, seeking instead to engage them economically and win their hearts by presenting a renewed association with Georgia as a path to Europe. Thus, Tbilisi's policies included a mix of carrots and sticks. This mix, however, never gained coherence.

From Moscow's vantage point, Georgia's assertiveness and success were the chief regional threats to the emerging "Putin doctrine"— according to which Russia would resume its domination and control over the states of the former Soviet Union. Indeed, the Kremlin saw Georgia's revolution as having inspired the Ukrainian revolution the next year and potentially beginning a wave of democratic revolutions that would bring Western-oriented leaders to power throughout the post-Soviet world. This would clearly be an obstacle to Putin's ambitions of restoring Moscow's empire, and eventually a threat to the power of the authoritarian kleptocracy in the Kremlin.

Peacekeeping Russian-Style

Moscow's response to Georgia's actions was gradual but strong, and included a set of instruments to which no other former Soviet state had been exposed. First, Russia undermined Georgia's statehood and independence by intervening more boldly than before in the unresolved civil wars that Moscow itself had helped instigate. Even before Saakashvili came to power, Russia had imposed a discriminatory visa regime on Georgia, requiring visas of Georgians but exempting residents of Abkhazia and South Ossetia. Subsequently, Moscow began to distribute Russian passports en masse to the populations of these two regions, in violation of international law.

This was followed by a claim that Russia had a right to defend its citizens abroad, through military means if necessary—which turned out to be exactly the pretext Russia used when it invaded Georgia. Not stopping at this, Russia's political leadership began floating the possibility of annexing Abkhazia and South Ossetia. Meanwhile, Moscow staunchly resisted all efforts to internationalize mediation, negotiation, and peacekeeping in the conflict zones.

Facing little international reaction to these aggressive moves, Moscow by 2004 essentially dropped any pretense of neutrality in the Georgian conflicts. It began appointing Russian officials to the military and security services of the breakaway regions' self-styled governments. Hence Russian general Sultan Sosnaliev served as Abkhazia's defense minister. Likewise, South Ossetia's defense minister, Major General Vasily Lunev (former commander of the Siberian military district), and its security chief, Anatoly Barankevich, were among several Russian military officers in that breakaway republic's government.

These moves made a mockery of Russia's claim to playing a peacekeeping and mediation role in the conflicts, as well as of any pretense that the separatist governments operated independently from Moscow. Yet these blatant interventions within Georgian territory were at most obliquely criticized by Western leaders, who did nothing to seek a transformation of the negotiation mechanisms, let alone of the peacekeeping forces.

Moscow also exercised economic instruments of policy. In 2006, coinciding with the Russian-Ukrainian energy crisis, energy supplies from Russia to Georgia were cut off after mysterious explosions on Russian territory destroyed the pipelines and power lines that carried gas and electricity to Georgia. Only months later, Russia imposed a total ban on imports of Georgian and Moldovan wine, citing bogus quality concerns (Russia consumed about 80 percent of both countries' wine exports). In September 2006, after Georgia arrested several alleged Russian spies, a full embargo was imposed—all transport, trade, and postage links with Georgia were ended. Georgians living in Russia were systematically harassed.

In 2007, Moscow escalated its policies to include military provocation. In March of that year, Russian attack helicopters shelled administrative buildings in the Kodori Gorge, while on August 6—a year to the day before the descent to war in 2008—a Russian aircraft attacked a Georgian radar station near South Ossetia. When a bomb that was dropped failed to explode, international investigators were able to prove its Russian origin. But Western leaders, mostly on summer vacation, took days to formulate a response, and when it came it turned out to be soft-spoken. By 2008, Putin had explicitly linked the conflicts in Georgia to the forthcoming Western recognition of Kosovo's independence.

On April 16, 2008, Putin signed a decree instructing his government agencies to open direct trade, transportation, and political ties to Georgia's separatist republics, and to open offices there. He then dispatched several hundred paratroopers as well as heavy artillery into Abkhazia—according to Moscow, as part of its peacekeeping operation. Utilizing troops to repair the railroad linking Russia and Abkhazia may have seemed an oddity, but repairs were completed on July 30. Thousands of Russian troops and hundreds of tanks sped down the line 10 days later, opening an entirely unprovoked second front to the war that had just started in South Ossetia.

Raising the Hammer

By August 7, 2008, days of escalating shelling of Georgian posts and villages by Russia's South Ossetian proxies in the South Ossetian conflict zone had led the Georgian army to increase its deployment of troops there. What happened next is a matter of dispute. Russia claims its invasion began after Georgia indiscriminately shelled Tskhinvali, the South Ossetian capital; Georgia says it began an attack only after a Russian tank column had already crossed the Roki Tunnel into Georgian territory.

The way the war began provides key insights about Russian motivations, and therefore also about the war's broader implications. The prevailing Western view is that Russia may have provoked Georgia, but that Saakashvili foolishly gave Moscow a pretext for intervention when he sent Georgian troops into Tskhinvali. While Westerners agree that Moscow's opportunistic invasion widely exceeded any legitimate right to action that Moscow may have had, there is also

a sense that Saakashvili has himself to blame for starting a war with Russia. But closer analysis indicates that this explanation is at best simplistic. A growing body of evidence suggests that Russia was determined in any event to wage war with Georgia this summer.

During the spring and early summer of 2008 it was Abkhazia, not South Ossetia, that was the scene of rising tensions—and in fact it is likely that Moscow planned to begin its war there. In the spring, statements by Russian and Abkhaz leaders regarding the Kodori Gorge grew increasingly belligerent, involving veiled threats to take control of this Georgian-administered region by force unless Georgia withdrew. Moreover, when Georgia sent unarmed drones over Abkhazia to monitor Russian troop movements, the Russian air force shot them down. One such incident was dramatically captured on camera. In late June, a leading Russian military analyst, Pavel Felgenhauer, said the Russian leadership had in April made the political decision to attack Georgia by August.

All these developments contributed to a growing sense of panic in Tbilisi. For years, Western partners had told the young Georgian leadership to stay calm in the face of escalating Russian assertiveness, and to stick to existing peacekeeping structures in spite of any flaws. The term "exercise restraint," so dear to Western leaders, became a standing joke in Tbilisi.

Indeed, the West's lame response to Putin's April 16 decree and the August 6 missile attack led Georgians to conclude that no one would check Moscow's now overt territorial claims, and that Abkhazia and South Ossetia were likely being lost, perhaps irreversibly. Seeing this, the more hawkish members of Saakashvili's entourage contemplated a military option. Yet the president himself and the majority of his government saw the futility of military action, instead accelerating efforts to encourage a stronger Western diplomatic response.

In late July, tensions suddenly shifted to South Ossetia, which differs in two important respects from Abkhazia. Whereas in Abkhazia a clear front line along the Inguri River separated Georgian from Abkhaz forces, South Ossetia was a patchwork of Georgian and Ossetian villages under the respective control of the Georgian government and the Russian-backed separatists, with each side controlling about half of the territory. Second, while Abkhazia's elite maintained a modicum of distance from Russia, the South Ossetian leaders answered to Moscow rather than to their own people.

Following a July 3 attempt on the life of Dmitry Sanakoyev, a leading pro-Georgian official in the territory, tensions escalated. South Ossetian forces started shelling Georgian posts and villages, which elicited fire from Georgian forces. Russian jets also conducted overflights of South Ossetia, and unlike on previous occasions, did not bother to deny these violations of Georgian airspace.

Across the mountains in the North Caucasus, Russia used the summer months to finalize an impressive military buildup. Starting on July 15, Russia conducted a major military exercise dubbed "Kavkaz-2008." When the exercise ended on August 2, the troops involved did not return to their barracks—though some of them had come from posts in faraway Pskov and Novorossiysk. They remained on alert in North Ossetia, just across the border from Georgia. The Black Sea fleet, based in Sevastopol, was meanwhile made ready for military action.

Striking the Blow

There is little dispute that on the late evening of August 7 Georgian forces began an attack on Tskhinvali. Russia claims it sent "additional forces" into South Ossetia only on the afternoon of August 8. But the Georgian forces, which had taken control of most of the city overnight, were pushed back at noon of that day by Russian artillery and air attacks. To carry out such an offensive by mid-day, Russian forces would have had to begin moving from their bases in North Ossetia on the evening of the previous day, at the very latest. In other words, whether the Russian tank column reached Georgian territory before or after the Georgian forces began their attack on Tskhinvali, the order to send troops across the border must have been given before Georgia began its attack.

That Moscow's invasion of Georgia was premeditated is also borne out by the extremely rapid and coordinated deployment to Georgia's Black Sea coast of the Black Sea fleet and by air force bombardments of Georgia's interior; as well as by the fact that a second front in Abkhazia was opened the very next day, followed by the landing in Abkhazia of over 6,000 troops by sea and railroad.

Saakashvili can certainly be blamed for the limited shelling of civilian areas that the Georgian military apparently committed (which even Saakashvili's supporters strongly deplore). Yet it is also clear that Russia intentionally inflated that assault's magnitude, claiming that more than 2,000 civilians had been killed though only about 100 deaths could be independently confirmed. In fact, most of the destruction in Tskhinvali was caused by Russia's air attack on Georgian positions. Beyond that, the only thing Saakashvili might be blamed for is falling into a trap that Russia had prepared for months.

The only thing Saakashvili might be blamed for is falling into a trap that Russia had prepared for months.

If, however, one accepts the premise that the Georgian advance took place against the imminent threat of a Russian army column moving toward the region, a compelling military logic justifies taking Tskhinvali. The city sits like a cork in a bottle: Had Russian troops been able to continue down the mountain roads to Tskhinvali, they could easily have moved from there toward Gori and even Tbilisi in a matter of hours, if that was their intention. By forcing Moscow to fight for Tskhinvali, the Georgian army—albeit at a devastating price—probably slowed the invasion by 48 hours. This gave Europe and America time to wake up, and perhaps saved the country's capital from occupation.

What Moscow Wants

Russia's invasion of Georgia in any case had little to do with South Ossetia. The aims were larger and strategic, and they reached well beyond Georgia. But as far as Georgia was concerned, Russia's invasion sought to punish Saakashvili's government for its Western orientation and its obstinate refusal to yield to Russian pressure. The Kremlin's ambition was in all likelihood to ensure the downfall of a president whom Putin is known to hate viscerally.

While that ambition was not met, at least in the short term, Moscow succeeded in crippling Georgia's military capacity and in dealing a devastating blow to the country's economy and infrastructure. Indeed, the war was a disaster for an economy largely dependent on growing Western investment.

Moscow's refusal to withdraw from Georgia, and its establishment of occupation zones deep in Georgian territory that threaten key transportation arteries, all indicate that the purpose of the invasion was to negate Georgia's independence and to reduce the country to a pliant satellite. The war was also obviously aimed at killing Georgia's integration into Euro-Atlantic structures. It capitalized on the assumption that European states would never seek to integrate a country that is partly occupied by Russian forces.

On a regional level, the war served to restore Moscow's control over the South Caucasus—a geo-politically crucial region with a unique position between Russia and Iran, and one that links the Black and Caspian seas. The Caucasian isthmus forms the access route between the West and Central Asia, enabling the transportation of Caspian oil to the West and providing NATO with a logistical link from Europe to its operations in Afghanistan (practically all flights between NATO territory and Afghanistan cross Georgian and Azerbaijani airspace). As such, the war indirectly targeted Azerbaijan's independence as much as Georgia's.

While oil-rich Azerbaijan has sought to maintain working relations with both Moscow and Tehran, there has been no doubt that the country's economic and strategic orientation has been toward the West. Indeed, Azerbaijan and Georgia are tightly connected—to the extent that they have come to be understood as a tandem that either stands or falls together. Without access to the West through Georgia, Azerbaijan loses its outlet for oil exports, and is also separated from Turkey, its closest ally. And without Azerbaijan, Georgia's strategic importance would be much reduced. The weak Western response to Russia's invasion of Georgia puts Azerbaijan in a quandary. While Moscow's actions undermine all that Baku has been working for in the past decade, the country cannot speak out too loudly, for fear it might be next to experience Moscow's wrath.

Moscow's war has broader significance, too, for the Caspian energy game. Moscow resented the building of twin oil and gas pipelines from Azerbaijan to Turkey across Georgia. While Russia has not yet directly attacked these pipelines, it has certainly sought to increase prohibitively the political risk of building any further pipelines along the same route—most specifically, the EU-championed Nabucco project, which would connect Turkmen or Kazakh reserves to Europe via the South Caucasus energy corridor. Moscow has thus dealt a further blow to Europe's attempts to diversify its energy imports and may have effectively ended any notions that Central Asian leaders had entertained about a Western export option.

But the country most on Moscow's mind when it invaded Georgia, other than Georgia itself, was probably Ukraine. Like Georgia, Ukraine is a candidate for NATO membership, but Russian elites see Ukraine as a historic part of Russia and not a separate nation. At NATO'S April 2008 Bucharest summit, Putin even warned US President George W. Bush that if Ukraine entered NATO it would be dismembered.

Also ominously, Russia since the spring of this year has been making more emphatic claims to the Crimean peninsula—not coincidentally home to Russia's Black Sea fleet. As it had in Georgia's breakaway regions, Russia has begun massive distributions of Russian passports to residents of the Crimea, many of whom are ethnic Russians. And territorial claims by leading official and semiofficial Russian figures on the peninsula have grown significantly. It is little surprise that Ukrainian leaders fear they will now have to choose between accepting a role as a Russian satellite or pressing on with a Western-oriented foreign policy—at the risk of meeting a fate similar to Georgia's.

Finally, Russia's aggression against Georgia sent a strong message to the West: that the South Caucasus and the entire former Soviet Union are parts of Moscow's exclusive sphere of influence, and the West should stay out. As such, Russia clearly indicated its desire to return to a cold war–style division of Europe into spheres of influence. Russia thus is mounting the largest challenge since the end of the cold war to the norms and principles of European security.

If Russia achieves its aims, Europe will become a place where whole nations are denied their sovereign right to run their own affairs and are instead subjugated to Russian control, regardless of their own national interests. Democracy would be impossible to maintain in areas under Russian domination because, as during Soviet times, Russia has failed to become a force of attraction and can only dominate its neighbors through intimidation. Moscow's ambitions therefore directly undermine the entire European project of peace, freedom, and prosperity as embodied by the European Union. And it is unclear at this juncture how far Moscow's ambitions extend: Does Russia wish to dominate even the Baltic states and Poland, despite their membership in NATO and the EU?

As during Soviet times, Russia has failed to become a force of attraction and can only dominate its neighbors through intimidation.

Might, Might Not

Whether Russia will succeed in its ambitions—in terms of achieving domination over Georgia, the South Caucasus, and the broader post-Soviet world, as well as in terms of changing the character of European security—will depend to a great degree on the West's ability to react correctly to the challenge. Unfortunately, the West's response in the weeks following the invasion was not encouraging, as Western leaders seemed taken aback by events and unable to find instruments to confront them.

French President Nicolas Sarkozy, serving also as EU president, did react rapidly to secure a cease-fire. But rather than mustering unity within the EU and seeing the agreement through to implementation, Sarkozy simply congratulated himself on a mission accomplished when, in fact, Russia had showed little if any inclination to respect its commitments. NATO was similarly muted, managing to gather only enough courage to say that "business as usual" with Russia would not be possible under these circumstances. European states in the EU and NATO remained divided on whether to move more assertively to punish Russia, with eastern members strongly supporting such plans and southern ones displaying more reluctance.

In the United States, which had invested tremendous prestige and political capital in Georgia, the Bush administration took several days to realize the magnitude of the crisis and to formulate a response—which primarily consisted of tough rhetoric. America did act by rapidly airlifting Georgian soldiers home from Iraq, where they had represented the third-largest foreign contingent of troops—a remarkable fact for a country of less than 5 million people. Washington also promised aid amounting to 1 billion dollars. But the initial Western reaction failed to attach any concrete cost to Russia's aggressive behavior—just as the West had offered only verbal, not substantive, reactions on the other occasions in recent years when Russia had acted provocatively against its neighbors.

With Europe divided and America overcommitted around the world, will Russia succeed in its effort to reestablish dominance in the post-Soviet space? This is by no means certain. In fact, while Russian success in this project is an entirely plausible outcome, so is failure. While Moscow's invasion of its southern neighbor is a sign of might, it is not necessarily a sign of strength. Indeed, it exposes several ways in which Russia may be weak.

While Moscow's invasion of its southern neighbor is a sign of might, it is not necessarily a sign of strength.

First, Russia's invasion proved that Moscow had failed to accomplish its political objectives in the South Caucasus without recourse to the ultimate instrument of power, war. The war, moreover, destroyed much of what remained of Western illusions about Russia.

Second, the fact that Russia's first foreign military adventure since 1979 took place at a time of murky "cohabitation" between now–Prime Minister Putin and Russian President Dmitri Medvedev may not be a coincidence. Russia's military adventures in its borderlands have often been related to domestic politics—indeed, the 1999 war in Chechnya was what brought Putin to power. Was the war in Georgia intended to secure Putin's control over Russia's foreign and security policies? If so, Russia is less stable than generally understood.

Third, it is likely that Moscow has mobilized international forces that will be difficult to contain. Russia's actions have cemented an alliance among the Baltic states, Poland, and Ukraine that is likely to develop further. This alliance will form a powerful force for action within the EU and NATO. And in Western Europe and North America, the war helped many people make up their minds about the nature of the regime in the Kremlin.

Given Europe's divisions, much of the burden of containing Russia will inevitably fall to the United States. As indicated by the strong reaction to the war by both US presidential candidates and by leading lawmakers from both parties, Georgia is a bipartisan issue in Washington. No matter who wins November's election, the next American president is unlikely to spend much time debating whether or not Russia is an ally, and will probably—unlike other recent presidents—pursue a much more forceful policy toward Russia and the post-Soviet space. In this sense, international reaction to Russia's military adventurism may prove to resemble a tsunami—slow, but massive in the end. Whether Western action will come in time to secure Georgia's freedom is another question.

SVANTE E. CORNELL is research director of the Central Asia–Caucasus Institute & Silk Road Studies Program, a joint center affiliated with the School of Advanced International Studies at Johns Hopkins University and the Stockholm-based Institute for Security and Development Policy.

The Long March to Be a Superpower

The People's Liberation Army is investing heavily to give China the military muscle to match its economic power. But can it begin to rival America?

The sight is as odd as its surroundings are bleak. Where a flat expanse of mud flats, salt pans and fish farms reaches the Bohai Gulf, a vast ship looms through the polluted haze. It is an aircraft-carrier, the *Kiev,* once the proud possession of the Soviet Union. Now it is a tourist attraction. Chinese visitors sit on the flight deck under Pepsi umbrellas, reflecting perhaps on a great power that was and another, theirs, that is fast in the making.

Inside the *Kiev,* the hangar bay is divided into two. On one side, bored-looking visitors watch an assortment of dance routines featuring performers in ethnic-minority costumes. On the other side is a full-size model of China's new J-10, a plane unveiled with great fanfare in January as the most advanced fighter built by the Chinese themselves (except for the Ukrainian or Russian turbofan engines—but officials prefer not to advertise this). A version of this, some military analysts believe, could one day be deployed on a Chinese ship.

The Pentagon is watching China's aircraft-carrier ambitions with bemused interest. Since the 1980s, China has bought four of them (three from the former Soviet Union and an Australian one whose construction began in Britain during the second world war). Like the *Kiev,* the *Minsk* (berthed near Hong Kong) has been turned into a tourist attraction having first been studied closely by Chinese naval engineers. Australia's carrier, the *Melbourne,* has been scrapped. The biggest and most modern one, the *Varyag,* is in the northern port city of Dalian, where it is being refurbished. Its destiny is uncertain. The Pentagon says it might be put into service, used for training carrier crews, or become yet another floating theme-park.

American global supremacy is not about to be challenged by China's tinkering with aircraft-carriers. Even if China were to commission one—which analysts think unlikely before at least 2015—it would be useless in the most probable area of potential conflict between China and America, the Taiwan Strait. China could far more easily launch its jets from shore. But it would be widely seen as a potent symbol of China's rise as a military power. Some Chinese officers want to fly the flag ever farther afield as a demonstration of China's rise. As China emerges as a trading giant (one increasingly dependent on imported oil), a few of its military analysts talk about the need to protect distant sea lanes in the Malacca Strait and beyond.

This week China's People's Liberation Army (PLA), as the armed forces are known, is celebrating the 80th year since it was born as a group of ragtag rebels against China's then rulers. Today it is vying to become one of the world's most capable forces: one that could, if necessary, keep even the Americans at bay. The PLA has little urge to confront America head-on, but plenty to deter it from protecting Taiwan.

The pace of China's military upgrading is causing concern in the Pentagon. Eric McVadon, a retired rear admiral, told a congressional commission in 2005 that China had achieved a "remarkable leap" in the modernisation of forces needed to overwhelm Taiwan and deter or confront any American intervention. And the pace of this, he said, was "urgently continuing". By Pentagon standards, Admiral McVadon is doveish.

In its annual report to Congress on China's military strength, published in May, the Pentagon said China's "expanding military capabilities" were a "major factor" in altering military balances in East Asia. It said China's ability to project power over long distances remained limited. But it repeated its observation, made in 2006, that among "major and emerging powers" China had the "greatest potential to compete militarily" with America.

Since the mid-1990s China has become increasingly worried that Taiwan might cut its national ties with the mainland. To instil fear into any Taiwanese leader so inclined, it has been deploying short-range ballistic missiles (SRBMs) on the coast facing the island as fast as it can produce them—about 100 a year. The Pentagon says there are now about 900 of these DF-11s (CSS-7) and DF-15s (CSS-6). They are getting more accurate. Salvoes of them might devastate Taiwan's military infrastructure so quickly that any war would be over before America could respond.

Much has changed since 1995 and 1996, when China's weakness in the face of American power was put on stunning display. In a fit of anger over America's decision in 1995 to allow Lee Teng-hui, then Taiwan's president, to make a high-profile trip to his alma mater, Cornell University, China fired ten unarmed DF-15s into waters off Taiwan. The Americans, confident that China would quickly back off, sent two aircraft-carrier battle groups to the region as a warning. The tactic worked. Today America would have to think twice. Douglas Paal, America's unofficial ambassador to Taiwan from 2002 to 2006, says the "cost of conflict has certainly gone up."

The Chinese are now trying to make sure that American aircraft-carriers cannot get anywhere near. Admiral McVadon worries about their development of DF-21 (CSS-5) medium-range ballistic missiles. With their far higher re-entry velocities than the SRBMs, they would be much harder for Taiwan's missile defences to cope with. They could even be launched far beyond Taiwan into the Pacific to hit aircraft-carriers. This would be a big technical challenge. But Admiral McVadon says America "might have to worry" about such a possibility within a couple of years.

Once the missiles have done their job, China's armed forces could (so they hope) follow up with a panoply of advanced Russian weaponry—mostly amassed in the past decade. Last year the Pentagon said China had imported around $11 billion of weapons between 2000 and 2005, mainly from Russia.

China knows it has a lot of catching up to do. Many Americans may be unenthusiastic about America's military excursions in recent years, particularly about the war in Iraq. But Chinese military authors, in numerous books and articles, see much to be inspired by.

On paper at least, China's gains have been impressive. Even into the 1990s China had little more than a conscript army of ill-educated peasants using equipment based largely on obsolete Soviet designs of the 1950s and outdated cold-war (or even guerrilla-war) doctrine. Now the emphasis has shifted from ground troops to the navy and air force, which would spearhead any attack on Taiwan. China has bought 12 Russian Kilo-class diesel attack submarines. The newest of these are equipped with supersonic Sizzler cruise missiles that America's carriers, many analysts believe, would find hard to stop.

There are supersonic cruise missiles too aboard China's four new Sovremenny-class destroyers, made to order by the Russians and designed to attack aircraft-carriers and their escorts. And China's own shipbuilders have not been idle. In an exhibition marking the 80th anniversary, Beijing's Military Museum displays what Chinese official websites say is a model of a new nuclear-powered attack submarine, the *Shang*. These submarines would allow the navy to push deep into the Pacific, well beyond Taiwan, and, China hopes, help defeat American carriers long before they get close. Last year, much to America's embarrassment, a newly developed Chinese diesel submarine for shorter-range missions surfaced close to the American carrier *Kitty Hawk* near Okinawa without being detected beforehand.

American air superiority in the region is now challenged by more than 200 advanced Russian Su-27 and Su-30 fighters China has acquired since the 1990s. Some of these have been made under licence in China itself. The Pentagon thinks China is also interested in buying Su-33s, which would be useful for deployment on an aircraft-carrier, if China decides to build one.

During the Taiwan Strait crisis of 1995–96, America could be reasonably sure that, even if war did break out (few seriously thought it would), it could cope with any threat from China's nuclear arsenal. China's handful of strategic missiles capable of hitting mainland America were based in silos, whose positions the Americans most probably knew. Launch preparations would take so long that the Americans would have plenty of time to knock them out. China has been working hard to remedy this. It is deploying six road-mobile, solid-fuelled (which means quick to launch) intercontinental DF-31s and is believed to be developing DF-31As with a longer range that could hit anywhere in America,

as well as submarine-launched (so more concealable) JL-2s that could threaten much of America too.

All Dressed up and Ready to Fight?

But how much use is all this hardware? Not a great deal is known about the PLA's fighting capability. It is by far the most secretive of the world's big armies. One of the few titbits it has been truly open about in the build-up to the celebrations is the introduction of new uniforms to mark the occasion: more body-hugging and, to howls of criticism from some users of popular Chinese internet sites, more American-looking.

As Chinese military analysts are well aware, America's military strength is not just about technology. It also involves training, co-ordination between different branches of the military ("jointness", in the jargon), gathering and processing intelligence, experience and morale. China is struggling to catch up in these areas too. But it has had next to no combat experience since a brief and undistinguished foray into Vietnam in 1979 and a huge deployment to crush pro-democracy unrest ten years later.

China is even coyer about its war-fighting capabilities than it is about its weaponry. It has not rehearsed deep-sea drills against aircraft-carriers. It does not want to create alarm in the region, nor to rile America. There is also a problem of making all this Russian equipment work. Some analysts say the Chinese have not been entirely pleased with their Su-27 and Su-30 fighters. Keeping them maintained and supplied with spare parts (from Russia) has not been easy. A Western diplomat says China is also struggling to keep its Russian destroyers and submarines in good working order. "We have to be cautious about saying 'wow'," he suggests of the new equipment.

China is making some progress in its efforts to wean itself off dependence on the Russians. After decades of effort, some analysts believe, China is finally beginning to use its own turbofan engines, an essential technology for advanced fighters. But self-sufficiency is still a long way off. The Russians are sometimes still reluctant to hand over their most sophisticated technologies. "The only trustworthy thing [the Chinese] have is missiles," says Andrew Yang of the Chinese Council of Advanced Policy Studies in Taiwan.

The Pentagon, for all its fretting, is trying to keep channels open to the Chinese. Military exchanges have been slowly reviving since their nadir of April 2001, when a Chinese fighter jet hit an American spy plane close to China. Last year, for the first time, the two sides conducted joint exercises—search-and-rescue missions off the coasts of America and China. But these were simple manoeuvres and the Americans learned little from them. The Chinese remain reluctant to engage in anything more complex, perhaps for fear of revealing their weaknesses.

The Russians have gained deeper insights. Two years ago the PLA staged large-scale exercises with them, the first with a foreign army. Although not advertised as such, these were partly aimed at scaring the Taiwanese. The two countries practised blockades, capturing airfields and amphibious landings. The Russians showed off some of the weaponry they hope to sell to the big-spending Chinese.

Another large joint exercise is due to be held on August 9th-17th in the Urals (a few troops from other members of the Shanghai Co-operation Organisation, a six-nation group including Central Asian states, will also take part). But David Shambaugh of George Washington University says the Russians have not been very impressed by China's skills. After the joint exercise of 2005, Russians muttered about the PLA's lack of "jointness", its poor communications and the slowness of its tanks.

China has won much praise in the West for its increasing involvement in United Nations peacekeeping operations. But this engagement has revealed little of China's combat capability. Almost all of the 1,600 Chinese peacekeepers deployed (including in Lebanon, Congo and Liberia) are engineers, transport troops or medical staff.

A series of "white papers" published by the Chinese government since 1998 on its military developments have shed little light either, particularly on how much the PLA is spending and on what. By China's opaque calculations, the PLA enjoyed an average annual budget increase of more than 15% between 1990 and 2005 (nearly 10% in real terms). This year the budget was increased by nearly 18%. But this appears not to include arms imports, spending on strategic missile forces and research and development. The International Institute for Strategic Studies in London says the real level of spending in 2004 could have been about 1.7 times higher than the officially declared budget of 220 billion yuan ($26.5 billion at then exchange rates).

This estimate would make China's spending roughly the same as that of France in 2004. But the different purchasing power of the dollar in the two countries—as well as China's double-digit spending increases since then—push the Chinese total far higher. China is struggling hard to make its army more professional—keeping servicemen for longer and attracting better-educated recruits. This is tough at a time when the civilian economy is booming and wages are climbing. The PLA is having to spend much more on pay and conditions for its 2.3m people.

Keeping the army happy is a preoccupation of China's leaders, mindful of how the PLA saved the party from probable destruction during the unrest of 1989. In the 1990s they encouraged military units to run businesses to make more money for themselves. At the end of the decade, seeing that this was fuelling corruption, they ordered the PLA to hand over its business to civilian control. Bigger budgets are now helping the PLA to make up for some of those lost earnings.

The party still sees the army as a bulwark against the kind of upheaval that has toppled communist regimes elsewhere. Chinese leaders lash out at suggestions (believed to be supported by some officers) that the PLA should be put under the state's control instead of the party's. The PLA is riddled with party spies who monitor officers' loyalty. But the party also gives the army considerable leeway to manage its own affairs. It worries about military corruption but seldom moves against it, at least openly (in a rare exception to this, a deputy chief of the navy was dismissed last year for taking bribes and "loose morals"). The PLA's culture of secrecy allowed the unmonitored spread of SARS, an often fatal respiratory ailment, in the army's medical system in 2003.

Carrier Trade

The PLA knows its weaknesses. It has few illusions that China can compete head-on with the Americans militarily. The Soviet Union's determination to do so is widely seen in China as the cause of its collapse. Instead China emphasises weaponry and doctrine that could be used to defeat a far more powerful enemy using "asymmetric capabilities".

The idea is to exploit America's perceived weak points such as its dependence on satellites and information networks. China's successful (if messy and diplomatically damaging) destruction in January of one of its own ageing satellites with a rocket was clearly intended as a demonstration of such power. Some analysts believe Chinese people with state backing have been trying to hack into Pentagon computers. Richard Lawless, a Pentagon official, recently said China had developed a "very sophisticated" ability to attack American computer and internet systems.

The Pentagon's fear is that military leaders enamoured of new technology may underestimate the diplomatic consequences of trying it out. Some Chinese see a problem here too. The anti-satellite test has revived academic discussion in China of the need for setting up an American-style national security council that would help military planners co-ordinate more effectively with foreign-policy makers.

But the Americans find it difficult to tell China bluntly to stop doing what others are doing too (including India, which has aircraft-carriers and Russian fighter planes). In May Admiral Timothy Keating, the chief of America's Pacific Command, said China's interest in aircraft-carriers was "understandable". He even said that if China chose to develop them, America would "help them to the degree that they seek and the degree that we're capable." But, he noted, "it ain't as easy as it looks."

A senior Pentagon official later suggested Admiral Keating had been misunderstood. Building a carrier for the Chinese armed forces would be going a bit far. But the two sides are now talking about setting up a military hotline. The Americans want to stay cautiously friendly as the dragon grows stronger.

Israeli Military Calculations towards Iran

Iran's apparent interest in a nuclear-weapons capability, which it denies, has sparked concerns in Israel mirroring those of the United States, the Gulf Cooperation Council, France, Germany and the United Kingdom. Yet there is a unique edge to Israel's worries: the concentration of three-quarters of its population on a narrow strip of coastline from Ashkelon to Haifa makes it extremely vulnerable to nuclear strikes. Israel's presumed second-strike capability might severely damage its attacker, but there would be no Israeli state left to take satisfaction.

I sraelis are not the first to notice this asymmetry. Former Iranian president Ali Akbar Hashemi Rafsanjani remarked five years ago that "the use of even one nuclear bomb inside Israel will destroy everything. However, it will only harm the Islamic world. It is not irrational to contemplate such an eventuality."

Converging Concerns

Several developments have reignited Israeli concerns about the prospect of an undeterrable adversary in its vicinity. The first was alleged Iranian progress in mastering uranium enrichment against a background of deception in Tehran's dealings with the International Atomic Energy Agency (IAEA). Israel is said to have told the U.S. that Iran has not only been working on centrifuge cascades, but has also made progress toward fabricating the explosive shell essential to compressing the fissile core of a nuclear device to produce a yield. The source is a secret agent whose reporting has not been confirmed by U.S. analysts. Given the trouble previously caused by "Curveball", a German intelligence asset whose inaccurate reporting on Saddam Hussein's supposed WMD efforts buttressed the case for war against Iraq, Israel's claims have been met with scepticism by the CIA, which is reported to have concluded that Iran does not, at this point, have a weapons programme.

Secondly, Israel, like other concerned Western countries, relates Iran's putative efforts to develop a nuclear weapons capability with advances Tehran claims to have made towards an intermediate ballistic missile capability in the form of the SHAHAB III. Given the range arcs connecting hypothetical launch sites in eastern Iran to the Mediterranean coast, Israel would have no more than two or three minutes' warning of impact. Such short lead-time would inevitably limit Israel's response options and strain its command-and-control arrangements.

Thirdly, Israel perceives Iran to be on the offensive. Tehran's interventions in Israel's dispute with the Palestinians in the West Bank and Gaza strike Israelis as gratuitously provocative. Iran's ideological and rhetorical commitment to the Palestinian cause is taken for granted by most Israelis, but the extension of this commitment to financing, training and equipping Hamas and Palestine Islamic Jihad is not. To Israeli minds it suggests a willingness to take risks for a purpose that does not contribute directly to the security of the Iranian state; it seems expressive, not rational and evokes a mindset unsuited to a strategic relationship involving nuclear weapons and underpinned by deterrence. The level of Iranian support for Hizbullah before, during and after recent hostilities in Lebanon has strengthened suspicions that Iran's posture toward Israel has taken a harder, more aggressive and somewhat risk-prone turn.

Rhetorical Offensive

The context for the current tensions was set by a sequence of carefully crafted and intentionally outrageous statements by Iranian President Mahmoud Ahmadinejad. He denied the Holocaust, threatened to wipe Israel off the map, characterised the Jewish state as "artificial" and predicted that Israel would disappear shortly.

These verbal attacks serve several purposes perhaps only tangentially related to the Iranian–Israeli bilateral relationship. They are popular in the Arab world, which makes it awkward for regional regimes to side openly with the U.S. in its efforts to win support for sanctions against Iran. They also serve Ahmadinejad's determination to breathe new life into the Islamic Revolution, which had not been launched as a Shia revolt but was originally envisaged as a pan-Islamic movement. By openly challenging Israel's legitimacy, let alone viability, as a state, the Iranian President enhances the primacy of Iran even as he papers over Sunni-Shia tensions that, in Iraq, are tearing at the fabric of society. Not coincidentally, he deflects attention from the continuing poor performance of Iran's economy under his leadership.

There is thus little likelihood that Ahmadinejad will temper his rhetoric, and just as little incentive for Supreme Leader Ali Khamene'i to push him towards a more tempered presentational approach. Meanwhile, Israelis are not focusing on the collateral objectives of Ahmadinejad's words, but rather on their face value.

Israeli Adjustments

The government of Israeli Prime Minister Ehud Olmert would like this problem to go away. The nearly universal disappointment—and, in some quarters, anger—over Olmert's handling of the confrontation with Hizbullah has put the government under pressure to be resolute. This pressure has been compounded by the continued firing of Qassam rockets from Gaza, where another Israeli soldier remains captive. It is therefore imperative politically that Olmert more overtly address the issue of Iran's nuclear ambitions and the interplay between these designs and Ahmadinejad's periodic out-bursts.

A Nuclear Anti-Nuclear Option?

In early January 2006, the "Sunday Times" revealed that the Israeli military has been planning to use nuclear weapons for a possibly attack against Iran's nuclear facilities, an most particularly the enrichment plant at Natanz. According to the article in the "Sunday Times," the use of nuclear weapons would be justified by the fact that the enrichment facilities at Natanz are protected by an estimated 20m of rock and concrete and are thus effectively outside reach of even the most powerful earth-penetrating bomb. However, any new use of nuclear bombs for combat purposes after Hiroshima and Nagasaki would have exceedingly heavy political and strategic implications.

Although Israeli Foreign Ministry spokesman Mark Regev formally denied the claim and restated the official stance that Israel was committed to a diplomatic solution and supported the UN Security Council resolution imposing sanctions on Iran, there are little doubts that the "tweaks" that arguably led to the newspaper's article were a deliberate move, in order to warn Iran (and the rest of the world) that Israel does have nuclear weapons and was prepared to use them. Much the same logic would seem to apply to Prime Minister Ehud Olmert's apparent "slip of the tongue" during his visit to Germany in December 2006, when he included Israel in a list of responsible nuclear powers (in contrast to Iran), and thus for the very first time indirectly acknowledged the existence of Israel's nuclear arsenal.

In addition to (re)asserting Israel deterrent vis-à-vis Iran, the calculate leaks about a conceivable Israeli pre-emptive nuclear strike might also be intended to force Washington's hand to launch a conventional attack of its own against Iran, or, at the very least, to give backing for Israel to do so.

Accordingly, Olmert has brought Avigdor Lieberman into the cabinet as part of a coalition deal that gives the newcomer the Iran portfolio. Lieberman is a right-wing politician who believes that Israel's enemies cannot be placated and must be subdued. Effie Eitam, another hardliner and former general who at one time seemed to favour the expulsion of Palestinians from the West Bank, also sits on Olmert's flank.

But the problem with being more vocal for domestic political purposes is that a prior foreign policy objective—to keep Israel out of the U.S.-UN-Iran diplomatic equation—has necessarily been compromised. The failure of the UN Security Council to agree on and enforce sanctions capable of raising the cost to Iran of pursuing its enrichment programme has reduced Olmert's room for manoeuvre. Nor is there much confidence in the willingness of third parties to deal with the problem militarily. The deputy defence minister, Ephraim Sneh, summed up Israeli sentiment by saying that the countries that would not bomb Auschwitz were not going to bomb Iran's nuclear production facilities.

American Mixed Messages

The U.S. appears to be giving Israel mixed signals regarding its own intentions to move beyond diplomacy, should this prove unavailing. Olmert met President George W. Bush in Washington on 14 November and emerged from his two-on-two meeting, at which Iran was presumed to be the main agenda item, saying that he was very happy with the discussion. Political analysts generally interpreted this to mean that Bush had given him assurances that, one way or another, Iran would not be allowed to obtain a nuclear-weapons capability. The implication drawn by some will have been that, if all else failed, the U.S. would consider facilitating an Israeli attack. But there is virtually no chance that approval would have been given by the White House at this encounter, or sought by Israel.

A crucial issue in any military calculations is the gap between the "red lines" of Israel and America. For Israel, Iranian mastery of the enrichment process represents a point of no return. For the U.S., which prudently has not specified a red line, that point would be further down the road, perhaps the moment when Iran was shown to have moved towards weaponisation. The gap between the two countries on this point could complicate diplomatic or military coordination over the next two years.

A conflicting and disconcerting message was also heard by Israelis who perceived that the defeats suffered by Republicans in the mid-term elections, which had taken place the week before Olmert's visit, ruled out the possibility of an American attack on Iran. The logic was that the White House, confounded by Iraq and under pressure from Republicans to do nothing more to damage the party's prospects in the 2008 general election, would abandon whatever plans might have been contemplated regarding military action against Iran. Donald Rumsfeld's replacement as Secretary of Defense by Robert Gates, who is on record as endorsing a dialogue with Iran, reinforced this view.

Despite the apparently encouraging substance of Bush's private remarks to Olmert, the Israeli delegation was hearing to them rather discouraging noises from others.

Military Planning

The complexities of an attack against Iran's nuclear facilities are daunting. The targets within Iran are much further from Israeli bases than was Iraq's Osirak reactor, destroyed by the Israeli Air Force in 1981. Yet Israel has reshaped its air force for deep strike missions of this kind. Its F-15s and F-16s have conformal fuel tanks that, in addition to drop tanks, increase the ability to fly long distances and reduce the need to refuel. For long-range missions such as this, however, tankers based on the C-130 and B-707 airframes are avaiiabie to support strike aircraft. The latter are big enough to loiter at refuelling stations for long periods and dispense the fuel needed to allow the raiders back to their bases after striking their targets.

Israel's air-force is sufficiently large to deploy a strike package of perhaps 50 jets—25 F-16s and 25 F-15s—which would be just enough to attack three key targets: the Natanz enrichment facility; the Arak research reactor; and the uranium conversion facility at Isfahan. The size of the attacking force would be determined by the number of aircraft needed to deliver a given amount of munitions, assuming a relatively low attrition rate. Israel has many weapons, such as 2,000-pound BLU-109 and 5,000 pound BLU-113 hardened penetration bombs, that could be used for such purposes. These can be released at standoff ranges and programmed to detonate above or below ground for maximum effect. Generating overpressures of about $0.7kg/cm^2$, these munitions are unlikely to leave much more than rubble. To assist precise targeting, Israel could use its LITENING targeting pods in combination with GPS systems. The Israelis would probably expect all but one or two of the aircraft to hit their targets. This is an expectation shaped by historical data on similar strikes conducted against an enemy that was well aware that an attack was coming.

There is the question of how Israeli planes would get to Iran. The attackers would have to traverse Turkish air space if they chose a northern route, which would skirt the Turkish bases at Diyarbakir and Incirlik. Standing against the risk of Turkish interference would be the advantage of refuelling over international Mediterranean waters. A central route would require them to overfly Syria or Jordan and Iraq. The Syrians would certainly shoot at the intruders; the Jordanians would probably not, but King Abdullah, a tacit Israeli friend, would be gravely humiliated. If the U.S. were fully supportive and willing to be identified unambiguously with an Israeli strike, it could facilitate overflight of Iraq and provide a secure orbit in Iraqi airspace for Israeli refuelling aircraft. A southern route would require overflight of Saudi Arabia.

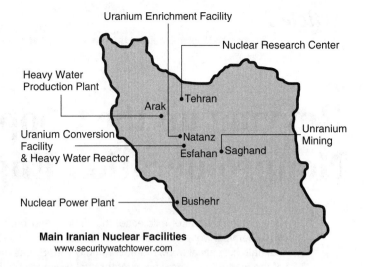

Main Iranian Nuclear Facilities
www.securitywatchtower.com

Since Iraq has faded as a rival to the Kingdom, and Saudi military alert levels are correspondingly lower, it is extremely improbable that the raiders would be detected, let alone successfully engaged. It seems unlikely at this juncture that the U.S. would be eager to accept the diplomatic and retaliatory costs entailed by any of these options.

Iranian retaliation does not loom large in Israel's thinking. Israelis are certainly vulnerable to Iranian reprisal in third countries, as Tehran proved when it collaborated in attacks against Jewish targets in Argentina in the early 1990s. But Hizbullah, despite its evident resilience, is no match for the Israeli Defense Force, especially if ground forces were fully unleashed, as many Israelis think they should have been recently in Lebanon. Tehran's Syrian ally would not be in a position to respond on Iran's behalf. And from an Israeli viewpoint, Iran is already pressing the Palestinian militant button as hard as it can.

For now, matters stand in delicate balance. The uncertainties regarding access are probably the ones that render the idea of attacking Iranian nuclear-related installations most unappetising to Israel. But Israel has tended to take risks in the past when it has felt most isolated and threatened. Israel's confidence in its nuclear deterrence will counterbalance the impulse to undertake the hazards of air strikes against Iran; and it is not yet clear to Israelis whether Iran would be more aggressive as a nuclear power, or more cautious and in fear of escalation. International inaction, an America with no appetite for confrontation, and an Iran whose leaders ruminate publicly on the destruction of Israel are precisely the conditions to upset this delicate balance.

From *Military Technology,* January 2007, pp. 258–260. Copyright © 2007 by Mönch Publishing Group. Reprinted by permission.

Revving up the Cooperative Nonproliferation Engine

In its sixteen years of existence, the Nunn-Lugar program has successfully dismantled nuclear, biological, and chemical weapons in the former Soviet Union. Washington's periodic disagreements with Russia should not halt this critical work. Moreover, the United States must expand the Nunn-Lugar principles to new regions of the world and to new types of threats. It is particularly vital to give Nunn-Lugar the authority to work with countries under conditions where U.S. legal obstacles might otherwise bar such cooperation, and to eliminate red tape and bureaucratic burdens on the Defense Threat Reduction Agency so it can respond to unforeseen contingencies. For example, Nunn-Lugar already has destroyed a chemical weapons stockpile in Albania, and it should be given the flexibility to work in North Korea if a future agreement makes that possible. Nunn-Lugar should be expanded so the United States can work cooperatively to control stockpiles of conventional weapons, train foreign governments in the interdiction of dangerous weapons and materials, and assist in responding to attacks involving weapons of mass destruction.

SENATOR RICHARD G. LUGAR

During the sixteen years that the Nunn-Lugar Cooperative Threat Reduction (CTR) process has been in operation, I have never considered "Nunn-Lugar" to be merely a program, or a source of funding, or a set of agreements. Rather, it is a concept through which we attempt to address a persistent global threat. It is an engine of nonproliferation cooperative and expertise that can be applied to many situations around the world. For a cooperative endeavor like Nunn-Lugar to work, new opportunities for partnership must be pursued creatively and relentlessly. The United States should be sending the clear message that we are willing to go anywhere in pursuit of preventing the proliferation of nuclear, biological, and chemical weapons.

That starts with Russia. Both the United States and Russia must accept the fact that we need each other. We must be as energetic in searching for common ground as we have been lately in voicing our dissatisfaction. Kremlin rhetoric will swing from one end of the strategic spectrum to the other. Commitments will be made and then put on hold. Projects will be on and then off. Our frustration level will be high. But we must not lose patience or miss the opportunities for cooperative threat reduction.

Critics argue that Russia's recent energy income windfall renders U.S. dismantlement and nonproliferation assistance unnecessary. Others attempt to resuscitate the fungibility argument, which asserts that every dollar we spend in Russia frees up dollars that Moscow can apply elsewhere. But we should recall that the Nunn-Lugar program was created to safeguard U.S. national security interests, and these interests exist regardless of the current state of Russia's financial fortunes.

Russia may well assume greater dismantlement and nonproliferation responsibilities in the years ahead, or it may refuse assistance even when it is needed. Washington cannot impose the Nunn-Lugar program on Russia. Moscow must make its own decisions and threat calculations. What we can do is effectively complete the work to which we are already committed and remain prepared to move quickly should new requests for cooperation occur.

The United States must seek new ways to remain active in Russia. The 2002 Moscow Treaty (also called the Strategic Offensive Reductions Treaty) did not contain any verification procedures, and the verification regime of the Strategic Arms Reduction Treaty (START) could expire next year. Discarding START's verification regime would be a mistake and would carry with it the seeds of greater distrust between the two sides. Under such a scenario, we have only one mechanism for verification and transparency—Nunn-Lugar. National technical means such as reconnaissance satellites cannot replace on-site verification.

We also must expand beyond Russia. In 2003, Congress authorized $50 million in Nunn-Lugar funding to be used outside the former Soviet Union. This authority has already been put to good use in Albania to destroy chemical weapons, an experience that taught us some important lessons. The Nunn-Lugar program must have the flexibility to adjust to unforeseen contingencies. The $50 million limit on work outside the former Soviet Union should be removed. The secretary of defense must have the authority to operate in difficult political and strategic environments without the risk that critical operations could be suspended because of the unintended consequences of executive or legislative action.

Today, the Nonproliferation and Disarmament Fund (NDF) at the State Department is the only U.S. nonproliferation program that operates with "notwithstanding authority." This authority allows the administration to do nonproliferation work in any nation or environment irrespective of U.S. legal obstacles—such as sanctions—that might otherwise block action. While useful, the NDF is not a substitute for a Nunn-Lugar program. The NDF's annual budget is only about $30 million, as opposed to a Nunn-Lugar budget of almost $500 million. The NDF operates with resource, management, and expertise limitations, some of which have been cited by the State Department Inspector General and the Government Accountability Office. It concerns me that if we experience a break-through in talks with North Korea that allowed us to begin helping that nation to fully secure and dismantle its nuclear program, NDF is the only option available to the administration under current law to carry out such operations.

Granting notwithstanding authority to Nunn-Lugar would not mean that Congress could not adjust or restrict the program. But it would mean that Nunn-Lugar would have the ability to respond rapidly to new nonproliferation opportunities that could be vital to our national security. We should not allow bureaucratic inertia to impede potentially historic transformations in North Korea or elsewhere.

Likewise, we must expand beyond Nunn-Lugar's traditional focus on strategic weapons. Two years ago, I introduced legislation with Senator Barack Obama (Democrat of Illinois) to jump-start the U.S. government's response to threats from conventional weapons stockpiles. We were concerned that leadership was lacking and that the budgetary commitment was not equal to the threat. Our bill called for a global effort to seek out and destroy surplus and unguarded stocks of conventional armaments.

The State Department has significantly increased funding for these efforts, but it is clear that the State Department budget does not have the capacity to focus the necessary funding and attention needed to address this threat. In my opinion, this means that the Department of Defense and the Defense Threat Reduction Agency (DTRA) must make a greater investment in conventional weapons elimination. I would recommend linking conventional weapons dismantlement with traditional Nunn-Lugar program activities.

We must also make the CTR process more streamlined. Over the last several years, I have worked to reduce the red tape associated with implementing Nunn-Lugar projects. The thirteen-step, nearly yearlong certification process for each Nunn-Lugar recipient must be eliminated. In some years, Nunn-Lugar funds for dismantlement projects have not been available for more than half of the fiscal year due to the cumbersome bureaucratic process. Hundreds of working hours by the intelligence community, the State Department, the Department of Defense, and other departments and agencies are routinely wasted complying with these requirements. Instead of interdicting weapons shipments, identifying the next A.Q. Khan, or locating hidden stocks of chemical and biological weapons, our nonproliferation experts spend their time compiling reports and assembling certification or waiver determinations.

I am pleased to report that this year, Congress will eliminate the certification requirements. This is good news, but it is just the tip of the iceberg of what must be done to streamline the process. I will keep looking for other opportunities to reduce bureaucratic burdens, and I urge DTRA to review its project implementation process in hopes of speeding dismantlement contracting and implementation.

While Nunn-Lugar is our country's first line of defense against weapons and materials of mass destruction, we need to bolster the second line of defense: our ability to stop weapons of mass destruction (WMD) that have been stolen from existing stockpiles but have not yet reached the United States.

To strengthen the second line of defense, we must improve the capabilities of other nations. We need the cooperation of like-minded nations to detect and interdict such threats. In 2003, the United States launched the Proliferation Security Initiative (PSI), which enlisted the participation of other nations in the interdiction of illicit nuclear, biological, and chemical weapons, and their components. PSI is an excellent step forward, but what is lacking is a coordinated effort to improve the capabilities of our foreign partners so that they can play a larger detection and interdiction role.

Nunn-Lugar has made important progress in this area. I have seen firsthand the effectiveness of the patrol ships, equipment, and training we have provided to Azerbaijan. In Ukraine, I witnessed WMD detection technology at border crossings and ground and sea surveillance in open areas. A number of countries including Afghanistan and Indonesia have asked to discuss possible Nunn-Lugar programs with their governments.

I recommend that Nunn-Lugar and DTRA make the provision of counterproliferation assistance a priority in the years ahead. In my view, this will make President George W. Bush's PSI more effective in stopping, interdicting, or deterring the proliferation of WMD. DTRA should also lead the way in providing expertise, equipment, and training to international partners in responding to potential WMD attacks. In other words, we must extend our cooperation to domestic preparedness. I recommend establishing bilateral and multilateral cooperation programs to assist in the development of decontamination and remediation capabilities. The response, mitigation, and restoration of public services following a WMD attack will be critical.

Our nation should make maximum use of the Nunn-Lugar program. The experts at DTRA are committed to protecting this country. They are an incalculable strategic asset for U.S. national security. We must find ways to help them do their job better and reduce the burdens we impose upon them.

Over the years, I have described our work with foreign governments to address threats posed by weapons of mass destruction as a "window of opportunity." We never know how long that window will remain open. We must not restrict or encumber our ability to act. Nor should we ignore opportunities to reduce the number of nuclear warheads or enhance the verification regime attendant to those drawdowns. Our government has the experience and capabilities to strengthen our role as the world leader in nonproliferation and counterproliferation. Our challenge is to devise the best way to implement programs devoted to these ends.

Acknowledgements—This viewpoint is adapted from testimony originally delivered before a review panel of the Defense Threat Reduction Agency in December 2007.

Pakistan: It's Déjà Vu All over Again

Pakistan lied, stole, and conned its way to becoming a nuclear weapons power. Now it's doing the same as a nuclear broker. Will the United States do anything about it?

LEONARD WEISS

Yogi Berra's famous quote can certainly be applied to recent revelations about nuclear weapon-related transfers to Iran and Libya from a Pakistani-generated, worldwide nuclear-materials black market. The current story also includes a remarkable display of public insouciance by the current U.S. government to the worst case of conscious proliferation in history.[1]

But the larger story is no surprise to those of us who have followed Pakistan's nuclear activities for the past 25 years. There is a long history to Pakistan's nuclear mendacity and the U.S. abandonment of nonproliferation goals in South Asia for short-term advantage in other policy areas.

Pakistani nuclear assistance to Iran and Libya is nothing new. News reports in 1988 revealed that Pakistan was assisting Iran on nuclear enrichment technology; reports of a Pakistan–Libya nuclear connection appeared as early as 1979.[2] In 1987, a BBC documentary film revealed that Libya had provided financing for the Pakistani bomb project in 1973. The Saudis were also involved as bankrollers in those early days.[3]

Despite President Pervez Musharraf's claim that the nuclear transfers to Iran and Libya (and North Korea) are the result of personal greed on the part of "the father of the Pakistani bomb," Abdul Qadeer (A. Q.) Khan, who "confessed" and was immediately pardoned, no serious observer believes that Khan's was a "rogue" operation unknown to the highest levels of the Pakistani military. While the complete story is yet to be told, it is well to remember the words of Musharraf's predecessor, the late Gen. Mohammed Zia ul-Haq, who said: "It is our right to obtain [nuclear] technology. And when we acquire this technology, the entire Islamic world will possess it with us."[4] (Zia failed to mention that Pakistan would also be sharing its nuclear secrets with North Korea, but that was before North Korea could help Pakistan with missile technology as a quid pro quo.)

Zia's bold statement was itself a paraphrase of a statement by his predecessor, Zulfikar Ali Bhutto, who wrote in his 1979 memoirs: "We know that Israel and South Africa have full nuclear capability. The Christian, Jewish, and Hindu civilization have this capability. The Communist powers also possess it. Only the Islamic civilization was without it, but that position was about to change."[5]

Khan's Early Network

Khan's illicit nuclear trading activities are merely an extension of his activities in the 1970s and 1980s. He began by stealing blueprints for uranium-enrichment centrifuges from Urenco, a European consortium, and then set about buying the materials and components needed for manufacturing highly enriched uranium. Here is some of what Khan was able to purchase in the 1980s:[6]

- 6,200 tubes of maraging steel, used to construct centrifuges, from a firm in the Netherlands;
- vacuum valves and a gas feed system to regulate streams of uranium hexafluoride gas into and out of the centrifuge system from a company in Switzerland;
- inverters from companies in Britain, Germany, and the United States;
- other electronic equipment for centrifuges from firms in the United States by way of Canada and Turkey;
- a metal-finishing plant from Britain;
- special measuring equipment from the Netherlands;
- a tritium extraction plant, special steel and aluminum, optical equipment, and other sensitive goods from Germany;
- vessels and tanks for Pakistan's fledgling reprocessing plant from Italy; and
- precision equipment for a reprocessing plant from Switzerland.

These acquisitions enabled Pakistan to get maximum benefit from the nuclear weapon design and supplies of uranium it received from China in 1983.[7]

In the ongoing investigation of how Libya was able to obtain sophisticated sensitive components for its nuclear program from Malaysia and other countries, the Malaysian police's inspector general reported that "the supply of components by middlemen . . . involved suppliers from other countries to blur the source of the components. Some of the suppliers were believed to be aware that these components could be for uranium enrichment centrifuges. Generally, these suppliers, mostly from Europe, were those who had had dealings with [A.Q. Khan] since the 1980s, at a time when Pakistan was developing its nuclear technology."[8] *Der Stern* reported on March 21, 1989, that more than 70 German firms helped Pakistan get materials and equipment needed to manufacture the bomb.

Some of the firms from which Khan made his purchases in the 1980s may no longer be involved in the trade, but the ease with which Khan was able to find so many suppliers to satisfy his more recent nuclear demands shows that an international black market was readily created and has been sustained. This is the legacy of the many years during which the United States turned a blind eye to Pakistan's nuclear activities.

Pakistan's brazenness during the 1980s is illustrated by its attempts to purchase and export materials from the United States—5,000 pounds of zirconium metal in 1981, and electronic parts known as krytrons for use in nuclear triggers in 1984. In July 1984 a man named Nazir Ahmed Vaid was arrested for the latter crime, but despite the fact that the government was in possession, on the day of his arrest, of information showing clearly that the intended recipient of the krytrons was the Pakistani Atomic Energy Commission, Vaid's indictment was rewritten to exclude any mention of the nuclear use of krytrons. He was then permitted to plea bargain to a reduced offense, thus avoiding a jury trial, and a gag order was placed on the case. He was found guilty of one count of export violation and quietly deported less than three weeks later. As in the current case with A. Q. Khan, the Pakistani government insisted that Vaid acted on his own, with no government authorization.[9] It was one of many denials of the obvious during the period.

No Nuclear Ambitions Here

During the 1970s and 1980s, when all this illicit nuclear activity was going on, Pakistan denied to the West that it was developing nuclear weapons or had any interest in nuclear weapons. As President Zia told the Foreign Policy Association on December 9, 1982:

"I would like to state once again . . . that our ongoing nuclear program has an exclusively peaceful dimension and that Pakistan has neither the means nor, indeed, any desire to manufacture a nuclear device. I trust that this distinguished gathering will take note of my assurance, which is given in all sincerity and with a full sense of responsibility."

A. Q. Khan himself weighed in two years later in an interview on February 10, 1984, saying that "the 'Islamic bomb' is a figment of the Zionist mind."

Starting in the late 1970s, when the U.S. government became aware of Pakistan's nuclear weapon-related activities, I was engaged in seeking to stop or slow the program through congressional investigations and legislative action. My boss at the time was Ohio Democratic Sen. John Glenn, who gave me free rein to work on the issue and became the Senate's voice of protest against Pakistan's nuclear activities. Frustration was more often than not the end result of much of our work.

I either crafted or was otherwise involved in numerous legislative actions designed to stop the Pakistanis through the threat of sanctions. These actions were passed by Congress and dutifully signed into law by three presidents, but their implementation was nearly always blocked because of other foreign policy considerations.

It didn't start off that way. Pakistan had been cut off from economic and military assistance in 1979 under the Symington and Glenn amendments to the Foreign Assistance Act, after it imported unsafeguarded nuclear enrichment technology and equipment. (The Pakistanis said the cutoff stemmed from the influence of "Zionist circles" seeking to protect Israel from the Muslim world.)[10] The Soviet invasion of Afghanistan later that year changed U.S. priorities.

Cold War Considerations

When Ronald Reagan arrived in the White House in 1981, his administration came with a desire to send arms to the Afghani mujahideen. They could only be delivered through Pakistan, and nonproliferation took a back seat to Cold War politics. The new administration was so intent on sending arms that as then–Assistant Secretary of State Robin Raphel later admitted, "There was no explicit agreement . . . no explicit quid pro quo" that in return for U.S. assistance Pakistan would not develop nuclear weapons.[11]

The Pakistanis got the message when there was no adverse U.S. reaction to a tough position articulated by Agha Shahi, then–foreign minister of Pakistan, in a meeting with James Buckley, then–U.S. undersecretary of state. On December 14, 1981, Shahi described the meeting to the Council of Pakistani Editors:

"We told Mr. Buckley that our program is only for peaceful purposes . . . and we are fully aware of the concerns of the United States over our atomic energy program, which we think to be baseless, unwarranted, unjustified. But we understand and we have taken note of this concern. So if we decide to carry out an explosion, then we would be prepared to forgo this [U.S. aid] program. That is a matter for our judgment, but we have given no undertaking to Mr. Buckley about explosions."

Despite Shahi's "in-your-face" position, James Buckley subsequently told Congress: "We believe that a program of support which provides Pakistan with a continuing relationship with a significant security partner and enhances its sense of security may help remove the principal underlying incentive for the acquisition of a nuclear weapons capability. With such a relationship in place we are hopeful that over time we will be able to persuade Pakistan that the pursuit of a weapons capability is neither necessary to its security nor in its broader interest as an important member of the world community."[12]

Sanctions Lifted

One month after Buckley's testimony, Congress passed the first of a series of legislated waivers of penalties under the Symington Amendment that lasted until the Soviets left Afghanistan in 1990. Although the legislation stipulated that a cutoff could still occur if Pakistan were to explode a nuclear device, the Pakistanis did not act worried that U.S. opposition to nuclear proliferation would put their bomb program in jeopardy.

During the U.S. presidential election season in 1984, President Zia told the *Wall Street Journal* on July 10 that he was "confident that U.S. politics won't disrupt the flow of American weaponry to Pakistan." His confidence was not misplaced. Indeed, it must have been reinforced by the contemporaneous Vaid case, whose lesson to the Pakistanis could only be that the United States would bend over backwards to keep the arms flowing, even in the case of overt nuclear smuggling attempts by Pakistan from within the United States. It must also have satisfied him to read that Richard Kennedy, then-ambassador at large for nonproliferation, had said: "We accept President Zia ul-Haq's statement that Pakistan's nuclear program is devoted entirely to power generation."[13] Ironically, the State Department had written a secret memorandum the year before stating that the United States had "unambiguous evidence that Pakistan is actively pursuing a nuclear weapons development program. . . . We believe the ultimate application of the enriched uranium produced at Kahuta, which is unsafeguarded, is clearly nuclear weapons."[14]

The Solarz and Pressler Amendments

As a result of the outrageous outcome of the Vaid case, Congress passed a law, known as the Solarz Amendment to the Foreign Assistance Act, prohibiting military and economic assistance to any non-weapon state that illegally exports or attempts to export U.S. items that would contribute significantly to the ability of that country to make a nuclear explosive device.

The Solarz and Pressler amendments were signed into law on August 8, 1985. The Pressler Amendment made continued military assistance to Pakistan contingent on an annual presidential certification that Pakistan did not possess a nuclear explosive device and that U.S. assistance would significantly reduce the risk that Pakistan would possess a nuclear explosive device. The Pressler Amendment was the last barrier to Pakistan's construction of a device, but the Pakistanis treated it with the same contempt they showed other efforts to condition U.S. assistance on nuclear restraint.

On September 12, 1984, a year before the Pressler Amendment was passed, President Reagan sent a letter to Zia warning the Pakistanis not to "cross the red line" of enriching uranium beyond 5 percent or face "grave consequences."[15] In response, President Zia pledged not to do so, and high-level officials kept repeating that pledge, which was itself repeated by administration spokesmen in congressional hearings.[16]

It was revealed some months later that the Pakistanis had already passed the 5 percent level at the time of Reagan's letter. But crossing the "red line" resulted in no action by the administration, and when Prime Minister Benazir Bhutto visited President George H. W. Bush in June 1989, the subject was not even mentioned.[17]

This undoubtedly reinforced the Pakistanis' feeling that they were under no limits by the administration save possibly for testing, and that Congress was equally feckless, with few exceptions. Attempts at smuggling materials from the United States continued, and another smuggler was caught in 1987. A Canadian citizen of Pakistani extraction named Arshad Pervez was arrested for illegally trying to buy and export a quantity of beryllium, along with 25 tons of maraging steel for centrifuges from an American manufacturer. He was ultimately convicted of the beryllium charge and of lying to investigators, but escaped conviction on the remaining charges on the grounds of entrapment, even though American intelligence officials found evidence that the Pakistani embassy in London was directly involved.[18] Pervez, who went to prison, admitted that he was working for a retired Pakistani brigadier general and that the final customer was the Pakistani nuclear program, thereby establishing a violation of the Solarz Amendment. But the U.S. government once again refused to sanction Pakistan, and the Pakistani nuclear program rolled on.

Pakistan Gets the Bomb

In an interview with Indian journalist Kuldip Nayar, A. Q. Khan admitted that Pakistan had enriched uranium to weapons grade, and added that Pakistan could build nuclear weapons.[19] In March 1987, Senator Glenn testified before the Senate Foreign Relations Committee, arguing that "Pakistani nuclear weapons production will, sooner or later, whether by design or by espionage, result in the wider transfer of nuclear weapons technology to countries in the Middle East." Despite such warnings, and clear evidence that U.S. assistance was not reducing the risk that Pakistan would possess a nuclear explosive device, presidential certifications were issued in 1988 by Reagan and in 1989 by Bush. On November 26, 1987, a United Press International story by Richard Sale quoted unnamed intelligence sources as saying that Pakistan had a workable nuclear device, although it was deemed too big "by those who have seen the new bomb" to be delivered by an F-16.

> **We are essentially back where we started with Pakistan in the 1980s. It has engaged in dangerous nuclear mischief, yet suffered no loss in its relationship with the United States.**

Too Little and Too Late

By 1990, the fiction that Pakistan might not possess the bomb was completely unsustainable. The Soviets had left Afghanistan, so no certification was issued by President Bush and assistance was cut off. Having been the recipient of extreme indulgence for so long, the Pakistanis were surprised by the action, which halted a shipment of F-16s that they had already paid for. Nonetheless, 40 F-16s had already been delivered, at least some of which were being modified to carry nuclear warheads in contravention of the conditions under which the planes were originally transferred. Thus, in service to the Cold War, the United States suffered more than a decade of Pakistani lies and false promises about their nuclear activities, did not enforce its own laws or restrictions on Pakistan's nuclear program when it counted, and left Pakistan with a U.S.-made nuclear weapons delivery system.

Senator Glenn's response to this outrageous history was encapsulated in an op-ed: "The Reagan and Bush administrations have practiced a nuclear nonproliferation policy bordering on lawlessness. In so doing, they have undermined the respect of other countries for U.S. law and have done great damage to the nuclear nonproliferation effort. Keep this in mind the next time someone in the administration extols the need for military action to deal with some power hungry dictator who is seeking to acquire nuclear weapons in the Middle East or elsewhere."[20]

After 9/11

Unfortunately, the story did not end with the cutoff of 1990. Pakistan had the bomb, but it still had not tested a nuclear weapon. So, in a triumph of hope over experience, legislation was passed in 1994 requiring the imposition of draconian sanctions in the event of a test, in the hope of deterring both Pakistan and India.

When both countries exploded nuclear test devices in 1998, the severe economic sanctions in the law were automatically triggered. But once again, Congress removed them, in part because of domestic considerations involving agricultural exports. The prohibition on military assistance continued, however, until after 9/11, when the current Bush administration issued a waiver ending the implementation of nearly all other sanctions because of the perceived need for Pakistani assistance in the fight against Al Qaeda and the Taliban in Afghanistan. This was the height of irony—it was U.S. support for Pakistan and the mujahideen in the 1980s that helped bring the Taliban and Al Qaeda to prominence in Afghanistan in the first place.

We are essentially back where we were with Pakistan in the 1980s. It is apparent that it has engaged in dangerous nuclear mischief with North Korea, Iran, and Libya (and perhaps others), but thus far without consequences to its relationship with the United States because of other, overriding foreign policy considerations—not the Cold War this time, but the war on terrorism.

But now there is a major political difference. It was one thing for Pakistan, a country with which the United States has had good relations generally, to follow India and produce the bomb for itself. It is quite another for Pakistan to help two-thirds of the "axis of evil," and the perpetrators of Pan Am 103, all of whom have, at one time or another, been accused of being sponsors of terrorism, to get the bomb as well.

The President's Dilemma

The waivers given to Pakistan after 9/11 are only good with respect to past behavior. Anything the Pakistanis have done since the waivers were issued that is proscribed by law require

new waivers to be issued. If the reports about the timing of Pakistan's exports are true—that some of the transfers occurred after the date of the most recent waivers—and the Pakistani government authorized the exports directly or indirectly, then Pakistan is in violation of U.S. laws and unprotected by past waivers. The same would be true if the Pakistani government was, as is likely, behind the recent incident of an Israeli businessman, operating out of South Africa, attempting illegally to buy and export nuclear trigger components for the Pakistani weapons program.[21]

No cutoff of the generous assistance that is being given and has been promised will occur unless and until the president makes a determination as to Pakistan's guilt. As in the 1980s with the Pressler Amendment, turning a blind eye means not having to make a difficult decision. And so far, the Bush administration appears to be pretending that Musharraf's claim of being the victim of a rogue operation headed by A. Q. Khan is the truth. It is reported that, in return, Musharraf has made some concessions facilitating the hunt for Osama bin Laden in northwest Pakistan.[22] But if the only concessions Pakistan makes because of the Khan case have to do with some immediate tactical advantage in the war on terror, and the nuclear program remains untouched, it is questionable whether U.S. national security has been enhanced in the longer term.

The president wants to be seen as not only a president fighting terrorism, but also as a staunch proponent of nonproliferation. Having gone to war with Iraq ostensibly to stop Iraq's possible proliferation, the president is now faced with a more serious violation of nonproliferation norms.

If the president does issue a new waiver for Pakistan, presumably on the grounds of the need for its support in the war on terror, he risks being accused of conducting business as usual. And, as indicated earlier, some will see this as a wholesale retreat from the nonproliferation rhetoric that fueled public support for the war in Iraq, and it will once again raise issues of U.S. credibility. A frequently voiced opinion abroad is that the United States does not oppose proliferation by its friends.

If, on the other hand, the president doesn't issue a waiver and pretends that no violation by the government of Pakistan has occurred, he risks being accused of misfeasance for having failed to carry out U.S. laws.

If the president wants to preserve U.S. credibility on nonproliferation, he can tell the Pakistanis that he is prepared to declare them in violation and impose sanctions unless they agree to a set of conditions that would cap their nuclear program and ensure the end of their illegal and immoral trade in nuclear weapons technology.

Among these conditions should be a demand that Pakistan sign a verifiable agreement to end its production of fissile material and make its nuclear trading records transparent to the International Atomic Energy Agency (IAEA) so the world can know what it is doing and with whom it has been dealing. An interrogation of A. Q. Khan by the IAEA should also be part of the deal. These conditions, if met, could enable the United States, in concert with its allies, to roll up much of the current black market in nuclear materials and equipment.

The president should also announce that greater intelligence resources will be devoted to Pakistan's export activities, with interdiction ready to be carried out under the administration's new Proliferation Security Initiative whenever indicated. In return for Pakistan's cooperation, the United States should be willing to help the Pakistanis improve their own security in ways that do not exacerbate the tensions in the area and are not perceived as assisting their nuclear weapons program.

It's Santayana All over Again

Some will argue that national pride would prevent Pakistan from accepting such terms and that the United States would lose a valuable ally in the fight against Al Qaeda if sanctions were imposed. Moreover, they will argue, sanctions could plunge Pakistan into economic and political chaos, with the possibility of takeover by a radical Islamic contingent that would then inherit Pakistan's nuclear weapons.

These arguments (just replace "Al Qaeda" with "communism") have been used for two decades in defense of a weak nonproliferation policy in South Asia that has brought nothing but grief. They do not take into account American credibility and the effect on other real or potential proliferators. It is true that Pakistan may be more prone to destabilization in response to economic stress than some other countries in the region, but it should be Pakistan's choice as to whether it wishes to belong to the community of responsible nations and receive the benefits it needs from that community. In any case, there needs to be an effective contingency plan for preventing Pakistan's weapons from falling into the hands of radical undemocratic elements in the country, something that could happen regardless of U.S. policy.

Pakistan presents a real and ongoing test of the seriousness of the Bush administration on the issue of nonproliferation. The choice between fighting proliferation or fighting terrorism is ultimately a false one. Sacrificing one for the other would have disastrous consequences for national security. George Santayana once wrote that those who forget the past are doomed to repeat it. In the case of Pakistan, we haven't forgotten, but the Bush administration insists on repeating it anyway.

Notes

1. Seymour Hersh, "The Deal," *New Yorker*, March 8, 2004.

2. O. Gozani, "Pakistan 'Aiding Iran' in Nuclear Weapons Venture," *Daily Telegraph*, Nov. 26, 1988. See also Farzad Bazoft, "Iran Signs Secret Atom Deal," *London Observer*, June 12, 1988, p. 1; John Fialka, "West Concerned by Signs of Libyan-Pakistan A-Effort," *Washington Star*, Nov. 25, 1979.

3. E. Lenhart, "Saudis Offer to Help Zia Build H-Bomb," *Sunday Times* (London), Jan. 18, 1981.

4. Interview in *Akhbar al-Khalij*, March 13, 1986, p. F4. Translated by Foreign Broadcast Information Service, FBIS-SAS-86-053, March 19, 1986.

5. See F. Hassan, "An Analysis of Propaganda Against Pakistan's Peaceful Nuclear Program," *Nawa-I-Waqt* (Lahore), March 16, 1984. See also Robert Windrem, "Pakistan: 'The Crazy Soup,'" MSNBC, February 8, 2004; Steve Weissman and Herbert Krosny, "Pakistan," in *The Islamic Bomb* (New York: New York Times Books, 1981), pp. 161–226.

6. Congressional Record, October 20, 1981, p. 24505; Mark Hibbs, "German Firms Exported Tritium Purification Plant to Pakistan," *Nuclear Fuel*, February 6, 1989, p. 6.

7. K. Malik, *Times of India*, Jan. 13, 1989, p. 1.

8. Press Release, "Inspector General of Police (Polis Diraja), Malaysia, in Relation to Investigation on the Alleged Production of Components for Libya's Uranium Enrichment Program," February 20, 2004, p. 3.

9. Seymour Hersh, "Pakistani in U.S. Sought to Ship A-Bomb Trigger," *New York Times*, Feb. 25, 1985, p. 1.

10. R. Trumbull, "Pakistan Denies It Plans A-Bomb; Denounces Washington Aid Cutoff," *New York Times*, April 9, 1979, p. 1.

11. Assistant Secretary of State Robin Raphel, testimony before the South Asia Subcommittee of the Senate Foreign Relations Committee, September 14, 1995.

12. James Buckley, testimony before the Senate Foreign Relations Committee, November 12, 1981.

13. Interview with Richard Kennedy, in *Pakistan Affairs* (newsletter), November 2, 1984.

14. U.S. State Department, Assessment of Pakistan's Nuclear Program, June 23, 1983. Declassified and released in March 1992 to the National Security Archive, Washington, D.C.

15. Simon Henderson, *Financial Times*, Dec. 7, 1984; Hedrick Smith, "A Bomb Ticks in Pakistan," *New York Times Sunday Magazine*, March 6, 1988, p. 38.

16. Simon Henderson, "Netherlands Drops Proceedings Against Nuclear Scientist," *Financial Times*, July 16, 1986, p. 3; Deputy Assistant Secretary of State Robert Peck, congressional testimony, July 31, 1987.

17. David Ottaway, "U.S. Relieves Pakistan of Pledge Against Enriching Uranium," *Washington Post*, June 15, 1989, p. A38.

18. Mark Hosenball and J. Adams, "A-Bomb Plot is Linked to Embassy," *Sunday Times* (London), July 26, 1987.

19. Shyam Bhatia, "Pakistan has the A-Bomb," *London Observer*, March 1, 1987, p. 1.

20. John Glenn, "On Proliferation Law, a Disgraceful Failure," *International Herald Tribune*, June 26, 1992.

21. David Rohde, "Pakistani Linked to Illegal Exports Has Ties to Military," *New York Times*, Feb. 20, 2004, p. 8.

22. Seymour Hersh, "The Deal."

LEONARD WEISS, now a consultant, was a staff director on the Senate Committee on Governmental Affairs, a position he held from 1977–1999.

From *Bulletin of the Atomic Scientists*, May/June 2004, pp. 52, 54–57. Copyright © 2004 by Bulletin of the Atomic Scientists, Chicago, IL. 60637. Reprinted by permission of the Atomic Scientists: The Magazine of Global Security, Science, and Survival.

Evolving Bioweapon Threats Require New Countermeasures

HELEN PURKITT AND VIRGEN WELLS

To better understand possible development and uses of biological weapons by nations and terrorist groups, we have studied past covert government programs in South Africa and Iraq, and recent trends in civilian biotechnology in South Africa.

U.S. monitoring of bioweapon threats is geared primarily toward uncovering large-scale, highly sophisticated programs, like that of the former Soviet Union during the cold war. But covert bioweapon development has become more diffuse, and many potential actors have far different goals than they did then. We think the United States needs to work with other nations to build new norms of transparency and greater international cooperation in regulating the operation of civilian-biotechnology laboratories and the dispersal of relevant data that may have military applications. Only through such global cooperation can we effectively monitor trends in potential bioweapon research and look for early-warning signs of covert biowarfare-weapons development by nation-states or by terrorists and other nonstate actors.

Our research indicates that terrorists are likely to use biological weapons not to inflict mass destruction but to commit blackmail or fuel political discontent, panic, or economic disruption. That's important because the development of biological weapons of mass disruption no longer requires large capital investment, great expertise, vast infrastructure, and sophisticated delivery devices like medium- or long-range missiles. Policy analysts and some policy makers have made similar points, but many of the United States' biosecurity priorities and policies do not reflect the new realities.

In the 1960s and 70s, a common pattern for developing countries was to send the "best and brightest" of their young scientists abroad for advanced study or training. Many of those scientists went on to work in their countries' covert bioweapons programs. For instance, Rihab Rashid Taha al-Azzawi al-Tikriti, a microbiologist (nicknamed "Dr. Germ" by U.N. weapons inspectors) who headed Iraq's bacterial program at al-Hakim for several years, earned a doctorate from the University of East Anglia, in England, where she studied plant disease. Huda Salih Mahdi Ammash, who was dubbed "Mrs. Anthrax" by U.S. intelligence services for her work reconstructing Iraq's biological weapons facilities after the 1991 Persian Gulf war, studied for a master-of-science degree in microbiology at Texas Woman's University, in Denton, and later earned a doctorate in microbiology at the University of Missouri at Columbia. Also, biowarfare scientists recruited to work on covert programs in developing countries were often trained in fields other than biology. For example, South Africa's former covert bioweapons program, Project Coast, recruited many of its first researchers from among veterinarians with advanced degrees in at least two scientific fields. Some Iraqi and South African researchers participated in American or English training exercises at military and government

installations, and in scientific exchanges. But the United States closed down a defensive bioweapons-research program in the 1970s, and as concerns grew about Iraqi and South African politics and development of weapons of mass destruction, it became, by the late 1980s, more difficult for scientists from those countries to travel abroad.

The United States further reduced foreign students' and scientists' access to American universities after the terrorist attacks of September 11, 2001, and the still-unsolved anthrax-letter incidents the following month. Unfortunately, the belief that students and scientists from developing countries must obtain their higher education in the West in order to acquire the skills needed to work with and weaponize biological agents is misguided and out-of-date. Today there are premier research universities throughout the world.

Visa restrictions and the rising cost of an American education have led many graduate students and scientists in the biological and physical sciences, especially from Middle Eastern countries, to study or work in countries in their own region or in Europe, Asia, or Africa. Moreover, the online availability of the information necessary to produce many biological pathogens, including step-by-step protocols, means that terrorists can obtain the requisite knowledge and even academic credentials while living almost anywhere.

If information is easy to come by, so are pathogens or potential pathogens. Before they shifted to genetic-modification techniques, both South African and Iraqi biowarfare scientists explored the feasibility of using naturally occurring pathogens. In their initial efforts, Iraqi scientists studied fungal toxins (for instance, mycotoxins and aflatoxins), anthrax spores, and a variety of other toxins, bacteria, and viruses, including those that cause botulism, cholera, polio, and influenza. Other early research involved creating deadly compounds from wheat and castor beans. Similarly, early South African experiments allegedly involved having military forces use biological agents to poison wells and putting cholera in some rivers in southern Africa. Project Coast scientists explored common viruses and bacteria and worked extensively with anthrax, which occurs naturally throughout southern Africa.

Those projects strongly suggest that covert-biowarfare scientists and terrorists are likely to use readily available, naturally occurring pathogens in initial attempts to create bioweapons. So thought the vast majority of the 43 scientists and researchers we interviewed in South Africa during 2003. Several of them noted that hundreds of different fungi found on the diverse plants and trees in rural areas throughout the world could easily be processed to form new biowarfare pathogens.

Some government officials are becoming alert to the prospect that natural pathogens could be used as a fast and easy way to acquire a seed stock for immediate use or further research on creating pathogenicity. To try to counter this emerging threat, 39 nations and the European Commission—all participants at the 2004 plenary session of the Australia Group—agreed to add five plant pathogens to its list of restricted items, the first expansion of the list since 1993. (The Australia Group is an informal network of countries that seeks to harmonize national export-licensing measures to stem the proliferation of chemical and biological weapons.)

Cloning techniques are another underestimated source of potential small-scale biological weapons. In 2003 three researchers in South Africa used an "in house" protocol for cloning that required minimal equipment and expertise to produce the first African cloned cow at a remote research station. Once scientists identify a gene that can cause disease, other scientists or terrorists can clone the gene and introduce it into common host bacteria by using a cloning kit readily available in catalogs of lab equipment.

Although cloning is a relatively common process that does not require a complex lab, safely conducting research on many viruses does demand a Biosafety Level 3 facility. Work with the most serious viruses—infectious diseases that are transmitted through the air and for which there is no known cure—require a BSL-4 laboratory. In BSL-3 labs, researchers wear protective gear to work in negative-pressure environments with transmissible infectious agents like tuberculosis. BSL-4 labs are highly secure areas for the study of the most infectious diseases, like the Ebola virus, and have multiple locked chambers, with constant monitoring of directed air flow. Scientists at those facilities wear suits with their own air supplies and work on infectious agents in special cabinets, also with their own air. The BSL-4 facilities require very careful construction, with holes for electrical, plumbing, piping, and camera outlets embedded ahead of time in their concrete walls.

Those needs have long been thought to limit the activities of scientists or terrorists working in poor countries. Recent technological advances, however, make it possible to set up a modular mobile BSL-3 lab within days, even in a remote location. As far as we know, all such facilities now are in the hands of agencies such as the U.S. Centers for Disease Control and Prevention. But recent changes in the Australia Group's export-control list reflect concern about smaller and more mobile equipment that could be used for covert biowarfare. In 2002, for instance, the group passed new export restrictions on small fermenters that could be used in the production of bacteria. But that type of equipment is already available for sale on the Internet, and if it hasn't already, it could soon fall into the wrong hands.

A great deal of public attention has focused on the use or genetic modification of extremely dangerous diseases such as Ebola or smallpox. A large portion of the money committed to date in contracts for the United States' Project BioShield ($877-million out of $5.6-billion) is for a program to buy 75 million doses of anthrax vaccine from a single company, VaxGen, even though the plan to inoculate all military personnel has run into legal, scientific, and production delays. The public concerns and large government efforts to counter those pathogens are understandable in the aftermath of the 2001 anthrax letters and public discussion of future terrorist scenarios involving Ebola, smallpox, or highly refined anthrax. However, any government or terrorist group would probably find it simpler to use common pathogens such as E. coli and salmonella, which are easier and cheaper to purchase, reproduce, and use.

Despite a flurry of recent research focused on the potential use of civilian biotechnology as a weapon, there have been remarkably few empirical studies of biotech trends in developing countries, especially African ones.

The online availability of the information necessary to produce many biological pathogens means that terrorists can obtain the requisite knowledge while living almost anywhere.

That lack of interest is unfortunate because nearly every country in the developing world is seeking to create the scientific and industrial capacity needed to compete in the biotech revolution. Even Zimbabwe, a failing state, recently passed a national biotechnology plan. Most such efforts focus on civilian biotechnology, which is widely viewed as a way to develop new high-value, high-tech products and processes for export, creating new jobs. Several countries in the developing world have also formed special-purpose transnational networks, like the Developing Country Vaccine Manufacturers Network, with a common focus like producing generic drugs for common infectious diseases. But terrorist groups interested in acquiring biotechnology expertise and products have also been reported to be forming transnational networks.

Public and private laboratories in the developing world are also gaining access to sophisticated bioinformatics-computing facilities and gene, tissue, and protein libraries. For example, the South African National Bioinformatics Institute has the long-term goal of connecting researchers at various sites in a transnational network. It will eventually permit scientists across the continent to access a common bioinformatics computer architecture, the power of the one high-speed Cray computer in South Africa, shared access to gene and protein libraries, and the computational tools necessary to conduct sophisticated bioinformatics research on shared problems.

Those trends suggest that before long the world may simultaneously face biological-weapons threats from naturally occurring pathogens and genetically modified organisms. Governments need to develop new approaches to monitor and manage this still poorly understood class of threats.

Traditional control strategies are unlikely to prevent the development of covert bioweapons by either nations or terrorists. The last major effort to ensure compliance with the 1975 Biological and Toxin Weapons Convention was in 2001–2 when a draft protocol was presented to member nations for a vote. The United States rejected it on the grounds that it was an ineffective arms-control approach, would compromise national-security and confidential business information, and would benefit would-be proliferators. But the failure to find evidence of any active WMD programs in Iraq and the suspected Iraqi mobile labs that are now believed to have been hydrogen-production units for weather balloons underscore how difficult it is to verify the existence of a covert biological-weapons program in the absence of sustained, intrusive inspections by neutral outside observers.

Many experts argue that the nature of biotech research is such that greater transparency and cooperation among nations and corporations may be the only way to monitor it. While the U.S. government worries about roughly three dozen countries that may have covert biowarfare programs, the number of possible bioterrorism threats seems limitless. One approach that might help would be to categorize possible threats emanating from different types of countries, and tailor monitoring and security efforts to each category.

Most biotechnology research and development is currently located in the United States, Europe, Japan, and Australia. However, India and China have many public and private biotech companies that are nearing the cutting edge.

A second tier of countries fosters a much smaller scale of biotech research. For example, Argentina and Brazil are significant producers of biotech agricultural crops and rank second and third, behind the United States, in the number of hectares devoted to such crops. Countries as diverse as Cuba, Egypt, Israel, South Africa, and South Korea play host to private and public biotech R&D activities. Much of that consists of civilian efforts to find a niche market in arenas dominated by large multinational businesses or to invent a unique product or process that could be sold to a multinational business. The governments of those countries share a commitment to help stimulate further biotech R&D, for which there is a modest amount of capital available from local or foreign sources. Despite their similarities, however, the countries differ in their degree of foreign collaboration, the extent of engagement in the global economy, and whether the government is a member of the biological-weapons convention.

Before long the world may simultaneously face biological-weapons threats from naturally occurring pathogens and genetically modified organisms.

A third tier consists of most other countries, which have limited civilian biotech research and little chance of closing the economic and technological gap between themselves and Tiers 1 and 2. These countries—such as Dubai, Kenya, Thailand, and the United Arab Emirates—primarily function as junior partners, labor reserves, or offshore tax shelters for multinational biotech companies.

A final tier are countries that have no functioning central government (like Somalia) or have large ungoverned and lawless spaces (like Colombia). In those nation-states the large, lawless areas can serve as attractive locations for terrorist activities.

Given that range, greater transparency seems to be a better approach than traditional control strategies. For example, Western governments should focus more attention on standardizing Good Laboratory Practice (GLP) and safety standards at public and private laboratories. GLP guidelines include inspections of active laboratories, university labs, foreign labs, and inactive labs. Those inspections are focused on standard practices and safety—for example, accountability for reagents and equipment certifications, maintenance of laboratory records, and specimen and sample tracking. The guidelines may help to control access to reagents and equipment, or to monitor illegal labs in remote areas or suburban-kitchen labs operated by terrorists or lone dissidents. But they might also, in the long term, promote greater transparency in biotechnology research and further the development of new international norms about what constitutes public and proprietary information and activities.

We need new regulations for the publication and other dissemination of peer-reviewed research that has possible biowarfare uses. Of course, creating such regulations would involve thorny, fundamental issues regarding the scientific process and the free press. On March 4, 2004, the Bush administration announced the creation of a new federal advisory board designed to help ensure that terrorists cannot make use of federally supported biological research. The new 25-member National Science Advisory Board for Biosecurity is intended to advise federal departments and agencies that conduct or support research of interest to terrorists on how best to keep it out of their hands. The creation of the board was one recommendation of a recent National Academies' National Research Council report (known as the Fink report) that focused on how to keep genetically engineered viruses and other works from being used in bioterrorism. Of course, the board's mandate does not cover research that receives no federal funds or that is conducted abroad, so there is an enormous security gap waiting to be filled.

Most of the scientists we interviewed cautioned that if handled clumsily, efforts to regulate the dissemination of federally supported biological research could damage the United States' position as a research leader. In a global world of science, American and foreign researchers working in the life sciences in America today have many options, including: opting out of research programs related to biosecurity, relying on private or foreign funds for research, or pursuing their research in other countries.

Many of the scientists also conveyed serious concerns about new restrictions on travel for graduate students. Some foreign students who left the United States to visit their home countries have had trouble returning to their American labs. The scientists were also concerned that many talented foreign graduate students who had been accepted into their programs were experiencing difficulties obtaining U.S. visas. Although entry restrictions have eased somewhat, continuing limits and bureaucratic obstacles have led many foreigners to go elsewhere for their education or advanced research. Such restrictions have been imposed in the name of security, but in the long run, they may become one of America's most serious security problems as they gradually erode our centrality in biotech innovation.

We support a significant easing of restrictions on foreigners seeking advanced scientific education or jobs in the West, but also the establishment of an enhanced monitoring system that would include more reliable procedures to ensure that all visa applicants undergo background investigations and checks. And we recommend a new reporting system that would allow the government to better track the whereabouts of foreign graduate students and scientists during their stays in the United States. We also recommend that more attention be given by relevant U.S. agencies to tracking the activities of foreign scientists and students after they have completed their work or studies and have left the United States. Perhaps if such a reporting requirement was incorporated as a condition for the initial visa it would be less controversial.

None of our suggestions would solve the host of problems created by the proliferation of biological expertise, equipment, and supplies. However, an important first step in improving security is to recognize that we face a range of biological threats from many different types of perpetrators, and that although we can monitor and reduce the dangers, we can never fully guard ourselves against attack. Enhancing our national security while also keeping American biotech research at the cutting edge are complementary goals. We can make progress toward both if we strive for greater international norms and transparency, while gauging threats in a more thoughtful and case-specific manner.

HELEN PURKITT is a professor of political science at the U.S. Naval Academy. VIRGEN WELLS, a microbiologist, is a former fellow at the American Association for the Advancement of Science. Their research cited here was supported by the Advanced Systems and Concepts Office of the Defense Threat Reduction Agency, the Institute for National Security Studies at the U.S. Air Force Academy, and the U.S. Naval Academy. However, the views expressed here are those of the authors and not those of the U.S. government.

UNIT 3

Foreign Policy Decision Making

Unit Selections

Key Points to Consider

- What is a foreign policy strategy and how do foreign policy decisionmakers and military planners use strategy?

- What is the meaning of national security, human security, and collective security?

- What are some policy areas where two or more of these security concerns overlap?

- Should future U.S. military strategy be based on the views of the Crusaders or Conservatives among returning Iraqi War officer veterans?

- What military lessons should be drawn from the U.S. involvement in Iraq and how do these lessons related to U.S. involvement in Vietnam?

Student Web Site

www.mhcls.com

Internet References

Carnegie Endowment for International Peace
   http://www.ceip.org
The Heritage Foundation
   http://www.heritage.org

Even before the Republican Party lost control of both the Senate and House of Representatives in 2006, the Bush's policy of the preventive use of force was being revised to emphasize other instruments of foreign policy and greater reliance on multilateral diplomacy. What to do in the future in terms of the United States' military involvement in Iraq, Afghanistan, and how to fight the War on Terrorism in the future were also central issues in the 2008 President election campaign. While President-elect Obama has yet to formulate new foreign policy priorities and guidelines, the Obama Administration has promised to reduce U.S. military involvement in Iraq. Given the growing economic crisis, there are sure to be changes in future U.S. foreign policies but only time will tell what priorities will receive the most attention given new economic constraints and changing realities throughout the world.

Despite President Obama's campaign emphasis on the need for changes in U.S. foreign policies, Israel will no doubt remain central to the United States policies in the Middle East, as will a preoccupation with the future policies of major powers, such as China, Russia, and India. A focus on how to maximize a nation-states' vital, important, and secondary interests have been the mainstay of a nation-states' foreign policy decision makers' calculus since the formation of the nation-state system. However, as the size of the world's population and the number of people lacking the most basic needs in terms of food, water, shelter, and personal security grows exponentially in future years, there will be a greater recognition that traditional national security interests increasingly intersect with policies designed to improve human security in the developing world. The nexus between traditional and human security concerns has become more salient to U.S. foreign policy decision makers and military leaders as they have had to modify existing strategies to achieve more successful counter-insurgency operations in Iraq. A growing recognition that the two types of security are intertwined was also a core consideration on the minds of the architects who established a new unified military command, AFRICOM, for the African continent in the fall of 2008. Similar reorganization policies have occurred in the U.S. military command, SOUTHCOM that has operational responsibility for Latin America and the Caribbean. SOUTHCOM has adopted a similar core mission of promoting security and helping where feasible to promote economic development by working with representatives of other U.S. national agencies in countries within the region. While the increased involvement of U.S. military stationed abroad in non-traditional military missions is still controversial, most U.S. decision makers and analysts stress that these new organizational changes merely reflect budgetary realities and realities on the ground. The U.S. military often is the only agency with the operational capacity to help in emergency and non-emergency situations.

© Department of Defense

A generalized recognition that a third type of threat, collective security threats that might harm all of humankind, may be growing, has led many policy makers and analysts to stress the future impact of collective security threats that may occur from such worldwide phenomenon as global warming and the spread of new, incurable infectious diseases. The potential threat to world civilizations in the event of a nuclear war was always present during the Cold War. However, today there is a greater possibility that national and human security issues will coincide with global collective security. Thus, the new president in the U.S. is likely to face a host of novel challenges as he tries to move U.S. policies toward a longer-term, sustainable security approach.

Prior to World War II, many realist analysts in the West assumed that foreign policy decision makers used the same maximizing logic worldwide to identify their country's important national interests. Thus, classical realists such as Hans Morgenthau talked about the vital and important interests of nation-states in universal terms. However, as recent debates over whether the United States should continue its special relationship with Israel illustrates, there is rarely a consensus on the definition of vital or important national interests within the national homeland. There are debates about what constitutes a nation-states vital national interest, especially within democracies, because what constitutes states most important interests is not an objective, or universal set of values. Thus, the questions of how best to maximize a country's national interests are always a topic of political debates. This is particularly true during times of war.

The recognition that countries do not have an invariant set of national interests is bolstered by a great deal of research in International Relations in recent decades that have focused on how foreign policy decision makers actually make decisions. One type of factor that is important in understanding how and why leaders make their decisions is the concept of images. Understanding the shared images that foreign policy decision makers have of their own country and perceived enemies can help analysts make predictions about future foreign policy choices. Since the 1950s, research on shared images of political leaders has confirmed that leaders and their key advisers often maintain "mirror images" of their adversary. Thus, many analysts have concluded that senior U.S. decision makers underestimated the intensity of the opposition that would result from the decision to disband Saddam Hussein's old army. The U.S. decision unwittingly unleashed century-old struggles for power and control of the security forces in Iraq among Sunni, Shi'ite and Kurdish communities. In order to cope with the ensuring sectarian conflict and increased attacks engineered by al Qaeda terrorists and other militia groups, the U.S. military had to devise a new military strategy named after the general who formulated it, the Petraeus Doctrine. While U.S. military leaders recognize that conditions in Afghanistan will require a modified strategy, many American combat veteran officers in Iraq are now committed to using Iraq-style counterinsurgency doctrines to shape the future of U.S. ground forces. This is particularly true within the U.S. Army where extensive modernization and rebuilding after nearly a decade of armed conflict. Andrew J. Bacevich in "The Petraeus Doctrine," describes the contours of a great debate within the U.S. Army between two camps of Iraqi War veterans: the Crusaders and the Conservatives. A central question in this debate is how should the lessons of Iraq inform future policy? Bacevich argues that unless the next President weighs in on this and related fundamental debates, decisions by default may well devolve to soldiers. Over time such a situation could tarnish the United States image as the leading democratic nation-state based on a few key principles, including the sanctity of civilian control of the military and the importance of political leaders in determining America's role in the world.

Strategy and the Search for Peace

For foreign policy and military planners, the future strategic environment is anything but certain. A defense expert explains why some of the most practical strategic objectives are also the most noble.

GREGORY D. FOSTER

There clearly is much about the future we can't predict, such as whether China and Taiwan will war, reconcile, or divorce; whether Russia will truly democratize or remilitarize; when or whether the two Koreas will reunify; what will happen in post-Castro Cuba or even in post-Saddam Iraq; or what will become of OPEC, NATO, Palestine, Kashmir, Chechnya, AIDS, global warming, al Qaeda, or any of the endless number of other things that concern us.

On the other hand, there is a more general future whose contours are already quite clear. This future will be marked by greater levels of global interconnectedness, more information becoming available to more people, and more world events seeming "local." It will see higher expectations of government and media-driven magnification of events, along with a broader definition of what constitutes a crisis.

Tomorrow's military decision makers will have to work in a climate of reduced response time and increased disaster potential. There will likely be less public and military tolerance for casualties, continuing confusion over the lengths and limits of sovereignty, new subliminal forms of aggression and intervention, and further diffusion of power from state actors to nonstate entities such as corporations and religious or ethnic groups.

Likewise, the coming period will also be one of proliferating levels of violence, a profusion of undeclared internal "non-wars," and accelerated technological obsolescence. In every sense, it will be a future of profound complexity, ambiguity, and turbulence that will admit of no easy explanations or simple solutions.

One of the defining features of this future will be a continuation of the convergence that has already occurred between the tactical and the strategic domains of human and military activity. In other words, even the most obscure incidents or conditions in the most remote locations may have almost instantaneous reverberations at other points across the globe. This reverberation can effect a shift in strategy, so strategies are more likely to change as a result of on-the-ground or "tactical" developments. Such magnification distorts decision making, compresses deliberation, multiplies the gravity of consequences and the impact

of responses, and, in the case of military decision making in particular, places those on the ground under constant scrutiny and reproach.

Potentially even more important than this convergence of the strategic and the tactical is the more sweeping evolutionary trajectory of war itself. We are on the cusp of a grand evolution of war. We have gone from an extended historical period of "hot war," dating to antiquity, in which the actual use of force was the central element of statecraft, to a highly compressed period of "cold war," involving two over-muscled adversaries who engaged in the unrestrained accretion of capabilities and tacit threat-making so as to avoid the actual use of force. Now, we are in a period of "new war," in which non-military instruments of power and nontraditional uses of the military are becoming more the norm than military and foreign-policy planners care yet to concede.

The logical extension of this grand evolutionary trend suggests an eventual end-state of "no war." In this scenario, large-scale collective violence is largely eschewed for its ultimate ineffectiveness, and militaries as we have known them will become essentially irrelevant. The plausibility, desirability, and feasibility of this heretofore unrealized (and largely unimagined) end-state will be a function of our inclination to step outside the binding intellectual constraints of the past and to exercise the free will that purportedly distinguishes humans from other living species.

Key Elements of Strategic Thinking

The importance of being strategic in confronting the future should be self-evident. To begin with, it is a moral obligation of government—foreign-policy and military planners in particular—to look ahead, to take the long view, to consider the big picture (and the attendant interrelatedness of virtually all things), to anticipate and influence events before they occur, and to take due account of the after effects and the unintended consequences of action or inaction.

Being strategic inoculates us against crises that demand the redirection of time, energy, and attention away from preferred goals, thereby testing the limits of public trust and confidence in government.

Strategic thinking enhances civilian control of the military because it forces civilian authorities and uniformed professionals alike to appreciate the higher aims they are both charged with serving. It also compels a better understanding and greater acceptance of the military as a subordinate player in the affairs of state. Also of great importance, being strategic provides the basis for achieving sustainable consensus by providing the coherent framework of stated objectives and the means to achieve them. Such frameworks help to galvanize people in common cause, especially in the face of complexity and ambiguity.

Being strategic is the basis for true strategic leadership—the quality of leadership we should expect from occupants of high office and from great powers. This type of leadership is about motivating and moving equals with minds of their own, rather than directing dutiful subordinates.

To be strategic is, above all else, to understand the essential nature of strategy: Rudimentary as that may seem, strategy entails much more than being a mere instrumentality of policy.

Strategy is a philosophy of global conduct, a collective set of assumptions and beliefs that underlie our interpretation of the world and our approach to dealing with it. Whether we realize it or not, most of us have internalized opinions and perceptions that influence the way we answer questions and meet challenges. We respond to the situations as we perceive them, and our first and most immediate perceptions almost always rise from bias. Does an objective reality exist (threats and national interests, for example)? Is it waiting to be grasped by the vigilant and discerning among us, or do we construct such "reality" in our minds? Is war inevitable, or is it a preventable outgrowth of conscious human decisions? Does force have demonstrable utility for resolving disputes and solving problems, or is it capable only of producing provocation and the escalation of violence? Is preparing for war the best (or only) way to produce peace? These problems are fundamentally existential, but they have real-world implications.

Managing Perceptions

Strategy is also about the effective management of perceptions—creating and projecting images, manipulating symbols, and constructing, deconstructing, and reconstructing reality. When we talk about strength or weakness, success or failure, victory or defeat, or aggression or self-defense, we are talking about mental constructs that are representations of the reality we see (or don't see).

Consider why we would care whether the Pentagon is called the Department of Defense rather than the Department of War or the Department of Peace. Consider why we would outfit military troops in camouflage battledress and berets rather than in pastel jumpsuits and baseball caps, why one would care about the shape of and seating arrangements at a negotiating table, or why the president would choose to deliver a major policy address from the Oval Office rather than on the tarmac at Andrews Air Force Base. Or consider why one might want to

be seen as having capabilities one doesn't actually possess—as Saddam Hussein presumably sought to do with (virtual) weapons of mass destruction. The strategic significance of perception brings to mind the observation once offered by social activist Saul Alinsky: "Power is not only what you have but what the enemy thinks you have." Perceptual matters such as these and countless others beg to be carefully attended and managed, as they produce credibility—the entirely intangible but priceless measure of standing and influence in the world.

No less significant perceptually is credibility's antithesis, hypocrisy, the costly disjunction between words and actions. When one preaches peace but practices war (invariably in the name of prudence), when one preaches arms control but practices arms proliferation (invariably in the name of practicality), when one preaches the rule of law but practices selective disregard for the law (invariably in the name of urgency), such hypocrisy never goes unnoticed and always diminishes difficult-to-replenish credibility.

Policy makers regularly play the perceptions game, rarely stating their aims unambiguously, but there is an obvious need in a democracy to clearly articulate the ends one seeks in the interest of generating public support. Clearly stated aims, after all, are the basis for judging actual performance and thus for holding politicians accountable. Precisely for this reason, politicians are almost invariably vague about their purposes so they later can claim success (even where it doesn't exist) and deny failure (even where it does exist). Similarly, in issuing threats to elicit desired behavior from adversaries, policy makers typically rely on tacit or implied threats (speaking in code or signaling through behavior) rather than explicit threats ("Do this or else . . .") that could be openly defied and might provoke unwanted escalatory response.

The Linkage between Ends and Means

Thinking strategically forces us to recognize the close link between ends and means and the need to address a number of crucial questions: What ends should we seek? Should they be realistic, attainable ends, or is it appropriate to pursue seemingly idealistic, unattainable ones (such as lasting universal peace)? Should they be worthy, or are less-than-worthy aims (assassinating despicable foreign leaders, say, or destabilizing hostile foreign governments) warranted to deal with the harsh realities of international politics?

Should ends dictate means? That is, should the aims we seek determine the means we use and whether or how we use them? Do the ends we seek justify any means considered necessary and useful, or are some means (like torture) demonstrably unacceptable for reasons like morality or credibility? Should the means available constrain, or even determine, the ends we seek? Do limited means demand limited aims, and do unlimited (or at least plentiful) means license unlimited aims?

Such ends-means questions are closely tied to strategy's most central meaning: the effective exercise of power. In fact, the measure of strategic effectiveness is essentially twofold: the extent to which the ends we seek are actually achieved, and the perceptions we generate in the process (responsiveness, reliability, consistency, resolve, unity, and the like). Power is the mechanism for determining such strategic effectiveness.

Strategy is a philosophy of global conduct, a collective set of assumptions and beliefs that underlie our interpretation of the world and our approach to dealing with it.

The Exercise of Power

Power may be characterized in several ways: getting what you want (or achieving your aims), getting your way (even if you don't know what you want), or bending others to your will or imposing your will on others.

There are three ways to employ power: coercion, persuasion, or inspiration.

Coercion, the most common form of power, may use threats that play on fear to produce unwilling deference. Such unwilling deference reflects and feeds underlying resentment and a desire for retribution that almost inevitably resurfaces over time.

Persuasion is the use of positive incentives, or "carrots," in lieu of the negative stick of coercion; it's basically a bribe that plays on someone's desires in order to elicit concessionary deference. But this concessionary deference is purely contingent—quid pro quo, tit for tat—and carries with it an intrinsic expectation of future payback.

Inspirational power, rarely acknowledged, is the least costly yet most conclusive and enduring form of power. It relies on setting an example—walking the talk, practicing what one preaches—to engender respect. Inspirational power thus produces willing deference, which is the source of true moral authority that gives leadership credibility.

The moral authority that derives from inspirational power underscores the critical nexus between strategy and morality. Some would argue that strategy and morality are independent of one another, perhaps even antithetical. However, moral behavior that accords with moral ideals offers untold strategic value. Consider the strategic value of the following moral ideals and what each says about power:

- **Balanced reciprocity:** treating others as you would want to be treated. Balanced reciprocity is the Golden Rule applied to the realm of international relations— what some would consider naïve, others would consider a necessary antidote to the lowest-common-denominator mentality of many self-professed realists.
- **Principled consistency:** acting consistently in accord with principle, regardless of circumstance. Principled consistency is the recognition that the pursuit of particular ends and the use of particular means on the grounds of situational prudence and pragmatism are often hypocritical and nothing more than a shallow cover for expediency.

- **Disciplined restraint:** refraining from exploiting advantage over others unless absolutely necessary. Disciplined restraint is the purest demonstration of true power—the conscious choice to refrain from exercising power (or at least its most overwhelming forms and levels) over others precisely because one can.

Such ideals have everything to do, philosophically, with whether, how, and under what circumstances power is employed and how it is perceived.

Four Strategic Imperatives

The differences between the world of yesterday—our Cold War past—and the world of today and tomorrow are palpable. We have moved:

- From a world guided largely by the precepts of *realpolitik* to one in which *idealpolitik,* the pursuit of heretofore unattainable though salutary ideals, now commands our assent.
- From a world driven by narrow national interests to one that demands attention to larger, supranational interests.
- From a long-standing fixation with unilateral capabilities and responses to a realization of the need for multilateral and even "polylateral" approaches; that is, permanent institutionalized relationships with both state and nonstate partners.
- From a predominant focus on the international dimension of security to a greater concern with the domestic dimension of security.
- From relying mainly on hard (predominantly military and economic) power to appreciating more fully so-called soft (primarily cultural and informational) power.
- From preparing for the most critical threats and contingencies to responding to the most likely ones on a regular basis.
- From possessing superior capabilities to bolstering national will as the necessary precondition for sustainable action.
- From making tacit threats in order to produce uncertainty to performing successfully and consistently in order to enhance credibility.
- From military effectiveness to strategic effectiveness as the standard for judging military utility.
- From unquestioning acceptance of the necessity for secrecy, opacity, and unaccountability to fuller appreciation of the need for and effectiveness of greater openness, transparency, and accountability.

Achieving comparative strategic advantage over those who would be our enemies in the face of such dramatic change requires that our actions not only be informed by a more sophisticated understanding of strategy, but that they be guided by the following four strategic imperatives, which are especially attuned to the demands of the postmodern world.

The first imperative is what we might call *targeted causation management*—orienting one's posture and actions on eliminating or ameliorating the underlying causes (e.g., poverty, injustice, environmental degradation) of unwanted conditions of conflict, along with other unwanted conditions, such as state failure and societal collapse. Employing this strategy is an altogether preferable alternative to reacting, as most governments do, to more visible but less controllable symptoms that have mutated out of control and thereby demand costly, forceful responses.

A second strategic imperative is the associated need for *institutionalized anticipatory response*—formalizing and regularizing the measures necessary to facilitate initiative and enable preventive action.

Appropriate situational tailoring is the third imperative. It refers to establishing and maintaining the capabilities necessary to deal with particular circumstances or contingencies on their own terms, rather than imposing preferred, available capabilities on situations that are geographically, politically, and culturally inappropriate and ineffective.

Balanced reciprocity is the golden rule applied to the realm of international relations—what some would consider naïve, others would consider necessary.

Finally, a fourth imperative is *comprehensive operational integration*—fully integrating the organizational, technological, and procedural dimensions of one's strategic posture to achieve unity of purpose, effort, and action while minimizing waste and delay.

To achieve a future we have yet to experience—that of lasting universal peace, for example—will depend on our ability to envision such a state by thinking strategically, and then on our willingness to act strategically. Thankfully, the future need not repeat the past.

GREGORY D. FOSTER is a professor at the Industrial College of the Armed Forces, National Defense University. He has published widely on a range of public policy and international security issues. His address is National Defense University, Washington, D.C. 20319. Telephone 202-685-4166; e-mail Fosterg@ndu.edu.

Originally published in the November/December, 2006, pp. 19–22 issue of *The Futurist*. Copyright © 2006 by World Future Society, 7910 Woodmont Avenue, Suite 450, Bethesda, MD 20814. Telephone: 301/656-8274; Fax: 301/951-0394; http://www.wfs.org. Used with permission from the World Future Society.

In Search of Sustainable Security

Linking National Security, Human Security, and Collective Security to Protect America and Our World

Gayle E. Smith

Introduction and Summary

Not long ago I conducted an informal survey during a trip to East Africa, asking everyone I met how they view America. My interlocutors were from Africa, the Middle East, and Asia. They were, in the main, educated and working in the private sector, the policy world, or government. Many of them hold dual passports.

Their answers were strikingly similar. Most of them said in one way or another that the "idea" of America has changed for the worse, and most asserted that they are less interested in traveling to, working in, or working with the United States now than in the past. But most disconcerting was the hope, expressed with striking consistency, that China would soon attain its full power so that American hegemony could be brought in check.

This was not for any love of China's ideology or even the aggressive aid and investment strategies Beijing is deploying in the developing world. It was, as a young woman attorney explained, because "America used to be the champion for all of us, and now it is the champion only for itself."

That much of the world has lost faith in America bodes ill for our national security because our role in the world is secured not simply by our military power or economic clout, but also by our ability to compel other nations to follow our lead. The next president will have the opportunity to craft a modern national security strategy that can equip the United States to lead a majority of capable, democratic states in pursuit of a global common good—a strategy that can guide a secure America that is the world's "champion for all of us."

But positioning America to lead in a 21st century world will take more than extending a hand to our allies, fixing a long list of misdirected policies, or crafting a new national security strategy that is tough but also smart. With globalization providing the immutable backdrop to our foreign policy, America is today competing on a global playing field that is more complex, dynamic, and interdependent and thus far less certain than in the past.

Leading in this new world will require a fundamental shift from our outdated notion of national security to a more modern concept of sustainable security—that is, our security as defined by the contours of a world gone global and shaped by our common humanity. Sustainable security combines three approaches:

- *National* security, or the safety of the United States
- *Human* security, or the well-being and safety of people
- *Collective* security, or the shared interests of the entire world

Sustainable security, in short, can shape our continued ability to simultaneously prevent or defend against real-time threats to America, reduce the sweeping human insecurity around the world, and manage long term threats to our collective, global security. This new approach takes into account the many (and ongoing) changes that have swept our planet since the end of the Cold War and the fall of the Soviet Union. To understand the efficacy of this new doctrine, though, requires a quick look at this new global landscape.

The New Realities of the 21st Century

During his presidency, Bill Clinton spoke often and passionately about our global interdependence and of positioning America to cross a "bridge to the 21st century." Once across, however, the Bush administration took a sharp right turn. In the wake of the September 11 terrorist attacks on the United States, the administration narrowly defined the quest for America's security, distinct from and uninformed by the interests of the larger world we inhabit.

The challenge before us, President Bush asserted, was the struggle between good and evil, our strategy was to wage his so called "war on terror," and our goal was to shape a "world without tyranny." Our primary tool was a strong military backed by the resolve to use force without seeking a "permission slip" from the international community. And our object was the "axis of evil," and the rest of the world was either "with us or against us." Anyone who suggested that it might not be quite that simple was quickly and effectively discounted as "soft on terrorism."

Despite ambitious rhetoric about the promotion of our core values—of leading "the long march to freedom" and pursuing the "non-negotiable demands of human dignity"—the Bush administration has culled its allies not from among those countries most committed to democracy, but from among those who have oil. The Bush administration had to leverage all of its diplomatic and economic clout to persuade the so-called "Coalition of the Willing" to participate at all in the invasion of Iraq. Then, the administration offered up not the shining example of an America where human and civil rights prevail, but an America where Guantanamo, Abu Gharaib, and illegal wire-tapping are justified by an elusive, greater purpose.

The United States has for the last five years defined America's role in the world with near exclusive reference to the invasion of Iraq. The deaths of 4,000[1] American soldiers, maiming of tens of thousands more, and the expenditure of well over $400 billion,[2] has failed to lay the foundations for either stability or democracy. And as defined by the Bush administration, the "War on Terror" has fared no better: Al Qaeda has not been defeated, and Osama bin Laden, its leader and the mastermind of the September 11 attacks, has yet to be captured.

Our losses, however, extend far beyond the edges of a failed Iraq policy or the shortcomings of an ill-defined "war on terror." We have also lost precious time, and are well behind the curve in our now tardy efforts to tackle the global challenges that are already shaping our future—climate change, energy insecurity, growing resource scarcity, the proliferation of illegal syndicates moving people, arms, and money—all of them global challenges that have been steadfastly ignored and in some cases denied by an ideologically driven Bush administration lodged firmly in its own distinct version of the here and now.

Perhaps most damaging, however, is this: We have lost our moral standing in the eyes of many who now believe that the United States has only its own national interests at heart, and has little understanding of or regard for either global security or our common humanity. Just as potent as the unsustainable federal budget deficit George W. Bush will leave in his wake is the unsustainable national security deficit that he will pass on to his successor. Whoever prevails in November will face a daunting list of real-time national security imperatives, among them:

- A spiraling crisis in Iraq
- Afghanistan's steady implosion
- A fragile Pakistan
- An emboldened Iran
- A raging genocide in Sudan
- The growing insecurity of our oil supplies
- A nuclear North Korea
- An increasingly dangerous Arab–Israeli conflict

Just to name a few. But the next president will also face looming and less tangible threats to our national security in a world where power has grown more diffuse and threats more potent—a world in which our security depends not only on the behavior of states, but also on a host of transnational threats that transcend national borders, such as terrorism, pandemics, money laundering, and the drug trade.

And finally, the next president will be confronted by the more subtle but potent threats and moral challenges arising from sweeping human insecurity in a world divided by sharp disparities between rich and poor, between those nations actively engaged in fast-paced globalization and those left behind, and between people who have tangible reasons to believe in a secure and prosperous world and those who daily confront the evidence that violence is a more potent tool for change than is hope.

Sustainable Security Is the Answer

The world has changed profoundly during the last 50 years, but our concept of national security has not. The concept of national security came into being after World War II, and has had as its primary focus a world dominated by the nation state. In this new era of globalization, we continue to rely upon the narrow definition offered by George Kennan, who in 1948 described our national security as "the continued ability of the country to pursue the development of its internal life without serious interference, or threat of interference, from foreign powers."[3] While Kennan's definition might have been relevant to the era of containment, it is insufficient in today's integrated and interdependent world.

A modern concept of national security demands more than an ability to protect and defend the United States. It requires that we expand our goal to include the attainment of *sustainable* security.

A modern concept of national security demands more than an ability to protect and defend the United States.

The pursuit of sustainable security requires more than a reliance on our conventional power to deflect threats to the United States, but also that we maintain the moral authority to lead a global effort to overcome threats to our common security. With its global scope, sustainable security demands that we focus not only on the security of nation states, but also of people, on *human* security. An emerging concept borne of multidisciplinary analyses of international affairs, economics, development, and conflict, human security targets the fundamental freedoms—from want and from fear—that define human dignity.

National security and human security are compatible but distinct. National security focuses on the security of the state, and governments are its primary clients, while human security is centered on the security of individuals and thus on a diverse array of stakeholders. National security aims to ensure the ability of states to protect their citizens from external aggression; human security focuses on the management of threats and challenges that affect people everywhere—inside, outside, and across state borders.

A national security strategy is commonly crafted in real time and focused on tangible, proximate threats, while a human security strategy aimed at improving the human condition assumes a longer-term horizon. Sustainable security combines the two, thus allowing for a focus on the twin challenges of protecting the United States while also championing our global humanity—not simply because it is the right thing to do, but also because our security demands it.

For a majority of the world's people, security is defined in the very personal terms of survival. The primary threats to this *human* security have far less to do with terrorism than with poverty and conflict, with governments that cannot deliver or turn on their own citizens, and with a global economy that offers differentiated access and opportunities to the powerful and the powerless. For literally billions of the world's people, weapons of mass destruction are not nuclear bombs in the hands of Iran, but the proliferation of small arms. For them, freedom is not defined simply by the demise of dictators, but also by the rise of economic opportunity.

Ensuring our security in today's world, however, also requires a focus on collective security. Among the major challenges that the United States will face over the coming decades are climate change, water scarcity, food insecurity, and environmental degradation. These are challenges that will threaten the economic well-being and security of all countries on earth, and by dint of their global nature, their effects cannot be overcome unless we adopt a global perspective and strategy.

Take the example of the world food crisis that emerged in the spring of 2008. No single cause triggered the near doubling of world food prices. Indeed, the causes included the skyrocketing price of oil, the growth of the middle class in the developing world (and thus rising demand in China and India), droughts in Australia and Ukraine, a weak dollar, and the expansion of bio-fuels production in the United States and Europe.

The consequent rise in food prices triggered riots or protests in Europe, Mexico, Egypt, Afghanistan, and several other countries, and plunged millions in the developing world into abject poverty. In the United States, the number of Americans seeking assistance from food banks rose 20 percent to 25 percent.

Or consider "transnational threats," such as money laundering, terrorism, and international drug and crime syndicates, all of which transcend state borders. These are threats that pose risks to the United States, but also to the well-being of our allies, to global stability, and to the world economy.

A national security approach seeks to prevent or reduce the effects of these trends and threats to the United States; a collective security approach, in contrast, assumes that the United States must act globally—in partnership with allies and in coordination with international institutions—to prevent or manage them.

Sustainable Security in Practice

Crafting a sustainable security strategy requires three fundamental steps. The first is to prioritize, integrate, and coordinate the global development policies and programs pursued by the United States. While our military power provides a critical and effective tool for managing our security, our support for the well-being of the world's people will not only provide us with a moral foundation from which to lead but will also enhance our ability to manage effectively the range of threats and trends that shape the modern world.

Second, we must modernize our foreign aid system in order to allow the United States to make strategic investments in global economic development that can help us to build capable states, open societies, and a global economy that benefits the world's majority. Third, we must re-enter the international arena, stepping up to the plate to lead the reform of international institutions that have not kept pace, and to create new institutions that are needed to manage our collective security.

In the pages that follow, this paper will present the challenges that threaten our national, human, and collective security in order to show just how important it is for the next president to embrace

these sustainable security policies. As this report will demonstrate, changing course will be difficult, but changing course is imperative to secure the future prosperity of humanity— an original and time-tested American value.

Human Security Under Threat

In today's world, human security is elusive. There are six billion people in the world. Nearly half of them live on less than two dollars per day, and over one billion people survive on half that amount.[4] These are not people waiting idly for a hand-out from the international community. The vast majority of them are working men and women who earn for their daily labors less than it costs to rent a DVD, and who annually take home to their families less than half of what the average American will spend on a summer vacation this year.

Women and children are the hardest hit. According to the United Nations, 70 percent of the world's poor and two-thirds of the world's illiterate are women, and though they provide the backbone for rural economies, women own only one percent of the world's titled land and control only a small percentage of rural capital.[5] Over ten million children die before their fifth birthday each year, mostly from preventable diseases,[6] while roughly a quarter of all children in the developing world do not finish primary school.[7]

More than a billion people do not have safe supplies of water,[8] and more than twice as many have no access to basic sanitation.[9] Only one-third of the world's people enjoy the kind of access to energy that we take for granted, another third have only intermittent access, and the remaining third—some two billion people— live without modern energy supplies.[10] This means that they don't have lights to read by, or refrigerators to preserve vaccines, or trucks to get their goods to market.

The antidote to economic decline is increased borrowing. Developing world debt increased to almost 3 trillion dollars early in this decade, meaning that developing countries spend on average $13 on debt repayment—to wealthy countries and private creditors in the developed world—for every one dollar they receive in grants.[11] The international debt relief supported by the current and past administrations may have staunched the bleeding, but it has not closed the wound for the poor, who remain dangerously vulnerable to external shocks because they have little or nothing to fall back on.

For this reason, shocks to already fragile societies, such as climate change, have a greater effect on the poor than on other, wealthier communities. According to the United Nations Development Program, over 250 million people were affected by climate disasters annually from 2000 to 2004, and over 98 percent of them were in the developing world. In the world's developed countries, one in 1,500 people was affected by climate disaster; in the world's poorest countries, it was one in 19.[12]

Similarly, the rising price of oil is an enormous shock to the world's poor. The fiscal gains of a majority of countries that have received debt relief through the Heavily Indebted Poor Countries Initiative, for example, had by last year been wiped out by the increase in the world price of oil. Those same countries now face a near doubling in the world market price of basic food commodities. Theirs is a losing game of catch up, and the consequences of the vicious cycle of poverty are clear—more than 50 countries are poorer today than they were in 1990.[13]

A Vicious Cycle and Downward Spiral

This stunning privation feeds on itself, in part because poverty increases the risk of war. War is development in reverse—a civil war reduces a country's growth rate by 2.3 percent, a typical seven-year war leaves a country 15 percent poorer,[14] and wars speed both the "brain drain" and the flow and volume of capital flight. The costs of conflict are also borne by citizens—largely as a consequence of war, one in every 120 people on earth is either internally displaced or a refugee.[15]

It is estimated that Africa is losing $18 billion per year to conflict, or almost twice what the continent spends on health and education.[16] Or consider Sri Lanka, where a long-running civil war has cost the country over two years of GDP. Defense expenditures average four percent to six percent of GDP while those for health and education combined run just four percent to five percent.[17] Meanwhile one quarter of Sri Lankans live in poverty.

Finally, the world's donor countries incur tremendous costs over many years. Conflict drives U.S. spending on humanitarian assistance to levels that well exceed expenditures on economic development and conflict prevention. Recent wars, most of them in the developing world, triggered the authorization of 26 new UN peacekeeping missions between 1988 and 1995.[18] Today, the UN is leading 17 peacekeeping operations, and providing support to three more.[19] Each of these missions is expensive, especially to the United States, which bears almost one quarter of the cost, and several have ended in failure.

Finally, the recovery costs are enormous. According to a study by the Center for Global Development, it takes the world's donors between 15 to 27 years to exit from a conflict country because it takes that long for post-war economies to generate sufficient internal revenues to reduce the need for the external assistance that is provided by the United Nations, the United States, and other donors.[20] As the costs of war mount, neither the victims nor the world's donors can realistically keep up.

Against this backdrop, sweeping demographic changes are altering the contours of the global socioeconomic landscape, and providing new fuel for the cycle of poverty and new triggers for instability. While the developed world is now incurring the economic burdens of an aging population, over 100 countries are grappling with an expanding youth bulge. Today, 85 percent of young people between the ages of 15 and 24 live in developing countries,[21] where educational and job opportunities are few. This means that millions of young women are denied opportunities for economic independence and that millions of young men face a future devoid of either hope or prosperity.

Urban populations have grown fourfold over the last 50 years,[22] and by 2025, 60 percent of the world's population will live in cities.[23] Many of them—Cairo, Lagos, Nairobi, and Mumbai—are ill-equipped to provide the jobs, housing, and services that this expanded urban population will require. These vast demographic convulsions will exert increased pressure on already overstretched natural resources and exacerbate growing poverty.

As the future hurtles towards us, we will see even greater threats to human security borne of our ecological interdependence. The world is facing a threefold increase in energy use by 2050.[24]

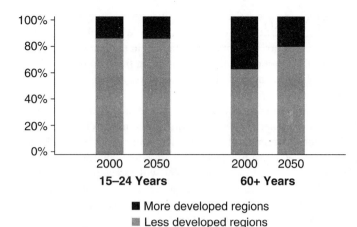

The proportions of youth and older persons in the total world population, 2000 and 2050.

Source: United Nations, *World Population Prospects: The 2002 Revisions: Volume II: Sex and Age* (Sales No. 03. XII.7).

World demand for fresh water has doubled over the last 50 years,[25] and the number of people living in water-stressed countries is expected to increase to 3 billion by 2025.[26] As global production, consumption, and population expand, so too will the competition for increasingly scarce resources. At the same time, the worst effects of climate change will reverberate in the world's poorest countries, which bear the least responsibility for global warming and have the least capacity to manage its impact.

A Different Take on "Us" and "Them"

Sweeping human insecurity also widens the gap between the world's rich and poor, a gap that might be more accurately described as a gulf. Although they constitute only 14 percent of the world's population, the world's ten wealthiest countries account for 75 percent of global GDP, and are 75 times richer than the ten poorest.[27] With the expansion of the Internet and satellite television, globalization is making this disparity more visible, including to those on the bottom.

Even with significant expansion, meanwhile, global trade has yet to yield sustainable benefits or to narrow this gap. Only two-thirds of the world's countries are engaged effectively in globalization. Low-income countries account for only three cents of every dollar generated through exports in the international trading system,[28] and the world's poorest region—sub-Saharan Africa—receives less than one percent of the total global flow of foreign direct investment.[29]

Global trade talks aimed at addressing this imbalance under the banner of the "Doha Development Round" have failed to deliver. Instead, these negotiations have all but collapsed under the weight of sharp disagreement between the world's rich and poor countries over the high subsidies paid out by the European Union and the United States to their agricultural producers.

What's worse, low- and middle-income countries bear 90 percent of the global disease burden yet they benefit least from global gains in treatment.[30] According to the Worldwatch Institute, only one percent of the over 1,200 new drugs that reached the global marketplace between 1975 and 1997 were applicable to the infectious tropical diseases that account for the most deaths around the world.[31] This is a human security problem of potentially immense proportions.

Total Youth Unemployment, 1995, 2004, and 2005

	Youth Unemployment (thousands)			
	1995	**2004**	**2005**	**% Change 1995–2005**
World	74,302	84,546	85,278	14.8
Developed Economies and European Union	10,281	8,997	8,481	−17.5
Central and Eastern Europe (non-EU) and CIS	5,962	5,724	5,900	−1.0
East Asia	13,149	11,840	12,076	−8.2
South East Asia and the Pacific	5,242	9,687	9,727	85.5
South Asia	11,765	13,561	13,662	16.1
Latin America and the Caribbean	7,722	9,263	9,495	23.0
Middle East and North Africa	7,209	8,380	8,525	18.2
Sub-Saharan Africa	12,972	17,095	17,414	34.2

Source: ILO, 2006:16.

Challenges to Our Collective Security

Democracy is making great gains, but so, too, are its opponents. Since 1974, some 90 countries have embraced democracy,[32] a positive gain to be sure, but one that is yet to be locked in. Many of the world's new democracies remain exceedingly fragile as their governments and citizens grapple simultaneously with profound political transitions, the legacies of war and repression, and the strains of poverty. Seemingly stable democracies in Kenya, Cote d'Ivoire, Georgia, and Thailand have proven to be vulnerable, while in many countries, structural poverty and corruption have precluded the delivery of a tangible democracy dividend.

In many countries, meanwhile, the failure of rulers to deliver economically or politically is speeding the rise of extremism. Across much of the Middle East, Africa, and Asia, extremism is forging a new political construct shaped by Islam, and with it the rise of a hostile, transnational political identity. In some regions, extremism takes the form of predatory movements, such as northern Uganda's Lord's Resistance Army, that prey on civilians and particularly on children.

In struggling democracies such as the Democratic Republic of the Congo, the echoes of the Rwandan genocide and the legacy of colonialism and post-colonial mis-rule reverberate in the form of militia wars, skyrocketing death rates, and rampant rape. Violence continues to threaten democratic gains in Nepal, Turkey, Sri Lanka, and the Philippines. And at the far worst and still-too-common end of the spectrum, genocide continues to rear its ugly head in places such as Darfur where, five years on, people still await a meaningful response from the international community.

The Power of Weak States

Both economic development and democracy are under further strain from the fact that a billion people live in states that do not deliver for their citizens. A recent study by the Brookings Institution notes that of the world's 193 countries, 28 qualify as weak and another 28 are critically weak or failed. Eighty-five percent of these countries have experienced conflict in the past 15 years, and the United Nations—and in some cases the United States—has had to deploy peacekeepers or observers to half of them.[33]

Governments in these countries lack the will or capacity to provide basic security or control their borders, cannot or do not meet the basic human needs of their citizens, and fail to provide either legitimate or effective governance. They are unable to adapt to the technological innovations that drive economic progress, establish the institutional foundations that are required for democratic stability, or function as reliable members of the international community.

They are equally incapable of meeting the challenges posed by environmental degradation, are more vulnerable to transnational threats than their more capable counterparts, and are unable to provide barriers to the spread of these threats across borders. Most important, they are unable (or unwilling) to offer their people economic opportunity, political freedom, or hope.

These weak and failing states include countries such as the Democratic Republic of the Congo, which by dint of the unresolved conflict in its eastern Kivu region is winning a fierce global competition for the worst humanitarian crisis on earth. They include Nigeria, where vast oil reserves have led not to prosperity but to sweeping systemic corruption, and to the rise of a pernicious insurgency in the Niger Delta. And they include Myanmar, where an authoritarian regime has not only failed to protect its citizens in the wake of a devastating cyclone, but has also prevented the world from aiding them.

These are countries often consigned to the bottom of our foreign policy priority list, but countries where unchecked instability and limited capacity risk the lives of millions. State weakness in these countries not only portends hopelessness for many of their citizens. It also poses a threat to global peace and security. Though viewed by many as of lesser import than countries in the Middle East or Asia, these African countries matter—Nigeria provides more than eight percent of our imported oil, and resource-rich Congo has, among other assets, uranium. Their security matters—to their people, and also to us.

Our Shared Interests

Americans are right to ask their government why they should add the costly charge of promoting human security and collective security to the already heavy burden of the spiraling federal budget deficit, rising gas and food prices, a home mortgage crisis, and multiple security challenges already on our national plate. The first reason is simple: It is the right thing to do. By championing the cause of the world's least powerful, the United States can build a stronger moral foundation from which to lead and a compelling example for the world to follow.

There is precedent on which to build, as both security imperatives and moral convictions have led the United States to help improve the lives of the world's poor throughout our modern history. In his inaugural address in 1961, President John F. Kennedy highlighted this commitment of the American people:

"To those peoples in the huts and villages across the globe struggling to break the bonds of mass misery, we pledge our best efforts to help them help themselves, for whatever period is required—not because the Communists may be doing it, not because we seek their votes, but because it is right. If a free society cannot help the many who are poor, it cannot save the few who are rich."[34]

Almost 50 years later, General Anthony Zinni (USMC-ret.) and Admiral Leighton Smith Jr. (USN-ret.) put it this way:

"It is time to repair our relationship with the world and begin to take it to the next level—a level defined not only by our military strength but also by the lives we save and the opportunities we create for the people of other nations . . . today our enemies are often conditions—poverty, infectious disease, political instability and corruption, global warming—which generate the biggest threats. By addressing them in meaningful ways, we can forestall crises."[35]

The second reason is more pragmatic but just as compelling. If we fail to act now, we will be forced to pay later, both financially and with our own national security. Human insecurity feeds on itself, laying the ground for conflict and the extreme vulnerability that causes people to fall over the economic edge when weather, wars, or world market prices disrupt their fragile, subsistence economies.

The United States leads the world in responding to the humanitarian crises that arise out of this acute vulnerability. Today, we spend more on emergency relief to treat the symptoms of these crises than we do to promote the development that might prevent them. The United States, for example, spends far more on food aid than it invests in agricultural development, and with food prices surging globally, we have had to increase spending on emergency food aid to forestall famine and food riots in the world's poorest countries.

Experts predict that our humanitarian and military expenditures will increase further unless the vulnerability of the world's poor to climate change is substantially reduced. A 2007 report by 11 former U.S. generals and admirals found that "Climate change can act as a threat multiplier for instability in some of the most volatile regions of the world, and it presents significant national security challenges for the United States."[36] When these new crises arise, the United States will be expected to respond.

We also pay for our failure to address our collective security. Globalization has spawned an interconnected world where capital, goods, people, and threats move freely across borders. These potent transnational threats affect the lives of ordinary Americans, whether in the form of the West Nile virus or a spike in oil prices triggered by the sabotage of oil pipelines by Nigerians desperate for fuel they cannot afford.

Moreover, threats to our collective security—the money laundering that fuels terrorist networks, crime syndicates and the drug trade, uranium smuggling and illegal weapons shipments—can be neither contained nor controlled by the United States alone. We need competent, capable partners, in all corners of the globe.

Shifting to Sustainable Security

America's power is unmatched. We account for roughly half of all global defense spending, and generate 20 percent of all global output. But in an interdependent world where power has grown more diffuse and threats more diverse, our military and economic superpower status is not enough to provide for sustainable security for us or the world we live in.

If our goal is simply to protect and defend America against external interference, then reliance on military force and a wall on the border with Mexico might suffice. But if our aim is to ensure the sustainable security of the United States in a fast-moving, rapidly-changing world driven by complex, global threats and challenges, we need to bring to bear all of the tools we can muster.

Offered up by academia and Washington's think tanks, the concepts of "soft power," "integrated power," and "smart power" bear in common the counsel that America must recalibrate its foreign policy to rely less on military power and more on other tools that can foster change and enhance our security. One of these is enhanced and robust diplomacy; the other is development.

A statement endorsed by eight former Secretaries of State, five former Secretaries of Defense, and four former National Security Advisors, put it this way: "Our increasingly interconnected world requires strong U.S. leadership to strengthen democratic governance, harness economic potential, alleviate global poverty and improve human conditions. American investments in these goals will reaffirm America's tradition of moral leadership, reduce our vulnerability to threats from destabilizing forces and improve America's image abroad."[37]

Secretary of Defense Robert Gates, meanwhile, recently called for the development of "a permanent, sizeable cadre of immediately deployable experts with disparate skills,"[38] and for beefing up our capacity to promote global development. Clearly, there is growing recognition that our sustainable security requires that we beef up our diplomatic capabilities and also strengthen our capacity to promote the development of capable, democratic states and healthy societies.

But when it comes to development, we've got it half right and upside down. Development dollars are up, but we have neither a development policy nor a development strategy. Our foreign aid system is chaotic, but instead of fixing it we are appending to it multiple new tools that, though necessary, risk complicating it further. And instead of balancing our military power with civilian-led capabilities to support development, we are giving the development lead to the Department of Defense.

> **When it comes to development, we've got it half right and upside down. The dollars are up, but we have neither a policy nor a strategy.**

Development Earns Widespread Support

On the positive side of the ledger, we have seen during the last eight years a dramatic increase in development funding legislated with strong bipartisan support. A new milestone was set this year when 186 members of Congress—from both sides of the aisle—wrote to President Bush urging him to increase next year's (fiscal year 2009) International Affairs Budget consistent with the 2006 National Security Strategy, which states that, "Development reinforces diplomacy and defense, reducing long-term threats to our national security by helping to build stable, prosperous, and peaceful societies."[39] President Bush responded by increasing the fiscal year 2009 budget for international affairs to $39.5 billion, a 16 percent increase over the previous year.[40]

Support for two major Bush administration initiatives has also been strong. In January 2004, the United States established and pledged $4.8 billion to the Millennium Challenge Corporation (MCC), a grant-making government agency targeted to countries that are performing well against set economic and political criteria. By the end of fiscal year 2007, 14 countries had signed MCC compacts and 14 more were on the "threshold," making efforts to adhere to the social, judicial, and political reform indicators set forth under the program.[41]

The MCC has been the object of budget battles and the target of criticism for the significant gap between the Bush administration's stated ambitions and the agency's actual implementation, but it has garnered support from both Republicans and Democrats. Bipartisan support for PEPFAR—the President's Emergency Program for AIDS Relief—is even more robust, with both parties in Congress supporting both initial outlays as well as President Bush's 2008 call to double program funding.

Moreover, there is today a growing constituency for action. Driven largely by young people and faith-based communities and elevated to media visibility by celebrities, major campaigns focused on global poverty and Darfur, for example, have caught the attention of the public, Capitol Hill, and the White House. Support for development initiatives such as these was once a predominantly liberal cause, but today it stretches across the political spectrum, and is increasingly prominent among conservatives.

Among young evangelicals, for example, global poverty and human trafficking are gradually overtaking abortion and gay marriage as top priorities. The leading champions for Darfur on Capitol Hill, meanwhile, are Senator Sam Brownback (R-KS) and Representative Donald Payne (D-NJ), two men who disagree on a host of issues but are firmly united in their conviction that America has a moral obligation to end the suffering in Sudan.

Most Americans also want their leaders to do more. A 2007 Gallup poll found that 56 percent of Americans were "dissatisfied" with the current role of the United States in global affairs.[42] Another poll showed that 65 percent of Americans—and the majority of both Republicans and Democrats—support increasing global poverty reduction expenditure to 0.7 percent of GDP.[43] Doing more to improve the lives of the poor is one way in which Americans believe they can restore our global image—and a key way, they believe, for the next president to be an effective and representative global leader.

But Development Gets Short Shrift

On the negative side of the ledger, development remains the poor stepchild of defense and diplomacy. Even with substantial increases in our foreign aid budget, 95 percent of the total outlays for national security in the fiscal year 2007 federal budget were for defense, compared with 3.5 percent for development.[44] Nearly half of that development allocation goes to ten countries, including Egypt, Colombia, Pakistan and Jordan, while the world's poorest receive only six percent.[45] And where foreign aid allocations are at their highest, short-term security imperatives dominate and development comes last.

Consider the case of Pakistan, a country where the United States has used aid to enhance the security of the Pakistani state, with only brief interruptions, since the 1980s. Despite the $24 billion invested by the United States in Pakistan over the last 25 years, we now face a more dangerous mixture of political instability, entrenched poverty, and extremism than existed in the early 1980s—all in a country that possesses nuclear weapons.

According to an August 2007 report from the Center for Strategic and International Studies, the bulk of the $10.5 billion in assistance provided by the U.S. to Pakistan since 9/11 "has not been directed to Pakistan's underlying fault lines, but to specific short-term counterterrorism objectives."[46] Only 10 percent of overall funding has gone for development or for meeting humanitarian needs,[47] and in the Federally Administered Tribal Areas along the country's north-western border with Afghanistan, development assistance comprises only one percent of our total aid package.[48]

In part because development has not been a priority, our heavy financial investment in Pakistan has neither reduced the security threats that Pakistan poses nor earned us the allegiance of the Pakistani people. Our consistent disregard for human security has borne a high cost. Deaths from internal terrorist attacks have skyrocketed since 2001, from 189 in 2003 to 648 in 2005 and 3,599 in 2007.[49] But as a recent Stanley Foundation report highlighted, "most Pakistanis are much more likely to suffer a premature death as a result of poverty or non-existent medical services as they are from an Islamist attack."[50]

Thirty-five percent of Pakistanis live in abject poverty. According to the World Food Program, food insecurity is on the rise, with 60 million people unable to secure an adequate nutritional intake, and an additional 18 million affected by the recent surge in global food prices.[51] Agricultural livelihoods are further threatened by untended environmental changes as the Indus River, upon which a majority of Pakistan's rural population depends for both drinking water and irrigation, begins to go dry.

Nearly half of all Pakistanis are illiterate, literacy rates for women stand at 30 percent, and only three percent of people in Federally Administered Tribal Areas—where some believe Osama bin Laden is hiding—can read or write.[52] Of the billions of dollars in aid provided by the United States since 2001, aid allocated to education represents at most 4.2 percent of the total package—an average of less than $2 per Pakistani child per year.[53] Unable to read, with few job prospects, and angered by U.S. military action within Pakistani borders, the strong financial incentives offered by extremist groups[54] are increasingly a welcome alternative. A recent public opinion poll, meanwhile, found that 72 percent of Pakistanis have unfavorable views of the United States, and only 38 percent of Pakistanis have a favorable view of our ally, President Pervez Musharraf. The same poll showed that free elections, a free press, and an independent judiciary are the most important long-term priority for a majority of Pakistanis.[55] Each of these remains elusive and none of them is a priority in our $10 billion aid package.

Even if there was sufficient political will to elevate development alongside defense and diplomacy, it would be practically impossible because our foreign aid system is irretrievably broken. In 2007, the bipartisan HELP Commission, appointed by Congress and mandated to review U.S. foreign aid, reported that of over 100 government officials (both civilian and military), aid practitioners, foreign policy experts, academics, and private-sector representatives consulted, "not one person appeared before this Commission to defend the status quo."[56]

The System Is Broken

America's ability to invest in global development is seriously constrained. The United States has neither a global development policy nor a strategy. The legislation governing foreign aid was written in 1961, and has since been amended to include 33 goals, 247 directives, and 75 priorities,[57] rendering it so cumbersome that it provides neither coherent guidance to the executive branch nor a roadmap for oversight to the legislative branch. In the absence of a policy, strategy, or effective guiding legislation, aid programming is driven in the main by congressional earmarks, presidential directives, and reaction.

Development programming was once the purview of the U.S. Agency for International Development (USAID), an agency that had a permanent staff of 15,000 during Vietnam but just 3,000 today, and is therefore compelled to rely heavily on expensive outside contractors to manage programs in over 150 countries.[58] Presently, over half of all aid programs are administered by agencies other than USAID, and development funding is arrayed across more than 20[59] government agencies, departments, and initiatives, each with its own goals, priorities, and procedures. No single individual or agency has the authority or the responsibility to oversee or coordinate these myriad programs.

The colossal failure of reconstruction efforts in Iraq and Afghanistan, meanwhile, has rightly focused Washington's attention on crisis management, and has led to the creation of even more instruments and initiatives. In 2004, Congress authorized funds to create an Office of Reconstruction and Stabilization in the State Department, and last year the House and Senate introduced legislation calling for the creation of an expert civilian response capability to carry out our reconstruction and stabilization activities.

The Department of Defense has established a Commanders' Emergency Response Program to meet emergency and reconstruction needs in Iraq and Afghanistan, and the 2006 National Defense Authorization Act created the "1206" fund to assist countries engaged in counter-terrorism and stability operations.

The Pentagon is now seeking to make these temporary crisis management authorities permanent through the "Building Global Partnerships Act."

President Bush deserves credit for dramatic increases in U.S. aid levels and global leadership in the fight against HIV/AIDS. But the changes the U.S. foreign aid system has undergone over the last several years have exacerbated rather than repaired the flaws in the system. These changes have also set far-reaching and potentially detrimental precedents.

The State Department's 2006 "Transformational Diplomacy" plan, for example, established a new Deputy Undersecretary for Foreign Aid in the State Department as a means of achieving greater coordination and policy coherence within the Executive Branch. But the pretense of coordination is more potent than is its practice. Although "Transformational Diplomacy" consolidated some aid accounts, the new Deputy Undersecretary has no jurisdiction over the growing development aid budget managed by the military, and provides guidance to but does not have authority over either the Millennium Challenge Corporation or the anti-AIDs program PEPFAR.

The continued lack of coordination not only leads to inefficiencies in the management of taxpayer funds, but it also places an enormous burden on international development partners who are forced to deal with multiple agencies, requirements, and procedures. It also fosters policy incoherence. Research conducted by the HELP Commission, for example, found that the United States collects more in tariffs from countries eligible for funding from the Millennium Challenge Account than is provided in aid. This fact was news to senior policymakers, who missed it for the simple reason that there is no coordination between our trade agencies and our aid agencies.

Moreover, the administration has launched robust, discrete initiatives without benefit of an overarching policy or strategy, and thus allowed significant gaps to emerge. For example, although agriculture represents almost 40 percent of GDP, 35 percent of exports, and 70 percent of employment in developing countries, less than two percent of the proposed fiscal year 2009 development budget targets agricultural development.

Robust funding to fight the HIV/AIDS pandemic, meanwhile, has not been matched by parallel investments in other sectors. Clearly, global health issues like HIV/AIDS are of paramount importance, but so too are education, agricultural development, institution-building, and job creation.

Consider the case of Kenya, a country that serves as the economic anchor for east and central Africa and has for over two decades functioned—at least in the eyes of the outside world—as an island of stability in a sea of turmoil. Kenya has for years provided staging and overflight rights for U.S. military operations, is the hub for emergency relief efforts throughout the region, regularly contributes troops to U.N. peacekeeping efforts, and has been a staunch ally of the United States in our campaign against global terrorist networks since the U.S. embassy there was bombed by Al Qaeda in 1998.

Close elections late last year brought Kenya's internal contradictions to the surface, however, as the country exploded in a wave of stunning violence that led to the deaths of over 1000 people and economic losses estimated to be in the range of $3 billion.[60]

The most effective tool on hand for the United States to foster stability and functional democracy in Kenya is foreign aid, and the goal of U.S. development efforts in Kenya is in fact to build an economically prosperous country. But of the over $700 million that Kenya now receives annually, over $500 million is earmarked for HIV/ AIDS, over $120 million goes for food aid, and most of the balance is for security and counter-terrorism programs. The net result is that there is little or no funding available to counter the economic or political conditions that gave rise to Kenya's destabilizing post-electoral crisis or to consolidate the fragile peace achieved by the recent formation of a unity government.

A broken, incoherent, and understaffed foreign aid system has allowed for the emergence of some isolated successes, but has also created a vacuum. The United States has neither the policies nor the people it needs to make development an effective foreign policy tool. What may prove to be the most far-reaching of the Bush administration's efforts in the development sphere is its decision to give the lead in filling this vacuum to the Department of Defense.

The Pentagon Steps Up to the Plate

Traditionally, the role of the Department of Defense (DoD) in development has been restricted to three key areas: support for humanitarian operations; engagement in small-scale community development projects linked to training missions and site visits; and, with the Department of State, "train and equip" programs for foreign militaries. But major deployments in Iraq, Afghanistan, and the Horn of Africa have taught the Pentagon three lessons.

First, from Iraq and Afghanistan it became clear that the fragile peace that can be won with military force cannot be sustained without a tangible peace dividend alongside a robust stabilization effort linked to long-term, sustainable development. The second lesson came from the deployment of U.S. forces to Djibouti under the banner of the Combined Joint Task Force-Horn of Africa, where the military has been mandated to conduct counter-terrorism operations and support the efforts of regional governments to contain and prevent the spread of terrorist networks.

It soon became clear that poor countries with weak governments cannot protect or defend their borders without also providing essential services to and securing the allegiance of the citizens who live in the vast, ungoverned spaces that are most vulnerable to terrorist infiltration. The third lesson was that with USAID's staffing eroded to bare bones levels, and with the State Department both non-operational and otherwise occupied, no government agency except the Department of Defense has the personnel or the proclivity to fill these gaps.

The Defense Department is responding, reflecting the observation of Defense Secretary Gates that "the non-military instruments of America's national power need to be rebuilt, modernized, and committed to the fight."[61] The Pentagon's development budget has soared from 5.6 percent of the executive branch total in 2002 to 21.7 percent, or $5.5 billion, in 2005,[62] and is slated to increase further. New authorities have been secured, new programs have been initiated, and with DoD Directive 3000.05, the U.S. military is now mandated to treat stability operations as a core mission on par with combat operations.[63]

But the Department's expanding role goes further than stability operations. In 2007, the Pentagon launched AFRICOM, a unified military headquarters for Africa that is focused on "war prevention," and is designed to "better enable the Department of Defense and other elements of the U.S. government to work in concert and with partners to achieve a more stable environment in which political and economic growth can take place." AFRICOM not only gives a regional military command a development mandate, it also operates with an integrated interagency staff, and thus provides the platform for the coordination of other U.S. government agencies.

The plan for AFRICOM's forward deployment in Africa, however, was poorly received by most African governments, which were not widely consulted in advance of its unveiling, and by civic groups across the continent, which opposed what they viewed as a permanent U.S. military presence in Africa. AFRICOM is thus slated to remain in Germany for the time being, but the AFRICOM model is spreading to other regional commands. SOUTHCOM's latest strategy document, for example, proposes that the command coordinate all relevant government agencies, including civilian, to address the full range of regional challenges in Latin America and the Caribbean.

There are those who believe that DoD's expanded role in development is a sign of the Department's intention to militarize foreign aid. The more plausible explanation is that the Pentagon is stepping in to fill a vacuum that has been left wanting by USAID's dire circumstances, and by the State Department's lack of intent. In much the same way that she ceded control over the Iraq war to the Pentagon during her tenure as National Security Advisor in the early years of the Bush administration, Secretary of State Condoleezza Rice has posed no visible or effective opposition to the Pentagon's expanded role in areas traditionally considered the purview of civilian agencies.

DoD's role has also grown more prominent because it is operational and capable. In contrast, the State Department is not operational, and a weakened USAID no longer has the capacity to tackle all of the development challenges the United States faces. Congress, therefore, is more inclined to allocate aid dollars to the Pentagon than to its weaker and less capable counterparts.

The greatest peril lies not in the fact that the Defense Department has stepped in to fill the development vacuum and pick up the slack on inter-agency coordination, or even that the Pentagon has no expertise or experience in the field of development. The hazard lies in the fact that the frontal face of America's support for development in the poorest corners of the world is our military, and not our civilian agencies. As the lukewarm reception to AFRICOM has made clear, this places our interest in human security squarely in the frame of our national security and, in particular, the war on terrorism—and not, as it should be, in the context of our shared commitment to the global common good.

Three Steps toward Sustainable Security

Adapting to today's world and achieving sustainable security requires that we pursue not only our national security, but also global and human security. This more modern approach can afford us the ability to deal simultaneously with short-term, nation-state based threats and with the global challenges that transcend state borders. Importantly, this sustainable security approach allows us to lead from a position of moral strength. But getting there requires three core elements:

- An organizing principle that can unite a majority of the world's people
- The elevation and strategic utilization of the full range of our foreign policy tool
- A revitalized international system that reflects not just the challenges that existed when it was created in the wake of World War II, but also the realities of today

It also requires that the next president establish the predicate for change, and speak truth to the American people. Over the course of two terms, the Bush administration has posited that the combination of its moral certitude and America's military might are sufficient to secure our national interests, and has treated threats to our global security—whether climate change or energy security—as electives rather than imperatives.

The next president instead must update and advise the American people, making clear that our ability to lead on the world stage demands not only awesome power but also moral authority, and that our interests are best served when we act in pursuit of our global security and common humanity.

The shift toward a sustainable security approach will take time, and the next president will face a daunting list of immediate challenges. But there are several steps that can be taken in 2009 to lay the ground for an increased and practical focus on the profound moral challenges of our world, to modernize our foreign aid system, and to lay the ground for the increased international cooperation that is necessary going forward. Specifically, the next president should:

- Add a third and powerful tool to our foreign policy apparatus, in addition to defense and diplomacy, by elevating, integrating, and coordinating U.S. global development policies and programs.
- Take immediate steps to modernize our foreign aid system so that a new administration can move nimbly and effectively to invest in building capable states, open societies, and a global marketplace that serves the world's majority.
- Move swiftly to re-engage on the international stage by signaling America's willingness to lead in the reform of international institutions and the creation of new mechanisms for managing our shared global interests.

The shift toward a sustainable security approach will take time, and the next president will face a daunting list of immediate challenges.

These three steps, in turn, require detailed action to ensure success. All three of these overarching policy proposals, when examined in detail, would elevate sustainable security to an active policy of global engagement within the first term of the next administration.

Prioritize, Integrate, and Coordinate Development

It will take presidential leadership to elevate development, a strong hand to integrate the concept of human security across the range of our foreign policy agencies, and high-level action to coordinate the myriad foreign aid agencies, instruments, and initiatives now spread across the executive branch. There are four key steps that the next president can take to lay the ground for progress in all three areas.

First, the president should use the administration's first National Security Strategy to lay the ground for a sustainable security approach by focusing on traditional national security, collective security, and human security. Though required by law, National Security Strategies are often boilerplate documents that provide little other than a narrative list of foreign policy priorities. The next president should use his first NSS as a tool for pivoting to sustainable security.

Second, the president should appoint a third Deputy National Security Advisor (NSA) for long-term strategic planning. In a White House facing the pressures of competing global and domestic crises, 24-hour news coverage, and a four-year election cycle, there is little time for thinking about and planning for the long term. A designated Deputy NSA mandated to think and plan ahead will not only allow the administration to make up for the time lost by the Bush administration on issues like climate change, but will also allow an administration to get out ahead of future threats like resource scarcity and new global pandemics.

Third, as the first step toward formulating a government-wide policy on development and crafting a whole-of-government development strategy, the president should issue a Presidential Directive providing initial guidance to the multiple agencies, departments, and offices that are now pursuing their own individual agendas. The guidance should neither be so vague—by pointing to, for example, "reducing global poverty"—as to be meaningless, nor so prescriptive that it undercuts the ability of professionals on the ground to make informed decisions.

Instead, it should focus on the priorities that serve our national interests and reflect a global common good, for example by building the capacity of governments and civil society; reducing the vulnerability of the poor; laying the ground for improved resource management; and enhancing the access of poor communities and low-income countries to capital and markets.

Fourth, the president should create a directorate, led jointly by the National Security Council and National Economic Council, to initiate and oversee the coordination of all foreign aid agencies, initiatives, departments, and programs. Given the growing role of non-governmental organizations, philanthropic groups, and corporations in humanitarian and development efforts overseas, the directorate should also ensure that the U.S. government is in regular consultation with these prominent partners.

Modernize Our Foreign Aid System

There is an urgent need to reform the structure, operations, and staffing of our foreign aid system, and an equally important need to coordinate a sweeping reform process with the Congress. Reform will likely require new legislation to replace the almost 50-year old Foreign Assistance Act, as well as an overhaul of critical internal procedures ranging from evaluation to procurement.

A growing number of development experts, NGOs, corporate leaders, and foreign-policy specialists are lending support to the creation of an independent, cabinet-level development agency, similar to Britain's Department for International Development, which was created by former Prime Minister Tony Blair and has been given an even more prominent role by his successor, Gordon Brown. The rationale is that because development is a field distinct from either defense or diplomacy, it warrants its own department and leadership, and a seat at the foreign policy-making table.

There is also a need, advocates argue, to bring our various foreign aid agencies under one roof. As well, there is growing recognition of the need to insulate the development portion of our foreign aid budget from the pressure of short-term security imperatives, and instead focus on long-term development objectives across the span of successive administrations.

The proposal is that military aid, including "train and equip" programs for foreign militaries, peacekeeping funds, and economic security funds, or ESF, would remain under the jurisdiction of the Departments of Defense and State. Humanitarian and development aid—including PEPFAR and the MCA—would be centralized under a new, professionally staffed department, insulated from short-term imperatives and focused on long-term goals.

Critics argue that the development portfolio should remain within State and be made a priority by the secretary. They point to the problems incurred by the creation of the Department of Homeland Security as evidence that a new independent agency will not work, and argue that an independent development agency will inevitably be sidelined. Further, there is concern that the creation of a separate development department would weaken and compete with the Department of State.

The "uber State Department" is clearly the easier option, but given the experience of USAID over the years, and the structural flaws in the State Department's "Transformational Diplomacy," it is also the least likely to bring about a fundamental change to the status quo. First of all, the State Department is not operational and is thus not equipped to manage the development portfolio. Second, the independent agency proposal entails uniting agencies and departments with common mandates, and not, as was the case with the Department of Homeland Security, creating a department that combines multiple operational agencies with distinct and varied mandates.

And third, a cabinet-level development agency reinforced by the Executive Office of the President and backed by the development budget is no more likely to be marginalized than is an office housed within the State Department. What's more, concerns about weakening the State Department overlook two salient facts.

First, development and diplomacy are two entirely different tasks that are undertaken on the basis of different time horizons, require distinct expertise and different capabilities, and entail separate and contrasting approaches. Past policy has been hindered by the assumption that development requires little expertise other than an understanding of international affairs and a concern for the plight of the poor, and that the development aspect of a given policy can thus be easily handled by either the Department of State or the Department of Defense. The dangers of this flawed assumption are now evident, however, in Iraq,

Afghanistan, Pakistan, Egypt, and countless other cases where we have failed to bring a development perspective to bear.

Second, this concern misdiagnoses the current weakness of the State Department, which has less to do with its authority over foreign aid and more to do with its failure to craft and act on a modern diplomatic agenda and its willingness to concede influence to the Department of Defense.

In the next administration, the State Department must take the foreign policy lead, including on reforming the international institutions that make up our global architecture and on crafting and implementing the policies that can enable the U.S. to manage a host of global threats and challenges. State's strength will and should derive from its leadership in formulating these and other policies that guide the use of all of our foreign policy tools—diplomacy, defense, and development.

But the next president needs to hear views forged from each of these perspectives. Just as the State and Defense Departments craft their own unique strategies, oversee their own budgets, and bring their own specific expertise and distinct perspectives to the decision-making table in the White House, so too should a department for development.

The next president, however, cannot create a new department without extensive internal deliberation or consultation with Congress. Fortunately, leading members of Congress have already taken on the cause of modernizing our foreign aid system.

The next president should immediately engage with this ongoing congressional process and appoint, during the transition, a high-level White House official to consult within and outside of government and develop options for rationalizing and modernizing our foreign aid system during his first term. Because traditional institutional imperatives may cause a new Secretary of State to oppose an independent cabinet-level agency, the president should also secure the support of the new secretary to consider the full range of options.

Re-Enter the International Arena

The next president has the opportunity to re-engage the international community and reposition America to lead. But this will take clear signals from the White House that the new administration is ready and willing to engage, and recognition that just as our own foreign policy architecture is out of date, so too is the international architecture in urgent need of reform. The next president can move on both fronts by taking four steps.

The next president has the opportunity to re-engage the international community and reposition America to lead.

First, he should work with Congress to ensure that the United States can fully cover its U.N. arrears within the first year of a new administration. As happened during the 1990s, the failure of the United States to pay its dues both hinders U.N. operations in critical areas such as peacekeeping, but also undermines our ability to make the case for, or demand, critical reforms.

Second, in an effort to begin reconciling our national interests and our global security, the next president should work with Congress, across the whole of government, and with allies from the developed and developing worlds to craft a strategy for global food security. The worldwide crisis that erupted when food prices nearly doubled exposed the need to harmonize policies in an interconnected world, and has affected consumers in every country in the world. In some cases, the crisis has triggered riots and instability, in others it has pushed millions over the edge from subsistence to hunger, and in the United States it has fostered economic hardship and a spike in demand for food stamps and other nutritional programs.

By the time the next president is sworn in, the Doha "Development Round" of trade talks will likely be dead on the mantle of disagreement between the world's rich and poor countries on agricultural policies. And barring some radical and unforeseen change, the global food market will still be volatile. Rationalizing America's agricultural policies to conform to a new global environment will take heavy political lifting, but the opportunity and indeed imperative created by collapsed trade talks and the global food crisis provide a window for starting the discussion.

Third, the next president should initiate the next phase of PEPFAR. While giving full credit to President Bush for launching and robustly funding the initiative, the next president should provide a larger share of HIV/AIDS funding through the Global Fund for AIDS, Tuberculosis, and Malaria, signaling our willingness to work collectively to address the global challenge that these diseases represent. A new and improved PEPFAR should also invest more resources in capacity-building and the ability of the world's poorest countries to manage future epidemics and health crises.

Fourth and finally, the next president should make Darfur—and indeed the issue of crimes against humanity across the globe—a top priority. There is little chance that the Darfur crisis will be resolved by next January, but there are plenty of other places where crimes against humanity are going untended by the world.

The Darfur genocide is now entering its sixth year, and cries of "never again" and pledges of "not on my watch" ring hollow. The next president needs to dedicate his time, and that of the secretary of state, to show the world that America is ready to stand up to the worst of all threats to human security, genocide, so that America's claim to global leadership will be shaped not only by the actions we take but also by those that we do not.

Conclusion

Few would envy the task of handling the long list of first priorities that awaits the next president. But while protecting and defending America's national security will be first on the list, so too should be adapting to the modern concept of sustainable security.

At the dawn of the 21st century, in a world seized by far-reaching and tumultuous change, President Bush dedicated eight years to waging a "war on terror" and reminding the rest of the world of what America is *against*. It is time for our next president to remind the rest of the world that we stand *for* the sustainable security of our shared world. To do otherwise would be to diminish our collective security and abandon our common humanity.

Notes

1. Iraq Coalition Casualty Count, available at http://www .icasualties.org/oif/ (last accessed May 2008).

2. Amy Belasco, "The Cost of Iraq, Afghanistan, and Other Global War on Terror Operations Since 9/11" (Washington: Congressional Research Service, 2008), available at http:// www.fas.org/sgp/crs/natsec/RL33110.pdf (last accessed May 2008) p. 16.

3. George F. Kennan, "Comments on the General Trend of U.S. Foreign Policy" (Princeton: George F. Kennan Papers, August 20, 1948).

4. The United States Commission on Helping to Enhance the Livelihood of People around the Globe, "Beyond Assistance: The HELP Commission Report of Foreign Assistance Reform" (2007). p. 10.

5. Dr. Fareda Banda, "Project on a Mechanism to Address Laws that Discriminate Against Women" (The United Nations' Office of the High Commissioner for Human Rights, March 6 2008), available at http://www.reliefweb.int/rw/lib.nsf/db900sid/ PANA-7DHGQM/$file/ohchr_mar2008.pdf?openelement (last accessed May 2008).

6. The United States Commission on Helping to Enhance the Livelihood of People around the Globe, "Beyond Assistance: The HELP Commission Report of Foreign Assistance Reform" (2007) p. 12.

7. William Easterly, *The White Man's Burden: Why the West's Efforts to Aid the Rest Have Done So Much Ill and So Little Good* (New York: Penguin Books, 2006) p. 8.

8. The Millennium Project of the World Federation of UN Associations, "Water: How Can Everyone Have Sufficient Clean Water Without Conflict?" available at http://www .millennium-project.org/millennium/Global_Challenges/ chall-02.html (last accessed May 2008).

9. The World Health Organization, "Statement from WHO's Director General" (2008), available at http://www.who.int/ water_sanitation_health/hygiene/iys/about/en/index.html (last accessed May 2008).

10. Energy Future Coalition, "Challenge and Opportunity: Charting a New Energy Future," available at http://www .energyfuturecoalition.org/pubs/EFCReport.pdf (last accessed May 2008) p. 36.

11. The United Nations, "Poverty Briefing," available at http:// www.un.org/Pubs/CyberSchoolBus//briefing/poverty/ poverty.pdf last accessed May 2008).

12. The United Nations Development Programme, "Human Development Report 2007/2008, Fighting Climate Change: Human Solidarity in a Divided World," (New York: The United Nations, 2007), available at http://hdr.undp.org/en/media/ hdr_20072008_en_complete.pdf (last accessed May 2008) p. 8.

13. The United Nations Development Programme, "Human Development Report 2003: Millenium Development Goals: A Compact Among Nations to End Human Poverty," (New York: Oxford University Press, 2003), available at http://hdr.undp .org/en/media/hdr03_complete.pdf (last accessed May 2008) p. 34.

14. Paul Collier, *The Bottom Billion: Why the Poorest Countries are Failing and What Can Be Done About It,* (New York: Oxford University Press, 2007) p. 27.

15. Robert Muggah and Martin Griffiths, "Reconsidering the Tools of War: Small Arms and Humanitarian Action" (Humanitarian Practice Network, 2002) p. 13.

16. Oxfam, Saferworld, and International Action Network on Small Arms, "Africa's Missing Billions: International Arms Flows and the Costs of Conflict" (October 2007), available at http://www.oxfam.org/en/files/bp107_africas_missing_billions_0710.pdf/download (last accessed May 2008) p. 9.

17. The World Bank, "Sri Lanka: Recapturing Missed Opportunities," Report No: 20430-CE, (June 16, 2000), available at http:// siteresources.worldbank.org/SRILANKAEXTN/Resources/Missed-opportunities/full_report.pdf (last accessed June 2008). NOT SURE

18. Larry Minear and Ian Smillie, *The Charity of Nations: Humanitarian Action in a Calculating World,* (Connecticut: Kumarian Press, 2004) p. 10.

19. The United Nations, "United Nations Peacekeeping Operations" (March 2008), available at http://www.un.org/Depts/dpko/dpko/bnote.htm (last accessed May 2008).

20. Satish Chand and Ruth Coffman, "How Soon Can Donors Exit From Post-Conflict States?" (Center for Global Development, Working Paper Number 141, February 2008), available at http://www.cgdev.org/content/publications/detail/15464 (last accessed May 2008).

21. The United Nations, "World Youth Report 2005: Young people Today, and in 2015," (2005), available at http://www.un.org/esa/socdev/unyin/documents/wyr05book.pdf (last accessed May 2008).

22. Dapo Oyewole, "Participation of Youth As Partners in Peace and Development in Africa: An Overview of Issues and Challenge" (Paper presented at the Expert Group Meeting on Youth in Africa: Participation of Youth as Partners in Peace and Development in Post-Conflict Countries, Windhoek, Namibia, November 14–16, 2006), available at http://www.un.org/esa/socdev/unyin/documents/namibia_overview.pdf (last accessed May 2008).

23. The United Nations, "The State of World Population: Population Change and Peoples Choice" (1999), available at http://www.unfpa.org/swp/1999/chapter2d.htm (last accessed May 2008).

24. The World Business Council for Sustainable Development, "Facts and Trends to 2050: Energy and Climate Change" (2004), available at http://www.wbcsd.org/DocRoot/FjSOTYajhk3cIRxCbijT/Basic-Facts-Trends-2050.pdf (last accessed May 2008) p. 1.

25. Lester Brown, "How Water Scarcity Will Shape the New Century" (Keynote speech presented at Stockhold Water Conference, August, 14, 2000), available at http://www.earth-policy.org/Transcripts/Transcript1.htm (last accessed May 2008).

26. The United Nations Environment Programme, "Water-Two Billion People are Dying for It" (2003), available at http://www.unep.org/wed/2003/keyfacts.htm (last accessed May 2008).

27. Oxfam International, "Rigged Rules and Double Standards: Trade, Globalization, and the Fight Against Poverty" (2002), available at http://www.oxfam.org.uk/resources/papers/downloads/trade_report.pdf (last accessed May 2008) p. 7.

28. Ibid, p. 9–10.

29. Ibid, p. 177.

30. Phillip Stevens, "Diseases of Poverty and the 10/90 Gap" (International Policy Network: London, 2004), available at http:// www.fightingdiseases.org/pdf/Diseases_of_Poverty_FINAL.pdf (last accessed May 2008) p. 3.

31. Worldwatch Institute, "Vital Signs: The Trends that are Shaping our Future" (London: W.W. Norton Company, 2001), available at http://www.worldwatch.org/system/files/EVS103.pdf (last accessed May 2008) p. 21.

32. Larry Diamond, "The Democratic Rollback" *Foreign Affairs,* March/April 2008.

33. Stewart Patrick and Susan E. Rice, "Index of State Weakness in the Developing World" (Washington: The Brookings Institution, 2008) p. 17.

34. President John F. Kennedy, "Inaugural Address" (January 20, 1961), available at http://www.bartleby.com/124/pres56.html (last accessed May 2008).

35. Leighton W. Smith Jr. and Anthony C. Zinni, "A Smarter Weapon: Why Two Retired Military Officers Believe It's Essential that the Next President Use Outreach, Good Deeds and a Strong Military to Make the United States Safer" *USA Today,* March 27, 2008, available at http://www.usatoday.com/printedition/news/20080327/oplede_wednesday.art.htm (last accessed May 2008).

36. The CNA Corporation, "National Security and the Threat of Climate Change" (2007), available at http://securityandclimate.cna.org/report/National%20Security%20and%20the%20Threat%20of%20Climate%20Change.pdf (last accessed May 2008).

37. Center for U.S. Global Engagement, "A 21st Century Vision of U.S. Global Leadership: Building a Better Safer World" (2007), available at http://www.usglobalengagement.org/SignonStatement/tabid/890/Default.asp#Signatories (last accessed May 2008).

38. Robert M. Gates, "Landon Lecture, Kansas State University" (November 26, 2007), available at http://www.defenselink.mil/speeches/speech.aspx?speechid=1199 (last access May 2008).

39. The White House, "The National Security Strategy of the United States of America" (March 2006), available at http://www.whitehouse.gov/nsc/nss/2006/nss2006.pdf (last accessed May 2008) p. 33.

40. The United States Department of State, "Summary and Highlights: International Affairs Function 150, Fiscal Year 2009 Budget Request" (2008), available at http://www.state.gov/documents/organization/100014.pdf (last accessed May 2008) p. 6.

41. The United States of America Millennium Challenge Corporation, "Changing Lives: 2007 Annual Report," available at http://www.mcc.gov/documents/mcc-2007-annualreport.pdf (last accessed May 2008) p. 6.

42. WorldPublicOpinion.org, "US Role in the World," available at http://www.americans-world.org/digest/overview/us_role/general_principles.cfm (last accessed May 2008).

43. Program on International Policy Attitudes and Knowledge Networks, "Americans on Addressing World Poverty" (June 30, 2005), available at http://www.pipa.org/OnlineReports/ForeignAid/WorldPoverty_Jun05/WorldPoverty_Jun05_rpt.pdf (last accessed May 2008).

44. Oxfam America, "Smart Development: Why US Foreign Aid Demands Major Reform" (Oxfam America Inc. 2008), available at http://www.oxfamamerica.org/newsandpublications/publications/briefing_papers/smart-development/smart-development-may2008.pdf (last accessed May 2008) p. 5–6.

45. Ibid.

46. Craig Cohen, "A Perilous Course: U.S. Strategy and Assistance to Pakistan" (Washington: Center for Strategic and International Studies, August 2007), available at http://www.csis.org/media/csis/pubs/071214_pakistan.pdf (last accessed May 2008) pg. viii.

47. Ibid, p. 26.

48. United States Government Accountability Office, "Combating Terrorism: The United States Lacks Comprehensive Plan to Destroy the Terrorist Threat to Close the Safe Haven in Pakistan's Federally Administered Tribal Areas" (April 2008), available at http://www.gao.gov/new.items/d08622.pdf (last accessed May 2008) p. 12.

49. South Asia Intelligence Review, "Casualties of Terrorist Violence in Pakistan," available at http://satp.org/satporgtp/countries/pakistan/database/casualties.htm (last accessed May 2008).

50. Owen Bennett-Jones, "US Policy Options Toward Pakistan: A Principled and Realistic Approach" (Iowa: The Stanley Foundation, February 2008) p. 4.

51. "Half of Pakistan's population is 'food insecure': WFP," *The News-International*, April 23, 2008, available at http://www.thenews. com.pk/daily_detail.asp?id=108337 (last accessed May 2008).

52. Craig Cohen, "A Perilous Course: U.S. Strategy and Assistance to Pakistan" (Washington: Center for Strategic and International Studies, August 2007), available at http://www.csis.org/media/csis/pubs/071214_pakistan.pdf (last accessed May 2008) p. 27.

53. Ibid, p. 26.

54. The United States Institute of Peace, "Islamic Extremists: How Do They Mobilize Support?" (July 2002, Special Report 89), available at http://www.usip.org/pubs/specialreports/sr89.pdf (last accessed May 2008) p. 4.

55. Terror Free Tomorrow, "Pakistanis Reject US Military Action against Al Qaeda; More Support bin Laden than President Musharraf: Results of a New Nationwide Public Opinion Survey of Pakistan" (2007) available at http://www.terrorfreetomorrow.org/upimagestft/Pakistan%20Poll%20Report.pdf (last accessed May 2008).

56. The United States Commission on Helping to Enhance the Livelihood of People around the Globe, "Beyond Assistance: The HELP Commission Report of Foreign Assistance Reform" (2007) p. 1.

57. Steven Radelet, "Foreign Assistance Reforms: Successes, Failures, and Next Steps" (Testimony for the Senate Foreign Relations Subcommittee on International Development, Foreign Assistance, Economic Affairs, and International Environmental Protection, June 12, 2007), available at http://www.senate.gov/~foreign/testimony/2007/RadeletTestimony070612.pdf (last accessed May 2008).

58. Robert M. Gates, "Landon Lecture, Kansas State University" (November 26, 2007), available at http://www.defenselink.mil/speeches/speech.aspx?speechid=1199 (last access May 2008).

59. The United States Commission on Helping to Enhance the Livelihood of People around the Globe, "Beyond Assistance: The HELP Commission Report of Foreign Assistance Reform" (2007) p. 63.

60. Cathy Majtenyi, "Economic Impact of Election Violence on Display in Western Kenyan City," *Voice of America,* March 4, 2008, available at http://www.voanews.com/english/archive/2008-03/2008-03-04-voa29.cfm (last accessed May 2008).

61. Robert M. Gates, "Address to the Marine Corps Association" (July 18, 2007), available at http://smallwarsjournal.com/blog/2007/07/secretary-gates-addresses-the/ (last accessed May 2008).

62. Kaysie Brown and Stewart Patrick, "The Pentagon and Global Development: Making Sense of the DoD's Expanding Role" (Washington: The Center for Global Development Working Paper Number 131, November 2007), available at http://www.cgdev.org/content/publications/detail/14815/ (last accessed May 2008).

63. United States Department of Defense, "Directive 3000.05" (November 28, 2005), available at http://www.dtic.mil/whs/directives/corres/pdf/300005p.pdf (last accessed May 2008) p. 2.

The Petraeus Doctrine

Iraq-style counterinsurgency is fast becoming the U.S. Army's organizing principle. Is our military preparing to fight the next war, or the last one?

Andrew J. Bacevich

For a military accustomed to quick, easy victories, the trials and tribulations of the Iraq War have come as a rude awakening. To its credit, the officer corps has responded not with excuses but with introspection. One result, especially evident within the U.S. Army, has been the beginning of a Great Debate of sorts.

Anyone who cares about the Army's health should take considerable encouragement from this intellectual ferment. Yet anyone who cares about future U.S. national-security strategy should view the debate with considerable concern: it threatens to encroach upon matters that civilian policy makers, not soldiers, should decide.

What makes this debate noteworthy is not only its substance, but its character—the who and the how.

The military remains a hierarchical organization in which orders come from the top down. Yet as the officer corps grapples with its experience in Iraq, fresh ideas are coming from the bottom up. In today's Army, the most creative thinkers are not generals but mid-career officers—lieutenant colonels and colonels.

Like any bureaucracy, today's military prefers to project a united front when dealing with the outside world, keeping internal dissent under wraps. Nonetheless, the Great Debate is unfolding in plain view in publications outside the Pentagon's purview, among them print magazines such as *Armed Forces Journal,* the Web-based *Small Wars Journal,* and the counterinsurgency blog Abu Muqawama.

The chief participants in this debate—all Iraq War veterans—fixate on two large questions. First, why, after its promising start, did Operation Iraqi Freedom go so badly wrong? Second, how should the hard-earned lessons of Iraq inform future policy? Hovering in the background of this Iraq-centered debate is another war that none of the debaters experienced personally—namely, Vietnam.

The protagonists fall into two camps: Crusaders and Conservatives.

The Crusaders consist of officers who see the Army's problems in Iraq as self-inflicted. According to members of this camp, things went awry because rigidly conventional senior commanders, determined "never again" to see the Army sucked

into a Vietnam-like quagmire, had largely ignored unconventional warfare and were therefore prepared poorly for it. Typical of this generation is Lieutenant General Ricardo Sanchez, once the top U.S. commander in Baghdad, who in late 2003 was still describing the brewing insurgency as "strategically and operationally insignificant," when the lowliest buck sergeant knew otherwise.

Younger officers critical of Sanchez are also committed to the slogan "Never again," but with a different twist: never again should the officer corps fall prey to the willful amnesia to which the Army succumbed after Vietnam, when it turned its back on that war.

Among the Crusaders' most influential members is Lieutenant Colonel John Nagl, a West Pointer and Rhodes Scholar with a doctorate from Oxford University. In 2002, he published a book, impeccably timed, titled *Learning to Eat Soup With a Knife: Counterinsurgency Lessons From Malaya and Vietnam.* After serving in Iraq as a battalion operations officer, Nagl helped rewrite the Army's counterinsurgency manual and commanded the unit that prepares U.S. soldiers to train Iraqi security forces. (Earlier this year, he left the Army to accept a position with a Washington think tank.)

To Nagl, the lessons of the recent past are self-evident. The events of 9/11, he writes, "conclusively demonstrated that instability anywhere can be a real threat to the American people here at home." For the foreseeable future, political conditions abroad rather than specific military threats will pose the greatest danger to the United States.

Instability creates ungoverned spaces in which violent anti-American radicals thrive. Yet if instability anywhere poses a threat, then ensuring the existence of stability everywhere—denying terrorists sanctuary in rogue or failed states—becomes a national-security imperative. Define the problem in these terms, and winning battles becomes less urgent than pacifying populations and establishing effective governance.

War in this context implies not only coercion but also social engineering. As Nagl puts it, the security challenges of the 21st century will require the U.S. military "not just to dominate land operations, but to change entire societies."

Of course, back in the 1960s an earlier experiment in changing entire societies yielded unmitigated disaster—at least that's how the Army of the 1980s and 1990s chose to remember its Vietnam experience. Crusaders take another view, however. They insist that Vietnam could have been won—indeed was being won, after General Creighton Abrams succeeded General William Westmoreland in 1968 and jettisoned Westmoreland's heavy-handed search-and-destroy strategy, to concentrate instead on winning Vietnamese hearts and minds. Defeat did not result from military failure; rather, defeat came because the American people lacked patience, while American politicians lacked guts.

The Crusaders' perspective on Iraq tracks neatly with this revisionist take on Vietnam, with the hapless Sanchez (among others) standing in for Westmoreland, and General David Petraeus—whose Princeton doctoral dissertation was titled "The American Military and the Lessons of Vietnam"—as successor to General Abrams. Abrams's successful if tragically aborted campaign in Vietnam serves as a precursor to Petraeus's skillfully orchestrated "surge" in Iraq: each demonstrates that the United States can prevail in "stability operations" as long as commanders grasp the true nature of the problem and respond appropriately.

For Nagl, the imperative of the moment is to institutionalize the relevant lessons of Vietnam and Iraq, thereby enabling the Army, he writes, "to get better at building societies that can stand on their own." That means buying fewer tanks while spending more on language proficiency; curtailing the hours spent on marksmanship ranges while increasing those devoted to studying foreign cultures. It also implies changing the culture of the officer corps. An Army that since Vietnam has self-consciously cultivated a battle-oriented warrior ethos will instead emphasize, in Nagl's words, "the intellectual tools necessary to foster host-nation political and economic development."

Although the issue is by no means fully resolved, the evidence suggests that Nagl seems likely to get his way. Simply put, an officer corps that a decade ago took its intellectual cues from General Colin Powell now increasingly identifies itself with the views of General Petraeus. In the 1990s, the Powell Doctrine, with its emphasis on overwhelming force, assumed that future American wars would be brief, decisive, and infrequent. According to the emerging Petraeus Doctrine, the Army (like it or not) is entering an era in which armed conflict will be protracted, ambiguous, and continuous—with the application of force becoming a lesser part of the soldier's repertoire.

Nagl's line of argument has not gone unchallenged. Its opponents, the Conservatives, reject the revisionist interpretation of Vietnam and dispute the freshly enshrined conventional narrative on Iraq. Above all, they question whether Iraq represents a harbinger of things to come.

A leading voice in the Conservative camp is Colonel Gian Gentile, a Berkeley graduate with a doctorate in history from Stanford, who currently teaches at West Point. Gentile has two tours in Iraq under his belt. During the second, just before the Petraeus era, he commanded a battalion in Baghdad.

Writing in the journal *World Affairs,* Gentile dismisses as "a self-serving fiction" the notion that Abrams in 1968 put the United States on the road to victory in Vietnam; the war, he says, was unwinnable, given the "perseverance, cohesion, indigenous support, and sheer determination of the other side, coupled with the absence of any of those things on the American side." Furthermore, according to Gentile, the post-Vietnam officer corps did not turn its back on that war in a fit of pique; it correctly assessed that the mechanized formations of the Warsaw Pact deserved greater attention than pajama-clad guerrillas in Southeast Asia.

Gentile also takes issue with the triumphal depiction of the Petraeus era, attributing security improvements achieved during Petraeus's tenure less to new techniques than to a "cash-for-cooperation" policy that put "nearly 100,000 Sunnis, many of them former insurgents, . . . on the U.S. government payroll." According to Gentile, in Iraq as in Vietnam, tactics alone cannot explain the overall course of events.

All of this forms a backdrop to Gentile's core concern: that an infatuation with stability operations will lead the Army to reinvent itself as "a constabulary," adept perhaps at nation-building but shorn of adequate capacity for conventional war-fighting.

The concern is not idle. A recent article in *Army* magazine notes that the Army's National Training Center in Fort Irwin, California, long "renowned for its force-on-force conventional warfare maneuver training," has now "switched gears," focusing exclusively on counterinsurgency warfare. Rather than practicing how to attack the hill, its trainees now learn about "spending money instead of blood, and negotiating the cultural labyrinth through rapport and rapprochement."

The officer corps itself recognizes that conventional-warfare capabilities are already eroding. In a widely circulated white paper, three former brigade commanders declare that the Army's field-artillery branch—which plays a limited role in stability operations, but is crucial when there is serious fighting to be done—may soon be all but incapable of providing accurate and timely fire support. Field artillery, the authors write, has become a "dead branch walking."

Gentile does not doubt that counterinsurgencies will figure in the Army's future. Yet he questions Nagl's certainty that situations resembling Iraq should become an all-but-exclusive preoccupation. Historically, expectations that the next war will resemble the last one have seldom served the military well.

Embedded within this argument over military matters is a more fundamental and ideologically charged argument about basic policy. By calling for an Army configured mostly to wage stability operations, Nagl is effectively affirming the Long War as the organizing principle of post-9/11 national-security strategy, with U.S. forces called upon to bring light to those dark corners of the world where terrorists flourish. Observers differ on whether the Long War's underlying purpose is democratic transformation or imperial domination: Did the Bush administration invade Iraq to liberate that country or to control it? Yet there is no disputing that the Long War implies a vast military enterprise undertaken on a global scale and likely to last decades. In this sense, Nagl's reform agenda, if implemented, will serve to validate—and perpetuate—the course set by President Bush in the aftermath of 9/11.

Gentile understands this. Implicit in his critique of Nagl is a critique of the Bush administration, for which John Nagl serves as a proxy. Gentile's objection to what he calls Nagl's "breathtaking" assumption about "the efficacy of American military power to shape events" expresses a larger dissatisfaction with similar assumptions held by the senior officials who concocted the Iraq War in the first place. When Gentile charges Nagl with believing that there are "no limits to what American military power . . . can accomplish," his real gripe is with the likes of Dick Cheney, Donald Rumsfeld, and Paul Wolfowitz.

For officers like Nagl, the die appears to have been cast. The Long War gives the Army its marching orders. Nagl's aim is simply to prepare for the inescapable eventuality of one, two, many Iraqs to come.

Nagl's aim is simply to prepare for the inescapable eventuality of one, two, many Iraqs to come.

Gentile resists the notion that the Army's (and by extension, the nation's) fate is unalterably predetermined. Strategic choice—to include the choice of abandoning the Long War in favor of a different course—should remain a possibility. The effect of Nagl's military reforms, Gentile believes, will be to reduce or preclude that possibility, allowing questions of the second order (How should we organize our Army?) to crowd out those of the first (What should be our Army's purpose?).

The biggest question of all, Gentile writes, is "Who gets to decide this?" Absent a comparably searching Great Debate among the civilians vying to direct U.S. policy—and the prospects that either Senator McCain or Senator Obama will advocate alternatives to the Long War appear slight—the power of decision may well devolve by default upon soldiers. Gentile insists—rightly—that the choice should not be the Army's to make.

ANDREW J. BACEVICH is a professor of history and international relations at Boston University. His new book, *The Limits of Power: The End of American Exceptionalism,* was published in August.

UNIT 4

Great Power Interstate Conflicts and Rivalries

Unit Selections

Key Points to Consider

- What should the U.S. and European allies do to improve relations and achieve a concrete partnership?

- Why do Henry Kissinger and George P. Shultz believe more joint cooperation between the United States and Russia is necessary for stability in Europe and the world?

- How is China creating a political and economic zone of influence throughout Southeast Asia?

Student Web Site

www.mhcls.com

Internet References

Archive of European Integration
http://aei.pitt.edu/
ISN International Relations and Security Network
http://www.isn.ethz.ch
The Henry L. Stimson Center—Peace Operations and Europe
http://www.stimson.org/fopo/?SN = FP20020610372
Central Europe Online
http://www.centraleurope.com
Europa: European Union
http://europa.eu.int
NATO Integrated Data Service
http://www.nato.int/structur/nids/nids.htm.
Russia Today
http://www.russiatoday.com
**Russian and East European Network Information Center,
University of Texas at Austin**
http://reenic.utexas.edu/reenic/index.html
Inside China Today
http://www.insidechina.com
Japan Ministry of Foreign Affairs
http://www.mofa.go.jp

The refusal of most European countries, including France and Germany, to support the U.S. military intervention in Iraq in 2003 or answer the call of the Untied States to join the "coalition of the willing" was an unprecedented breach in the Western Alliance. Many analysts interpreted this policy breach within the context of longer term changes in the structure of the international system as the world moves from a unipolar to a multipolar world. This longer term perspective views conflicts between the United States and Europe as inevitable as the Untied States aims to assert its hegemony over Europe while France and Germany seek to create a European counter balance to U.S. hegemony.

In "The Transatlantic Turnaround," Charles A. Kupchan describes how the Bush Administration, after hitting rock bottom in 2003 with the U.S. invasion of Iraq, made progress in repairing relations with Atlantic alliance partners in recent years. Recent events and trends such as the Russian invasion in Georgia, Taliban advances in the war in Afghanistan against NATO forces, and the worsening global economic crisis during 2008 further served to stimulate a search for greater solidarity among NATO allies. These trends also underscore the merits of trying to engaging Russia and China in multinational diplomatic efforts to settle conflicts and find coordinated solutions to the global economic crisis.

The existing cleavages among European countries, the United States, Russia, and China along with simultaneous requirements that the major powers need to cooperate to maintain peace and prosperity were dramatically on view in rounds of meetings of presidents and prime ministers from around the world during the fall of 2008 in Washington DC. Various meetings of the G-8 and G-20 nation-states were held in an attempt to negotiate agreements on the shape of future global financial regulations. While European heads of states generally pushed for new roles for international organizations to monitor banks operating across borders, the Bush administration was reluctant to grant new powers to international organizations. The Chinese joined their European counterparts in calling for an overhaul of current regulatory systems but made clear that they would stop short of supporting a proposal for a worldwide organization with significant power that could affect the sovereignty of countries.

Russia's role in the current economic crisis has less impact on relations among the major nation-state actors than the country's more aggressive foreign policies. In recent years, Russia's more assertive foreign policies have play a key role in shaping relations between Europe and the United States. The fatal radioactive poisoning of a former Russian spy, Alexander Litvinenko, who was living in Great Britain when he was poisoned, reminded many of the type of intrigue that was more commonplace during the Cold War. Now that the Cold War is over, the relations between the Russian and Western states are expected to follow traditional norms of diplomacy. This expectation may be one reason why Russia's military invasion of Georgia

© Digital Vision/Getty Images

caught many statesmen and observers by surprise. However, Russia's foreign policy has always contained complex and often contradictory trends. These contradictions are due in part to the fact that the current Russian political economic system and government has quickly transitioned over the past 13 years from a communist state, to a fledgling democracy and capitalist system, to a "managed democracy" with many features of the old authoritarian regime. Worsening economic conditions facilitated a shift back to state control that has accelerated under the tutelage of former KGB leader and former President Vladimir Putin. Putin stepped down from the Presidency in May of 2008 and now holds the position of Prime Minister for a second time. Most Russians supported Putin's policies of re-consolidating power in the central government, the government's hard-line approach to dealing with Chechen rebels, and the recent military intervention into Georgia. Most observers expect the new President, Dmitry Medvedev, to play a supporting role to Putin who is widely thought to continue exercising power from his new position as Prime Minister. Events in the former Soviet Union are also complex because the former USSR is a region composed of 15 independent nation-states, with each state trying to define separate national interests as they experience severe economic problems. Many ex-Soviet citizens share a sense of disorientation and "pocketbook shock" as their standard of living is lower today than it was under communism. About half of the states are experiencing political instability and growing discontent.

Since the end of the Cold War, many Western statesmen and observers have either forgotten or tend to minimize the complex factors that shape policies in Russia and other former Soviet Union-controlled nation-states. Two icons of the U.S. foreign policy establishment, Henry Kissinger and George Shultz recently warned that the drift towards confrontation with Russia after its military invasion in Georgia must end. In "Building on Common Ground with Russia," the two elder statesmen point out that the

Georgian crisis originated in a series of miscalculations. They go on to note that while America has an important stake in the territorial integrity of an independent Georgia, the U.S. must also use diplomacy and appreciate Russian perceptions of recent events in dealings with a former adversary. They point out that a document known as the Sochi agreement that President Bush and then-President Putin agreed to in April 2008 outlined a program of joint cooperation to deal with long-term requirements of world order. Kissinger and Shultz argue that this document can provide a useful road map for the U.S. government's dealing with Europe and Russia.

The changing power structure of the world system means that informed observers of International Relations must pay closer attention to trends outside of the Western axis of the United States, Europe, and Russia. In "Lifting the Bamboo Curtain," Robert Kaplan helps us understand changing trends in Asia by describing how China is quietly working to create a political and economic zone of influence throughout Southeast Asia. China's foreign policies include plans for a new port, oil refinery, and hub for oil and natural gas for resources coming from East Africa and the Middle East. According to Kaplan, India is current working to avoid being blocked from her access to ports along the coast in this region. Kaplan underscores the importance of understanding the context and dynamics of local politics in his concluding assessment that the struggle over the eastern part of the Indian Ocean may "come down to who deals more adroitly with the Burmese hill tribes."

The Transatlantic Turnaround

CHARLES A. KUPCHAN

The Atlantic alliance has made a remarkable recovery over the course of President George W. Bush's second term. Relations between the United States and Europe hit rock bottom after the US-led invasion of Iraq in 2003, raising the prospect of an irreparable transatlantic rift. Although the war won grudging support from some European governments, it was staunchly opposed by many of the continent's citizens. Acrimony and recriminations engulfed diplomacy as well as public debate. The Atlantic community faced its most serious crisis since World War II.

This crisis and the charged rhetoric that accompanied it have since abated. Over the past three years, the Bush administration and its European counterparts have worked hard to mend fences—with impressive results. And it is not only the atmospherics that have changed. The United States and its European partners are fighting together in Afghanistan. They are working jointly to rein in Iran's nuclear program, negotiate peace between Israelis and Palestinians, and ease Kosovo toward formal independence.

From the European perspective, the Bush administration continues to fall short of expectations on several fronts—especially curbing climate change. But even on this issue, which President Bush effectively dismissed during his first term, Washington has now moved forward, agreeing to multilateral negotiations over a successor to the Kyoto Protocol and supporting measures to reduce consumption of fossil fuels.

Recognizing Reality

The improvement in Atlantic relations has been a matter of necessity, not choice. The Bush administration once thought the United States was strong enough to run the world on its own. The debacle in Iraq proved otherwise. For their part, many Europeans initially welcomed a distancing from Washington. With the end of the cold war and with the European Union's growing economic and political muscle, it was time—the argument went—for the EU to countenance life without its American guardian. But with the Atlantic link on the verge of being severed, the EU soon found itself adrift and deeply divided. Both Americans and Europeans, after getting a glimpse of what it would be like to go it alone, realized they remained each other's best partners.

Recognition of this strategic reality was reflected in—but also fostered by—changes in key leadership positions on both sides of the Atlantic. In Washington, though President Bush and Vice President Dick Cheney remained in charge, their top echelon of foreign advisers changed dramatically. Out were Paul Wolfowitz, John Bolton, Douglas Feith, Donald Rumsfeld, and others responsible for the ideological excesses of the first term. In were Condoleezza Rice, Robert Zoellick, Robert Kimmitt, Robert Gates, and others associated with a more pragmatic and centrist brand of internationalism.

In Europe, elections rather than political appointments were the main driver of change. Bush's main allies in Europe—Tony Blair in Great Britain, José María Aznar in Spain, and Silvio Berlusconi in Italy—all lost the confidence of their citizens and are no longer in office. But also gone are Gerhard Schröder of Germany and Jacques Chirac of France, the two leaders who led the charge against the Iraq War. Curiously, these leaders' successors—Angela Merkel in Berlin and Nicolas Sarkozy in Paris—are far more Atlanticist and pro-American than were their predecessors. Both Merkel and Sarkozy campaigned primarily on domestic issues, not foreign policy. But it nonetheless speaks volumes that even after the ill will toward the United States provoked by the Iraq War, both Germans and Frenchmen voted into office leaders intent on repairing Atlantic relations.

The White House no doubt misses Blair, its most stalwart ally, especially because his successor, Prime Minister Gordon Brown, has been keeping his distance from the Bush administration. On balance, however, Washington has more leverage in Europe today than it did when Blair was in office. Working through London had a major drawback for the United States: Britain's own reluctance to integrate fully into the EU (the United Kingdom, for example, remains outside the euro zone) means that its influence in Europe is limited. Washington in this respect is better off dealing directly with Berlin and Paris, long the dual locomotives of European integration, instead of working through its offshore ally.

This year's election in the United States has the potential to advance further the repair of the Atlantic link. President Bush, despite the conciliatory overtures of his second term, remains a singularly unpopular figure in Europe. The bitter legacy of the Iraq War, Bush's stingy approach to fighting climate change, his refusal to negotiate with Iran, his policies on treatment of detainees—all these continue to generate ire. Should the Democrats prevail in the presidential contest, transatlantic relations are poised to receive a new boost. Indeed, Europe awaits with bated breath the arrival of a Democrat in the White House.

High Expectations

Although a change of leadership in Washington will no doubt brighten the prospects for transatlantic comity, both Americans and Europeans should keep their expectations in check. A Democratic administration would not be satisfied with just a warm welcome from Europe; the new US government would also expect the Europeans to shoulder more international burdens. In the probably correct belief that the EU had not gone out of its way to do favors for the Bush administration, a Democratic White House would seek greater European assistance in Afghanistan, Iraq, and other trouble areas. The Democratic candidates, after all, are promising the electorate that the United States will benefit not just from renewed respect abroad, but also from a reduction in the nation's onerous overseas commitments.

Some such help may be forthcoming from Europe—but not much. EU member states simply do not have the personnel and military assets needed to undertake a substantial expansion of their missions abroad. To be sure, the union is in the midst of reforming its institutions in order to allow greater coherence on foreign policy. But that project will advance only slowly. And as casualties mount in Afghanistan, EU member states will find the war increasingly unpopular—even if a Democrat controls the White House.

Meanwhile, Europeans will be expecting an about-face in foreign policy from a Democratic administration. Yet, while some change will be in the offing, the next US president will not hold a strong hand of cards. Wars in Iraq and Afghanistan, instability and extremist violence in Pakistan, nuclear ambitions in Iran, an economic downturn at home, a deeply divided electorate—these inauspicious conditions will constrict the administration's room for maneuver as it seeks to pursue a new brand of statecraft.

An ebullient transatlantic reunion may be in store come January 2009. But then the hard realities of transatlantic cooperation will set in. The good news is that Americans and Europeans alike have realized that they will need each other for the foreseeable future. The sobering news is that transforming this recognition into concrete partnership will remain difficult—no matter who holds power on the two sides of the Atlantic.

An ebullient transatlantic reunion may be in store come January 2009. But then the hard realities of cooperation will set in.

CHARLES A. KUPCHAN is a professor of international affairs at Georgetown University and a senior fellow at the Council on Foreign Relations.

Building on Common Ground with Russia

Henry A. Kissinger and George P. Shultz

In 1914, an essentially local issue was seen by so many nations in terms of established fears and frustrations that it became global in scope and led to the First World War. There is no danger of general war today. But there is the risk that a conflict arising out of ancestral passions in the Caucasus will be treated as a metaphor for a larger conflict, threatening the imperative of building a new international order in a world of globalization, nuclear proliferation and ethnic conflicts.

The presence of Russian troops on the territory of a state newly independent from the old Soviet empire was bound to send tremors through the other countries that established themselves after the collapse of the Soviet Union. This has evoked a rhetoric of confrontation, reciprocal threats and retaliatory countermeasures: American naval forces have been in the Black Sea; Russian military and economic capability has been displayed in the Caribbean, as if from a 19th-century balance-of-power playbook.

The Georgian crisis is cited as proof that Vladimir Putin's Russia is committed to a strategy of unraveling the post-Soviet international order in Europe. A strategy of isolating Russia has been advocated in response. Until a recent meeting between Secretary of State Condoleezza Rice and Russian Foreign Minister Sergey Sergei Lavrov, the United States and Russia had been without high-level contact since early August. Nongovernmental contacts have been curtailed.

This drift toward confrontation must be ended. However appropriate as a temporary device for showing our concern, isolating Russia is not a sustainable long-range policy. It is neither feasible nor desirable to isolate a country adjoining Europe, Asia and the Middle East and possessing a stockpile of nuclear weapons comparable to that of the United States. Given Russia's historically ambivalent and emotionally insecure relations with its environment, this approach is not likely to evoke considered or constructive responses. Even much of Western Europe is uneasy about such a course.

In 1983, when the Soviets shot down a Korean airliner that had wandered into their airspace, the United States vigorously invited all countries to join in sharp condemnation. Yet President Ronald Reagan ordered our arms-control negotiators back to Geneva. Strength and diplomacy remained in step.

Like most wars, the Georgian crisis originated in a series of miscalculations. Tbilisi misjudged its scope for military action and the magnitude of Russia's response. For its part, Moscow may have been surprised by the West's reaction to the scale of its intervention. It also may not have fully considered the impact that recognition of South Ossetia and Abkhazia as independent states would have on other countries with geographically distinct ethnic minorities, or the precedent this action might establish, even for some regions of Russia.

Yet these miscalculations should not be allowed to dominate future policy. America has an important stake in the territorial integrity of an independent Georgia but not in a confrontational diplomacy toward Russia by its neighbors. Russia needs to understand that the use or threat of military force evokes memories that reinforce the very obstacles to cooperative relations that are the basis of its grievances. America must decide whether to deal with Russia as a possible strategic partner or as a threat to be combated by principles drawn from the Cold War. Of course, should Russia pursue the policies its detractors assign to it, America must resist with all appropriate measures. Those of us who had responsibilities in conducting the Cold War would take the lead in supporting such a strategy.

We are not yet at this point. Russia's leaders undoubtedly deplore the dissolution of the Russian and Soviet empire. But if they have any realism—and in our experience they do—they know that it is impossible and dangerous to seek to reverse Russia's history by military means.

Russian history displays a tale of ambivalent oscillation between the restraints of the European order and the temptations for expansion into the strategic vacuums along its borders in Asia and the Middle East. These vacuums no longer exist. In the west, NATO is a formidable strategic presence. In the east, there is a resurgent Asia, to which the center of gravity of world affairs is shifting. In the south, Russia faces a partly radicalized Islam along a lengthy border. Internally, demographic prospects are for decline in the total population and a relative rise in the percentage of its Muslim portion, which is partly disaffected. Russia has not been able to address its infrastructure and health deficit adequately. With a gross domestic product less than one-sixth that of the United States (in purchasing power parity terms) and a defense budget significantly smaller than those of the European Union and the United States, Russia is not well placed to conduct a superpower struggle. Whatever their rhetoric, Russian leaders know this.

What they have sought, sometimes clumsily, is acceptance as equals in a new international system rather than as losers of a Cold War to whom terms could be dictated. Their methods have occasionally been truculent. Understanding the psychology of its international environment has never been a Russian specialty—partly because of the historic difference in domestic evolution between Russia and its neighbors, especially in the West.

But fairness requires some acknowledgment that the West has not always been sensitive to how the world looks from Moscow. Consider the evolution of NATO. For its first 50 years, NATO legitimized itself as a defensive alliance. In undertaking a war of choice against Yugoslavia in 1999, NATO proclaimed the right to achieve its moral aspirations by offensive military action. (We strongly supported NATO policy at the time.) The war to stop Serbian human rights violations in Kosovo, ended in part by Russian mediation, provided for an autonomous Kosovo under titular Serbian sovereignty but de facto European Union supervision. Earlier this year, that status was changed by, in effect, a unilateral decision of a group of European nations and the United States to declare independence for Kosovo without U.N. endorsement and over strenuous Russian objection.

The Kosovo decision occurred nearly simultaneously with publication of the plan to move anti-ballistic missiles into Poland and the Czech Republic as well as a proposal to invite Ukraine and Georgia to join NATO. Moving the East-West security line, in a historically short period, 1,000 miles to the east while changing the mission of NATO and deploying advanced weapons technology on the territory of former Soviet satellites was not likely to be met with Russian acquiescence.

This narrative explains some of Russia's motivations; it does not seek to justify every response or the confrontational rhetoric occasionally employed. But it suggests the importance of viewing the current conflict with some historical and psychological perspective.

Immediate crises should not deflect us from long-term responsibilities. The six points put forward by French President Nicolas Sarkozy provide a framework for a solution of the Georgian crisis formally accepted by all the parties: a genuinely independent Georgia, within its existing borders, while the status

of South Ossetia and Abkhazia—disputed since the founding of Georgia—continues as the subject of negotiation within the security framework in Sarkozy's points.

In April, President Bush and then-President Putin met in Sochi and outlined a program of joint cooperation to deal with the long-term requirements of world order. It included such subjects as nonproliferation, Iran, energy, climate change, methods to defuse the impact of the anti-ballistic missile deployment in Eastern Europe, and a possible linking of some American and Russian anti-ballistic missile defense systems. The two countries possess more than 90 percent of the world's nuclear weapons; cooperation is imperative if proliferation is to be stopped.

The Sochi document provides a useful road map. Russia, of course, should not be allowed to use the invocation of the common interest as a way to achieve its special concerns by military pressure and intimidation. Those of us who question the urgency with which NATO membership was pursued for Georgia and Ukraine are not advocating a sphere of influence for Russia in Eastern Europe. We consider Ukraine an essential part of the European architecture, and we favor a rapid evolution toward E.U. membership. We do believe that the security of Ukraine and Georgia should be placed in a larger context than mechanically advancing an integrated NATO command to a few hundred miles from Moscow. NATO has already agreed to the principle of membership for Ukraine and Georgia. Delaying its implementation until a new U.S. administration is able to consider its options is not a concession but responsible management of the future.

Finally, our ability to conduct effective foreign policy toward Russia requires energetic efforts to restore our domestic strength. Our financial house must be put in order, regarding not just the immediate crisis but also the structure of entitlement programs. We are far too dependent on oil imports. We need legislation that gives a long-term horizon to comprehensive and determined efforts to end this state of affairs.

Diplomacy without strength is sterile. Strength without diplomacy tempts posturing. We believe that the fundamental interests of the United States, Europe and Russia are more aligned today—or can be made so—even in the wake of the Georgian crisis, than at any point in recent history. We must not waste that opportunity.

HENRY A. KISSINGER was secretary of state from 1973 to 1977.
GEORGE P. SHULTZ was secretary of state from 1982 to 1989.

Lifting the Bamboo Curtain

As China and India vie for power and influence, Burma has become a strategic battleground. Four Americans with deep ties to this fractured, resource-rich country illuminate its current troubles, and what the U.S. should do to shape its future.

ROBERT D. KAPLAN

Monsoon clouds crushed the dark, seaweed-green landscape of eastern Burma. Steep hillsides glistened with teak trees, coconut palms, black and ocher mud from the heavy rains, and tall, chaotic grasses. As night came, the buzz saw of cicadas and the pestering croaks of geckos rose through the downpour. Guided by an ethnic Karen rebel with a torchlight attached by bare copper wires to an ancient six-volt battery slung around his neck, I stumbled across three bamboo planks over a fast-moving stream from Thailand into Burma. Any danger came less from Burmese government troops than from those of its democratic neighbor, whose commercial interests have made it a close friend of Burma's military regime. Said Thai Prime Minister Samak Sundaravej recently: the ruling Burmese generals are "good Buddhists" who like to meditate, and Burma is a country that "lives in peace." The Thai military has been on the lookout for Karen soldiers, who have been fighting the Burmese government since 1948.

"It ended in Vietnam, in Cambodia. When will it end in Burma?" asked Saw Roe Key, a Karen I met shortly after I crossed the border. He had lost a leg to a Toe Popper antipersonnel mine—the kind that the regime has littered throughout the hills that are home to more than a half-dozen ethnic groups in some stage of revolt. Of the two dozen or so Karens I encountered at an outpost inside Burma, four were missing a leg from a mine. Some wore green camouflage fatigues and were armed with M-16s and AK-47s; most were in T-shirts and traditional skirts, or *longyis*. Built into a hillside under the forest canopy, the camp was a jumble of wooden-plank huts on stilts roofed with dried teak leaves, with a solar panel and an ingenious water system. Beyond the camp beckoned perfect guerrilla country.

Sawbawh Pah, 50, small and stocky with only a tuft of hair on his scalp, runs a clinic here for wounded soldiers and people uprooted from their homes, of whom there have been 1.5 million in Burma. The Burmese junta, known as the State Peace and Development Council (SPDC), has razed more than 3,000 villages in Karen state alone—one reason *The Washington Post* has called Burma a "slow-motion Darfur." With a simple, resigned expression that some might mistake for a smile, he told me, "My father was killed by the SPDC. My uncle was killed by the SPDC. My cousin was killed by the SPDC. They shot my uncle in the head and cut off his leg while he was looking for food after the village was destroyed." Over a meal of fried noodles and eggs, I was inundated with life stories like Pah's. Their power lay in their grueling repetition.

Major Kea Htoo, the commander of the local battalion of Karen guerrillas, had reddened lips and a swollen left cheek from chewing betel nut. Like his comrades, he told me he saw no end to the war. They were fighting not for a better regime composed of more enlightened military officers, nor for a democratic government that would likely be led by ethnic Burmans like Aung San Suu Kyi, but for Karen independence. Tu Lu, missing a leg, had been in the Karen army for 20 years. Kyi Aung, the oldest at 55, had been fighting for 34 years. These guerrillas are paid no salaries. They receive only food and basic medicine. Their lives have been condensed to the seemingly unrealistic goal of independence; since Burma first fell under military misrule in 1962, nobody has ever offered them anything resembling a compromise. Although the junta has trapped the Karens, Shans, and other ethnics into small redoubts, its corrupt and desertion-plagued military lacks the strength for the final kill. So the war continues.

Endless conflict and gross, regime-inflicted poverty have kept Burma primitive enough to maintain an aura of romance. Like Tibet and Darfur, it offers its advocates in the post-industrial West a cause with both moral urgency and aesthetic appeal. In 1952, the British writer Norman Lewis published *Golden Earth,* a spare and haunting masterpiece about his travels throughout Burma. The insurrections of the Karens, Shans, and other hill tribes make the author's peregrinations dangerous, and therefore even more uncomfortable. He found that only a small region in the north, inhabited largely by the Kachin tribe, was "completely free from bandits or insurgent armies." Lewis spends a night tormented by rats, cockroaches, and a scorpion, yet wakes none the worse in the morning to the "mighty whirring of hornbills flying overhead." His bodily sufferings seem a small price to pay for the uncanny beauty of a country of broken roads and no adequate hotels, where "the condition of the soul replaces that of the stock markets as a topic for polite conversation." More than 50 years later, what shocks about this book is how contemporary it seems. A Western relief worker arriving in the wake of last spring's devastating cyclone could have followed Lewis's itinerary and had similar experiences. By contrast, think of all the places where globalization has made even a 10-year-old travel guide out of date.

But Burma is more than a place to feel sorry for. And its ethnic struggles are of more than obscurantist interest. For one thing, they precipitated the military coup that toppled the country's last civilian government almost a half century ago, when General Ne Win took power in part to forestall ethnic demands for greater autonomy. With one-third of Burma's population composed of ethnic minorities living in its fissiparous borderlands (which account for seven of Burma's 14 states and divisions), the demands of the Karens and others will return to the fore once the military regime collapses. Democracy will not deliver Burma from being a cobbled-together mini-empire of nationalities, even if it does open the door to compromise among them.

Moreover, Burma's hill tribes form part of a new and larger geopolitical canvas. Burma fronts on the Indian Ocean, by way of the Bay of Bengal. Its neighbors India and China (not to mention Thailand) covet its abundant oil, natural gas, uranium, coal, zinc, copper, precious stones, timber, and hydropower. China especially needs a cooperative, if not supine, Burma for the construction of deepwater ports, highways, and energy pipelines that can open China's landlocked south and west to the sea, enabling its ever-burgeoning middle class to receive speedier deliveries of oil from the Persian Gulf. These routes must pass north from the Indian Ocean through the very territories wracked by Burma's ethnic insurrections.

Burma is a prize to be contested, and China and India are not-so-subtly vying for it. But in a world shaped by ethnic struggles, higher fuel prices, new energy pathways, and climate-change-driven natural disasters like the recent cyclone, Burma also represents a microcosm of the strategic challenges that the United States will face. The U.S. Navy underscored these factors in its new maritime strategy, released in late 2007, which indicated that the Navy will shift its attention from the Atlantic to the Indian Ocean and the western Pacific. The Marines, too, in their new "Vision and Strategy 2025" statement, highlight the Indian Ocean as among their main theaters of activity in coming years.

But toward Burma specifically, U.S. policy seems guided more by strategic myopia. The Bush administration, like its predecessors, has loudly embraced the cause of Burmese democracy but has done too little to advance it, either by driving diplomatic initiatives in the region or by supporting any of the ethnic insurgencies. Indeed, Special Operations Command is too preoccupied with the western half of the Indian Ocean, the Arab/Persian half, to pay much attention to Burma, which lacks the energizing specter of an Islamic terror threat. Meanwhile, the administration's reliance on sanctions and its unwillingness

to engage with the ruling junta has left the field open to China, India, and other countries swayed more by commercial than moral concerns.

But some Americans are consumed by Burma, and they offer a window onto different, and perhaps more fruitful, ways of engaging with its complex realities. I saw Burma through the eyes of four such men. In most cases, I cannot identify them by name, either because of the tenuousness of their position in neighboring Thailand, whose government is not friendly to their presence, or because of the sensitivity of what they do and whom they work for. Their expertise illustrates what it takes to make headway in Burma, while their goals say a great deal about what is at stake.

The Son of the Blue-Eyed Shan

While the mess in Iraq has made the virtues of cultural expertise newly fashionable, champions of such experience often conveniently forget that many of America's greatest area experts have been Christian missionaries. American history has seen two strains of missionary area experts: the old Arab hands and the Asia, or China, hands. The Arab hands were Protestant missionaries who in the early 19th century traveled to Lebanon and ended up founding what became the American University of Beirut. From their lineage descended the State Department Arabists of the Cold War era. The Asia hands have a similarly distinguished origin, beginning, too, in the 19th century and providing the U.S. government with much of its area expertise through the early Cold War, when, during the McCarthy era, a number of them were unjustly purged. One American who counseled me on Burma is descended from several generations of Baptist missionaries from the Midwest who ministered to the hill tribes beginning in the late 19th century. His father, known as "The Blue-Eyed Shan," escaped Burma ahead of the invading Japanese and was conscripted into Britain's Indian army, in which he commanded a Shan battalion. Among my acquaintance's earliest childhood memories was the sight of Punjabi soldiers ordering work gangs of Japanese prisoners of war to pick up rubble in the Burmese capital of Rangoon. With no formal education, he speaks Shan, Burmese, Hindi, Thai, and the Yunnan and Mandarin dialects of Chinese. He has spent his life studying Burma, though the 1960s saw him elsewhere in Indochina, aiding America's effort in Vietnam.

During our conversation, he sat erect and cross-legged on a raised platform, wearing a *longyi*. Gray-haired, with a sculpted face and an authoritative, courtly Fred Thompson voice, he has the bearing of an elder statesman, tempered by a certain gentleness. "Chinese intelligence is beginning to operate with the antiregime Burmese ethnic hill tribes," he told me. "The Chinese want the dictatorship in Burma to remain, but being pragmatic, they also have alternative plans for the country. The warning that comes from senior Chinese intelligence officers to the Karens, the Shans, and other ethnics is to 'come to us for help—not the Americans—since we are next door and will never leave the area.'"

At the same time, he explained, the Chinese are reaching out to young military officers in Thailand. In recent years, the

Thai royal family and the Thai military—particularly the special forces and cavalry—have been sympathetic to the hill tribes fighting the pro-Chinese military junta; Thailand's civilian politicians, influenced by lobbies wanting to do business with resource-rich Burma, have been the junta's best allies. In sum, democracy in Thailand is momentarily the enemy of democracy in Burma.

But the Chinese, the Son of the Blue-Eyed Shan implied, are still not satisfied: they want *both* Thailand's democrats and military officers on their side, even as they work with *both* Burma's junta and its ethnic opponents. "A new bamboo curtain may be coming down on Southeast Asia," he worried. This would not be a hard-and-fast wall like the Iron Curtain; nor would it be part of some newly imagined Asian domino theory. Rather, it would create a zone of Chinese political and economic influence fostered by, among other factors, American neglect. While the Chinese operate at every level in Burma and Thailand, top Bush-administration officials have skipped summits of the Association of Southeast Asian Nations. My friend simply wanted the United States back in the game.

"To topple the regime in Burma," he says, "the ethnics need a full-time advisory capability, not in-and-out soldiers of fortune. This would include a coordination center inside Thailand. There needs to be a platform for all the disaffected officers in the Burmese military to defect to." Again, rather than a return to the early Vietnam era, he was talking about a more subtle, more clandestine version of the support the United States provided the Afghan mujahideen during the 1980s. The current Thai administration would be hostile to that, but the government in Bangkok, and its policies, routinely changes. The military could yet return to power there, and even if it doesn't, if the U.S. signaled its intent to support the Burmese hill tribes against a regime hated the world over, the Thai security apparatus would find a way to assist.

"The Shans and the Kachins near the Chinese border," my friend went on, "have gotten a raw deal from the Burmese junta, but they are also nervous about a dominant China. They feel squeezed. And unity for the hill tribes of Burma is almost impossible. Somebody from the outside must provide a mechanism upon which they can all depend." Larger than England and France combined, Burma has historically been a crazy quilt of vaguely demarcated states sectioned by jungly mountain ranges and the valleys of the Irrawaddy, Chindwin, Salween, and Mekong rivers. As a result, its various peoples remain distinct: the Chins in western Burma, for example, have almost nothing in common with the Karens in eastern Burma. Nor is there any community of language or culture between the Shans and the Burmans (the ethnic group, not the nationality, which is Burmese), save their Buddhist religion. Indeed, the Shans have much more in common with the Thais across the border.

But Burma should not be confused with the Balkans, or with Iraq, where ethnic and sectarian differences simmering for decades under a carapace of authoritarianism erupted once central authority dissolved. After so many years of violence, war fatigue has set in here, and the tribes show little propensity to fight each other after the regime unravels. They are more disunited than they are at odds. Even among themselves, the

Shans, as my friend told me, have been historically subdivided into states led by minor kings. As he sees it, such divisions open a quiet organizing opportunity for Americans of his ilk.

The Father of the White Monkey

Tha-U-Wa-A-Pa, or "The Father of the White Monkey" in Burmese, is also the son of Christian missionaries, originally from Texas. Except for nine years in the U.S. Army, including in Special Forces, from which he retired as a major, he has been, like his parents, a missionary in one form or another. He also speaks a number of the local languages. He is much younger than my other acquaintance and much more animated, with a ropy, muscular body in perpetual motion, as if his system were running on too many candy bars. Whereas my other contact has focused on the Shan tribes near the Chinese border, the Father of the White Monkey—the sobriquet comes from the nickname he has given his daughter, who often travels with him—works mostly with the Karen and other tribes in eastern Burma abutting Thailand, though the networks he operates have ranged as far as the Indian border.

In 1996, he met the Burmese democracy leader Aung San Suu Kyi in Rangoon, while she was briefly not under house arrest. The meeting inspired him to initiate a "day of prayer" for Burma, and to work for its ethnic unity. During the 1997 Burmese army offensive that displaced more than 100,000 people, he was deep inside the country, alone, going from one burned-out village to another, handing out medicine from his backpack. He told me about this and other army offensives that he witnessed, in which churches were torched, children disemboweled, and whole families killed. "These stories don't make me numb," he said, his eyes popping open, facial muscles stretched. "Each is like the first one. I pray always that justice will come and be done."

In 1997, after that trip inside Burma, he started the Free Burma Rangers, a relief group that has launched more than 300 humanitarian missions and has 43 small medical teams among the Karens, Karennis, Shans, Chins, Kachins, and Arakanese— across the parts of highland Burma that embrace on three sides the central Irrawaddy River valley, home to the majority Burmans. As he told it, the Free Burma Rangers is an unusual nongovernmental organization. "We stand with the villagers; we're not above them. If they don't run from the government troops, we don't either. We have a medic, a photographer, and a reporter/intel guy in each team that marks the GPS positions of Burmese government troops, maps the camps, and takes pictures with a telephoto lens, all of which we post on our Web site. We deal with the Pentagon, with human-rights groups . . . There is a higher moral obligation to intervene on the side of good, since silence is a form of consent.

"NGOs," he went on in a racing voice, "like to claim that they are above politics. Not true. The very act of providing aid assists one side or another, however indirectly. NGOs take sides all the time." The Father of the White Monkey takes this hard truth several steps further. Whereas the Thais host Burmese refugee camps on their side of the border, and the ethnic insurgents run camps inside Burma for internally displaced people—even as the Karens and other ethnics have mobile clinics near Burmese army concentrations—the backpacking Free Burma Rangers operate *behind* enemy lines.

Like my other acquaintance, the Father of the White Monkey is a very evolved form of special operator. One might suspect that the Free Burma Rangers is on some government payroll in Washington. But the truth is more pathetic. "We are funded by church groups around the world. Our yearly budget is $600,000. We were down to $150 at one point; we all prayed and the next day got a grant for $70,000. We work hand to mouth." For him, Burma is not a job but a lifelong obsession.

"Burma is not Cambodia under the Khmer Rouge," he told me. "It's not genocide. It's not a car wreck. It's a slow, creeping cancer, in which the regime is working to dominate, control, and radically assimilate all the ethnic peoples of the country." I was reminded of what Jack Dunford, the executive director of the Thailand Burma Border Consortium, had told me in Bangkok. The military regime was "relentless, building dams, roads, and huge agricultural projects, taking over mines, laying pipelines," sucking in cash from neighboring powers and foreign companies, selling off natural resources at below market value—all to entrench itself in power.

Once, not long ago, the Father of the White Monkey was sitting on a hillside at night, in an exposed location between the Burmese army and a cluster of internal refugees whom the army had driven from their homes. The Karen soldiers he was with had fired rocket-propelled grenades at the Burmese army position, and in response the Burmese soldiers began firing mortar rounds at him. At that moment, he got a message on his communications gear from a friend at the Pentagon asking why the United States should be interested in Burma.

He tapped back a slew of reasons that ranged from totalitarianism to the devastation of hardwood forests, from religious persecution of Buddhist monks to the use of prisoners as mine sweepers, and much else. But, ever the missionary, the Father of the White Monkey barely touched on strategic or regional-security issues. When I asked him his denomination, he responded, "I'm a Christian." As such, he believes he is doing God's work, engaged morally first and foremost, especially with the Karens, who number many Christians, converted by people like his parents. He is the kind of special operator the U.S. security bureaucracy can barely accept, for becoming one involves taking sides and going native to a degree. And yet, operatives like him offer the level of expertise that the United States desperately needs, if it is to have influence without being overbearing in remote parts of the globe.

The Colonel

Timothy Heinemann, a retired Army colonel from Laguna Beach, California, does think strategically. He is also a veteran of Special Forces. I first met him in 2002 at the Command and General Staff College at Fort Leavenworth, Kansas, where he was the dean of academics. He now runs Worldwide Impact, an NGO that helps ethnic groups, as well as a number of crossborder projects, particularly sending media teams into Burma

to record the suffering there. Another kind of special operator, Heinemann, with his flip-flops and his engaging manner, embodies the subtle, indirect approach to managing conflict emphasized in the 2006 Quadrennial Defense Review, one of the Pentagon's primary planning documents. Heinemann says that he "privatizes condition-setting." He explains: "We are networkers on both sides of the border. We try to find opportunities for NGOs to collaborate better in supporting ethnic groups' needs. I do my small part to set conditions so that America can protect national, international, and humanitarian interests with real savvy. Our work is well known to various branches of the U.S. government. The opposition to the military dictatorship has no strategic and operational planning like Hezbollah does. Aung San Suu Kyi is little more than a symbol of the wrong issue—'Democracy first!' Ethnic rights and the balance of ethnic power are preconditions for democracy in Burma. These issues must be faced first, or little has been learned from the lessons of Afghanistan and Iraq." Heinemann, like the Father of the White Monkey, also lives hand to mouth, grabbing grants and donations from wherever he can, and is sometimes reduced to financing trips himself. He finds Burma "exotic, intoxicating."

Burma is also a potential North Korea, he says, as well as a perfect psychological operations target. He and others explained that the Russians are helping the Burmese government to mine uranium in the Kachin and Chin regions in the north and west, with the North Koreans waiting in the wings to supply nuclear technology. The Burmese junta craves some sort of weapons-of-mass-destruction capability to provide it with international leverage. "But the regime is paranoid," Heinemann points out. "It's superstitious. They're rolling chicken bones on the ground to see what to do next.

"Burma's got a 400,000-man army [the active-duty U.S. Army is 500,000] that's prone to mutiny," Heinemann went on. "Only the men at the very top are loyal. You could spread rumors, conduct information warfare. It might not take much to unravel it." (Burmese soldiers are reportedly getting only a portion of their salaries, and their weapons at major bases are locked up at night.) On the other hand, the military constitutes the country's most secure social-welfare system, and that buys a certain amount of loyalty from the troops. And yet, "there is no trust by the higher-ups of the lower ranks," according to a Karen resistance source. The junta leader, Than Shwe, a former postal clerk who has never been to the West, is known, along with his wife, to consult an astrologer. "He governs out of fear; he is not brave," notes Aung Zaw, editor of *The Irrawaddy,* a magazine run by Burmese exiles in the northwestern Thai city of Chiang Mai. "And Than Shwe rarely speaks publicly; he has even less charisma than Ne Win," the dictator from 1962 to 1988.

Heinemann and Aung Zaw each recounted to me how the regime suddenly deserted Rangoon one day in 2005 and moved the capital north, halfway to Mandalay, to Naypyidaw, "the abode of kings," which it built from scratch, with funds from Burma's natural-gas revenues. The date of the move was astrologically timed. The new capital lies deep in the forest and is fortified with underground bunkers designed to protect against an American invasion. Heinemann sees China, India, and other

Asian nations jockeying for position with one of the world's worst, weirdest, wealthiest, and most strategically placed rogue regimes, which is vulnerable to a coup or even disintegration, if only the United States adopted the kind of patient, low-key, and inexpensive approach that he and my other two acquaintances advocate.

Heinemann's last job in the military was as a planner for the occupation of Iraq, and he was an eyewitness to the mistakes of a massive military machine that disregarded local realities. He sees Burma as the inverse of Iraq, a place where the United States can do itself a lot of good, and do much good for others, if it fights smart.

The Bull That Swims

And then there is Ta Doe Tee, or "The Bull That Swims," another American, whom I met in his suite in one of Bangkok's most expensive hotels. His impeccably tailored black suit barely masked an intimidating physique—the reason for his Burmese nickname—and his business card defines him as a "compradore," an all-purpose factotum steeped in local culture, the kind of enabler who was vital to the running of the British East India Company. The Bull was a staff sergeant in Special Forces in the 1970s and now works in the security business in Southeast Asia.

He is of the Army Special Forces generation that was frustrated about having just missed service in Vietnam, with little to do overseas during the presidency of Jimmy Carter. Stationed at Fort Devens, Massachusetts, in the mid-1970s, he was mentored, commanded, and led by some of the Son Tay Raiders. "Dick Meadows, Greg McGuire, Jack Joplin, Joe Lupyak"—he recites their names with reverence—were SFs who stormed the Son Tay prison camp near Hanoi in 1970 in a failed attempt to rescue American prisoners of war. "Vietnam and Southeast Asia were all they ever talked about," he told me.

But in 1978, Jimmy Carter's head of the CIA, Admiral Stansfield Turner, fired or forced into early retirement almost 200 officers running agents stationed abroad who had been providing intelligence, and many of them were in Southeast Asia. The CIA's clandestine service was devastated. As the Bull tells the story, many of the fired officers would not simply "be turned off," and decided to maintain self-supporting networks, "picking up kids" like himself along the way, just out of Special Forces. They sent him to learn to sail and fly, and he became a certified ship's master for cargo vessels and an FAA-certified pilot. In the 1980s, he became involved in operations in Southeast Asia, such as bringing equipment to the Khmer Rouge in Cambodia. He blurred the line between such controversial and shadowy government operations and the illegal means sometimes used to sustain them: in 1988, while trying to bring 70 tons of marijuana to the West Coast of the United States with a Southeast Asian crew under his command, he was boarded by the U.S. Coast Guard. He served five years in prison in the U.S. and has been back in Southeast Asia ever since.

The Bull put on reading glasses and opened a shiny black loose-leaf notebook to a map of the Indian Ocean. A line drawn on the map went from Ethiopia and Somalia across the water past India, and then north up the Bay of Bengal, through the heart of Burma, to China's Yunnan province. "This map is just an example of how CNOC [the Chinese National Oil Company] sees the world," he explained.

He showed me another map, which zoomed in on Ethiopia and Somalia, with grid marks on the significant reserves of oil and natural gas in the Ogaden Basin on the Ethiopian-Somali border. A circle was drawn around Hobyo, a Somali port visited in the early 15th century by the Chinese admiral Zheng He, whose treasure fleets plied the same Indian Ocean sea lanes that serve as today's energy routes. "Oil and natural gas would be shipped from Hobyo direct to western Burma," the Bull said, where the Chinese are building a new port at Kyauk Phyu, in Burma's Arakan state, that will be able to handle the world's largest container ships. According to him, the map shows how easy it will be for the Chinese to operate all over the Indian Ocean, "tapping into Iran and other Persian Gulf energy suppliers." Their biggest problem, though, will be cutting through Burma. "The Chinese need to acquire Burma, and keep it stable," said the Bull.

There are other routes to energy-hungry inner China besides the one through Burma. The Chinese are also developing a deepwater port in Gwadar, in Pakistani Baluchistan, close to the Iranian border, and have plans to do the same in Chittagong in Bangladesh. Both ports would be closer than Beijing and Shanghai to cities in western China. But the Burmese route is the most direct from the Indian Ocean.

This whole development is part of the Chinese navy's "string of pearls" strategy, which—coupled with a canal that the Chinese may one day help finance across Thailand's Isthmus of Kra, linking the Bay of Bengal with the South China Sea—will give China access to the Indian Ocean. China is, in effect, expanding south, even as India, to keep from being strategically encircled by the Chinese navy, is expanding east—also into Burma.

Until 2001, India, the world's largest democracy, took the high road on Burma, condemning it for its repression and providing moral support for the cause of Aung San Suu Kyi, who had studied in New Delhi. But as senior Indian leaders told me on a recent visit, India could not just watch Chinese influence expand unchecked. Burma's jungles serve as a rear base for insurgents from eastern India's own mélange of warring ethnic groups. Furthermore, as Greg Sheridan, foreign editor of *The Australian,* has observed, India has been "aghast" to see the establishment of Chinese listening stations along Burma's border with India. So in 2001, India decided to provide Burma with military aid and training, selling it tanks, helicopters, shoulder-fired surface-to-air missiles, and rocket launchers.

India also decided to build its own energy-pipeline network through Burma. In fact, during the 2007 crackdown on the monks in Burma, India's petroleum minister signed a deal for deepwater exploration. Off the coast of Burma's western Arakan state, adjacent to Bangladesh, are the Shwe gas fields, among the largest natural reserves in the world, from which two pipeline systems will likely emerge. One will be China's at Kyauk Phyu, which will take deliveries of oil and gas from as far away as the Persian Gulf and the Horn of Africa, as well as from Shwe itself. The other pipeline system will belong to India, which is spending $100 million to develop the Arakanese port of Sittwe as a trade window for its own landlocked, insurgency-roiled northeast.

There is nothing sinister about any of this: it is the consequence of the intense need of hundreds of millions of people in India and China who will consume ever more energy as their lifestyles improve. As for China, it may not be a democracy, but little in its larger Indian Ocean strategy can be decried. China is not, and will likely never be, a truly hostile state like Iran.

But China's problems with Burma are actually just beginning, argues the Bull, and the United States must exploit them quietly. As he observed, the minutiae of tribal and ethnic differences can easily displace grand lines on a map and the plans of master strategists. Just look at Yugoslavia, at Iraq, at Israel-Palestine. Given the energy stakes, he sees the struggles of the Karens, Shans, Arakanese, and other minorities as constituting the "theater of activity" for his lifetime, something that the Turner firings had denied him. Burma is where the United States has to build a "UW [unconventional-war] capability," he said. Such would be the unofficial side of our competition with China, which should be forced over time to accept a democratic and highly federalized Burma, with strong links to the West.

Like the other three Americans, the Bull talked about the need to build and manage networks among the ethnic hill tribes, through the construction of schools, clinics, and irrigation systems. In particular, he focused on the Shan, the largest of the hill tribes, with 9 percent of Burma's population and about 20 percent of its territory. Allying with the Shans, he said, would give the United States a mechanism to curtail the flow of drugs in the area, and to create a balancing force against China right on its own border. In any Burmese democracy, the Shans would control a sizeable portion of the seats in parliament. More could be accomplished through nonmilitary aid to a specific Burmese hill tribe, he argued, than through some of the larger weapons and other defense programs the United States spends money on. The same strategy could be applied to the Chins in western Burma, with the help of India. Not just in Iraq, but in Burma, too, American policy in the coming years should be all about the tribes.

Winning the Endgame

But while the former Special Forces and other Asia hands I interviewed see Burma as central to American strategy, the active-duty Special Operations community does not, because it is under orders to focus on al-Qaeda. This, my acquaintances say, shows how America's obsession with al-Qaeda has warped its strategic vision, which should be dominated by the whole Indian Ocean, from Africa to the Pacific.

Larger U.S. policy toward the Burmese regime, meanwhile, has remained unchanged over several administrations. George H. W. Bush, Bill Clinton, and George W. Bush have all declared their support for Burmese democracy, even as they have demonstrated little appetite for supporting the ethnic insurgencies,

however covertly. In that respect, American policy toward Burma can seem more moralistic than moral, and President Bush in particular, despite Laura Bush's intense interest in Burma, may seem prone to the same ineffectual preachiness of which former President Jimmy Carter has often been accused. Bush, by some accounts, should either open talks with the junta, rather than risk having the U.S. ejected from the whole Bay of Bengal region; or he should support the ethnics in an effective but quiet manner. "Right now, we get peanuts from the U.S.," Lian Sakhong, general secretary of the Burmese Ethnic Nationalities Council, told me.

American officials respond that they have in fact backed their affirmations of democracy with actions. The United States has banned investment in Burma since 1997 (though the ban is not retroactive, thereby leaving Chevron, which took over its concession from Unocal, free to operate a pipeline from southern Burma into Thailand). The United States added new sanctions in 2003 and 2007 and provides humanitarian aid through NGOs operating from Thailand. As for cross-border support for the Karen and Shan armies, officials note that the moment the word of such a policy got out, America's embassy presence in Burma would be gutted. Of course, it's unclear what good the U.S. diplomatic presence in Burma is doing.

Nevertheless, according to a top member of the nongovernmental-aid community, the United States is the only major power that sends the junta a "tough, moral message, which usefully prevents the International Monetary Fund and World Bank from dealing with Burma." As a result, Burma has less money to build dams and roads to further despoil the landscape and displace more people. U.S. policy, this source went on, "also rallies Western and international pressure that has led to cracks in the Burmese military." The regime will collapse one day, maybe sooner than later; when it does, America would presumably be in excellent stead with the Burmese people.

Though the prospect of another mass uprising excites the Western imagination, what's more likely is another military coup, or something more nuanced—a simple change in leadership, with Than Shwe, 75 years old and in poor health, allowed to step aside. Then, new generals would open up talks with Aung San Suu Kyi and release her from house arrest. Even with elections, this would not solve Burma's fundamental problems. Aung San Suu Kyi, as a Nobel Peace Prize laureate and global media star, could provide a moral rallying point that even the hill tribes would accept. But the country would still be left with no public infrastructure, no institutions, no civil society, and with various ethnic armies that fundamentally distrust the dominant Burmans. As one international negotiator told me, "There will be no choice but to keep the military in a leading role for a while, because without the military, there is nothing in Burma." In power for so long, however badly it has ruled, the military has made itself indispensable to any solution. "It's much more complicated than the beauty-and-the-beast scenario put forth by some in the West—Aung San Suu Kyi versus the generals," says Lian Sakhong. "After all, we must end 60 years of civil war."

Burma must somehow find a way to return to the spirit of the Panglong Agreement of February 1947, the pact that the nationalist leader, General Aung San, negotiated among the country's tribes shortly before independence from Great Britain. It was based on three principles: a state with a decentralized federal structure, recognition of the ethnic chieftaincies in the hills, and their right of secession after a number of years. Failure to implement that agreement, which collapsed after Aung San's assassination that summer, has been the cause of all the problems since.

Meanwhile, the war continues. When I asked Karen military leaders in the Thai border town of Mae Sot what they needed most, they told me: assault rifles, C-4 plastic explosives to make Claymore mines, and .50-caliber sniper systems with optics to knock out the microwave relay stations and bull-dozers that the Burmese army uses to communicate and to build roads through Karen areas.

In his bunker in the jungle capital of Naypyidaw, Than Shwe sits atop an unsteady and restless cadre of mid-level officers and lower ranks. He may represent the last truly centralized regime in Burma's postcolonial history. Whether through a peaceful, well-managed transition or through a tumultuous or even anarchic one, the Karens and Shans in the east and the Chins and Arakanese in the west will likely see their power increased in a post-junta Burma. The various natural-gas pipeline agreements will have to be negotiated or renegotiated with the ethnic peoples living in the territories through which the pipelines would pass. The struggle over the Indian Ocean, or at least the eastern part of it, may, alas, come down to who deals more adroitly with the Burmese hill tribes. It is the kind of situation that the American Christian missionaries of yore knew how to handle.

UNIT 5

North-South Interstate Conflicts and Rivalries

Unit Selections

Key Points to Consider

- What must be done to provide viable alternatives to radical populist leaders such as Hugo Chavez in Venezuela?

- What are some of the unintended consequences of the United States' invasion of Iraq?

- What are some of the reasons why the U.S. military recently established a new, unified military command called AFRICOM?

Student Web Site

www.mhcls.com

Internet References

The National Defense University Website
http://www.ndu.edu
The North American Institute
http://www.northamericaninstitute.org
Inter-American Dialogue
http://www.iadialog.org
African Center for Strategic Studies (ACSS)
http://www.africacenter.org/
United States Africa Command (AFRICOM)
http://www.africom.mil/
Observatory of Cultural Policies in Africa (OCPA)
http://ocpa.irmo.hr/resources/index-en.html

Mao made famous the phrase the "Third World," to refer to the large number of countries that were united by their economic status and historical experiences. Mao and many others urged the countries in the "Third World" to remain apart from the Western "First World" or the former communist "Second World" during the Cold War and unite instead, in a new coalition. Since the 1960s, there has been a growing recognition that most of the developing countries of the "Third World" are located south of the equator and thus, share a number of common problems related to climate, geography, and transportation that make economic development more difficult.

The "North-South" label has increasingly been adopted to designate both an informal and formal grouping of nation-states based on their economic level of development, shared history, and common continuing problems. Negotiations over many issues between Northern and Southern countries take place in the United Nations General Assembly, and in more specialized U.N. organizations such as the United Nations Conference on Trade and Agricultural Development or UNCTAD. UNCTAD has continued to operate as a forum for dialogue between the poor and wealthy states. However, by the 1980s, the unity of the South's Group of 77 (G77) had largely collapsed. Most analysts cite the rise of OPEC and the newly industrialized countries in Asia as important trends that helped shatter the façade of a united developing world.

Although most observers today acknowledge that such labels as the "North-South conflict" are too simplistic to capture the diverse range of issues among countries at very different levels of development, the term continues to be used as a convenient short-hand label. The label is useful for referencing the fact that there are frequent conflicts between developed and developing countries on a host of non-traditional security issues (i.e., economic and environmental) that result in very different interests and experiences among large numbers of countries in the developed and developing world.

One region where the "North-South," and even the "Third World" label still resonate with many leftist politicians and intellectuals is Latin America. For nearly two centuries, the United States viewed Latin America as being within its exclusive sphere of influence. Over the past three decades, most countries in the region shifted from military dictatorships to democracies to civilian-led governments that adopted neo-liberal economic reforms. Political changes and economic growth occurred, but few economic benefits trickled down to most citizens. The result was a wave of leftist leaders elected in several Latin American countries who have promised to bring more tangible results to the people.

After two decades of privatization and trade liberalization across the hemisphere, leftist leaders were elected first in Venezuela with the election of Hugo Chávez and next in Brazil. Evo Morales was elected in Bolivia promising to exert more

state control over their nations' economies to promote wealth distribution. Rafael Correa, the U.S-educated economist, promised to apply the same prescription in his country, where three-fourths of its inhabitants live in poverty despite Ecuador being South America's fifth largest oil producer. The return of leftist even extends to Nicaragua where a nemesis of the Reagan administration, Daniel Ortega, was elected in 2006. Although Hugo Chávez ran for re-election in 2006 pleading to hold a referendum in 2010 to abolish a clause in the constitution that would restrict presidents to two consecutive six-year terms, few observers expect him to leave the political scene any time soon. While some analysts warn that recent leftist-populist alliances threaten U.S. interests in the region, others are not so alarmed. Chávez and other leftist leaders were losing support even before the financial crisis of 2008. Regardless of how one interprets the varying support for more radical leaders in key Latin American countries, a basic reality facing the current generation of leaders is that they must find ways to produce tangible results to everyday problems for increased numbers of middle class and poor citizens. In many countries in the region, the poorest citizens come from minority groups who are traditionally alienated from mainstream cultures. In "A New Path for Latin America?," Michael Shifter emphasizes that a central question for "the longer term is whether Venezuelans and their counterparts across Latin America will be able to find satisfactory responses to the grievances that gave birth to the Chávez phenomenon and its populist analogues elsewhere in the region."

Many of the same economic problems facing leaders and citizens in Latin America are also found throughout the Middle East. However, the region also contains multiple conflicts, including the long-running Arab-Israeli conflict, that often divide countries along the "North" and "South" continuum in forums such as the United Nations. However, the region is also home of several well-established nation-states who have been historical rivals and dominant civilizations in the region in earlier eras. Since 2003, the United States involvement in Iraq has been an epicenter of conflict and a trigger for shifting alignments in the region. Jeffrey Goldberg in "After Iraq," describes the many unintended consequences that may flow from the United States' future military disengagement. Whether this disengagement is a rapid or gradual process, Goldberg speculates that the ramifications could include Kurdish independence and the division of Iraq into three parts. Such a dramatic change could in turn result ultimately in the entire system of nation-states breaking apart.

One factor that continues to differentiate countries in the "South" in terms of resources that are of interest to foreign governments and corporations remains oil. As demand for oil continues to increase there is increased interest in exploiting new geographic sources of oil. Nowhere is this more apparent than in the Gulf of Guinea, off the coast of several West African countries. Advances in deep sea mining technologies are rapidly increasing oil exploration off the coast of such important African countries as Nigeria. As several African countries begin or expand existing off-shore oil concessions with companies based in the West and increasingly also with Chinese and other Asian based corporations, the strategic importance of Africa is increasing in importance for many countries in the developed "North."

Nowhere is this more apparent than in the United States. The United States recently declared the Gulf of Guinea an area of strategic national interest that might require military intervention at some point in the future by U.S. forces. Concerns about the possible need for a U.S. military intervention are increasing as signs continue to mount that the most important nation-state in the region, Nigeria, may someday in the not too distant future collapse. Concerns about the increased use of ungoverned spaces throughout the continent by al Qaeda affiliated groups and other Jihadist extremists are also fueling U.S. governmental attention to recent trends in Africa as is the increased attacks by pirates on commerce off the coast of Somalia. These issues contributed to the decision of the U.S. government to formulate new prevention strategies in their dealings with a number of different African countries. The increased importance but volatility of the African continent also led the United States to take the historic step of combining three different regional military commands into a single military command called AFRICOM. AFRICOM, a new command that incorporates geographical areas previously under three different COCOMS, officially came into existence in the fall of 2008. Lieutenant Commander Patrick J. Paterson describes the new organization and notes in "Taking Africa Seriously" that it is still uncertain whether the U.S. military will be effective as the lead U.S. agency in executing both security and non-traditional human security issues. Given an expanded set of missions, AFRICOM will no doubt be the subject of debate for years among analysts and senior officials in African and non-African countries.

A New Path for Latin America?

MICHAEL SHIFTER

Paradoxes abound in Hugo Chávez's Venezuela. The Venezuelan president sells most of the oil that has enabled him to accumulate power at home and abroad to his chief political adversary, the United States. Chávez justly criticizes the coup attempt that was made against him in April 2002, but he was only catapulted to national political prominence a decade earlier after he led a failed coup against a democratically elected government. In yet another twist, on December 2, 2007, Chávez lost a popular vote for the first time—along with his aura of invincibility—precisely as oil prices approached a record $100 per barrel.

In spite of his control of key Venezuelan institutions and of untold billions of dollars, Chávez failed to gain approval of a constitutional reform referendum on his plan for "twenty-first century socialism." The proposed changes would have allowed for the president's indefinite reelection and imposed what Chávez ominously called a new "geometry of power," in which elected local officials would have been supplanted with his own appointees.

Even for many *chavistas,* or Chávez supporters, a power grab as flagrant as this one crossed the line. His overreaching led university students to protest in the streets and pushed a former close ally of the president to decry the reform package as a "constitutional coup." Chávez, despite the many advantages he enjoys, lost the referendum because he could not generate enthusiasm for his proposed governing model or obscure its inherent defects.

Even without the constitutional amendments, Chávez's unbridled ambition and appetite for power have already produced virtual one-man rule, devoid of any institutional checks or constraints. For some time, the Venezuelan president has exhibited little inclination or capacity to actually govern the country, and has focused instead on consolidating his own power and building regional and international alliances. As a result, political vulnerabilities have emerged and multiplied. Chávez's core constituency, the very poor, has been hit particularly hard by a combination of inflation (at more than 20 percent, the highest rate in Latin America last year) and a scarcity of basic goods such as milk and sugar. Common crime, to some degree fueled by drug trafficking, is affecting more and more Venezuelans. And, unsurprisingly, absolute power has been accompanied by increasing accusations of government corruption. Latin America, it appears, must find other models for effective governance and sustainable prosperity.

Saying "No" to Chávez

Even more than many of its neighbors in booming Latin America, Venezuela has experienced impressively high growth rates in recent years. In addition, the government has prioritized its distributive and social-welfare functions to address the needs of those who have been marginalized and denied the fruits of economic progress. In this respect, Chávez is just one part of a region-wide pattern. Indeed, the principal message one can take from the 2006 wave of eleven Latin American presidential elections—as well as from the two that took place in 2007, in Guatemala and Argentina—is that the social agenda is of central importance in the region.

A social agenda, however, is not incompatible with democratic institutions. Although many observers believed that heightened attention to economic inequality in the region might presage a Chávez-led populist wave throughout Latin America, the Venezuelan president's defeat at the polls in December demonstrates that autocratic governance has limited appeal and, ultimately, does not work.

Chávez, the standard-bearer of this populist movement, was unable to muster sufficient support for his president-for-life ambitions despite the ample resources he devotes to social programs and despite his strong, personal bond with many Venezuelans. Indeed, the Venezuela vote can be plausibly construed as a proxy for popular rejection of any "twenty-first century socialism" in an authoritarian form. Chávez's experience should serve as a cautionary tale for other Latin American leaders on a similar course.

> **The Venezuela vote can be construed as a proxy for popular rejection of "twenty-first century socialism" in an authoritarian form.**

Two examples are especially relevant. Chávez's main South American ally, Bolivian President Evo Morales, has encountered tremendous resistance in his efforts to pass a new constitution that centralizes power and loosens term limits. At the same time, President Rafael Correa in Ecuador is embarking on his own constituent assembly project that also risks eroding checks and balances on executive power.

Continued Frustration

To be sure, both in Bolivia and Ecuador, constitutional changes are under way because the status quo had become so discredited that it was no longer workable. It would be a mistake, moreover, to interpret any reaction against the populist politics associated with Chávez as a ringing endorsement of liberal, representative democracy as practiced in the United States. That model of governance has been tried in Latin America—before Chávez in Venezuela, for instance, and before Morales in Bolivia—and it was deemed deficient in delivering services and satisfying basic demands.

Latin America has experienced sustained economic growth (2003–2007 is the best stretch in the past 25 years) and achieved welcome reductions in poverty and even inequality in some countries. But the most recent edition of the comparative Latin Barometer survey shows that most Latin Americans remain profoundly dissatisfied with their governments' performances and place scant confidence in key institutions. According to the survey, less than a third of people in the region trust their national legislatures, and only one in five has confidence in political parties. Public security, in particular, has become an increasingly serious problem in a number of countries, as the police and courts have proved ineffective at combatting crime.

Economic statistics, even if encouraging, reveal little about Latin America's political stability, much less about the quality of democracy in the region. In fact, dynamic economic performance and a benign international environment have only heightened political expectations. Higher expectations in turn have fostered uncertainty and strained the relatively fragile political institutions in many countries. Citizens have greater access than ever to communications technology and to information about social realities, and are better equipped to articulate grievances. They are aware that money is being made and they are demanding a bigger share of the pie.

Perhaps nowhere in Latin America is the combination of robust economic growth and keen political frustration more salient than in Peru. Peru's economy is booming, growing at around 8 percent per year. A free trade deal with the United States was finalized in December 2007, and there is serious talk about an agreement with China as well. Nevertheless, discontent among Peruvians is widespread. This is reflected in rock-bottom levels of political satisfaction as measured by the Latin Barometer survey and by plummeting approval ratings for President Alan García—especially in southern Peru, home to the country's most impoverished regions. Social indicators, meanwhile, remain dismal. In the World Economic Forum's 2007 rankings, which cover 130 countries, Peru is in last place in quality of primary education—behind Ethiopia.

Top Models

The Latin American countries that offer the greatest promise for forging a new course—one that upholds democratic, pluralist politics while using the fruits of growth to enhance social welfare—are Chile, Brazil, and Mexico. Brazil and Mexico, for example, are pioneers of successful conditional cash-transfer programs now being replicated worldwide. The Bolsa Familia and Oportunidades initiatives, respectively, are credited with dramatically reducing hunger and income inequality by giving monetary bonuses to impoverished families that meet certain requirements, such as sending their children to school and taking them to be vaccinated.

In Chile, under a series of democratic governments since the dictator Augusto Pinochet left power in 1990, a range of targeted social programs has helped the country grow at double the regional average while poverty levels have been halved. Inequality remains a top issue, and Michelle Bachelet won the presidency in 2006 by promising to focus on the social agenda. Indeed, the slow pace of reforms led to protests in 2006 and other difficulties for Bachelet, prompting her to intensify government efforts to reduce inequality.

Despite significant stumbling blocks, all three countries are, however gradually, strengthening their institutional capacity for democratic governance while also reducing poverty and even inequality. In the October 2007 International Monetary Fund report "Globalization and Inequality," for example, Brazil and Mexico are cited as rare and notable exceptions to a worldwide trend toward rising income inequality.

For Presidents Bachelet, Luiz Inácio Lula da Silva of Brazil, and Felipe Calderón of Mexico, the left-right divide is of little relevance as they forge policies to create and distribute wealth, all within the give-and-take of democratic politics.

It is hard to imagine that, in the wake of his December 2 defeat, Chávez will decide to follow the path pursued by these Latin American leaders. In contrast to Bachelet and Lula, who fought against military governments in their countries, Chávez is a consummate military man bound to push ahead doggedly with his grandiose agenda. With his oil money, seductive rhetoric, and shrewd political sense, he should not be underestimated. Despite discernible and growing fissures within *chavismo,* he maintains control of key institutions like the National Assembly and the armed forces. The opposition, moreover, is still highly fragmented. Recent history gives little indication that Chávez's opponents will be able to capitalize on their current opportunity to build an alternative political coalition with a viable social agenda.

The Turning Point

Nonetheless, the beginnings of decay in Chávez's rule are evident, and the president's problems are bound to intensify in the coming years. Chávez can distribute oil revenues to shore up his personal power, but that will not resolve problems like inflation, crime, corruption, and food shortages. Problems such as these can only be overcome with long-term, sensible public policies bolstered by democratic safeguards.

Chávez's loss at the polls marked a turning point, both in Venezuela and in the president's own aggressive regional political project. The president's confrontational outbursts in the weeks before the referendum may have appealed to his hard-core base, but it is doubtful that they helped him with undecided Venezuelan voters, let alone people elsewhere in the region. On November 25, 2007, Chávez exchanged verbal barbs with President Alvaro Uribe of Colombia, calling him a "shameless liar" and "pawn of the American empire." He continued his belligerence less than two weeks later at the Ibero-American Summit in Santiago.

In some respects, the summit offered an ideal opportunity for Chávez to assert his regional leadership. After all, the theme was "social cohesion," the meeting was held in Socialist-governed Chile, Cuba had high-level representation, and there was no one present from the United States (as is customary at these summits). Instead, Chávez called former Spanish President José María Aznar a "fascist," famously prompting King Juan Carlos to ask him to "shut up" and causing an intercontinental diplomatic spat. Even otherwise sympathetic leaders are wary of such divisive politics. The referendum setback, coupled with mounting difficulties on the foreign policy front, could well force Chávez to concentrate more on shoring up domestic political support and less on aggressive regional diplomacy.

The question for the longer term is whether Venezuelans and their counterparts across Latin America will be able to find satisfactory responses to the grievances that gave birth to the Chávez phenomenon and its populist analogues elsewhere in the region. Paradoxically, a fluid and dynamic process of constant political experimentation may now be paving the way for a more enduring and effective model of governance in Latin America.

MICHAEL SHIFTER, a *Current History* contributing editor, is vice president for policy at the Inter-American Dialogue and an adjunct professor at Georgetown University.

After Iraq

A report from the new Middle East—and a glimpse of its possible future.

JEFFREY GOLDBERG

Not long ago, in a decrepit prison in Iraqi Kurdistan, a senior interrogator with the Kurdish intelligence service decided, for my entertainment and edification, to introduce me to an al-Qaeda terrorist named Omar. "This one is crazy," the interrogator said. "Don't get close, or he'll bite you."

Omar was a Sunni Arab from a village outside Mosul; he was a short and weedy man, roughly 30 years old, who radiated a pure animal anger. He was also a relentless jabberer; he did not shut up from the moment we were introduced. I met him in an unventilated interrogation room that smelled of bleach and paint. He was handcuffed, and he cursed steadily, making appalling accusations about the sexual practices of the interrogator's mother. He cursed the Kurds, in general, as pig-eaters, blasphemers, and American lackeys. As Omar ranted, the interrogator smiled. "I told you the Arabs don't like the Kurds," he said. I've known the interrogator for a while, and this is his perpetual theme: close proximity to Arabs has sabotaged Kurdish happiness.

Omar, the Kurds claim, was once an inconsequential deputy to the now-deceased terrorist chieftain Abu Musab al-Zarqawi. Omar disputed this characterization. By his own telling, he accomplished prodigies of terror against the pro-American Kurdish forces in the northern provinces of Iraq. "You are worse than the Americans," he told his Kurdish interrogator. "You are the enemy of the Muslim nation. You are enemies of God." The interrogator—I will not name him here, for reasons that will become apparent in a moment—sat sturdily opposite Omar, absorbing his invective for several minutes, absentmindedly paging through a copy of the Koran.

During a break in the tirade, the interrogator asked Omar, for my benefit, to rehearse his biography. Omar's life was undistinguished. His father was a one-donkey farmer; Omar was educated in Saddam's school system, which is to say he was hardly educated; he joined the army, and then Ansar al-Islam, the al-Qaeda-affiliated terrorist group that operates along the Iranian frontier. And then, on the blackest of days, as he described it, he fell prisoner to the Kurds.

Kurdistan

Capital: Kirkuk
Population: 31.2 million
Form of Government: Parliamentary Democracy
Official Language: Kurdish
Major Export: Oil

The interrogator asked me if I had any questions for Omar. Yes, I said: Have you been tortured in this prison?

"No," he said.

"What would you do if you were to be released from prison right now?"

"I would get a knife and cut your head off," he said.

At this, the interrogator smacked Omar across the face with the Koran.

Omar yelped in shock. The interrogator said: "Don't talk that way to a guest!"

Now, Omar rounded the bend. A bolus of spit flew from his mouth as he screamed. The interrogator taunted Omar further. "This book of yours," he said, waving the Koran. " 'Cut off their heads! Cut off their heads!' That's the answer for everything!" Omar cursed the interrogator's mother once again; the interrogator trumped him by cursing the Prophet Muhammad's mother.

The meeting was then adjourned.

In the hallway, I asked the interrogator, "Aren't you Muslim?"

"Of course," he said.

"But you're not a big believer in the Koran?"

"The Koran's OK," he said. "I don't have any criticism of Muhammad's mother. I just say that to get him mad."

He went on, "The Koran wasn't written by God, you know. It was written by Arabs. The Arabs were imperialists, and they forced it on us." This is a common belief among negligibly religious Kurds, of whom there are many millions.

"That's your problem, then," I said. "Arabs."

"Of course," he replied. "The Arabs are responsible for all our misfortunes."

"What about the Turks?" I asked. It is the Turks, after all, who are incessantly threatening to invade Iraqi Kurdistan, which they decline to call "Iraqi Kurdistan," in more or less the same obstreperous manner that they refuse to call the Armenian genocide a genocide.

"The Turks, too," he said. "Everyone who denies us our right to be free is responsible for our misfortunes."

We stepped out into the sun. "The Kurds never had friends. Now we have the most important friend, America. We're closer to freeing ourselves from the Arabs than ever," he said.

To the Kurds, the Arabs are bearers of great misfortune. The decades-long oppression of Iraq's Kurds culminated during the rule of Saddam Hussein, whose Sunni Arab–dominated army committed genocide against them in the late 1980s. Yet their unfaltering faith that they will one day be free may soon be rewarded: the Kurds are finally edging close to independence. Much blood may be spilled as Kurdistan unhitches itself from Iraq—Turkey is famously sour on the idea of Kurdish independence, fearing a riptide of nationalist feeling among its own unhappy Kurds—but independence for Iraq's Kurds seems, if not immediate, then in due course inevitable.

In many ways, the Kurds are functionally independent already. The Kurdish regional government has its own army, collects its own taxes, and negotiates its own oil deals. For the moment, Kurdish officials say they would be satisfied with membership in a loose-jointed federation with the Shiite and Sunni Arabs to their south. But in Erbil and Sulaymani, the two main cities of the Kurdish region, the Iraqi flag is banned from flying; Arabic is scarcely heard on the streets (and is never spoken by young people, who are happily ignorant of it), and Baghdad is referred to as a foreign capital. In October, when I was last in the region, I called the office of a high official of the *peshmerga,* the Kurdish guerrilla army, but was told that he had "gone to Iraq" for the week.

The Bush administration gave many reasons for the invasion of Iraq, but the satisfaction of Kurdish national desire was not one of them. Quite the opposite: the goal was, and remains, a unified, democratic Iraq. In fact, key officials of the administration have a history of indifference to, and ignorance of, the subject of Kurdish nationalism. At a conference in 2004, National Security Advisor Condoleezza Rice stated, "What has been impressive to me so far is that Iraqis—whether Kurds or Shia or Sunni or the many other ethnic groups in Iraq—have demonstrated that they really want to live as one in a unified Iraq." As Peter Galbraith, a former American diplomat and an advocate for Kurdish independence, has observed, Rice's statement was disconnected from observable reality—shortly before she

spoke, 80 percent of all Iraqi Kurdish adults had signed a petition calling for a vote on independence.

Neoconservative ideologues never seemed much interested in, or knowledgeable about, the Kurdish cause. 'What's a Kurd, anyway?' Norman Podhoretz asked me a few years ago.

Nor were neoconservative ideologues—who had the most elaborate visions of a liberal, democratic Iraq—interested in the Kurdish cause, or even particularly knowledgeable about its history. Just before the "Mission Accomplished" phase of the war, I spoke about Kurdistan to an audience that included Norman Podhoretz, the vicariously martial neoconservative who is now a Middle East adviser to Rudolph Giuliani. After the event, Podhoretz seemed authentically bewildered. "What's a Kurd, anyway?" he asked me.

As America approaches the fifth anniversary of the invasion of Iraq, the list of the war's unintended consequences is without end (as opposed to the list of intended consequences, which is, so far, vanishingly brief). The list includes, notably, the likelihood that the Kurds will achieve their independence and that Iraq will go the way of Gaul and be divided into three parts—but it also includes much more than that. Across the Middle East, and into south-central Asia, the intrinsically artificial qualities of several states have been brought into focus by the omnivorous American response to the attacks of 9/11; it is not just Iraq and Afghanistan that appear to be incoherent amalgamations of disparate tribes and territories. The precariousness of such states as Lebanon and Pakistan, of course, predates the invasion of Iraq. But the wars against al-Qaeda, the Taliban, and especially Saddam Hussein have made the durability of the modern Middle East state system an open question in ways that it wasn't a mere seven years ago.

It used to be that the most far-reaching and inventive question one could ask about the Middle East was this: How many states, one or two—Israel or a Palestinian state, or both—will one day exist on the slip of land between the Mediterranean Sea and the Jordan River?

Today, that question seems trivial when compared with this one: How many states will there one day be between the Mediterranean and the Euphrates River? Three? Four? Five? Six? And why stop at the western bank of the Euphrates? Why not go all the way to the Indus River? Between the Mediterranean and the Indus today lie Israel and the Palestinian territories, Lebanon, Syria and Jordan, Iraq, Iran, Afghanistan, and Pakistan. Long-term instability could lead to the breakup of many of these states.

Islamic Emirate of Gaza

Capital: Gaza City
Population: 2.8 million
Form of Government: Sharia state
Official Language: Arabic

Shiite Islamic State of Iraq

Capital: Baghdad (administrative), Najaf (religious)
Population: 22.3 million
Form of Government: Mullah-ocracy
Official Language: Arabic
Major Export: Oil

All states are manmade. But some are more manmade than others. It was Winston Churchill (a bust of whom Bush keeps in the Oval Office) who, in the aftermath of World War I, roped together three provinces of the defeated and dissolved Ottoman Empire, adopted the name Iraq, and bequeathed it to a luckless branch of the Hashemite tribe of west Arabia. Churchill would eventually call the forced inclusion of the Kurds in Iraq one of his worst mistakes—but by then, there was nothing he could do about it.

The British, together with the French, gave the world the modern Middle East. In addition to manufacturing the country now called Iraq, the grand Middle East settlement shrank Turkey by the middle of the 1920s to the size of the Anatolian peninsula; granted what are now Syria and Lebanon to the French; and kept Egypt under British control. The British also broke Palestine in two, calling its eastern portion Trans-Jordan and installing a Hashemite prince, Abdullah, as its ruler, and at the same time promising Western Palestine to the Jews, while implying to the Arabs there that it was their land, too. As the historian David Fromkin puts it in *A Peace to End All Peace,* his definitive account of the machinations among the Great Powers that resulted in the modern map of the Middle East, the region

> became what it is today both because the European powers undertook to re-shape it and because Britain and France failed to ensure that the dynasties, the states, and the political system that they established would permanently endure.

Of course, the current turbulence in the Middle East is attributable also to factors beyond the miscalculations of both the hubristic, seat-of-the-pants Bush administration and the hubristic, seat-of-the-pants French and British empires. Among other things, there is the crisis within Islam, a religion whose doctrinal triumphalism—Muslims believe the Koran to be the final, authoritative word of God—is undermined daily by the global balance of power, with predictable and terrible consequences (see: the life of Mohammed Atta et al.); and there is the related and continuing crisis of globalization, which drives people who have not yet received the message that the world is now flat to find solace and meaning in their fundamental ethnic and religious identities.

But since 9/11, America's interventions in the region—and especially in Iraq—have exacerbated the tensions there, and have laid bare how artificial, and how tenuously constructed, the current map of the Middle East really is. By invading Iraq, the Bush administration sought not only to deprive the country of its putative weapons of mass destruction, but also to shake things up in Iraq's chaotic neighborhood; toppling Saddam and planting the seeds of democracy in Iraq would, it was hoped, make possible the transformation of the region. The region *is* being transformed; that transformation is just turning out to be a different, and possibly far broader, one than imagined. As Dennis Ross, who was a Middle East envoy for both Bill Clinton and George H. W. Bush, and is now with the Washington Institute for Near East Policy, puts it, the Iraq War has begun to produce "wholesale change"—but "it won't be the one envisioned by the administration." An independent Kurdistan would be just the start.

Envisioning what the Middle East might look like five or 10 or 50 years from now is by definition a speculative exercise. But precisely because of the scope of the transformation that's under way, imagining the future of the region, and figuring out a smart approach to it, should be at the top of America's post-Iraq priorities. At the moment, however, neither the Bush administration nor the candidates for the presidency seem to be thinking about the future of the Middle East (beyond the immediate situation in Iraq and the specific question of what to do about Iran's nuclear intentions) in any particularly creative way. At the State Department and on the National Security Council, there is a poverty of imagination (to borrow a phrase from the debate about the causes of chronic intelligence failure) about the shifting map of the region.

It's not just the fragility of the post-1922 borders that has been exposed by recent history; it's also the limitations of the leading foreign-policy philosophies—realism and neoconservatism. Formulating a foreign policy after Iraq will require coming to terms with a reshaped Middle East, and thinking about it in new ways.

Unintended Consequences

In an effort to understand the shape of things to come in the Middle East, I spent several weeks speaking with more than 25 experts and traveling to Iraq, Jordan, the West Bank, and Israel. Many of the conversations were

Sunni Republic of Iraq

Capital: Ramadi
Population: 10 million
Form of Government: Military dictatorship
Official Language: Arabic

colored, naturally, by the ideological predispositions of those I talked with. The realists quake at instability, which threatens (as they see it) the only real American interest in the Middle East, the uninterrupted flow of Arab oil. Iranophobes see that country's empowerment, and the threat of regional Shiite-Sunni warfare, as the greatest cause for worry. Pro-Palestinian academies blame Israel, and its friends in Washington, for trying to force the collapse of the Arab state system. The liberal interventionists lament the poor execution of the Iraq War, and wish that the Bush administration had gone about exporting democracy to the Middle East with more subtlety and less hypocrisy. The neoconservatives, who cite the American Revolution as an example of what might be called "constructive volatility," see no reason to regret instability (even as they concede that it's hard to imagine a happy end to the Iraq War anytime soon).

The list of the Iraq War's unintended consequences is without end and includes, notably, the likelihood of Kurdish independence and the division of Iraq into three parts.

Some experts didn't want to play at all. When I called David Fromkin and asked him to speculate about the future of the Middle East, he said morosely, "The Middle East has no future." And when I spoke to Edward Luttwak, the iconoclastic military historian at the Center for Strategic and International Studies in Washington, he said there was no reason to engage the subject: the West is unable to shape the future of the Middle East, so why bother? "The United States could abandon Israel altogether, or embrace the general Arab cause 100 percent," he said, but "the Arabs will find a new reason to be anti-American."

Many experts I spoke to ventured that it would be foolish to predict what will happen in the Middle East next Tuesday, let alone in 2018, or in 2028—but that it would also be foolish not to be actively thinking about, and preparing for, what might come next.

So what might, in fact, come next? The most important first-order consequence of the Iraq invasion, envisioned by many of those I spoke to, is the possibility of a regional conflict between Sunnis and Shiites for theological and political supremacy in the Middle East. This is a war that could be fought by proxies of Saudi Arabia, the Sunni flag-bearer, against Iran—or perhaps by Iran and Saudi Arabia themselves—on battlefields across Iraq, in Lebanon and Syria, and in Saudi Arabia's largely Shiite Eastern Province, under which most of the kingdom's oil lies. In 2004, King Abdullah II of Jordan, a Sunni, spoke of the creation of a Shiite "crescent," running from Iran, through Iraq, and into Syria and Lebanon, that would destabilize the Arab world. Jordan, which is an indispensably important American ally, is a Sunni country, but its population is also majority-Palestinian, and many of those Palestinians support the Islamist Hamas movement, one of whose main sponsors is Shiite Iran.

There are likely second-order consequences, as well. Rampant Kurdish nationalism, unleashed by the invasion, may spill over into the Kurdish areas of Turkey and Iran. America's reliance on anti-democratic regimes, such as Egypt's, for help in its campaign against Islamist terrorism could strengthen the Islamist opposition in those countries. An American decision to confront Iran could have an enduring impact on the Israeli-Palestinian peace process—a tenuous undertaking to begin with—because the chief enemies of compromise are the Iranian-backed terror groups Hamas and Hezbollah.

Then there are third-order consequences: in the next 20 years, new states could emerge as old ones shrink, fracture, or disappear. Khuzestan, a mostly Arab province of majority-Persian Iran, could become independent. Lebanon, whose existence is perpetually inexplicable, could become partly absorbed by Syria, whose future is also uncertain. The Alawites who rule Syria are members of a Shiite splinter sect, and they are a tiny minority in their own, mostly Sunni country (the Alawites briefly ruled an independent state in the mountains above the Mediterranean). Syria, out of a population of 20 million, has roughly 2 million Kurds, who are mostly indifferent, and sometimes hostile, to the government in Damascus.

Kuwait is another state whose future looks unstable; after all, it has already been subsumed once, and could be again—though, under another scenario, it could gain territory and population, if Iraq's Sunnis seek an alliance with it as a way of protecting themselves from their country's newly powerful Shiites. Bahrain, a majority-Shiite country ruled by Sunnis, could well be annexed by Iran (which already claims it), and Yemen could expand its territory at Saudi Arabia's expense. And the next decades might see the birth of one or two Palestinian states—and, perhaps, the end of Israel as a Jewish state, a fervent dream of much of the Muslim world.

Pashtunistan

Official Name: The Pathan Federation of Tribal Emirates
Capital: Kandahar
Population: 61 million
Form of Government: Tribal law
Official Language: Pashto
Major Industries: Weapons manufacturing, smuggling

Baluchistan

Capital: Gwadar
Population: 20.2 million
Form of Government: Tribal confederation
Official Language: Baluchi
Major Exports: Opium, hydrocarbon transit

And let's not forget Pakistan, whose artificiality I was reminded of by Pervez Musharraf, the Pakistani dictator, during an interview in the garrison city of Rawalpindi some years ago. At one point, he took exception to the idea that the Baluch, the quasi-nomadic people who inhabit the large deserts of Pakistan's west (and Irans' southeast), might feel unattached to the government in Islamabad. In so doing, he undermined the idea of Pakistan as a naturally unitary state. "I know many residents of Baluchistan who are appreciative of Pakistan and the many programs and the like that Pakistan has for Baluchistan," he said, referring to one of his states as if it were another country. He continued: "Why [is Pakistan] thought of as artificial and not others? Didn't your country almost come to an end in a civil war? You faced larger problems than we ever have."

Musharraf also made passing reference to the Afghan-Pakistan border, the so-called Durand Line. It was named after the English official who in 1893 forced the Afghans to accept it as their border with British India, even though it sliced through the territory of a large ethnic group, the truculent Pashtuns, who dominate Afghan politics and warmaking and who have always disliked and, accordingly, disrespected the line. Musharraf warned about the hazards of even thinking about the line. "Why would there be such a desire to change existing situations?" he said. "There would be instability to come out of this situation, should this question be put on the table. It is best to leave borders alone. If you start asking about this and that border or this and that arrangement . . ." He didn't finish the sentence.

All of this is very confusing, of course. Many Americans (including, until not so long ago, President Bush) do not know the difference between a Shiite and a Sunni, let alone between a Sindhi and a Punjabi. Just try to imagine, say, Secretary of State Podhoretz briefing President Giuliani on his first meeting with the leaders of the Baluchistan Liberation Army, and it becomes obvious that we may be entering a new and hazardous era.

Mapping the New Middle East

"Nobody is thinking about whether or not the map is still viable," Ralph Peters told me. Peters is a retired Army lieutenant colonel and intelligence expert who writes frequent critiques of U.S. strategy in the Middle East. "It's not a question about how America wants the map to look; it's a question of how the map is going to look, whether we like it or not."

In the June 2006 issue of *Armed Forces Journal*, Peters published a map of what he thought a more logical Middle East might look like. Rather than following the European-drawn borders, he made his map by tracing the region's "blood borders," invisible lines that would separate battling ethnic and sectarian groups. He wrote of his map,

> While the Middle East has far more problems than dysfunctional borders alone—from cultural stagnation through scandalous inequality to deadly religious extremism—the greatest taboo in striving to understand the region's comprehensive failure isn't Islam but the awful-but-sacrosanct international boundaries worshipped by our own diplomats.

Peters drew onto his map an independent Kurdistan and an abridged Turkey; he shrank Iran (handing over Khuzestan to an as-yet-imaginary Arab-Shiite state he carved out of what is now southern Iraq); he placed Jordan and Yemen on a steroid regimen; and he dismembered Saudi Arabia because he sees it as a primary enemy of Muslim modernization.

It was an act of knowing whimsy, he said. But it was seen by the Middle East's more fevered minds as a window onto the American imperial planning process. "The reaction was pure paranoia, just hysterics," Peters told me. "The Turks in particular got very upset." Peters explained how he made the map. "The art department gave me a blank map, and I took a crayon and drew on it. After it came out, people started arguing on the Internet that this border should, in fact, be 50 miles this way, and that border 50 miles that way, but the width of the crayon itself was 200 miles."

Given the preexisting sensitivities in the Middle East to white men wielding crayons, it's not surprising that his map would be met with such anxiety. There is a belief, prevalent in the Middle East and among pro-Palestinian American academics, that the Bush administration's actual goal—or the goal, at least, of its favored theoreticians—is to rip up the existing map of the Arab Middle East in order to help Israel.

"One of the most evil things that is happening is that a bunch of people who are fundamentally opposed to the existence of these nation-states have gotten into the control room," Rashid Khalidi, who is the Edward Said Professor of Arab Studies at Columbia University, told me. "They are irresponsible and highly ideological neoconservatives, generally, and they have been trying to smash the Arab state system. Their basic philosophy is, the smaller the Arab state, the better."

Neoeonservatives inside the administration deny this. "We never had the creation of new states as a goal," Douglas Feith, the former undersecretary of defense for policy, told me, and indeed, there is no proof that the administration sought the breakup of Iraq. On the contrary: shortly after the invasion, I saw Paul Wolfowitz, then the deputy secretary of defense, at the White House Correspondents' Association dinner, and I told him I had just returned from Kurdistan. Maybe he was just feeling snappish (a few minutes earlier he had had a confrontation with Al Franken that ended with Wolfowitz saying "Fuck you" to the comedian), but Wolfowitz looked at me and, as though he were channeling the Turkish foreign minister, said, "We call it northern Iraq. Northern *Iraq*."

Peters said he noticed early on as well that the administration was committed to a unified Iraq, and to the preexisting, European-drawn map of the Middle East. "This is how strange things are—the greatest force for democracy in the world has signed up for the maintenance of the European model of the world," he said. "Even the neocons, who look like revolutionaries, just want to substitute Bourbons for Hapsburgs," he continued, and added, "Not just in Iraq." (Peters acknowledged that neoconservatives outside the administration were more radical than those on the inside, like Feith and Wolfowitz.)

So just what did the neoconservatives, the most influential foreign-policy school of the Bush years, have in mind? Feith, whose (inevitable) book on the invasion and its aftermath will be published in March, told me that the neoconservatives—at least those inside the administration—did not hope to create new borders, but did see a value in "instability," especially since, in his view, the Middle East was already destabilized by the presence of Saddam Hussein. "There is something I once heard attributed to Goethe," he said, "that 'Disorder is worse than injustice.' We have an interest in stability, of course, but we should not overemphasize the value of stability when there is an opportunity to make the world a better or safer place for us. For example, during the Nixon presidency, and the George H. W. Bush presidency, the emphasis was on stabilizing relations with the Soviet Union. During the Reagan administration, the goal was to put the Communists on the ash heap of history. Those Americans who argued for stability tried to preserve the Soviet Union. But it was Reagan

who was right." Feith had hoped that the demise of Iraq's Baath regime would allow a new sort of governance to take hold in an Arab country. "We understood that if you did something as big as replacing Saddam, then there are going to be all kinds of consequences, many of which you can't possibly anticipate. Something good may come, something negative might come out."

So far, it's been mainly negative. The neoconservatives' big idea was that American-style democracy would quickly take hold in Iraq, spread through the Arab Middle East, and then be followed by the collapse of al-Qaeda, who would no longer have American-backed authoritarian Arab regimes to rally against. But democracy has turned out to be a habit not easily cultivated, and the idea that Arab political culture is capable of absorbing democratic notions of governance has fallen into disfavor.

In December of 2006, I went to the Israeli Embassy in Washington for a ceremony honoring Natan Sharansky, who had just received the Medal of Freedom from President Bush. Sharansky, the former Soviet dissident, had become the president's tutor on the importance of democratic reform in the Arab world, and during the ceremony, he praised the president for pursuing unpopular policies. As he talked, the man next to me, a senior Israeli security official, whispered, "What a child."

"What do you mean?" I asked.

"It's not smart . . . He wants Jordan to be more democratic. Do you know what that would mean for Israel and America? If you were me, would you rather have a stable monarch who is secular and who has a good intelligence service on your eastern border, or would you rather have a state run by Hamas? That's what he would get if there were no more monarchy in Jordan."

After the ceremony, I spoke with Sharansky about this critique. He acknowledged that he is virtually the lone neoconservative thinker in Israel, and one of the few who still believes that democracy is exportable to the Arab world, by force or otherwise.

"After I came back from Washington once," he said, "I saw [Prime Minister Ariel] Sharon in the Knesset, and he said, 'Mazel tov, Natan. You've convinced President Bush of something that doesn't exist.'"

A War about Nothing?

It is true that the neoconservatives' dream of Middle East democracy has proved to be a mirage. But it's not as though the neocons' principal foils, the foreign-policy realists, who view stability as a paramount virtue, have covered themselves in glory in the post-9/11 era. Brent Scowcroft, President George H. W. Bush's national security adviser and Washington's senior advocate of foreign-policy realism, told me not long ago of a conversation he had had with

Bedouin Autonomous Zone of the Sinai

Capital: El Tor
Population: 500,000
Form of Government: Local councils, Egyptian military administration
Official Language: Arabic
Major Industries: Seminomadic desert pastoralism, scuba-diving

Khuzistan

Official Name: The Arab State of Khuzistan
Capital: Ahvaz
Population: 2.4 million
Form of Government: Arab republic
Official Language: Arabic
Major Exports: Oil, petroleum, hydrocarbons, natural gas

his onetime protégée Condoleezza Rice. "She says, 'We're going to democratize Iraq,' and I said, 'Condi, you're not going to democratize Iraq,' and she said, 'You know, you're just stuck in the old days,' and she comes back to this thing, that we've tolerated an autocratic Middle East for 50 years, and so on and so forth. But we've had 50 years of peace." Of course, what Scowcroft fails to note here is that al-Qaeda attacked us in part because America is the prime backer of its enemies, the autocratic rulers of Egypt and Saudi Arabia.

It is conceivable, if paradoxical, that the actual outcome of the recent turmoil in the Middle East could be a new era of stability, fostered by realists in this country and in the region itself. This might be the most unlikely potential outcome of the Iraq invasion—that it turns out to be the Seinfeld War, a war about nothing (except, of course, the loss of a great many lives and vast sums of money). Everything changes if America attacks Iranian nuclear sites, of course—but the latest National Intelligence Estimate, which came out in early December and reported that Iran had shut down its covert nuclear-weapons program in 2003, makes it unlikely that the Bush administration will pursue this option. And the next one or two U.S. presidents, who will be inheriting both the Iraq and Afghanistan portfolios, will probably be hesitant to attack any more Muslim countries. It's not impossible to imagine that, in 20 years, the map of the Middle East will look exactly like it does today.

> The Middle East state system has become an open question: Israel and the Palestinian territories, Lebanon, Syria, Jordan, Iran, Iraq, Afghanistan, Pakistan, and others could all ultimately break apart.

"We tend to underestimate the power of states," Robert Satloff, the director of the Washington Institute for Near East Policy, told me. "The PC way of looking at the 21st century is that non-state actors—al-Qaeda, Hezbollah, general chaos—have replaced states as the key players in the Middle East. But states are more resilient than that." He added that a newfound fear of instability might even buttress existing states.

Jordan is an interesting example of this phenomenon. While it would seem eminently vulnerable to the chaos—Iraq is to its east, the Palestinians and Israel to its west, and Syria to the north—Jordan is, in fact, almost tranquil, in part because it is led by a savvy king (scion of a family, the Hashemites, who are quite used to living on the balls of their feet) and in part because most of its people, having viewed from orchestra seats the bedlam in Iraq, want quiet, even if that means forgoing all the features of Western democracy.

Jordan might be an exception, however. Even a passing look at a country like Saudi Arabia suggests that internally driven regime changes are real possibilities. In Egypt the aging Hosni Mubarak is trying to engineer his unproven younger son, Gamal, into the presidency. It does not seem likely, at the moment, that Gamal would succeed in the job. Egypt was once a country that could project its power into Syria; now its leaders are having trouble controlling the Sinai Peninsula, home to a couple hundred thousand Bedouin, who are Pashtun-like in their stiff-neckedness and who seem more and more unwilling to accept Cairo's rule. America, of course, continues to embrace Mubarak, seeing no alternative except the fundamentalist Muslim Brotherhood. This pattern is familiar in American diplomacy; President Bush's long embrace of Musharraf comes to mind, and there are various, bipartisan antecedents—such as, most notably, Jimmy Carter's support for the Shah of Iran.

Beyond Realism and Neoconservatism

In the years since his Iraq project fell into disrepair, President Bush has acted like a realist while speaking like a utopian neoconservative. He has touted the virtues of democracy to the very people subjugated by pro-American dictators. This is probably not a good long-term policy for managing chaos in the Middle East.

The problem is that Iraq has already proven—and Iran continues to prove—that Americans cannot make Middle Easterners do what is in America's best interest. "Whether the Middle East is unimportant or terrifically important, when it comes to doing anything about it, the actions undertaken are all ineffectual or counterproductive," Edward Luttwak told me. "In the Middle East, it doesn't help to be nice to them, or to bomb them."

A first step in restoring America's influence in the Middle East is to accept with humility the notion that America—like Britain before it—cannot organize the region according to its own interests. (Ideologues of varying positions tend to quote for their own benefit the theologian Reinhold Niebuhr on the proper use of American power—but perhaps what the debate needs is a version of Niebuhr's Serenity Prayer: "God grant me the courage to change the regimes I can, the grace to accept the regimes I can't . . .") What's called for is a foreign policy in which the neoconservative's belief in the liberating power of democracy is yoked to the realist's understanding of unintended consequences.

Of course, winning in Iraq—or at least not losing—would help fortify America's deterrent power, and check Iran's involvement in Lebanon, Gaza, and elsewhere. America's situation in Iraq is not quite so dire as it was a year ago; the troop surge has worked to suppress much violence, and there have been tentative steps by both Shiite and Sunni leaders to prevent all-out sectarian war. To be sure, very few experts predict with any assurance an optimistic future for Iraq. "Ten years is a reasonable time period to think that the sectarian conflict will need to play out," Martin Indyk, the director of the Saban Center for Middle East Policy at the Brookings Institution, told me. "The parties will eventually exhaust themselves. Perhaps they have already, although I fear that the surge has just provided a break for Sunnis and Shias to better position themselves for further conflict when American forces are drawn down. There's no indication yet that the Shias are prepared to share power or that the Sunnis are prepared to live as a minority under Shia majoritarian rule."

Erstwhile optimists about the prospects for democracy in the Middle East, myself included, have been chastened by recent events. But the U.S. would do well not to abandon the long-term hope that democracy, exported carefully, and slowly, can change reality. This would be not a five-year project, but a 50-year one. It would focus on aiding Middle Eastern journalists and democracy activists, on building strong universities and independent judiciaries—and on being discerning enough *not* to aid Muslim democracy activists when American help would undermine their credibility. If Arab moderates and democrats "begin this work now, in 10 or 15 years we will have a horse in this race," said Omran Salman, the head of an Arab reform organization called Aafaq. "We've sacrificed democracy for stability, but

The Alawite Republic

Capital: Latakia
Population: 4.5 million
Form of Government: Absolute monarchy under the House of Asad
Official Language: Arabic
Major Exports: Agricultural products

it's a fabricated stability. When someone's sitting on your head, it's not stable." Salman, a Shiite from Bahrain, said he opposes Western military intervention in certain cases, preferring American "moral intervention": The Americans "have to keep pressure on regimes to force them to make reforms and open their societies. Now what the regimes do is oppress liberals."

One problem is that American moral capital has been depleted, which only underscores the practical importance to national security of, among other things, banning torture, and considering carefully the impact an American strike on Iran would have on the typical Iranian. After 30 years of oppressive fundamentalist Muslim rule, many of Iran's people are pro-American; that could change, however, if American bombs begin to fall on their country.

The Next Phase

There is a way to go beyond merely managing the current instability, and to capitalize on it. I'm aware that this is not the most opportune moment in American history to disinter Wilsonian idealism, but America does now have the chance to help right some historic wrongs—for one thing, wrongs committed against the Kurds. (There are other peoples, of course, in the Middle East that the U.S. could stand up for, if it weren't quite so committed to the preservation of the existing map; the blacks in the south of Sudan—one of the most disastrous countries created by Europe—would surely like to be free from the Arab government that rules them from Khartoum.)

Iraq has been unstable since its creation because its Kurds and Shiites did not want to be ruled from Baghdad by a Sunni minority. So why not remove one source of instability—the perennially oppressed Kurds—from the formula? Kurdish independence was—literally—one of Wilson's famous Fourteen Points (No. 12, to be precise), and it is quite obviously a moral cause (and no less moral than the cause that preoccupies the West—that of Palestinian independence). There is danger here, of course: Kurdish freedom might spark secessionist impulses among other Middle Eastern ethnic groups. But these impulses already exist, and one lesson from the British and French management of the Middle East is that people cannot be suppressed forever.

For the moment, the Kurds of Iraq are playing the American game, officially supporting the U.S. and its flawed vision of Iraqi federalism, in part because the Turks fear Kurdish independence. Turkey has been an important American ally except for the one time when Turkey's friendship would have truly mattered—at the outset of the Iraq War, when Turkey refused to let the American 4th Infantry Division invade northern Iraq from its territory. The U.S. does not owe Turkey quite as much as its advocates think. The Kurds, on the other hand, are the most stalwart U.S. allies in Iraq, and their leaders are certainly the most responsible, working for the country's unity even while hoping for something better for their own people. "If Iraq fails, no one will be able to blame the Kurds," said Barham Salih, a Kurd who is Iraq's deputy prime minister.

T he next phase of Middle East history could start 160 miles north of Baghdad, in Kirkuk, which the Kurds consider their Jerusalem. One day, in the home of Abdul Rahman Mustafa, the Kurdish-Iraqi governor there, I learned about the mature position the Kurds are adopting. Over the course of its 20 years, Saddam's regime expelled Kurds from Kirkuk and gave their homes to Arabs from the south. The government now is slowly—too slowly for many Kurds—reversing the expulsions. A group of dignitaries had come to see the governor on Eid al-Fitr, the holiday that marks the end of the holy month of Ramadan. To reach the governor's office, you must navigate an endless series of barricades manned by tense-seeming Kurdish soldiers. The house itself is surrounded by blast walls. Kirkuk has a vigorous Sunni terrorist underground, and an enormous car bomb had killed seven people the day before.

I asked the governor, who is an unexcitable lawyer of about 60, if "his people"—I phrased it this way—were seeking independence from Iraq. "My people," he said, "are all the people of Kirkuk." The men seated about his living room nodded in agreement. "My job is to help all the people of Kirkuk have better lives." More nodding. "My friends here all know that we will have justice for those who were hurt in the regime of Saddam, but we will not hurt others in order to get justice." Even more nodding, and mumblings of approval.

Druzistan

Official Name: The Most Serene State of Jabal al-Duruz
Capital: Al Suwayde
Population: 1.1 million
Form of Government: Benevolent dictatorship
Official Language: Arabic

Four men eventually got up to leave. They kissed the governor and then left the house. The governor turned to me and said, "One of those men is Arab. Everyone is welcome here."

I told him I would like to ask my question again. "Do your people want independence from Iraq?"

"Yes, of course my people, most of them, want a new, different situation," he said. "I think—I will be careful now—I think that we will have what we need soon. Please don't ask me any more specific questions about what we need and want."

I asked, instead, for his analysis of the situation—did he think the Sunni-Shiite struggle would become worse, or would it burn out? He laughed. "I cannot predict anything about this country. I would never have predicted that I would be governor of Kirkuk. This is a city that expelled Kurds like me until the Americans came. So I couldn't predict my own future. I only know that we won't go back to the way it was before."

He went on, "I listen to television about the future, but I don't believe anything I hear."

Later that evening, as I was looking over my notes of the conversation, I recalled another comment, made by a man who thought he understood the Middle East. A little over a year ago, I ran into Paul Bremer, the ex–grand vizier of the Coalition Provisional Authority, the man who disbanded the Iraqi army, among other achievements. We were at Reagan National Airport; it was the day after the Iraq Study Group report was released, and I asked Bremer what he thought of it. He said he had not yet read it. I told him that from what I could tell, the experts were already divided on its recommendations. Bremer laughed, and said, with what I'm fairly sure was a complete lack of self-awareness, "Who really is an Iraq expert, anyway?"

JEFFREY GOLDBERG, an *Atlantic* national correspondent, is the author of *Prisoners: A Story of Friendship and Terror.*

From *The Atlantic,* January/February 2008, pp. 69–79. Copyright © 2008 by the Atlantic. Reprinted by permission.

Taking Africa Seriously

The U.S. government now knows that Africa is important—and dangerous. Formerly divided between three different strategic military regions, the entire continent (except Egypt) will soon fall under the purview of a new combatant command, AFRICOM.

PATRICK J. PATERSON

The White House has announced a new military headquarters dedicated solely to operations in Africa. African Command (AFRICOM), the first new headquarters since the Northern Command was established in 2002, will help stop the continent from careening into conflict and collapse, while also serving U.S. interests abroad and at home.

Tenacious insurgencies in Iraq and Afghanistan continue to occupy U.S. military and political attention, while China offers increasing strategic competition. This simultaneous focus of U.S. interests on the enormous continent of war-ravaged regions and vast expanses of ungoverned territory marks a monumental foreign policy shift for the United States, which has long avoided Africa because of its myriad problems and lack of strategic value. But now U.S. government leaders have seen the value of a proactive approach to solving Africa's problems.

AFRICOM was conceived soon after the attacks of 11 September 2001, because of growing concern that terrorists could use Africa for training new jihadist recruits. Senior Pentagon and State Department officials realized that the continent's porous borders, nascent security forces, and corrupt dictators could provide a sanctuary for senior al Qaeda members fleeing the fighting in Afghanistan and Iraq.

In mid 2006, Secretary of Defense Donald Rumsfeld established a committee to review the possibilities of creating a new military headquarters for operations in Africa. The completed proposal was forwarded to the White House, and on 15 December 2006 President George Bush authorized the creation of a new combatant command and a change in responsibilities for U.S. military regions across the globe.

AFRICOM's Enormous AOR

Aside from a huge area of responsibility, the new command faces a daunting mission: help stabilize the continent. The region encompasses 25 percent of the world's landmass and 20 percent of its coastline. The continent's 53 countries account for more than a quarter of nations globally.

On the second-largest continent, African culture is as diverse as its topography. More than 2,000 languages have been identified, and most countries include hundreds of ethnic tribes. North Africa is characterized by its Muslim inhabitants, while sub-Saharan Africa mixes Christianity with traditional African religions.

In accordance with the Pentagon's Unified Command Plan, for strategic military purposes the world's regions are divided into zones. Previously, Africa fell under the responsibility of three different headquarters (combatant commands in military parlance), which Secretary of Defense Robert Gates called "an outdated arrangement left over from the Cold War."[1] The European Command (EUCOM) in Stuttgart had responsibility for 43 of the 53 African nations. The Central Command (CENTCOM) in Tampa oversaw operations in eight African nations in the Horn of Africa, including Djibouti, Egypt, Eritrea, Ethiopia, Kenya, Somalia, Sudan, and Yemen. And the Pacific Command (PACOM) controlled events in the islands off the Pacific Coast, including Madagascar, Comoros, Seychelles, and Mauritius.

Where Are the Boundaries?

Exactly where the lines would be drawn was a subject of major debate. Most proponents of the new command insisted that the entire continent fall under the AFRICOM commander's responsibility. But transferring all the various African programs from three COCOMs to a new headquarters was deemed problematic and unnecessary.

Currently, the only U.S. base in Africa resides in Djibouti, home of the Combined Joint Task Force-Horn of Africa (CJTF-HOA). This is the first permanent U.S. military presence on the continent since Wheelus Air Base, near Tripoli, Libya, closed in 1970. Established after 9/11, when the United States was concerned about terrorists fleeing into the ungoverned spaces of Somalia, the task force rests under the responsibility of CENTCOM Commander Admiral William Fallon, based in Tampa.

Some Pentagon officials cited the difficulty of transferring control of a 1,800-person command to a new headquarters that initially will be manned by only 200–300 officers. Further, many on the new AFRICOM staff will be new to the political and social issues in Africa, and probably challenged by the magnitude of establishing a new headquarters. The Pentagon officials recommended permanently leaving the Horn of Africa under CENTCOM's responsibility.

That is not going to happen, but for these and other reasons, the standup of the new headquarters will be a gradual process, spread over the next 12 months. The headquarters for the transition team was established in early February 2007 near the European Command headquarters staff from which AFRICOM, at least initially, will draw much of its expertise. Rear Admiral Robert Moeller, formerly Director of Strategy, Plans, and Policy (J-5) for CENTCOM, manages the transition team, which organized the headquarters staff that will be declared initially operational capable in October.

Among their many tasks, this team developed directives for AFRICOM, identified resource and manpower requirements, organized the interagency staff, and established relations with U.S. embassy personnel in all of the 53 African countries. Moeller will eventually hand over responsibility to a four-star general officer, the first commander of the African Command.

By 30 September 2008, AFRICOM will be fully operational and, with a staff estimated at 700–800, designated as its own combatant command. At this point, AFRICOM will assume responsibility for the entire continent—with the exception of Egypt. Because of its unique diplomatic relationship with the United States, Egypt will remain under CENTCOM purview.

The responsibility for AFRICOM will fall on General Kip Ward, U.S. Army, previously assigned as Deputy Commander of the European Command. At EUCOM, Ward's day-to-day responsibilities included overseeing military operations in 43 African countries.

Currently awaiting congressional confirmation for his new assignment, Ward already has had extensive experience on the continent. He was a senior commander involved with the Somali Relief Mission during Operation Restore Hope in 1993, and later served as the chief of the U.S. military mission to Egypt. Only the fifth African American four-star general in U.S. history, Ward is known for his ambitious and resourceful leadership, someone with a can-do attitude. These will be important traits for tackling the enormous military and diplomatic problems on a continent bigger than the United States, Canada, and Europe combined.

The commander of AFRICOM will be in close contact with the President. With the Goldwater-Nichols Act of 1986, combatant commanders were given control of all military services operating in their regions: they report to the President through only the Chairman of the Joint Chiefs and the Secretary of Defense. Unlike other combatant commands, the AFRICOM commander will not have the support of each service working in the theater of operations. The headquarters will comprise a joint staff of officers from different military services—but, for the time being, separate subcomponent headquarters from the

Army, Navy, Air Force, and Marine Corps will not be established to support operations in the AOR.

Searching for a Home

Stuttgart may be only a temporary stop for the staff. No one has revealed where the AFRICOM headquarters will be permanently located, but most admit that it should be somewhere on the African continent. Of the five current geographic combatant commands, only the European Command headquarters is located outside the United States. President Bush has said, "We will work closely with our African partners to determine an appropriate location for the new command in Africa."[2]

But initial negotiations among numerous African countries have revealed a reluctance to host the new headquarters command. Much of this hesitancy stems from the U.S. invasion of Iraq and from suspicions regarding our intentions in Africa. Theresa Whelan, Deputy Assistant Secretary of Defense for African Affairs, recently spoke of the misconceptions of AFRICOM's purpose: "Some people believe that we are establishing AFRICOM solely to fight terrorism or to secure oil resources or to discourage China. That is not true. AFRICOM is about helping Africans build greater capacity to assure their own security."[3]

As a result of this lack of enthusiasm, recent discussions have focused on establishing a series of "nodes" on the continent from which AFRICOM's responsibilities can be distributed. Exactly how the nodes will be organized—functionally, geographically, by mission—is still under discussion.

A New Model for Regional Military Commands

As a new command significantly different from EUCOM and CENTCOM, AFRICOM will be, according to Pentagon sources, the clearing house for all humanitarian assistance and disaster relief efforts on the continent. Unlike traditional COCOM organizations, AFRICOM will attempt to coordinate and focus the efforts of myriad government, international, and nongovernmental relief agencies dedicated to improving Africa's deplorable public-health problems.

The headquarters will be heavily staffed with State Department and U.S. Agency for International Development representatives, including senior Foreign Service officer Ambassador Robert Loftis, who will serve as the military commander's civilian deputy. Loftis, who has served in embassies in Lesotho and Mozambique, said: "What we're really talking about is taking all of those activities that are already being done and consolidating them into one command."[4]

Current Military Missions

The U.S. military is already a presence in Africa, dedicated to alleviating the suffering caused by famine and disease. CJTF-HOA, currently commanded by CENTCOM's Navy Rear Admiral James Hart, consists of 1,800 personnel, including engineers, veterinarians, and doctors dedicated to goodwill missions. They assist some of the poorest nations on the planet in an area more than two-thirds the size of the United States.

By improving conditions there, the unit hopes to prevent disenfranchised youth from being lured toward radicalism and extremist sentiments. One of Hart's predecessors, Marine Major General Timothy F. Ghormley, said: "We're trying to improve the underlying conditions. Poverty itself doesn't bring about terrorism, but destitution with no way ahead brings about a turn to a more radical approach."[5]

Many officials believe the vast unpatrolled and ungoverned expanses of the Saharan Desert, a region as large as the continental United States, make it a sanctuary for terrorists fleeing Afghanistan and Iraq. In 2004 the Pentagon launched Operation Enduring Freedom-Trans Sahara (OEF-TS), its biggest anti-terrorist effort outside Iraq and Afghanistan, designed to provide security assistance to our African partners. The idea was to be proactive. As former European Commander Marine General James Jones said, "Modest near term investments will enable us to avert crises that may require costly U.S. intervention in the future."[6]

OEF-TS is a multi-year effort to improve military capacities of the African armed forces so they can govern the region more effectively. The operation, currently involving nine Sahara nations, includes $100 million of funding each year, through 2013, for U.S. special operations forces conducting training with African military partners.

U.S. experts also believe the region is ideally suited for terrorists to recruit and train new jihadists before exporting members to targets in Europe or Iraq. "The whole gist of this thing is to get ahead . . . before it becomes a really big problem," said former deputy commander of EUCOM Air Force General Charles Wald.[7]

But critics say the effort could risk destabilizing already shaky African regimes by generating resentment for cooperation with a United States that many perceive as anti-Islamic. John Prendergrast, an African specialist with the Brussels-based International Crisis Group, said that U.S. counter-terror efforts in sub-Sahara Africa are "very little, and the training is a drop in the ocean. The locals see right through it."[8]

Other skeptics claim the effort will bolster control of corrupt African authoritarian regimes guilty of human rights abuses and heavy-handed tactics against their constituents. Proponents such as General Jones argue, "We're trying to prevent Africa from becoming the next Afghanistan or Iraq."

Keeping the Peace

One of AFRICOM's most important programs will be training African peacekeeping forces. The continent currently hosts half (8 of 16) of all active U.N. peacekeeping missions; 81 percent of the 54,000 U.N. peacekeepers are serving in Africa.[9] The post-World War II withdrawal from Africa of colonial powers left a power vacuum that was often filled by wars of independence and civil conflict. More than 8 million Africans are estimated to have died from war or war-related causes since 1945, and another 9.5 million remain displaced from their homes, accounting for one of every three refugees on the planet.

The most urgent crisis is in the Sudanese province of Darfur. Fighting between government-backed militia and rebels has resulted in 250,000 deaths and 2.5 million displaced refugees. Despite economic sanctions leveled on Khartoum by the U.N. and a declaration of genocide by the United States, only African Union forces have responded by sending peacekeeping forces to the region.

The effort has failed; African troops, inadequately trained and poorly equipped, have been unable to prevent bloodshed and violence in the regions they are deployed to protect. Seven thousand African Union peacekeepers, mostly from Nigeria, Rwanda, and Kenya, have not stopped the fighting between warring factions in an area the size of France.

The United States and European nations, spread thin by the conflicts in Iraq and Afghanistan, have been reluctant to commit troops and have limited their contribution to airlifting AU forces into the area. Even the African Contingency Operations Training and Assistance (ACOTA) program, a $40 million-a-year U.S. effort to train and equip African peacekeepers, has not provided results.

The success of ACOTA, EUCOM's flagship peacekeeping training program in Africa, is of vital importance for the United States. Our foreign policy has seriously failed in previous disasters on the continent, including Somalia in 1993 and Rwanda in 1994. Today, despite a recent agreement on the deployment of a U.N. peacekeeping force, the suffering in Darfur continues with no end in sight.

U.S. Strategic Objectives

AFRICOM's new mission is of critical urgency for American national security experts. The desperate conditions that most Africans wrestle with every day—civil conflict, disease, broken infrastructure, government corruption, uncontrolled borders, dysfunctional security forces, piracy—result in massive populations susceptible to popular rhetoric. Deputy Assistant Secretary of Defense Theresa Whelan described the objective: "We want to prevent problems from becoming crises and crises from becoming catastrophes."[10]

Fifty percent of the African population is under 15 years old, and the population is expected to grow from 800 million to 2 billion by 2050. This "youth bulge" is perceived to be especially vulnerable to jihadist sentiment and antiAmericanism. Combined with extreme weather and poor infrastructure, the situation is dire. Former CENTCOM commander General Abizaid said: "The combination of these serious challenges creates an environment that is ripe for exploitation by extremists and criminal organizations."[12]

Military civil affairs units and AFRICOM-supported charity organizations will have the dual assignments of winning the hearts and minds of Africans while improving their desperate conditions. Collaborating closely with the nongovernmental organizations, these teams will conduct goodwill missions such as well-digging and providing medical assistance to tribal areas that rarely see outsiders.

The units will need to be aware of cultural intricacies. Diplomat-soldiers like the current pool of foreign area officers in each service will be critical to developing language skills and cultural sensitivity. "We don't have a lot of people who understand the region well," said former CJTFHOA commander Rear Admiral Richard Hunt of his mission among the eight nations of the Horn of Africa.[13]

Can We Do It?

Already bogged down countering a costly insurgency in Iraq, the United States may have little fight left for the problems in Africa. U.S. military forces, "stretched nearly to the breaking point by repeated deployments to Iraq," according to the Iraq Study Group report, will be hard-pressed to send adequate troops.[14] A multitude of African nations have an immediate need for training and advisement.

One staff officer involved with the AFRICOM planning effort calculated that the total annual financial assistance for all of Africa last year would last 16 hours in Iraq. A drawdown there may free additional troops for duty in Africa, but the heavily used equipment in Iraq will require years before it can be brought back into working condition. Another critical question is whether the new Democratic-led Congress will permit another military foray into uncharted territory.

There is no guarantee of success in an area with such enormous problems. Indeed, though most officials believe the standup of an African Command is long overdue, there is some pessimism about its ability to do much good on such a vast continent. "It's almost even asking too much to have one command for Africa, since there are such differences between northern Africa, sub-Sahara Africa, and even within the regions," said one strategist.[15]

The reputation of the United States—which many resent for having invaded two Muslim countries in the last five years—requires damage control if it's going to overcome suspicions on this continent. One West African representative at a recent maritime conference said to me: "You have invaded Iraq for its oil. Now we think that you are coming here for our oil."[16]

But regardless of perceptions, the best hopes of preventing an African apocalypse ride on the shoulders of the new African Command. (All opinions expressed here are my own and in no way reflect an official position of AFRICOM or Special Operations Command, Europe.)

Notes

1. Jim Garamone, "DOD Establishing U.S. Africa Command," American Forces Press Service, 6 February 2007.

2. White House press release, "President Bush Creates a Department of Defense Unified Combatant Command for Africa," 6 February 2007.

3. John Kruzel, "Pentagon Official Describes AFRICOM's Mission, Dispels Misconceptions," American Forces Press Service, 6 August 2007.

4. Vince Crawley, "U.S. Creating New African Command to Coordinate Military Efforts," U.S. Information Agency, 6 February 2007.

5. Vince Crawley, "Troops Tackle Humanitarian Projects in Horn of Africa," Navy Times, 24 October 2005.

6. General James Jones, USMC, U.S. Department of State, testimony to Senate Foreign Relations Committee, 28 September 2005.

7. Gordon Lubold, "Euro Command Wants a Heftier Presence in Northern Africa," Navy Times, 10 January 2005.

8. David Morgan, "Africa Key to Pentagon Counterterrorism Plan," Reuters News Agency, June 2006.

9. Stephan Faris, "Containment Strategy," Atlantic Monthly, December 2006, p. 34.

10. Deborah TaTe, "U.S. Officials Brief Congress on New Military Command for Africa," Voice of America News, 1 August 2007.

11. United Nations Population Fund, statement commemorating World Population Day, 11 July 2005, http://www.unfpa.org.

12. Mark Trueblood, The Spectrum, 18 October 2006.

13. Jim. Garamone, "Admiral Cites Complexity in Horn of Africa Mission," American Forces Press Service, 24 April 2006.

14. James A Baker III and Lee Hamilton, The Iraq Study Group Report (New York: Vintage, 6 December 2006). p. 51.

15. Joseph Giordono, "U.S. Military Aid in Tanzania a Huge Step Forward," Mideast Stars and Stripes, 17 September 2006.

16. Nigerian Ministry of Foreign Affairs representative, Gulf of Guinea Maritime Security Conference, Accra, Ghana, March 2006. Comments made to author.

Lieutenant Commander **PATRICK J. PATERSON,** a Navy Foreign Area Officer, recently completed an assignment with Special Operations Command Europe. He was a strategic planner for Operation Enduring Freedom-Trans Sahara (OEF-TS) and coordinated U.S. Special Operations Forces employment in 43 African countries.

UNIT 6

Conflicts among Nation-States in the Global South, Sub-National Conflicts, and the Role of Non-State Actors in an Interdependent World

Unit Selections

Key Points to Consider

- Is it too late for a diplomatic solution leading to a Palestinian state?

- Why are so many refugees leaving Iraq and what type of problems are they bringing to Iraq's neighbors?

- What non-state actors are likely to play important roles in the conflict dynamics of future political conflicts in the Middle East and Africa?

Student Web Site

www.mhcls.com

Internet References

Kubatana.net
   http://www.kubatana.net

AllAfrica.com
   http://allafrica.com/

Pajhwok Afghan News
   http://www.pajhwak.com/

ei: Electronic Intifada
   http://electronicintifada.net/new.shtml

IslamiCity
   http://islamicity.com

Palestine-Israel—American Task Force on Palestine
   http://www.americantaskforce.org

Private Military Companies (Mercenaries)
   http://www.bicc.de/pmc/links.php

Civil wars are now the most common form of warfare in International Relations. Civil conflicts are extremely costly in terms of the number of lives lost, the damage to the local economy and environment, and the violence and disruption that spills over into neighboring countries. The civil war in the Democratic Republic of the Congo (DRC) led to more lives being lost than during World War II.

In the Horn of Africa, there are several interlocking conflicts involving actors in Sudan and Somalia. In both countries, millions of civilians are at risk. During 2007, the government of Sudan finally agreed to accept 26,000 international peacemakers under the auspices of the United Nations and the African Union (AU) after extensive international pressures and publicity of ongoing atrocities in Darfur, Sudan, that the AU peacekeepers were unable to stop. The new peacekeepers were unable to prevent attacks on civilians in October 2007 by an unidentified rebel force that overran an African Union peacekeeping base in Darfur killing 10 personnel and wounding several more. No non-African member state of the United Nations have been willing to support the UNAMID peacekeeping force for Darfur with either more resources or troops even though the conflict in Darfur has spilled over into neighboring Chad.

Tensions between Arabs and Africans are also increasing in other parts of Sudan in 2008. The world also ignored a major violation of the Comprehensive Peace Accords (CPA) when Sudanese government troops violently took control of a disputed town on the border with Southern Sudan. Most observers are now predicting that a planned referendum to be held in 2010 to let the people of Southern Sudan decide whether or not to secede will probably not be held. Instead, both sides are now preparing for resumption of armed conflict in Africa's longest running civil war.

The fact that the government of Southern Sudan is actively purchasing additional arms in preparation for renewed fighting accidentally burst onto the front pages of western newspapers when a freighter registered in Lithuanian was seized by pirates off the coast of Somalia. The pirates were surprised to learn that the cargo included old Soviet tanks officially destined for Kenya. However, subsequent reports claimed that the ultimate destination of the tanks was to be the government of Southern Sudan. The fact that several actors, including private and publically foreign owned oil companies, are vying for the rights to exploit oil reserves in Southern Sudan suggest that any future conflict is likely to have international implications.

By November, pirates off the coast of southern Somalia had attacked more than 80 vessels in 2008. The pirates escalated their tactics by seizing the Sirius Star, a Saudi state-owned oil tanker that carried two million barrels of oil or a quarter of Saudi Arabia's daily exports. The Sirius Star was bound for the United States via the Cape of Good Hope. Although the Saudi Arabian government immediate announced that they would

© Ingram Publishing/SuperStock

join international efforts to battle piracy, the government also retained a private firm to negotiate the release of the Sirius Star crews from the pirates. As a failed state in a state of civil war, the Transnational Government that most Western states recognize can do nothing as the group is a government in name only. However, a week after the seizure of the Sirius Star, a spokesperson of the Islamic Courts coalition that recently retook major towns in the south, claimed that they would take action to find the pirates and return the vessel to Saudi Arabia as dictated by Shar'ia law. Thus, the incident illustrates how non-state actors in a failed state perform certain duties normally handled by governments.

The Sirius Star incident also illustrates how failed states negatively affect the stability of regional neighbors and occasionally the entire world. Some piracy has always occurred in the Gulf of Aden. However, older Somali pirates claim that they were forced to take up piracy in large numbers about a decade ago because they had no other way to earn a living after local fisheries collapsed due to over fishing by foreign commercial fish factory vessels. After a decade, the pirates operating in the Gulf of Aden have used profits and their experiences with successful seizures to buy larger boats, sophisticated weapons, and learned new tactics to seize increasingly larger vessels quickly. These operations are increasing despite increased number of foreign navies, including U.S. and NATO vessels.

Recent developments suggest that more than increased naval patrols and high technology, monitoring will be needed to solve the problem of piracy in East Africa. Most of the younger pirates claim they have no other way to earn a living. By the end of 2008, Somali journalists were also reporting that in several villages in southern Somali, young men claimed that no woman would consider marriage unless they were a pirate and that young children were singing songs about how they wanted to become pirates when they grew up. The *Sirus Star* incident may help to make visible some of the longer-term and usually invisible costs of ignoring collapsed states. In addition to creating a seriously growing humanitarian crisis, people are forced to adopt new economic livelihoods and cultural norms that are likely to make settlement of domestic conflicts even harder to resolve in the long run.

Often, the damage from modern civil wars is so great that it takes decades for the effected nation-state to fully rebuild and recover. Nearly every ongoing civil war must be of concern to foreign policy decisionmakers because there is always the danger that a civil war will escalate and spill over to other states. Also, several different types of outside parties are almost always involved in domestic conflicts such as providers of arms, allies for one or more factions in the fight, external nation-states who get involved for a variety of reasons, and neighboring states who often have tangible interests in preventing violence from spilling over their borders. The lack of a legitimate government was the rationale provided by the Ethiopian government for their military intervention into Somalia at the end of 2006; at the time, the Somali Courts had managed to take control of most of the cities and village in central and southern Somalia. The Ethiopian government had promised to leave Somalia quickly once they had overthrown the radical Islamic Courts. However, Ethiopian troops remain bogged down in central Somalia while factions aligned with the Islamic Courts have retaken most settlements in the south. Even though the Ethiopians were well-trained, well-armed, and aided initially by U.S. military airstrikes designed to eliminate al Qaeda training camps and kill the few remaining participants of the Kenya and Tanzania bombings, the rival factions have survived and continue to fight.

A similar spillover effect into neighboring countries is a continuing feature of the conflict between the Palestinians and the Israelis. This intractable conflict acquired a dangerous, new dimension in 2007 after Hamas seized control from Fatah forces in Gaza while Fatah remains in control in the West Bank. In "The Fragmentation of Palestine," Glenn E. Robinson describes the costly consequences of Hamas victory for Gaza residents. The continuing border closure between Israel and Gaza and international sanctions, implemented after Hamas seized power, are now threatening to cause the faltering economy in Gaza to completely collapse. No one is starving yet because UN food aid is being permitted into the area. However, many residents in Gaza ponder what to do about their increasingly bleak future. Despite recent sporadic rounds of diplomacy, Robinson concludes that "it may be too late to create a state of Palestinian territories splintered by factional politics and Israeli settlements."

Neighboring countries most often bear the costs of housing and feeding refugees who have fled the violence. Daniel L. Byman and Kenneth M. Pollack in "Carriers of Conflict" describe how the recent exodus of Iraqi refugees to neighboring countries, including Jordan, Lebanon, Syria, Saudi Arabia, Iran, Kuwait and Turkey, may be a precursor of future instability and war in the Middle East. Often neighboring states are helped by non-governmental organizations (NGOs) engaged in humanitarian relief for civilians in conflict ridden zones. Most of these organizations or national relief agencies are invisible to international publics, although some such as Doctors without Borders, have become quite well known. NGOs often function alongside or in coordination with programs run by the United Nations, other intergovernmental organizations, and some national relief efforts of neutral countries.

Increasingly, certain wealthy or famous individuals are also getting involved as informal mediators or spokespersons for groups that have no other voice. Although ex-officials and famous personalities have always played a role in international affairs, the potential influence of famous individuals has increased, as various media become more influential in the lives of citizens throughout the world. Wealthy individuals—such as Bill and Melinda Gates—are now having a significant effect on the way many governments in the developing world combat the spread of the HIV/AIDS pandemic and other infectious diseases through foundation contributions. In a similar fashion, another wealthy philanthropist, George Soros, through his own private foundation has given more than $5 billion in grants to populist causes that make a substantial difference on the ground in the developing world. During 2006, the Soros and Bill and Melinda Gates Foundations joined forces with another well-established actor, the Rockefeller Foundation, in order to build Millennium Villages in Africa. These villages are meant to be demonstration projects that involve a comprehensive approach to improving the lives of villages by providing wage jobs, better schools, health care, and better access via improved physical and electronic infrastructure to the outside world. Another fabulously wealthy private individual, Warren Buffett, also announced his decision to use the bulk of his fortune to address the world's most challenging inequities, including directing a large portion of his funds to the Bill and Melinda Gates Foundation.

Rock stars are also increasingly getting involved by working to ameliorate specific international problems. One of the most visible rock stars involved in global affairs is Bono from the band U2. Bono has been remarkably successful in his global campaign against disease and destitution. The actions of these celebrities, and millions of individuals who are not well known, illustrate how and why thousands of daily transactions and exchanges throughout the world are undermining the sovereignty of nation-states to such an extent that the future system may be very different than the one we know today. The potential influence of individuals, particularly those with worldwide name-recognition such as ex-U.S. presidents and famous movie or rock stars, seems to be growing as the role of media spreads around the world.

The Fragmentation of Palestine

Ironically, without concerted effort by all parties to forge a credible Palestinian state, the solution that almost nobody wants will gradually emerge: that of a single, binational state between the Jordan River and the Mediterranean Sea.

GLENN E. ROBINSON

The late Israeli Prime Minister Yitzhak Rabin once commented that he would not mind seeing Gaza sink into the Mediterranean Sea. Events during the past year suggest that not only would many Israelis concur with his sentiment, but many Palestinians would not object either.

The current year has marked a dismal nadir in Palestinian politics. A brief but perhaps unfinished civil war split the Hamas-led Gaza Strip from the Fatah-controlled West Bank. Gaza has rotted in its forced isolation, sending the occasional crude Qassam rocket into Israel, and receiving much more in return. The West Bank has continued to be fragmented by Israel into small insulated regions, with ever more land seized for settlements, a separation wall barring access to Israel, and more roads onto which Palestinians are not allowed. A late flurry of diplomatic activity by a Bush administration seeking to salvage something from its disastrous Middle East policies will likely prove to be too little, too late. Finding reasons for optimism in this morass is a Herculean task declined by nearly all observers.

Pluralism Palestinian-Style

The history itself is dispiriting to recount. The Bush administration, with its newfound zeal for elections, pushed hard following the death of Yasser Arafat in November 2004 for parliamentary elections in the Palestinian Authority (PA). The guiding belief was that democratic elections would naturally bring to power moderate, pro-Western representatives, especially after the election of the moderate Mahmoud Abbas (also known as Abu Mazen) to the PA presidency in January 2005. Given that the most recent parliamentary elections had been held in 1996, it was not unreasonable to argue that it was time for a new vote.

But the dominant political party, Fatah, proved incapable of engineering an election format that would allow it to win.

With Fatah's backing, the PA adopted a new, hybrid electoral law that would elect equal numbers of parliamentarians from national lists (under a proportional representation system) and from district elections (under a winner-take-all system). Hamas, the militant Islamist faction, detected an opening for success that did not exist in 1996, and agreed to participate in the elections.

Hamas tried to spin its participation as principled, but few took the argument seriously. Hamas had refused to run in the 1996 elections because the institutions at stake (parliament and the presidency) were direct results of the Oslo peace process, something Hamas rejected because it recognized Israel's existence. Hamas always maintained that it would run in municipal elections, since those bodies predated Oslo, and so it had—and successfully. Hamas's prospects for success in national elections were bolstered by its gains in these periodic municipal elections, by the new electoral law, and by the death of the iconic Arafat. Still, Hamas had to justify its volte-face on ideological grounds, so it declared that the second intifada, or uprising, had killed off the Oslo peace process, and thus the institution of parliament could now be considered independent of that now-defunct process. The argument broke down under even cursory scrutiny, but Hamas has always been a pragmatic and self-interested organization.

The January 2006 parliamentary elections gave Hamas an outright majority in parliament (74 seats out of 132, compared to Fatah's 34), but the party did not win a majority of the votes cast (it won 44 percent of the popular vote, compared to Fatah's 41 percent). The difference was the district elections, in which Hamas's party discipline won out. Hamas ran no more than one candidate per open seat. Officially, Fatah did likewise, but scores of Fatah-allied independents and Fatah cadres running as independents badly split the Fatah vote. On average, each Hamas candidate faced six opponents, most of whom were tied to Fatah. In Nablus, for example, 22 Fatah and Fatah-allied independent candidates received 300,000 total votes, but these candidates won only one seat of the six available. Hamas ran five candidates, and all five were victorious, even though they received only 204,000 votes combined. It was Hamas's party discipline, not majority support, that brought the party electoral success in 2006.

Hamas's election victory brought hard times to Palestinian society. The Bush administration, caught off guard, rejected the election result, and halted most aid to the Palestinians. Israel likewise cut ties to the PA, and halted the transfer of Palestinian tax revenues to the authority. Such transfers account for about two-thirds of the PA budget. Even the Europeans, after some hesitation, significantly cut back their support for the PA.

Nor did Fatah take the sudden transition from one-party rule to political pluralism lightly. Party cadres who had grown accustomed to the perquisites of power no longer had access to the patronage resources previously available. That the large majority of men under arms in the PA were loyal to Fatah provided a temptation to simply force Hamas out of power through force. Muhammad Dahlan, at the time Fatah's primary warlord in Gaza, argued for just such a militant approach. He was overruled by others in Fatah who believed that Hamas's reign would be brief, given its international isolation.

Still, Dahlan and his soldiers undertook a policy of armed provocation against Hamas. US policy, guided centrally by Elliot Abrams at the National Security Council, encouraged this Fatah militancy against Hamas. Together with Egypt and Jordan, the United States armed and trained a new elite Presidential Guard that would be loyal to Fatah's Abbas. Many analysts believed this unit would ultimately be responsible for initiating a coup against the Hamas government if and when a showdown occurred.

Hamas responded by creating its own 5,000-man paramilitary Executive Force, distinct from its long-time armed wing, the Izz al-Din al-Qassam Brigades. The Executive Force was based entirely in the Gaza Strip, since Israel still had full control of the West Bank. Meanwhile, Fatah militants repeatedly attacked Hamas ministries, the Hamas-controlled parliament, and other institutions associated with Hamas. The Fatah-allied Preventive Security Force often refused to take orders from its newly elected civilian leaders. In spite of constant and passionate calls by leading Palestinians to back away from the brink of civil war, by December 2006, assassinations and street battles in Gaza between Hamas and Fatah were occurring daily, with scores killed. Fatah's killings and abductions of Hamas cadres and their supporters were often undisciplined in their implementation. Hamas was generally more careful to focus its violence on the Fatah security apparatus instead of Fatah's broader political base.

Periodic interventions slowed the march toward civil war for brief periods. The most serious intervention occurred in February 2007 when Saudi King Abdullah, at a conference in Mecca, convinced Abbas, PA Prime Minister Ismail Haniya, and Khalid Mishal, Hamas's Damascus-based external leader, to agree on a power-sharing arrangement. The Bush administration, seeking to isolate Hamas, was not pleased with the Saudi effort and quietly rejected it. But King Abdullah had his own political reasons for his unprecedented display of diplomatic initiative: Iran's rising influence and regional ambitions, in which, as the Saudis recognized, the Palestine issue was of central importance.

The Hamas Putsch

The agreement reached in Mecca was short-lived because it did not address the key issue that was driving intra-Palestinian violence: the rejection of political pluralism by Fatah hardliners who sought to recreate one-party rule. While some of Fatah's major political leaders were willing to play ball with Hamas under certain conditions, Fatah's warlords and the armed elements they controlled were not so inclined. That they had American and Israeli backing to go after Hamas further encouraged the hardliners. Armed provocations and retaliations resumed before the ink was dry on the Mecca agreement.

In June 2007, in a well-organized campaign, Hamas overwhelmed Fatah's forces in Gaza after four days of fighting. Fatah put up surprisingly little resistance, in part because Dahlan was in Egypt recovering from knee surgery and could not rally his forces. Abbas immediately labeled Hamas's putsch a coup d'ètat, broke off all relations with Hamas, dissolved the unity government that had been formed just three months earlier, and dismissed Haniya as prime minister—replacing him with Salam Fayyad, a political independent who has the trust of Fatah's top leaders, Israel, the United States, and the European Union. Hamas, for its part, claimed that it was acting to protect a democratically elected government from an organized, armed attempt to overthrow it.

The timing of the putsch was not accidental—Hamas leaders believed, with some cause, that a Fatah coup was imminent. Under the leadership of Lt. Gen. Keith Dayton, the American security coordinator with the Palestinians, 3,500 Presidential Guards had been trained and armed. At least one battalion recently had been deployed in Gaza (and had been involved in clashes with Hamas several weeks before the putsch). The process of readying the Presidential Guard had been accelerated in the months since the Mecca power-sharing agreement. With half of Hamas's parliamentarians imprisoned in Israeli jails, the paralysis of the PA's government could have provided Abbas with a rationale for dismissing the Hamas government if he so chose, and Abbas increasingly had the forces necessary to beat back any resistance to such a decision. Hamas determined that it had to move soon if it wanted to maintain power, at least in Gaza, and it acted accordingly.

The Fatah Response

The Hamas putsch in Gaza has effectively split the West Bank and Gaza Strip into two separate political and administrative bodies, a new reality that is unlikely to change in the near future. After its takeover of Gaza, Hamas did not declare victory or seek a new political structure. It did not proclaim a new state in Gaza. Hamas continued to recognize the presidency of Abbas, but rejected Abbas's dismissal of Prime Minister Haniya and his cabinet. Indeed, Hamas vigorously justified its action as a defense of democracy and the rule of law against armed and extralegal attempts to reverse the outcome of the 2006 elections.

Fatah has responded to the Hamas putsch with anger and extralegal maneuvers. Initially, numerous Hamas cadres in the West Bank were beaten, some were killed, and Hamas institutions were attacked. Hamas activists in the West Bank have assumed a low profile, especially given that the armed elements of Hamas who could provide some protection are almost entirely based in Gaza.

On the political level, the basis for Fatah's response to the events in Gaza remains controversial. Fayyad, whom Abbas appointed as acting prime minister after he dismissed the Hamas government, is a respected economist, a former analyst with the World Bank and the International Monetary Fund, and a former PA minister of finance. The problem is that Fayyad's government clearly violates the PA's Basic Law. The authority's president may dismiss a prime minister and may appoint an acting prime minister (with some caveats). But the new prime minister and his cabinet must be confirmed by the parliament. Since Hamas controls the parliament, such confirmation is impossible, which is why many Palestinians, even those not associated with Hamas, view Fayyad's government as illegal. Abbas tried to get around this problem by simply suspending three articles of the Basic Law, an action that was also legally suspect. In short, the current PA government was constituted outside the legal framework and operates, *ipso facto,* through extra-constitutional fiat and political expediency, not legal legitimacy.

Many Palestinians, even those not associated with Hamas, view Fayyad's government as illegal.

Fatah has also signed on to efforts by Israel and the United States to isolate Gaza so thoroughly that the Hamas government loses popular support. Some humanitarian assistance is allowed into Gaza, but daily life there today is extremely harsh. Israel has direct control over two of Gaza's three land borders and indirect control over the third. Israel also controls Gaza's airspace and its seacoast. Because of this overarching control, many legal specialists maintain that Israel is still legally in occupation of the Gaza Strip, although its colonization efforts have ended. Since the Hamas putsch, Israel has tightened the borders into Gaza, limiting to a trickle the flow of goods and people across the border. The one exception has been Israeli agricultural products, which mostly indicates the power of Israel's farm lobby.

The closure of Gaza and its conversion into a large open-air prison, as many Palestinians call it, have led to economic devastation. The picture is bleak: Unemployment in Gaza tops 70 percent; the same percentage of Gazan households live below the poverty line; and, worse still, 42 percent of Gazan households live in extreme poverty. Most survive on humanitarian distributions from the United Nations Relief and Works Agency and nongovernmental organizations (many of which are affiliated with Hamas). Gaza is now poorer than Rwanda, a country only a few years removed from genocide. And the periodic military tit-for-tat between Israel and Hamas at times makes life even more miserable for Gazans. In September 2007, Israel declared Gaza a "hostile entity" and stated its intention to cut off electricity and fuel supplies.

The one area in which Hamas has enjoyed success is in law and order. Hamas effectively ended armed clashes with Fatah, and it has also disarmed some major gangs, and clans operating as gang networks. Public opinion surveys give Hamas high marks for bringing security and order to Gaza, if not for much else.

Hamas's putsch in Gaza temporarily unified Fatah, but it remains a deeply divided organization. Fatah's fissures, brought on by Oslo, have grown even wider since Arafat's death. Today, there are three Fatahs, with only loose ties holding the disparate parts together. There is the Fatah of the old guard, or Oslo elite, represented most prominently by Abbas. This is the smallest but most widely known branch of Fatah. It includes the Palestine Liberation Organization (PLO) cadres who returned from exile with Arafat in 1994 as part of the Oslo accords.

Then there is the Fatah of the young guard, or the intifada elite—cadres born and raised in the occupied territories who rose to local prominence with the first Palestinian uprising in 1987–1993. The most prominent leader of this group is Marwan Barghouti, currently in an Israeli prison. Widely viewed as a future Palestinian president, Barghouti is the most important leader in Palestine in terms of being able to deliver a peace deal with Israel.

The third Fatah is that of the young toughs—teenagers and twenty-somethings who came of age during the second uprising, or *intifadat al-Aqsa,* of 2000–2005. This Fatah has yet to coalesce around particular leadership, and is only loosely controlled by the other two Fatah factions. Often, these cadres are free agents, available for recruitment by Fatah's regional warlords. The dramatic rise in armed criminal behavior in Palestine in the past few years is also linked to this group.

The Divided West Bank

Life in the West Bank is not much better than in Gaza, as it has become nearly impossible for Palestinians to travel from one village to another. The West Bank is divided into scores of isolated fragments of land, each cut off from the rest of Palestinian society by some of the over 500 permanent Israeli checkpoints and road closures scattered throughout the occupied territory. On any given day, moreover, there are hundreds more "flying checkpoints," which generally remain in place for a few hours at a time. All of these closures are in addition to the enormous separation wall that Israel is building along the entire length of the West Bank. Higher than the Berlin Wall, it cuts some Palestinian communities in half and in many cases prevents farmers from reaching their land. Israel claims the wall is essential to its security, but Palestinians (and some Israeli human rights groups such as B'Tselem) see an ill-disguised land grab.

Israel has promised to ease the burdens on Palestinian internal travel in the West Bank as a political favor to Abbas, but has failed to fulfill this pledge. Israel has also promised the United States that it would remove recently built "outpost" settlements in the West Bank, but this has not been done yet either. The outposts, advocated by the former prime minister Ariel Sharon during attempts by then-Prime Minister Ehud Barak to make peace, were built in rural areas of the West Bank in order to prevent land contiguity for Palestinians even in lightly populated areas.

Israeli colonies in the West Bank are central to the fragmentation of Palestinian lands. The inexorable growth of the settlements also largely explains Palestinian skepticism about the Oslo peace process in the 1990s. For example, at the time of the Madrid conference in 1991, which initiated the Middle East peace process, there were 90,000 Israeli settlers in the West Bank (excluding East Jerusalem). When Rabin was assassinated in November 1995, the West Bank settlement population had grown to 135,000. At the time of the ill-fated Camp David talks in 2000, Israel's settler population in the West Bank had grown to 200,000. Today, it stands at 270,000, scattered across 140 settlements. Each settlement is accompanied by a network of checkpoints and "bypass roads" for use only by settlers and the army. These roads further fragment the West Bank. The settlements are in clear violation of international law, specifically the Fourth Geneva Convention, which prohibits an occupying power from transferring its own civilian population to the lands it is occupying. The settlers' presence poisons any hope for real peace.

For decades Israel claimed that the settlements were built on "state lands," not on confiscated private property. In fact, Israel's own data, obtained and published by B'Tselem in 2007, show that 39 percent of settlement lands consist of private Palestinian property confiscated by Israel, often under the guise of "security." The actual percentage of private property confiscated is no doubt even higher, since Israel, beginning with the government of Prime Minister Menachim Begin, has used tortured definitions of "state lands," dating back to the Ottoman Empire, to justify confiscation and settlement construction.

The extent of Israeli colonies in the West Bank today may well represent the victory of the Likud Party's ideology, an ideology seeking to populate the West Bank with so many Jews that it would be politically impossible for any future Israeli government to undertake a meaningful withdrawal as part of a peace treaty. The Israeli right also knew that no legitimate Palestinian leader would sign on to a peace agreement that returned only fragmented portions of the West Bank. The best way to block such an agreement and maintain permanent Israeli control of the West Bank—the goal of the Israeli right—was to build and expand settlements at a furious pace. That is exactly what has happened since 1981, when fewer than 20,000 settlers lived in the West Bank.

Analysts skeptical that any genuine two-state solution is still possible point to the settlements. Will any Israeli government really be willing to dismantle the settlement of Ariel, for example, which is deep inside the West Bank? Ariel alone has twice the number of settlers that were removed from all of the Gaza Strip in 2005. Even a peace deal mandating a level of annexation and land-swapping that the Palestinians could accept would still require Israel to remove tens of thousands of settlers from the West Bank. Likud's strategy to keep permanent Israeli control over the West Bank may very well have already achieved success.

Rice into the Maelstrom

US Secretary of State Condoleezza Rice has recently stepped into this bitter mess with a flurry of shuttle diplomacy that is designed, she says, to finally create a Palestinian state. It is still not clear how serious an effort this will be. Optimists point to several factors that could indicate a window of opportunity. First, they note that the Israel-Palestine issue is an enormous geostrategic liability for the United States, one that hinders American policy in Iraq, Iran, Syria, and elsewhere, and is the cornerstone for Al Qaeda recruitment propaganda throughout the Muslim world. The Bush administration, the argument goes, ignored the Palestine problem at its peril for years, but has run full force into it on every Middle East issue, and has thus finally "found religion." Second, optimists suggest that the legacy issue may be at work for both Rice and Bush, who are now seeking to pull a rabbit out of the hat for the sake of historical judgment. If they can manage an Israeli-Palestinian agreement, the catastrophe of Iraq may be partly mitigated. As a student of history, Rice may be especially motivated by such concerns. Third, the rejectionists on the Palestinian side—led by Hamas—are largely bottled up in Gaza and may not be in a strong position to undermine a deal on the West Bank. Since there are no settlers in the Gaza Strip, Gaza could always be added later to a peace deal fairly easily.

But skeptics outnumber optimists. Putting aside the sheer depth of Israel's occupation of the Palestinian territories, pessimists pose this question: Can a lame duck President Bush in his final year of office expend the kind of political capital necessary to forge a peace settlement? And not only is the US president in a position of weakness, so are Abbas and Israeli Prime Minister Ehud Olmert. Abbas's government, led by Fayyad, is unconstitutional. Olmert, still feeling the effects of Israel's disastrous 2006 war in Lebanon, has had approval ratings in Israel as low as 2 percent—below the margin of error! Skeptics argue that neither Olmert nor Abbas can really deliver on promises made as part of a peace deal.

Also, Rice appears to be doing battle inside the Bush administration. The most powerful neoconservative remaining in the Bush administration, Abrams, is widely seen as opposed to any substantive peace effort. Indeed, he famously told an audience of hawkish Israel supporters in the United States not to worry that Rice's shuttle diplomacy might bear fruit, because it was "just process" in order to keep the Europeans and moderate Arabs "on the team." President Bush, he assured his audience, was an "emergency brake" who would make sure Israel never had to sign an agreement it did not like. As previous Arab-Israeli negotiations have demonstrated, without a fully committed and involved US president, there will be no progress.

Skeptics note that on two other occasions the United States made promises to Abbas on which the Bush administration never delivered—weakening Abbas's position. In 2003, the United States strong-armed Arafat into agreeing to create a new position of prime minister, to which a great deal of authority would be transferred from the president's office. Abbas was named prime minister, also at Washington's urging. Yet no substantial political benefits then flowed to him: no settlements removed, no travel restrictions eased, no significant rhetorical support on major issues. Within months, an empty-handed Abbas resigned from office.

The same process unfolded when Abbas was elected president in January 2005. The United States had spent years arguing that Arafat was the core problem in the Israeli-Palestinian conflict and that no progress was possible with him at the helm. The Bush administration openly backed Abbas in the presidential election that followed Arafat's death. Once elected, however, Abbas was hung out to dry by the United States and Israel, which gave him no tangible rewards that could bolster supporters of peace on the Palestinian side. Even Israel's withdrawal from Gaza in 2005 was carried out unilaterally, and pointedly so, without Palestinian involvement. As a result, Abbas could not claim credit for compelling Israel to withdraw through negotiations. This allowed Hamas to claim credit for forcing Israel out with its militancy. Thus, Hamas's election victory after a year of fruitless rule by Abbas should not have surprised anyone.

Whether the US interest in the Israel-Palestine issue is "just process," as Abrams put it, or something more substantive, will largely determine the chances for success of the current peacemaking initiative by Rice and the Bush administration. Three strikes and Abbas is out.

Toward a Binational State

Ironically, without concerted effort by all parties to forge a credible Palestinian state, the solution that almost nobody wants will gradually emerge: that of a single, binational state between the Jordan River and the Mediterranean Sea. Israelis across the political spectrum reject a binational state, preferring instead the model of a Jewish state. Palestinians are more open to a binational state—indeed, an illiberal version of it was the PLO's choice before 1988—but by a large majority, they support a two-state solution today. A credible Palestinian state, however, will not emerge by itself, and it will require painful concessions by Israel if it is to exist at all. Is it already too late?

Some analysts, notably including Jerusalem's former deputy mayor, Meron Benvinisti, believe that the Rubicon has already been crossed, that the question is no longer whether there will be a binational state, but rather how best to manage and organize the reality of a binational state. But formal recognition of binationalism will not happen for at least two more generations, if indeed it ever does happen—and these generations likely will be drenched in blood, violence, and hatred.

Formal recognition of binationalism will not happen for at least two more generations, and these generations likely will be drenched in blood, violence, and hatred.

Israel has no consensus or long-term strategy on how to proceed. If a two-state solution is not forged now, and a binational state is rejected, what other possible solutions would there be? There are two, but neither one will be embraced by civilized nations. The first involves the ethnic cleansing of Palestinians west of the Jordan River—or "transfer," to use Israeli parlance. Once advocated by only the most extreme racists in Israel, the notion of transfer has gained a foothold in mainstream Israeli society and, it appears, even in the United States. Senator Sam Brownback of Kansas, when he was a candidate for the Republican presidential nomination, endorsed one version of "peaceful" ethnic cleansing. The problem with transfer, besides the obvious moral issue, is that it cannot work. There are 11 million people between the Jordan and the Mediterranean, split almost exactly between Jews and Palestinians. Ridding the land of 5 million Palestinians, or even a large number of them—even if it were done through "encouragement" rather than force—is a fool's dream that has no chance of success.

The other option is permanent occupation under conditions of apartheid. When the former US president Jimmy Carter described Israel's policies in the West Bank as resembling apartheid, he was strongly criticized in some quarters. But he was right on the facts. The West Bank is a geographical unit that contains two classes of people, each with separate and vastly unequal legal rights. The systematic legal discrimination goes beyond simple inequality in housing and education, for example; it extends to which roads are reserved for whom, who can ride which bus, and who has to stop at checkpoints. From my own experience in both places, the West Bank today does indeed resemble apartheid-era South Africa. No civilized country or person should embrace permanent occupation as a legitimate solution.

This observation returns us to the question that should give a sense of urgency to diplomatic efforts: a Palestinian state now, or a violent drift toward a binational state decades from now?

GLENN E. ROBINSON is an associate professor in the department of defense analysis at the Naval Postgraduate School. He is on leave this year at the Center for Middle Eastern Studies at the University of California at Berkeley.

The World in Numbers

Carriers of Conflict

For a preview of future instability and war in the Middle East, watch where Iraqi refugees are going.

Daniel L. Byman and Kenneth M. Pollack

Refugees from Iraq are on the move. More than 1.2 million of them have already fled the country, and recent anecdotal reports—a many-fold increase in the buses traveling daily from Baghdad to Jordan this summer, for example—suggest that the tempo of the exodus is increasing. If the violence in Iraq spreads, the number of Iraqis who flee to neighboring states may well triple. And if the nascent civil war in Iraq unfolds the way most other recent civil wars have, the refugees will remain outside Iraq for years.

All too often, where large numbers of refugees go, instability and war closely follow—as Middle Eastern history attests. Palestinian refugees, who with their descendants number in the millions, have been a source of regional violence and regime change for decades. They helped provoke the 1956 and 1967 Arab-Israeli wars by conducting cross-border attacks against Israel and inviting Israeli retaliation against the Arab states that hosted them. Later they turned against their hosts and catalyzed a civil war in Jordan (1970–71) and in Lebanon (1975–90). The "Palestinian question"—and the paltry Arab-state reaction to it—has also contributed to coups by militant Arab nationalists in Egypt, Iraq, and Syria.

The Palestinian experience in this regard is not unique. The fall of the Zairean ruler Mobutu Sese Seko, for instance, and the subsequent civil war in Zaire, which claimed roughly 4 million lives, can be traced directly to the arrival of Rwandan refugees in 1994. Refugees have a knack for upsetting the status quo.

The iconic image of the refugee is a bedraggled woman clutching her child as she stumbles into a blighted aid camp. But this picture is incomplete. Refugee camps, which are often under international protection but do not have international policing, can become sanctuaries for militia groups. Host governments often find it hard to stop these militias, even when they want to, either because they lack the military strength to do so or because fighters hide among innocent civilians. In fact, militia leaders sometimes

become the leaders of the refugee community, offering protection, imposing their will on any rivals, and recruiting new fighters from among the camp's many traumatized, jobless young men. Tribal elders and other leaders who might oppose violence may find themselves enfeebled by both the trauma of flight and the loss of their traditional basis of power (typically, control of land). As a result, refugee camps can become deeply radicalized communities, dangerous to their host countries in several ways. The mere presence of militias among the refugees tends to embroil the host country in war by making it a target.

Most Iraqi refugees are not in camps, but dispersed among local populations. But refugees, whether in camps or not, can also corrode state power from the inside, fomenting the radicalization of domestic populations and encouraging rebellion against host governments. The burden of caring for hundreds of thousands of refugees is heavy, straining government administrative capacity and possibly eroding public support for regimes shown to be weak, unresponsive, or callous. And the sudden presence of armed fighters with revolutionary aspirations can lead disaffected local clans or co-religionists to ally with the refugees against their own government, especially when an influx of one ethnic or religious group upsets a delicate demographic balance, as would likely be the case in some of Iraq's neighbors.

To date, Jordan and Syria have taken in the vast majority of fleeing Iraqis—in large part because those countries have been the most welcoming. But in the worst-case scenario of an all-out civil war, Iraq's other neighbors would not find it easy to resist the influx of refugees shows some of the places that might be most affected.

Daniel L. Byman is the director of Georgetown University's Center for Peace and Security Studies. **Kenneth M. Pollack** is the director of research at the Saban Center for Middle East Policy at the Brookings Institution.

UNIT 7

Asymmetric Conflicts: Trends in Terrorism and Counterterrorism

Unit Selections

Key Points to Consider

- What actions would you recommend the U.S. government to take in order to counter al Qaeda activities in the Middle East, Central Asia, and Europe?

- What is the "massive demographic tsunami" growing in much of the developing world? How is this demographic trend related to Jihadist terrorists' activities?

- What are some of the criminal scams being used by al Qaeda local cells and why are more terrorists turning to crime to support their attacks?

- What are the three integrated pillars of a successful counterinsurgency campaign?

- What are the counterinsurgency lessons that can be gleaned from the successful Rwandan Patriotic Army insurgency?

Student Web Site
www.mhcls.com

Internet References

Columbia International Affairs Online
http://www.ciaonet.org/cbr/cbr00/video/cbr-v/cbr-v.html

Combating Terrorism Center at West Point
http://ctc.usma.edu/

SITE: The Search for International Terrorist Entities
http://www.siteinstitute.org/index.html

Terrorism Research Center
http://www.terrorism.com

United States Government Counterinsurgency Initiative
http://www.usgcoin.org/

The terrorist attacks against the World Trade Center and the Pentagon on September 11, 2001, and the anthrax letter attacks the following month highlighted the vulnerabilities of economically developed societies to attacks by disaffected radicals who can now pursue their political goals by killing large numbers of civilians. The United States' decision to pursue the al-Qaeda terrorists using the military as the lead agency in the Global War on Terrorism (GWOT) resulted in an eight-year comprehensive offensive that has mobilized large amounts of the resources and time of the U.S. and allied governments. Although Osama bin Laden and Ayman al-Zawahiri remain at large, much of the leadership and organizational structure of al-Qaeda has been destroyed or disrupted.

For many observers, al-Qaeda's decision to take the fight directly to America was a strategic mistake since it prompted an unprecedented and largely effective response from a previously distracted giant, the United States. During the early years of the war many analysts believed that the United States had succeeded in its struggle against terrorism. However, many analysts and U.S. voters today have concluded that the United States was also wrong to attack Iraq rather than finish the hunt for Osama bin Laden and eliminate the residual Taliban threat in Afghanistan.

Peter Bergen in "Al Qaeda at 20 Dead or Alive?" describes the reasons why he believes al Qaeda's military and strategic campaign against the United States and 'near enemies' have failed. However, Bergen warns that "Al Qaeda's war for the hearts and minds continues." While he predicts that al Qaeda is unlikely to attack the United States and that Muslims will increasingly take a dim view of his group and its suicide bombers, Bergen warns that the links between radicals in such places as the United Kingdom and bin Laden remain a serious threat. Bergan warns that the "legacy will endure, even after al-Qaeda is defeated."

Close cooperation among U.S. allies in Europe and throughout the world appears to be an important part of an effective counterterrorism strategy. After the September 11, 2001, attacks in the United States, European investigators were surprised to learn that an extensive interlocking set of terrorist cells in Italy, Germany, Spain, Britain, France, Belgium, and numerous other countries remained in place. Al-Qaeda continues to recruit new members among disenchanted Muslims throughout Europe, Africa, and the Middle East who are looking for an alternative to the corrupt political center in which they live. Some recently foiled plots in Europe, such as the 2006 thwarted multiple Atlantic airline hijacking plot, had a few direct links to al-Qaeda Central. However, most of the 1,600 Muslims youths in the United Kingdom that MI5 acknowledged in November of 2006 they were monitoring as suspected foot soldiers for al-Qaeda throughout the United Kingdom, receive inspiration from, but had only a few direct links with, al-Qaeda Central. How to deal with

© Purestock/SuperStock

this threat is the subject of a great deal of debate. One reason is that the nature of the threat is actually quite complex in societies, such as the United Kingdom, with a large and growing Muslim population.

Cheryl Benard in "Toy Soldiers: The Youth Factor in the War on Terror" helps us understand one of the more basic levels of complexities found in both developed and developing societies. She notes that "membership in a clandestine terrorist cell" and the opportunity "to belong to a feared and seemingly heroic movement complete with martyrs" is inherently appealing to young people. Cheryl Benard explores some of the developmental and societal factors that may explain why the young, especially young men, join radical Jihadist terrorist cells and are willing to fight in remote conflicts. While the Western media tends to focus on the radical youths in societies such as the United Kingdom, Cheryl Benard warns that the large number of young people in many developing countries is a "massive demographic tsunami" that will continue to be a growing recruiting pool for terrorist cells in the future.

Today, some analysts stress that we are at the start of an asymmetric battle that may take 50 years to win. This more pessimistic view is based on several trends. Al-Qaeda has proven to be a highly adaptive movement in the face of a successful global War on Terrorism (GWOT) launched and led by the United States. Although al-Qaeda Central may be highly constrained and remain in hiding until Osama bin Laden is found or dies, the al-Qaeda movement has transformed itself into a looser, global collection of decentralized cells and groups. Some of these networks span the globe and are only loosely linked or linked only by shared political beliefs to al-Qaeda central run by Osama bin Laden and Ayman al-Zawahiri. Nearly all of the local cells fund their low-cost operations through criminal scams that are difficult to detect and thwart. Craig Whitlock in "Al-Qaeda Masters Terrorism on the Cheap," describes why such self-financing cells are difficult for authorities to detect by monitoring cash flows or bank transfers—the basis of many of the anti-terrorism financing laws in place today.

Another reason why most security analysts within the United States characterize the War on Terrorism as far from over is because there is a growing recognition that successful counterinsurgency campaigns are complicated affairs to implement effectively and often take a long time. David J. Kilcullen emphasizes in "Three Pillars of Counterinsurgency" that the last time the United States attempted to implement an inter-agency counterinsurgency doctrine was in 1962 and it didn't work very well. Kilcullen warns that the conflict environment today is even more complicated and that the U.S. government must mobilize all agencies of the U.S. government, along with host nations, multiple foreign allies and coalition partners, non-government organizations, media, community groups, and business in order to win the war. In his article, Kilcullen proposes an inter-agency counterinsurgency framework based on three integrated pillars—economic, political, and security activities.

A renewed interest in conditions necessary for counterinsurgency campaigns to succeed has also fueled an interest in learning more about the reasons why rebels are sometimes successful. In "The Boot Is Now on the Other Foot: Rwanda's Lessons from Both Sides of Insurgency," Greg Mills focuses on the Rwanda Patriotic Front's Army (RPA) that consists of soldiers who used to be insurgents. Mill's analysis is based on interviews with former rebels fighting to free Rwanda and finds three lessons why the RPA insurgents were successful against their Hutu opponents. Mills found that the RBA won because "their cause was just and had popular support; they used flexible tactics as circumstances changed; and there was no alternative to fighting until the regime in Kigali offered the Arusha peace agreement of 1993." Mills argues that these conditions can be used as general counterinsurgency lessons that are applicable to other parts of the world as well.

Al Qaeda at 20 Dead or Alive?

PETER BERGEN

Two decades after al-Qaeda was founded in the Pakistani border city of Peshawar by Osama bin Laden and a handful of veterans of the war against the Soviets in Afghanistan, the group is more famous and feared than ever. But its grand project—to transform the Muslim world into a militant Islamist caliphate—has been, by any measure, a resounding failure.

In large part, that's because Osama bin Laden's strategy for arriving at this Promised Land is a fantasy. Al-Qaeda's leader prides himself on being a big-think strategist, but for all his brains, leadership skills and charisma, he has fastened on an overall strategy that is self-defeating.

Bin Laden's main goal is to bring about regime change in the Middle East and to replace the governments in Cairo and Riyadh with Taliban-style theocracies. He believes that the way to accomplish this is to attack the "far enemy" (the United States), then watch as the supposedly impious, U.S.-backed Muslim regimes he calls the "near enemy" crumble.

This might have worked if the United States had turned out to be a paper tiger that could sustain only a few blows from al-Qaeda. But it didn't. Bin Laden's analysis showed no understanding of the vital interests—oil, Israel and regional stability—that undergird U.S. engagement in the Middle East, let alone the intensity of American outrage that would follow the first direct attack on the continental United States since the British burned the White House in 1814.

In fact, bin Laden's plan resulted in the direct opposite of a U.S. withdrawal from the Middle East. The United States now occupies Iraq, and NATO soldiers patrol the streets of Kandahar, the old de facto capital of bin Laden's Taliban allies. Relations between the United States and most authoritarian Arab regimes, meanwhile, are stronger than ever, based on their shared goal of defeating violent Islamists out for American blood and the regimes' power.

For most leaders, such a complete strategic failure would require a rethinking. Not for bin Laden. He could have formulated a new policy after U.S. forces toppled the Taliban in the winter of 2001, having al-Qaeda and its allies directly attack the sclerotic near-enemy regimes; he could have told his followers that, in strictly practical terms, provoking the world's only superpower would clearly interfere with al-Qaeda's goal of establishing Taliban-style rule from Indonesia to Morocco.

Instead, bin Laden continues to conceive of the United States as his main foe, as he has explained in audio- and videotapes that he has released since 2001. At the same time, al-Qaeda has fatally undermined its claim to be the true representative of all Muslims by killing thousands of them since Sept. 11, 2001. These two strategic blunders are the key reasons why bin Laden and his group will ultimately lose. But don't expect that defeat anytime soon. For now, al-Qaeda continues to gather strength, both as a terrorist/insurgent organization based along the Afghan-Pakistani border and as an ongoing model for violent Islamists around the globe.

So how strong—or weak—is al-Qaeda at 20? Earlier this year, a furious debate erupted in Washington between two influential counterterrorism analysts. On one side is a former CIA case officer, Marc Sageman, who says that the threat from al-Qaeda's core organization is largely over and warns that future attacks will come from the foot soldiers of a "leaderless jihad"—self-starting, homegrown radicals with no formal connection to bin Laden's cadre. On the other side of the debate stands Georgetown University professor Bruce Hoffman, who warns that al-Qaeda is on the march, not on the run.

This debate is hardly academic. If the global jihad has in fact become a leaderless one, terrorism will cease to be a top-tier U.S. national security problem and become a manageable, second-order threat, as it was for most of the 20th century. Leaderless organizations can't mount spectacular operations such as 9/11, which required years of planning and training. On the other hand, if al-Qaeda Central is as strong as Hoffman thinks it is, the United States will have to organize its policies in the Middle East, South Asia and at home around that threat for decades.

Sageman's view of the jihadist threat as local and leaderless is largely shared by key counterterrorism officials in Europe, who told me that they can't find any evidence of al-Qaeda operations in their countries. Baltasar Garzon, a judge who has investigated terrorist groups in Spain for the past decade, says that while bin Laden remains "a fundamental reference point for the al-Qaeda movement," he doesn't see any of the organization's fingerprints in his recent inquiries.

But this view is not shared by top counterterrorism officials in the United Kingdom and the United States. A 2007 U.S. National Intelligence Estimate concluded that al-Qaeda was growing more dangerous, not less.

Why the starkly differing views? Largely because U.S. and British officials are contending with an alarming new phenomenon, the deadly nexus developing between some militant British Muslims and al-Qaeda's new headquarters in Pakistan's lawless borderlands. The lesson of the July 2005 London subway bombings, the foiled 2006 scheme to bring down transatlantic jetliners and several other unnerving plots uncovered in the United Kingdom is that the bottom-up radicalization described by Sageman becomes really lethal only when the homegrown wannabes manage to make contact with the group that so worries Hoffman, al-Qaeda Central in Pakistan.

"Hotheads in a coffeehouse are a dime a dozen," said Michael Sheehan, who until 2006 was the deputy New York police commissioner responsible for counterterrorism. "Al-Qaeda Central is often the critical element in turning the hotheads into an actual capable cell." Which is why it's so worrisome that counterterrorism officials have noticed dozens of Europeans making their way to the tribal areas of Pakistan in the past couple of years.

That's a major shift. Until 2006, hardcore European jihadists would have traveled to Iraq. But the numbers doing so now have dwindled to almost zero, according to several European counterterrorism officials. That's because al-Qaeda's affiliate in Iraq has committed something tantamount to suicide.

Al-Qaeda in Iraq once held vast swaths of Sunni-dominated turf and helped spark a civil war by targeting Iraqi Shiites. But when the group imposed Taliban-style measures, such as banning smoking and shaving, on Iraq's Sunni population and started killing other insurgents who didn't share its ultra-fundamentalist views, other Sunnis turned against it. Today al-Qaeda in Iraq is dead, at least as an insurgent organization capable of imposing its will on the wider population. It can still perpetrate large-scale atrocities, of course, and could yet spoil Iraq's fragile truce by again attacking Iraqi Shiites. But for the moment, al-Qaeda in Iraq is on the run, demoralized and surrounded by enemies.

While that's good news for Iraq, there are alarming signs elsewhere. The border region of Pakistan and Afghanistan, an area where jihadists operate with something close to impunity, has become a magnet for foreign fighters. One particularly unwelcome development here: Al-Qaeda Central now exerts a great deal of ideological sway over Baitullah Mehsud, the new leader of the Taliban movement inside Pakistan, who has vowed to attack New York and London.

Next door in Afghanistan, the Taliban have also increasingly adopted bin Laden's worldview and tactics, which has helped them launch a dangerously effective insurgency based on sustained suicide attacks and the deft use of IEDs. And bin Laden's influence extends well beyond the Afghanistan-Pakistan theater. The same mainland European counterterrorism officials who are relieved not to be finding al-Qaeda Central cells in their own countries now worry that bin Laden's North African ally, al-Qaeda in the Islamic Maghreb, may be finding recruits among poorly integrated North African immigrants living in France, Belgium, Spain and Italy.

Al-Qaeda's war for hearts and minds goes on, too. Bin Laden once observed that 90 percent of his battle is waged in the media—and here, above all, he remains both relevant and cutting-edge. The most reliable guide to what al-Qaeda and the wider jihadist movement will do have long been bin Laden's public statements.

Since 9/11, bin Laden has issued more than two dozen video- and audiotapes, according to IntelCenter, a government contractor that tracks al-Qaeda's propaganda activities. Those messages have reached untold millions worldwide via TV, the Internet and newspapers. The tapes exhort al-Qaeda's followers to continue to kill Westerners and Jews, and some have also carried specific instructions for militant cells. In the past year, for instance, bin Laden has called for attacks on the Pakistani state—one of the reasons Pakistan saw more suicide attacks in 2007 than at any other time in its history.

Despite al-Qaeda's recent resurgence, I think it highly unlikely that the group will be able to attack inside the United States in the next five years. In the past, al-Qaeda terrorists trying to strike the U.S. homeland have had to slip inside from elsewhere, as the 9/11 hijackers did. No successful past plot has relied on al-Qaeda "sleeper cells" here, and there is little evidence that such cells exist today. Moreover, the United States is a much harder target than it was before 9/11. The U.S. government is on alert, as are ordinary citizens. (Just ask the would-be shoe-bomber, Richard Reid.)

Of course, homegrown terrorists inspired by al-Qaeda might carry out a small-bore attack inside the United States, although the U.S. Muslim community, which is far better integrated than its European counterparts, has produced few violent radicals. And al-Qaeda itself remains quite capable of attacking a wide range of U.S. interests overseas, killing U.S. soldiers in Iraq and Afghanistan and targeting U.S. embassies. But on balance, we have less to fear from al-Qaeda now than we did in 2001.

We would also be far better off if we managed to kill or capture al-Qaeda's innovative chief. So what is the U.S.-led hunt for bin Laden turning up? The short answer is nothing. Washington hasn't had a solid lead on him since radio intercepts placed him at the battle of Tora Bora in eastern Afghanistan in December 2001. U.S. intelligence officials widely assume that he is now in or near Pakistan's tribal areas—a particularly shrewd hiding place, according to Arthur Keller, a former CIA officer who ran a spy network there in 2006.

Keller told me that al-Qaeda's leaders have excellent operational security. "They have had a Darwinian education in what can give them away, and their tradecraft has improved as we have eliminated some of the less careful members of their organization," he noted. "They're hiding in a sea of people who are very xenophobic of outsiders, so it's a very, very tough nut to crack."

No matter what bin Laden's fate, Muslims around the world are increasingly taking a dim view of his group and its suicide operations. In the late 1990s, bin Laden was a folk hero to many Muslims. But since 2003, as al-Qaeda and its affiliates have killed Muslim civilians by the thousands from Casablanca to Kabul, support for bin Laden has nose-dived, according to Pew polls taken in key Muslim countries such as Indonesia and Pakistan.

At 20, al-Qaeda is losing its war, but its influence will live on. As Michael Scheuer, who founded the CIA's bin Laden unit in 1996, points out, "Their mission is accomplished: worldwide instigation and inspiration." To our grief, that legacy will endure, even after al-Qaeda is defeated.

PETER BERGEN is a fellow at both the New America Foundation and New York University's Center on Law and Security. He is the author of *The Osama bin Laden I Know*.

Toy Soldiers

The Youth Factor in the War on Terror

Membership in a clandestine terrorist cell; online linkages with glamorous, dangerous individuals; the opportunity to belong to a feared and seemingly heroic movement complete with martyrs—all of this is inherently appealing to young people.

CHERYL BENARD

"About the time of Easter . . . , many thousands of boys, ranging in age from six years to full maturity, left the plows or carts which they were driving, the flocks which they were pasturing, and anything else which they were doing . . . [and] put up banners and began to journey to Jerusalem. . . . They [said] that they were equal to the Divine will in this matter and that, whatever God might wish to do with them, they would accept it willingly and with humble spirit. Some were turned back at Metz, others at Piacenza, and others even at Rome. Still others got to Marseilles, but whether they crossed to the Holy Land or what their end was is uncertain. One thing is sure: that of the many thousands who rose up, only very few returned."

—From a description of the so-called
Children's Crusade in *Chronica Regiae Coloniensis
Continuatio prima,* translated by James Brundage

Much has been made of an ominous demographic reality prevalent in the Middle East. Although the exact number varies from country to country, any speaker who mentions the proportion of the population below age 20, or below age 16, can count on receiving gasps of surprise from Western audiences. Fifty percent of the population below age 19! Sixty-five percent below age 25! And no functioning economy to absorb them. It is clear even to a layperson that this spells trouble.

Experts will point out that it could also spell prosperity—in theory. In theory, a young population has the potential to be productive and to bless its society with a low dependency ratio: that is, with a larger segment of productive workers supporting a smaller segment of the elderly, the very young, the incapacitated, and otherwise nonproductive individuals who must count on tapping into the income of others. In reality, though, cultural, political, and economic factors can—and throughout much of the Islamic world do—stand in the way of productivity and prosperity. The youth overhang, instead of constituting a motor for growth, becomes what Isobel Coleman of the Council on Foreign Relations has called a potential "youthquake" and a "massive demographic tsunami."

Many young people in the Middle East, especially the famously more volatile young males, are deprived of sensible activities, bereft of real hope for a happy and independent future, unschooled in practical modes of thinking, and sexually frustrated in their strict and puritanical societies. Many are hammered with the rousing appeals of radical preachers and ideologues. Others are simply bored and purposeless. Clearly this is not a promising recipe for stable social advancement.

All of these social conditions and their implications in the region are being discussed and fretted over, and with good cause. But another variable in the situation has received less attention: the underlying mindset and mental development of young adults generally. I would argue that, beneath many of the conflicts tearing at the Middle East today, including the "war on terror," the Palestinian intifada against Israel, and the insurgency in Iraq—as indeed underneath probably most instances of major violence throughout history—there lies an unspoken, disturbing social contract in which older people pursue agendas by deploying the volatile weapon of mentally not-yet-mature younger men.

The Immature Brain

While this issue has important ethical dimensions, the question is raised more neutrally by recent neurological and developmental findings that in turn are the product of improved medical technology. Increasingly sophisticated Magnetic Resonance Imaging (MRI) of brains, in combination with research in experimental psychology, indicates that maturation may take place more gradually and conclude later than formerly presumed. A number of studies suggest that mental and behavioral development continues to be in considerable flux until somewhere between the ages of 22 and 24; that before this time, young people and particularly young men are inclined to show particular responses, behaviors, and mind-sets; and that these are of high relevance to their own personal safety and well-being and to those of others around them.

The findings can be summed up as follows: young men are strongly inclined to seek out situations of risk, excitement, and danger; and they also are likely to make fallacious judgments about their own abilities, overestimating their capacities and underestimating objective obstacles and dangers. In a variety of important interactive contexts, as a result, their reactions predictably veer toward the impulsive taking of unwise risks. All of this affects their ability not so much to understand, but to process and "believe in" the potential for negative outcomes and even catastrophic consequences of their decisions.

Not much of this, of course, really comes as a surprise. That young people are impulsive and that young men like to test themselves in situations of high risk is well known. Recent research, however, provides a much more specific window into the mechanics of youthful responses and decisions, as well as the situations that represent a particular risk for reactions that can be harmful to the individual or to others. It also reveals the inherence of some of these behaviors, which are not individual failings or errors but flow from a natural developmental process to which all individuals are subject—and which others might exploit.

The first conclusion that suggests itself from current research in neurological development is that adolescence and young adulthood conclude later than formerly assumed. Brain development is of course an ongoing process. Adolescence, however, is a time of particularly high change. Longitudinal studies following changes in the prefrontal cortex indicate that the changes do not wind down until age 22 or even later. The prefrontal cortex is jovially referred to by experts in this field as the "area of sober second thought." This is the part of the mind that carefully considers the consequences of a decision, weighs the pros and cons, reflects, and, depending on the evidence, may come to reconsider. In the absence of a fully developed prefrontal cortex, an individual will be more inclined to follow through on a spontaneous, impulsive decision.

In a 2004 study titled "Adolescent Brain Development and Drug Abuse," Ken Winters of the University of Minnesota noted that three brain structures that undergo maturation during youth—the nucleus accumbens, amygdale, and prefrontal cortex—have important implications for understanding adolescent behavior. "An immature nucleus accumbens is believed to result in preferences for activities that require low effort yet produce high excitement. . . . The amygdale is the structure responsible for integrating emotional reactions to pleasurable and aversive experiences. It is believed that a developing amygdale contributes to two behavioral effects: the tendency for adolescents to react explosively to situations rather than with more controlled responses, and the propensity for youth to misread neutral or inquisitive facial expressions of others as a sign of anger. And one of the last areas to mature is the prefrontal cortex . . . responsible for the complex processing of information, ranging from making judgments to controlling impulses, foreseeing consequences, and setting goals and plans. An immature prefrontal cortex is thought to be the neurobiological explanation for why teenagers show poor judgment and too often act before they think."

Recent MRI and brain mapping research has also focused on the cerebellum, a part of the brain formerly thought to relate primarily to physical movement, but now found to coordinate a variety of cognitive processes and to enable individuals to "navigate" social life. As Jay Giedd of the National Institute of Mental Health, among others, has pointed out, this portion of the brain is not fully developed until well into the early twenties.

Besides magnetic resonance imaging, a second strand of research employs experiments to measure the responses and the decision making of individuals in relation to an assortment of variables, among them, age and gender. These include tests that place an individual in simulated decision-making scenarios, such as a driving situation in which he or she must make a split-second decision on whether or not to proceed through an intersection; tests that require the individual to override a physical reflex, for example by deliberately not looking in the direction of a suddenly bright light; gambling tasks that measure

risk aversion; and many more. Young men perform very poorly on all of these tasks.

Thrill Seekers

In turn, outcomes suggested by the findings of both of these research methods are reflected in broader social data. Changes that begin with adolescence and conclude at the end of young adulthood incline young people, and young men in particular, to seek excitement, to misjudge situations, and to dismiss danger. These inclinations are clearly readable in morbidity rates, which increase by a dramatic 200 to 300 percent between childhood and full adulthood.

Roadside accidents, for example, are one arena in which this plays itself out. In a 2005 study commissioned by the Allstate Foundation, accident fatalities and car-related injuries to young drivers were studied in collaboration with Temple University, which brought neuropsychiatric and experimental findings to bear in an analysis of accident causation. The study noted that "key parts of the brain's decision-making circuitry do not fully develop until the mid-20s. So, in actual driving situations, teens may weigh the consequences of unsafe driving quite differently than adults do. This, combined with the increased appetite for novelty and sensation that most teens experience at the onset of puberty, makes teens more disposed to risk-taking behind the wheel—often with deadly results."

Males below the age of 24 have nearly three times as many accidents as their older counterparts; their accidents are significantly more likely to be fatal; and accident analysis reveals that the young men are almost always at fault. This is not attributable, as some might suppose, to a lack of experience or technical skill. Rather, the problem lies in the propensity of young men to take risks, to misjudge or ignore danger, and to make erroneous split-second decisions on the basis of factually unwarranted optimism and overconfidence. Young people are also substantially more likely to make the decision to drive while under the influence of alcohol or drugs.

The Allstate study found that conventional drivers' education programs are not effective in countering these dangerous youthful inclinations. They can enhance skill levels and convey information, including warnings about dangers and advice about safer decisions, but they do not affect the underlying impulses and motivators. Interestingly, the expedient of placing a female passenger in the vehicle with the young male driver effects more improvement in safe driving than a lecture or a class. Having him joined by another young male, on the other hand, will increase the likelihood of reckless driving.

Another example of how young adulthood differs from both childhood and full adulthood can be found in recent research on Post Traumatic Stress Disorder—in particular, a study published in the October 2006 issue of the *American Journal of Psychiatry*. Research conducted at Walter Reed Army Medical Hospital on veterans of combat in Afghanistan and Iraq found that soldiers below age 25 are 3.4 times more likely to experience Post Traumatic Stress Disorder than older soldiers. This is in accordance with other research showing that adolescence and young adulthood are a time of particular vulnerability to stress, and an age at which grief and loss are felt with enhanced severity.

A few caveats are in order before speculating on the political significance of these insights into young people's mentality. First, this research is fairly young and we may come, at some future point, to challenge or even reverse its findings. Second, the determinism of responses and behaviors varies. The mere fact that inclinations or reflexes push an individual in a certain direction does not mean that he or she is unable to override them; it just means that this may be more difficult.

Finally, the point being made by the research is that maturation is a process. The findings do not mean that individuals are irresponsible and volatile until, at some arbitrary point, be it 18 or 21 or 22 or 24, they suddenly emerge as mature and sober adults. Maturation unfolds at different rates and to different degrees; it seems reasonable to presume, though this has not yet been studied, that much will also depend on the surrounding societal circumstances, on education, and on other variables affecting the life circumstances and influences operating on the individual young adult.

It remains nonetheless a telling fact that, within the Middle East and Muslim communities worldwide, young males constitute the most numerous participants in violent behavior and pose the greatest security threat to Western societies. Indeed, Western European security agencies report that radicalization among European Muslim minority communities is manifesting itself at ever-younger ages, with 14 and 15 now the typical age at which young people are drawn into extremism. (The most effective recruiting tool today is the Internet.)

Better-adjusted male teenagers satisfy their craving for excitement with video games; those who belong to a disaffected minority may be drawn to the real thing.

It is not difficult to see that propensities inherent in this age group, and effective until age 24 or so, make this subpopulation an ideal audience for radical recruitment. Membership in a clandestine terrorist cell; online linkages with glamorous, dangerous individuals; the opportunity to belong to a feared and seemingly heroic movement complete with martyrs—all of this is inherently appealing to young people. And membership comes with flaming speeches, weapons, face-masks, and all the accoutrements of a forbidden armed struggle. Better-adjusted male teenagers satisfy their craving for excitement with video games; those who belong to a disaffected minority may be drawn, at least in some instances, to the real thing.

How Real Is Real?

After all, when you are an adolescent, how real is real? The question cannot yet be scientifically measured, but we can glimpse an answer in some of the Muslim suicide bomber videos circulating on the Internet. Do not look, for the moment, at the chanting group of celebrants surrounding the prospective bomber. Ignore the splendid, resolute text he is reading from his notes. Look instead at his face, and take note of the momentary expression of surprise, even shock. Did this young man, when he signed up to become a suicide bomber, truly understand that this moment would come, that it would feel like this, that it would be real and irreversible? His expression suggests otherwise, but there is no turning back, not with the video camera rolling and his cheering comrades ready to pack him into the truck—where in many cases, to strengthen his resolve, he will be handcuffed to the steering wheel.

Similarly, the teenagers who place improvised explosive devices (IEDs) on the streets of Baghdad may not have thought very far beyond the money, or the approbation of their clique, with which this act is rewarded. U.S. intelligence officers report seeing children, including a 14-year-old girl, placing roadside IEDs. Iraqi officials report capturing near the Syrian border a 10-year-old boy who had "come to wage jihad."

This is not to dismiss the more elaborate, complex approaches that are being put forward to explain and respond to the threat of Islamist radicalism, global terrorism, and the insurgency in Iraq. Certainly, political and ideological and cultural and ethnic and economic and perhaps religious reasons play a part. But with all of that, it would be a mistake to forget that most of the minds involved are very young and acting on impulses and a logic that any proposed solutions should take into account.

It is necessary to mention, as well, that the same is true on the other side of this conflict. If America's adversaries in Iraq, for example, are primarily young, then so are the soldiers that the United States is sending forward to confront them. There is some difficulty in criticizing Islamist recruitment videos aimed at teenage viewers, when the online game "America's Army" similarly seeks to rope in 14-year-olds for subsequent service. This multi-player interactive online game is a recruiting tool created by the U.S. military. It is popular because of its excellent graphics and because it is free. Research conducted by the U.S. military shows that the game is instrumental in the decision of numerous young people to join the actual armed services.

The point here obviously is not to equate the goal of these two "recruiting agencies." The point is that 14-year-old males are largely vulnerable to the promise of thrills and danger and largely oblivious to risk, and that—if the research cited above is correct—they will not have changed enough by 17 or 18 years of age to assure that their decision to join a war and risk death and dismemberment has been judicious, thoughtful, and taken in full understanding of what it can entail. Research on young people's brain development also implies that militaries ought, at a minimum, to consider some of the revealed inclinations and predispositions of young adults in their training and deployment of younger soldiers. Thus, a propensity to interpret facial expressions as reflecting hostility can clearly be detrimental in interactions with civilian populations, for example in house searches.

More generally, developmental research raises provocative questions for a U.S. intervention in Iraq in which the largest proportion of casualties is borne by troops aged 21 and below. Do optimistic risk assessments and split-second decisions in favor of the more dangerous path play a role? Does the United States really have a "volunteer army" if very young adults have an impaired ability to judge the consequences of their decisions? And perhaps most intriguingly of all: What would the "war on terror" look like if neither side could deploy large numbers of young men with high affect, operating on hair-trigger responses, and low on "sober second thought"?

CHERYL BENARD is a senior political scientist with the RAND Corporation and director of RAND's Initiative on Middle East Youth. She is the author of *Civil Democratic Islam* (Rand, 2004).

Al-Qaeda Masters Terrorism on the Cheap

CRAIG WHITLOCK

Al-Qaeda has increasingly turned to local cells that run extremely low-cost operations and generate cash through criminal scams, bypassing the global financial dragnet set up by the United States and Europe.

Although al-Qaeda spent an estimated $500,000 to plan and execute the Sept. 11 attacks, many of the group's bombings and assaults since then in Europe, North Africa and Southeast Asia have cost one-tenth as much, or less.

The cheap plots are evidence that the U.S. government and its allies fundamentally miscalculated in assuming they could defeat the network by hunting for wealthy financiers and freezing bank accounts, according to many U.S. and European counterterrorism officials.

In an ongoing trial here of eight men accused of planning to blow up airliners bound for the United States two years ago, jurors have been told how the accused shopped at drugstores for ingredients to build bombs that would have cost $15 apiece to assemble.

Similarly, the cell responsible for the July 7, 2005, transit bombings in London needed only about $15,000 to finance the entire conspiracy, including the cost of airfare to Pakistan to consult with al-Qaeda supervisors, according to official British government probes.

Investigations into several plots in Europe have shown that operatives were often flush with cash, raising far more than necessary through common criminal rackets such as drug dealing and credit card theft.

Testimony in the trial of the accused airliner plotters has shown that the defendants had enough money to buy a northeast London apartment for $260,000 shortly before their arrest, allegedly so they would have a safe place to mix liquid explosives for their bombs.

One of the July 2005 suicide bombers, a 22-year-old part-time worker at a fish-and-chips shop, left an estate worth $240,000 after he blew up a subway train. Neither his family nor authorities have explained where he got the money.

In Spain, the cell responsible for the March 2004 train bombings in Madrid needed $80,000 to finance the plot, according to Spanish court documents. But they had access to more than $2.3 million worth of hashish and other illegal drugs that they could have sold to raise more money, the documents showed.

Even the 9/11 hijackers wired back about $26,000 in surplus funds to accounts in the Persian Gulf area a few days before the attacks.

Authorities said it is often impossible to monitor fundraising by such cells because they generally keep so little in the bank. Instead of receiving wire transfers or making large deposits that would trigger automatic alerts, they move cash in person and are discreet about how they spend it.

"The groups operating in Europe don't need a lot of money. The cost of operations is very low," said Jean-Louis Bruguière, a former senior anti-terrorism judge in France who now works as an adviser to the European Union on terrorism financing. "But they are very skilled at obtaining money and using criminal systems to do it. They can collect thousands and thousands of dollars or euros in a few weeks. It is beyond our control."

Law enforcement officials in London said al-Qaeda cells are trained to plot and live on the cheap. Operatives lead ascetic lives, often keeping their day jobs or depending on their families to cover expenses. Above all, they are taught to build bombs that are lethal but crude and inexpensive. Almost every terrorist plot in Europe in recent years has followed a simple formula: homemade explosives stuffed into backpacks, shoes, suitcases or car trunks.

Outflanking the Laws

Thirteen days after the Sept. 11 hijackings, President Bush launched what the White House later described as the "first strike in the war on terrorism." He signed an executive order freezing the assets of 27 individuals and groups suspected of terrorism and forbidding anyone from doing business with them.

"Money is the lifeblood of terrorist operations," Bush said in the Rose Garden. "Today we're asking the world to stop payment."

A month later, Congress and Bush went further by adopting the USA Patriot Act, which required banks to report transactions larger than $10,000 to the Treasury and to check if any of their customers were on a database of suspected terrorists.

By December 2001, the government had frozen $33 million in assets and expanded its terrorism-financing blacklist to 153 names. In a report assessing its progress in the fight against al-Qaeda, the White House declared, "The United States and its allies have been winning the war on the financial front."

The measures, however, have failed to dry up the supply of money available to al-Qaeda and have had no discernible effect in preventing the network from carrying out attacks, according to several counterterrorism officials and experts in the United States and Europe.

Before Sept. 11, 2001, al-Qaeda and its affiliates rarely used the banking system in a manner that might arouse suspicion, officials and experts said. In response to the new anti-terrorism financing laws, the network has became even more cautious, relying on couriers to carry money across borders when necessary, authorities said.

Ibrahim Warde, an adjunct professor at Tufts University and an expert on financial systems in Islamic countries, said the Bush administration and its allies falsely assumed that al-Qaeda had stashed large sums in secret bank accounts.

"It got the entire financial bureaucracy started on a wild-goose chase," Warde said. "There's a complete disconnect between this approach and the underlying reality of how terrorism is funded."

Dennis M. Lormel, a former head of the FBI's Terrorist Financing Operations section, said the laws passed since 2001 have closed some gaps and addressed vulnerabilities that made it easy for al-Qaeda to raise and transfer money.

But he said the network has responded quickly. Its cells in Europe and elsewhere now raise money on their own instead of relying on financial transfers from external sources that could be tracked by law enforcement officials.

"Clearly, when you're dealing with groups that are self-funded, you're dealing with a different set of circumstances from when they put these laws in place," said Lormel, now a senior vice president at Corporate Risk International, a Reston-based firm.

"The bad guys, after a while, they realize what we're doing, so they're going to alter how they do business," he added. "Obviously, you're not going to stop them from getting money, and they're going to be able to adapt."

Inventive Fundraising

Al-Qaeda's self-financing cells in Europe have become increasingly creative in their fundraising methods, officials said.

After the July 2005 London transit bombings, police knocked on the door of a sheep farmer in Scotland to inquire about a livestock deal gone sour. The farmer, Blair Duffton, confirmed that he had lost more than $200,000 when he sent several truckloads of sheep to a slaughterhouse in Leeds, England, but never received payment.

The slaughterhouse specialized in halal meat, or food prepared according to Islamic law. Detectives informed Duffton that the person who had stiffed him for the sheep was an associate of Shehzad Tanweer, one of three bombers who had lived in Leeds.

"I almost went bankrupt," Duffton recalled in a telephone interview. "I couldn't believe it when they told me that this might have been connected to terrorism."

British authorities have not commented publicly on the sheep scam or said if any of the proceeds were used to finance the attacks. Three men accused of providing support to the suicide bombers are currently on trial in London.

In Germany, three Arab men were convicted in December on charges of attempting to raise $6.3 million for al-Qaeda by faking a death to collect on nine life insurance policies. In Switzerland and Spain in 2006, authorities broke up a cell that had stolen $2 million worth of computers, cars and home furnishings. Police said the group sold the goods on the black market and had couriers carry the cash, in $2,000 increments, to an al-Qaeda-affiliated network in Algeria.

In Britain, an al-Qaeda operative, Omar Khyam, was caught on a surveillance tape urging some of the July 2005 London suicide bombers to defraud banks and hardware stores by defaulting on loans of less than $25,000.

Khyam said the goal was not just to raise money for operations but to "rip the country apart economically, as well," according to court testimony in April at the trial of the three men accused of providing support to the bombers.

Acting on Khyam's advice, one of the bombers obtained and then defaulted on a $20,000 loan from HSBC Bank. Another secured a $14,000 line of credit from a building supply company.

Given the small scale of such transactions, banks or police would have had little reason to suspect the involvement of terrorists, officials said.

"That's the cleverness of these schemes—to keep it under the radar," said Stephen Swain, former head of Scotland Yard's international counterterrorism unit. "By doing this, they can raise significant amounts of money, fairly quickly, and there's no real way to detect it."

Cracking Down after the Fact

A few weeks after the Sept. 11 attacks, Gordon Brown, then Britain's chancellor of the exchequer, or finance minister, announced a major effort to "crack the code" of terrorist financing. He said Britain would press the entire European Union to hunt for al-Qaeda by combing through the international banking system.

"If fanaticism is the heart of modern terrorism, then finance is its lifeblood," said Brown, who is now Britain's prime minister.

In response to the July 2005 London transit bombings, Brown said the government would freeze the suspects' bank accounts and place additional controls on international financial transfers, even though there was no evidence the cell had received any money from outside sources. "There will be no hiding place for those who finance terrorism," he promised.

Two months after authorities broke up what they said was the plot to bomb transatlantic airliners in August 2006, Brown reiterated that the key to fighting terrorism was to disrupt al-Qaeda's bank accounts. He said Britain would use classified intelligence to freeze assets of people suspected of having links to terrorist groups and would exercise greater control over Islamic charities.

"We will take any necessary steps and find all necessary resources to ensure whether in Iraq, Afghanistan or anywhere else there is no safe haven for terrorists and no hiding place for terrorist finance," Brown said, echoing his 2005 comments.

Britain has frozen assets belonging to 359 individuals and 126 organizations suspected of assisting al-Qaeda, according to a Treasury report released last year. All told, about $2 million has been seized, the Treasury reported.

But the government's efforts have had little practical effect, several current and former British counterterrorism officials said. For instance, Britain froze the accounts of 19 suspects in the 2006 transatlantic airliner plot—but only after they were arrested. Officials said most of the accounts contained negligible amounts.

As part of the same investigation, British officials announced an inquiry into the operations of a charity, Crescent Relief, saying that it was suspected of providing money to the cell. Officials with the charity, which was set up to aid earthquake survivors in Pakistan, denied wrongdoing.

Two years later, however, the trial has yielded no public evidence linking the defendants to Crescent Relief. A spokeswoman for Britain's Charity Commission, which regulates nonprofit organizations, said the investigation is continuing but declined to comment further.

Swain, the former Scotland Yard counterterrorism official, said politicians often announce stricter anti-terrorism financing laws after an attack as a public relations measure. But he said they do little good in terms of actually preventing terrorism.

"I think there is a realization that they are not that effective," Swain said. "But they need to be seen as doing something to provide reassurance to the public that they're doing something. We're living in a false paradise if you think these things will stop it."

Needles in Haystacks

Some officials defended the anti-terrorism financing laws passed since 2001, saying that al-Qaeda would have a much easier time raising money if the measures weren't in place.

"We mustn't be wooed into the idea that because attacks are costing less and less, that there isn't a need for money, or that it isn't being provided," said Michael Chandler, who headed a U.N. panel that monitored financial sanctions against al-Qaeda and the Taliban from 2001 to 2004. "It's not just the money they need to make the explosive devices. It's the money they need for other things: to support the network, to recruit and to train."

Chandler also acknowledged that al-Qaeda and its affiliates have adapted and are having little difficulty financing their plots.

"Notwithstanding the successes we've had, groups associated or affiliated with al-Qaeda still appear to be able to carry out an attack, as and when they feel so inclined," said Chandler, a former British Army officer and U.N. diplomat, citing the Taliban and cells in Iraq and North Africa. "Either they had the money already when they needed it, or they have no problem getting it."

Law enforcement officials said terrorism-financing controls also make it easier to investigate cells that are under surveillance or after an attack. By retracing suspected plotters' financial footsteps, no matter how small, investigators can map their movements and develop new leads.

But Cliff Knuckley, a former chief money-laundering investigator for Scotland Yard, said it's difficult to detect potential terrorist plots just by monitoring cash flows or bank transfers—the basis of many of the anti-terrorism financing laws in place today.

"You're looking for a needle in a haystack, and unfortunately you have a field full of haystacks," Knuckley said.

Three Pillars of Counterinsurgency

Dr David J. Kilcullen[*]

Introduction

We meet today in the shadow of continuing counterinsurgencies that have cost thousands of lives and a fortune in financial, moral and political capital. And we meet under the threat of similar insurgencies to come. Any smart future enemy will likely sidestep our unprecedented superiority in traditional, force-on-force, state-on-state warfare. And so insurgency, including terrorism, will be our enemies' weapon of choice until we prove we can master it.[1] Like Bill Murray in *Groundhog Day,* we are going to live this day over, and over, and over again—until we get it right.

So we seek a common doctrine to integrate national power against the threat. This has happened before, it turns out.

The United States produced an inter-agency counterinsurgency doctrine in 1962. Called the *Overseas Internal Defense Policy* (OIDP),[2] it was "prepared by an Interdepartmental Committee consisting of representatives of State (Chair), DOD, JCS, USIA, CIA and AID."[3] It was approved under *National Security Action Memorandum 182* of 24 August 1962, signed by McGeorge Bundy[4] and overseen by a Special Group (Counter-Insurgency), comprising "the Chairman of the Joint Chiefs of Staff, the Deputy Secretary of Defense, the Director of Central Intelligence, the heads of AID and USIA, a staff member of the National Security Council, and . . . the Attorney General of the United States".[5] OIDP lays out a framework for whole-of-government counterinsurgency, assigns responsibilities and resources, and explains what each agency brings to the fight.

Why the history lesson? Because last time we tried this, it did not work very well. OIDP was classified, and while it informed senior leaders it filtered only fitfully down to the field. It was applied in only the minor campaigns of the day. And it lasted only until 1966. As Vietnam escalated, OIDP (used during the advisory phase of the war) was dropped and the campaign was handed off to the conventional military and the State Department's "A" Team of Europeanists and Cold Warriors.[6] And so, as many have observed, our problem is not that we lack doctrine but that we continually forget, relearn, discard our corporate knowledge, and treat as exceptional one of the most common forms of warfare.[7]

Today, things are even more complicated than in 1962. To be effective, we must marshal not only all agencies of the USG (and there are more than 17 agencies in the foreign policy arena alone[8]), but also all agencies of a host nation, multiple foreign allies and coalition partners, international institutions, non-government organizations of many national and political flavors, international and local media, religious and community groups, charities and businesses. Some have counterinsurgency doctrine that is more or less compatible with ours. Some have different doctrines, or none. Some reject the very notion of counterinsurgency—but all must collaborate if the conflict is to be resolved.

This means we need a way to generate purposeful collaboration between a host of actors we do not control. No doctrinal handbook will ever be flexible enough for such a fluid environment (though, something tells me, we will develop one anyway). Rather, we need an easily grasped mental model that helps individuals and agencies cooperate, creates platforms for collaboration, and forms a basis for improvisation. In conventional war we might call this an "operational design", or "commander's intent". I will call it a "model".

There are two parts to this model. The first is a description of the "conflict ecosystem" that forms the environment for 21st century counterinsurgency operations. The second is a tentative framework for whole-of-government counterinsurgency in that environment.

The Conflict Environment

An insurgency is a struggle for control over a contested political space, between a state (or group of states or occupying powers), and one or more popularly based, non-state challengers.[9] Insurgencies are popular uprisings that grow from, and are conducted through pre-existing social networks (village, tribe, family, neighborhood, political or religious party) and exist in a complex social, informational and physical environment.[10]

Think of this environment as a sort of "conflict ecosystem".

It includes many independent but interlinked actors, each seeking to maximize their own survivability and advantage in a

* Chief Strategist, Office of the Coordinator for Counterterrorism, U.S. Department of State. Correspondence address: 2201 C St NW Washington D.C. 20520 e-mail kilcullendj@state.gov This presentation represents the author's personal opinions only.

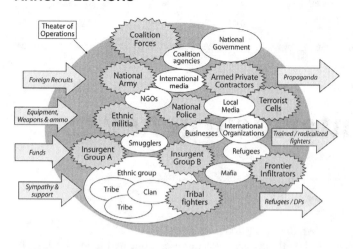

Figure 1 The Conflict Ecosystem.

chaotic, combative environment. Pursuing the ecological metaphor, these actors are constantly evolving and adapting, some seeking a secure niche while others seek to become "top predator" or scavenge on the environment. Some actors existed in the environment before the conflict. They include government, ethnic, tribal, clan or community groups, social classes, urban and rural populations, and economic and political institutions. In normal times, these actors behave in a collaborative or competitive way: but now, due to the internal power struggle, they are combative and destructive. The relatively healthy competition and creative tension that sustains normal society has spun out of control, and the conflict threatens to destroy the society.

This new state of the environment also produces new actors. These include local armed organizations, and foreign armed groups drawn into the conflict from outside. Often, that includes intervening counterinsurgent forces such as ourselves. Foreign terrorists are also increasingly "swarming" from one conflict to another in pursuit of their global agenda. In addition, the conflict produces refugees, displaced persons and sometimes mass migration. It creates economic dislocation, leading to unemployment and crime, and creating armed groups such as bandits, narcotics traffickers, smugglers, couriers and black marketeers.

This might be illustrated graphically as in Figure 1.

It is critically important to realize that we, the intervening counterinsurgent, are not outside this ecosystem, looking in at a Petrie dish of unsavory microbes. Rather, we are inside the system. The theater of operations is not a supine, inert medium on which we practise our operational art. Rather it is a dynamic, living system that changes in response to our actions and requires continuous balancing between competing requirements.

Where the counterinsurgent differs from other actors is largely a matter of intent. Like other players, we seek to maximize our survivability and influence, and extend the space which we control. But unlike some other players (the insurgents, for example) our intent is to reduce the system's destructive, combative elements and return it to its "normal" state of competitive interaction. This has sometimes been expressed as "bringing democracy" but, of course, democratic processes without the foundation of a robust civil society may simply create instabil-

ity and perpetuate conflict. Thus, whatever our political objective, our functional objective is to impose a measure of control on the overall environment. But in such a complex, multi-actor environment, "control" does not mean imposing order through unquestioned dominance, so much as achieving collaboration towards a set of shared objectives.

If this sounds soft, non-lethal and non-confrontational, it is not: this is a life-and-death competition in which the loser is marginalized, starved of support and ultimately destroyed. The actors mount a lethal struggle to control the population. There is no known way of doing counterinsurgency without inflicting casualties on the enemy: there is always a lot of killing, one way or another. But killing the enemy is not the sole objective—and in a counterinsurgency environment, operating amongst the people, force is always attended by collateral damage, alienated populations, feuds and other unintended consequences. Politically, the more force you have to use, the worse the campaign is going. Marginalizing and out-competing a range of challengers, to achieve control over the overall socio-political space in which the conflict occurs, is the true aim.

Remembering that this is simply a theoretical model, and thus a brutal oversimplification of an infinitely complex reality, how might we seek to operate in this environment?

A Framework for Inter-Agency Counterinsurgency

Obviously enough, you cannot command what you do not control. Therefore, "unity of command" (between agencies or among government and non-government actors) means little in this environment. Instead, we need to create "unity of effort" at best, and collaboration or deconfliction at least. This depends less on a shared command and control hierarchy, and more on a shared diagnosis of the problem, platforms for collaboration, information sharing and deconfliction. Each player must understand the others' strengths, weaknesses, capabilities and objectives, and inter-agency teams must be structured for versatility (the ability to perform a wide variety of tasks) and agility (the ability to transition rapidly and smoothly between tasks).

A possible framework for inter-agency counterinsurgency operations, as a means to creating such a shared diagnosis, is the "three pillars" model depicted at Figure 2.

This is a framework, not a template. It helps people see where their efforts fit into a campaign, rather than telling them what to do in a given situation. It provides a basis for measuring progress and is an aid to collaboration rather than an operational plan. And clearly, it applies not only to counterinsurgency but also to peace operations, Stabilization and Reconstruction, and complex humanitarian emergencies. The model is structured as a base (Information), three pillars (Security, Political and Economic) and a roof (Control). This approach builds on "classical" counterinsurgency theory, but also incorporates best practices that have emerged through experience in peacekeeping, development, fragile states and complex emergencies in the past several decades.

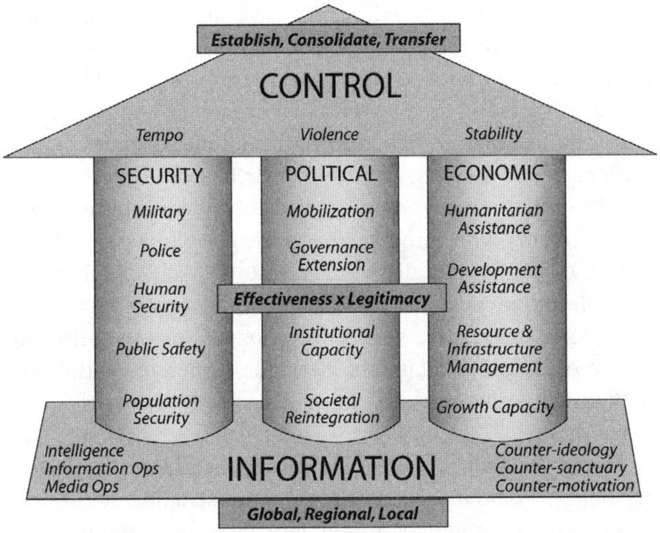

Figure 2 Inter-agency counterinsurgency framework.

Within this "three pillars" model, information is the basis for all other activities. This is because perception is crucial in developing control and influence over population groups. Substantive security, political and economic measures are critical but to be effective they must rest upon, and integrate with a broader information strategy. Every action in counterinsurgency sends a message; the purpose of the information campaign is to consolidate and unify this message. It includes intelligence collection, analysis and distribution, information operations,[11] media operations (including public diplomacy) and measures to counter insurgent motivation, sanctuary and ideology. It also includes efforts to understand the environment through census data, public opinion polling, collection of cultural and "human terrain" information in denied areas. And it involves understanding the effects of our operations on the population, adversaries and the environment. Clearly, not all actors will collaborate in these efforts; but until an information base is developed, the other pillars of counterinsurgency cannot be effective. Importantly, the information campaign has to be conducted at a global, regional and local level—because modern insurgents draw upon global networks of sympathy, support, funding and recruitment.

Resting on this base are three pillars of equal importance. Indeed, as Figure 2 illustrates, unless they are developed in parallel, the campaign becomes unbalanced: too much economic assistance with inadequate security, for example, simply creates an array of soft targets for the insurgents. Similarly, too much security assistance without political consensus or governance simply creates more capable armed groups. In developing each pillar, we measure progress by gauging effectiveness (capability and capacity) and legitimacy (the degree to which the population accepts that government actions are in its interest). This approach is familiar to anyone who has participated in a USAID conflict assessment, or worked on fragile states or complex humanitarian emergencies. It has a solid basis in empirical field experience in the aid and development community.[12]

The security pillar comprises military security (securing the population from attack or intimidation by guerrillas, bandits, terrorists or other armed groups) and police security (community policing, police intelligence or "Special Branch" activities, and paramilitary police field forces). It also incorporates human security, building a framework of human rights, civil institutions and individual protections, public safety (fire, ambulance, sanitation, civil defense) and population security. This "pillar" most engages military commanders' attention, but of course military means are applied across the model, not just in the security domain, while civilian activity is critically important in the security pillar also. Clearly, also, security is *not* the basis for economic and political progress (as some commanders and political leaders argue). Nor does security depend on political and economic progress (as others assert). Rather, all three pillars must develop in parallel and stay in balance, while being firmly based in an effective information campaign.

The political pillar focuses on mobilizing support. As for the other pillars, legitimacy and effectiveness are the principal dimensions in which it is developed. It comprises efforts to mobilize stakeholders in support of the government, marginalize insurgents and other groups, extend governance and further the rule of law. A key element is the building of institutional capacity in all agencies of government and non-government civil institutions, and social re-integration efforts such as the disarming, demobilization and reintegration (DDR)[13] of combatants. Like the security pillar for military forces, the political pillar is the principal arena for diplomatic and civil governance assistance efforts—although, again, civil agencies play a significant role in the security and economic pillars also.

The economic pillar includes a near-term component of immediate humanitarian relief, as well as longer-term programs for development assistance across a range of agricultural, industrial and commercial activities. Assistance in effective resource and infrastructure management, including construction of key infrastructure systems, is critically important. And tailoring efforts to the society's capacity to absorb spending, as well as efforts to increase absorptive capacity, underpin other development activities.

These three pillars support the overarching objective of control, which—as we have seen—is the counterinsurgent's fundamental aim. The aim is not (as some have argued) simply to create stability. Stability may actually not be our objective, as the President emphasized in his recent speech to the United Nations General Assembly, when he observed that "on 9/11, we realized that years of pursuing stability to promote peace left us with neither. Instead, the lack of freedom made the Middle East an incubator for terrorism. The pre-9/11 status quo was dangerous and unacceptable."[14] Moreover, even if we do seek stability, we seek it as a means to an end, a step on the way to regaining control over an out-of-control environment, rather than as an end in itself.

In achieving control, we typically seek to manage the tempo of activity, the level of violence, and the degree of stability in the environment. The intent is not to reduce violence to zero or to kill every insurgent, but rather to return the overall system to normality—noting that "normality" in one society may look different from normality in another. In each case, we seek not only to establish control, but also to consolidate that control and then transfer it to permanent, effective and legitimate institutions.

Operationalizing the "Three Pillars"

If this model represents a possible framework for inter-agency counterinsurgency, how might we apply it in practice? Arguably, the basis for doing so exists already, in National Security Presidential Directive 44 (NSPD 44) which authorizes the creation of civilian capabilities for stabilization and reconstruction. True enough, the words "insurgency", "insurgent" or "counterinsurgency" do not appear in NSPD 44, but it clearly envisages the need to deploy integrated whole-of-government capabilities in hostile environments.

Personnel policies to develop human capital also require effort, but might be less of a burden than we currently envisage. Rather than sweeping policy changes, we simply need relatively minor modifications such as the ability to identify and record civilian officials with appropriate skills for conflict environments, track them throughout their careers, provide financial and legal cover for deployments, give them the necessary individual and team training to operate in hostile areas, and create career structures (perhaps in the form of "additional skills identifiers") that recognize time in conflict zones as equivalent, for career purposes, to time in standard postings.

Organizations, again, perhaps need less modification that we might imagine. We already have a near-perfect instrument for inter-agency counterinsurgency in the form of the Country Team, a 1950s innovation that has proven highly effective in adapting to complex environments. It remains the only standing inter-agency organization in the USG that can deliver integrated whole-of-government effects. It is thus an extremely valuable tool that we should be working to improve even further. Other organizational approaches, such as the Provincial Reconstruction Team (PRT), provide a basis for adaptation. PRTs were invented in 2003 in Afghanistan and have often been treated as a panacea for civilian counterinsurgency. They are not. But careful analysis of why PRTs succeed in some areas and do less well in others can help tailor approaches for specific situations. In this context, the efforts of private firms like Aegis Defence Services, whose Reconstruction Operations Centres and Regional Liaison Teams are flexible inter-agency organizations that have worked extremely well in Iraq, are worth emulating. Similarly, while NSPD 44 envisions a civilian reserve corps deploying field personnel and middle-management into conflict environments, we could also use it to establish a smaller expert cadre of advisors who could assist Ambassadors, Country Teams or force commanders.

Systems capabilities (electronic and otherwise) require significant work. These might include skills registers, personnel databases, and field capabilities such as communications, transportation and protection equipment. We could also benefit from electronic platforms to enable sharing of information between agencies, including non-government organizations. ReliefWeb is a good example of this, allowing multiple agencies to post and share information, identify opportunities to collaborate, and deconflict efforts. Security protocols allow information to be shared only with authorized participants, while public information can be widely disseminated. ReliefWeb's Afghanistan page (http://www.reliefweb.int/rw/dbc.nsf/doc104?OpenForm&rc=3&cc=afg) covers many components of the "three pillars" model, in the context of a complex emergency. Building on this would be less difficult, and less expensive, than one might think.

Training and education (for civil, military, and non-government personnel) would also create shared understanding, and spread best practices throughout a "counterinsurgency community"—again helping us achieve collaboration across a wide variety of players whom we cannot control. Besides specific educational outcomes, these programs develop personal relationships and erode institutional paranoia. Specific training needs include the development of civilian teams capable of "early entry" into environments not yet secured by military or police forces, with the movement, communications and self-protection skills and equipment to operate in these areas. Other needs are a capability for "denied area ethnography" to collect human terrain and population data for effective planning, and education for military leaders in the significant body of expertise that aid, humanitarian assistance and development communities have built up over time.

Finally, doctrine—a common USG handbook, common funding and legal authorities, and common operating standards—might be useful. And so we come full circle, to the OIDP of 1962. But it should now be clear that, without a common mental model for the environment and the pillars of a counterinsurgency effort, and without the personnel, organizations, systems, training and education elements of capability in place, merely producing a doctrinal handbook is likely to be as little use in 2006 as it was in 1962.

Conclusion

These thoughts are tentative; they need a large amount of work. The "three pillars" model is clearly incorrect—all models are, in that they are systematic oversimplifications of reality. But this, or something like it, might be a basis for further development.

And time is of the essence: regardless of the outcome of current campaigns, our enemies will keep applying these methods until we show we can defeat them. Thus, this is one of the most important efforts that our generation of national security professionals is likely to attempt. Our friends and colleagues' lives, the security of our nation and its allies, and our long-term prospect of victory in the War on Terrorism may, in part, depend on it.

Notes

1. United States Department of Defense, *Quadrennial Defense Review Report 2006,* U.S. Government Printing Office, Washington D.C. 2006, Chapter 1 for a detailed exposition of this argument.

2. See State Department, Office of the Historian, *Foreign Relations of the United States, 1961–63,* Volume VIII, Document 106, U.S. Government Printing Office, Washington D.C., 1990, pp. 382–383

3. *Ibid.* p. 3

4. *Ibid,* Document 105.

5. Charles Maechling, "Camelot, Robert Kennedy, and Counter-Insurgency: A Memoir", in *The Virginia Quarterly Review,* at http://www.vqronline.org/printmedia.php/prmMediaID/7976 accessed Sep 06.

6. *Ibid.*

7. See Robert R. Tomes, "Relearning Counterinsurgency Warfare" in *Parameters,* Spring 2004, pp.16–28. See also John A. Nagl, *Learning to East Soup with a Knife: Counterinsurgency Lessons from Malaya and Vietnam,* 2nd Edition, University of Chicago Press, Chicago, 2005; Robert M. Cassidy, "Back to the Street Without Joy: Counterinsurgency Lessons from Vietnam and Other Small Wars" in *Parameters,* Summer 2004 pp. 73–83; and N. Aylwin-Foster, "Changing the Army for Counterinsurgency Operations" in *Military Review,* November–December 2005, pp. 2–15.

8. Including, but not limited to, the Department of State, Agency for International Development, Department of Homeland Security, Department of Justice, Federal Bureau of Investigation, Department of Treasury, Central Intelligence Agency, Department of Commerce (International Trade Administration), Department of Defense, Department of Energy (National Nuclear Security Administration), Department of Labor (Bureau of International Labor Affairs), International Trade Commission, National Security Agency, National Security Council, United States Trade Representative, etc.

9. This definition follows that put forward by Gordon H. McCormick, who suggests that "an insurgency is a struggle for power (over a political space) between a state (or occupying power) and one or more organized, popularly based internal challengers". (McCormick, "Things Fall Apart: The 'Endgame Dynamics' of Internal Wars," RAND, draft paper, forthcoming, p. 2). But, to take into account the trans-national nature of several contemporary insurgencies, I have replaced McCormick's notion of a single state entity facing an internal challenger with the broader concept of a state *or group of states* confronting one or more (internal or external) *non-state* challengers.

10. I am indebted to Dr. Gordon McCormick of the Naval Postgraduate School, Monterrey, and to Colonel Derek Harvey for insights into the "small world, scale-free" aspects of insurgent social networks and the enduring influence of the pre-war Iraqi oligarchy on the current Iraqi insurgency.

11. Including psychological operations, electronic warfare, computer network operations, military deception and operations security. See U.S. Department of Defense, *Joint Publication 3–13 Information Operations,* 13 February 2006.

12. For a description of this approach, see United States Agency for International Development, *Fragile States Strategy,* January 2005, PD-ACA-999, USAID, Washington D.C. 2005, p. 3 ff.

13. See United Nations, Department of Peacekeeping Operations, *Disarmament, Demobilization and Reintegration of ex-Combatants: Principles and Guidelines*, United Nations, New York, 1999, available online at http://www.un.org/Depts/dpko/lessons/DD&R.pdf

14. See The White House, "President Bush Addresses United Nations General Assembly" at http://www.whitehouse.gov/infocus/mideast/ accessed September 2006.

The Boot Is Now on the Other Foot
Rwanda's Lessons from Both Sides of Insurgency

GREG MILLS

Most writings on countering insurgencies are written on behalf of those attempting to do just that. Seldom have the insurgents—or in this case, former insurgents—used the opportunity to write about the strategy and tactics pursued by their opponents. If they did, they might be able to help answer a key question confounding militaries, governments and development agencies from Afghanistan to the Sudan: What can be done better to defeat insurgencies and enable peace?

The army of the Rwanda Patriotic Front (RPF) provides a valuable and unique study. The RPF, through its military wing the Rwanda Patriotic Army (RPA), did not just wage an insurgency in the four-year war against the Habyarimana regime in Kigali. Many of its cadres fought in Uganda as members of Yoweri Museveni's National Resistance Army (NRA) in deposing Milton Obote in 1985, and then afterwards in the Ugandan Army fighting various antigovernment insurgencies.

When Museveni's band of twenty-seven companions attacked the Military School at Kabamba (in Uganda) in February 1981 to snatch some weapons, Rwandan exiles Fred Rwigema and Paul Kagame (now President of Rwanda) were among their ranks. By January 1986, when Museveni's 13,000-strong NRA guerrillas stormed Kampala, there were around 4,000 Banyarwanda among them, though they comprised a higher percentage of the officer corps. Many Tutsi diaspora had joined in 1982–83 and worked their way up through the ranks. But when Major General Rwigema, the Deputy Army Commander and Deputy Minister of Defence of Uganda, was removed by President Museveni from his post in 1988, the Rwandan exiles realised their fight to end their condition of 'statelessness' had not ended.

Since taking power in Kigali in July 1994, bringing the genocide to a stop, the RPA—now the Rwanda Defence Force (RDF)—has fought a war against Hutu extremist insurgents in Rwanda and the Congo, along with a more conventional nine-month conflict which ejected President Mobutu Sese Seko from his Zairean throne in May 1997. The RDF now also provides a large component to the Darfur peacekeeping mission in the Sudan.

No army has probably fought more battles in recent times and certainly none so often both as insurgents and counter-insurgents.

No army has probably fought more battles in recent times and certainly none so often both as insurgents and counter-insurgents. It therefore provides an instructive study of insurgency through an examination of what is required for victory in the first place, and by showing how, with their roles swapped and the boot indeed on the other foot, they were victorious both abroad and domestically. Some key lessons emerge. For successful insurgency, belief in a just cause is vital. Tactical agility is also essential: circumstances can change quickly. But for counter-insurgents, political agility is also crucial; if an incumbent government does not offer an alternative to fighting, its victory will be virtually impossible. Indeed, peace ultimately requires a political solution to gradually erode social polarisation, whatever the context. But to win hearts and minds on such a scale is a long and difficult project.

Lessons from a 'Popular War'

During the struggle against Obote's government, the NRM had learned the importance of co-operation between the various anti-government forces, notably the Uganda Freedom Movement (UFM) and the federalist FEDEMU forces. While they might not have been able to agree to fight together, at least they agreed not to fight each other. By treating prisoners of war and local communities alike with respect they were able to win converts more easily notably among the Baganda (making up one in five of the Ugandan population), many of whom were dissatisfied with a northern-dominated army and were prepared to cross government lines to join the NRA. The rebels, Major-General Frank Mugambage[1] observes, had to remember all the while that 'the bad behaviour of just one or two soldiers could make your life very difficult—discipline was imperative.' They had also learned the importance of capturing and holding territory, making it impossible for the government to deny their cause.

These were translated across to their campaign to liberate Rwanda. Three overall lessons stand out for the RPA as insurgents against the Hutu regime. First, it was an immensely difficult struggle fraught with setbacks. It took the RPF four years of heavy and costly fighting to advance the 75 km from their Ugandan base, but just nine months to fight their way more than 2,000 km across the Congo to remove Mobutu from power. The opposition Rwandan government forces were well-armed and supported, especially by their French allies, and believed that they were fighting a life and death struggle. The insurgent had to make them believe they were not.

The *justness* of their cause was immensely important in galvanising both the RPA and its supporters. Initially their struggle, in part, was motivated by the'homelessness' of the Tutsi diaspora, ejected and marginalised after continuous pogroms before and after Rwanda's independence from Belgium in 1962. More than that, the RPF's cause was about a vision of a Rwanda where politics were inclusive, and the aim was a society free from sectarianism and poverty. This demanded the need for vigilance and discipline within the movement against 'ethnic' bias, and created ownership and participation by Hutus and Tutsis alike in the struggle.

Second, tactics changed to suit the circumstances. The initial 2,000-strong RPA incursion into Rwanda in October 1990 ended in virtual defeat. With the recall of then-Major Paul Kagame from the United States (where he was enrolled on command and staff course at Fort Leavenworth as a Ugandan officer) which involved a harrowing journey through Mengistu Haile Mariam's Ethiopia, the RPA changed tactics to avoid direct battle with the government Forces Armées Rwandais (FAR). The RPA retreated to the volcanic Virunga region to the northwest where it regrouped, but where the 5,000 metre altitude and cold cost the lives of several fighters. Supplies and food—mostly beans, maize and sorghum—had to be ferried up at night along slippery, difficult tracks from supporters among the local population. All the time the RPA kept another front open in the east forcing the FAR to divide its forces and avoid concentrating on the Virunga contingent.

On 23 January 1991, the RPA moved down at night from the Virunga range to carry out an attention-grabbing strike on nearby *préfecture* of Ruhengeri, President Juvenal Habyarimana's seat of power and the heartland of the Hutu regime. Akin to a Rwandan Tet offensive, this caused a national upheaval. The RPA also cut the road to Uganda, forcing traffic to use the more difficult route through Tanzania. As a front developed countrywide thereafter, the RPA would deliberately snipe around the edges, trying to draw out the FAR and catch them off guard, aiming to liberate areas as it went. The tempo of the campaign ensured that Habyarimana's government could not claim that the insurgency was simply a Ugandan ploy aimed at creating a Tutsi empire in the Great Lakes region, and aimed to stoke support within Rwanda for the RPA's cause. Its tactical battles against the government were focused on the strategic goal, in Kagame's words, of 'a popular protracted war'.[2] Kagame's disciplined approach and tactical and strategic *nous* was central to the success of the campaign. Lieutenant-General Romeo Dallaire, the Canadian head of the UN peacekeeping force in Rwanda (UNAMIR) at the time of the genocide, observes, 'They [the RPA] had won all recent contests because of their superior leadership, training, experience, frugality, discipline and morale. If Kagame was responsible for mobilising their force he was a truly impressive leader and perhaps deserved the sobriquet that the media had given him: the Napoleon of Africa.'[3]

All this time the FAR was growing at an exponential rate, from 5,200 in 1990 to 50,000 by 1994, and buying weapons on the international market (including from Egypt and apartheid South Africa). It also received support from around 600 French troops deployed after October 1990 to Rwanda where they were *inter alia* involved in directing artillery support and logistics, flying helicopters and providing airport security. The RPA increased fourfold to around 15,000 men by the time of the genocide in April 1994, recruiting heavily from the population inside Rwanda, its ammunition and weaponry coming from captured and other stocks, and funding through its diaspora.

Third, the regime in Kigali did not give the RPA much alternative but to fight on, at least until the Arusha peace agreement of 1993. When the Arusha negotiations stuttered at the start of 1993 over the issue of sharing power in the military, the RPA launched an offensive that took them to the outskirts of Kigali at Shyorongi and cut the Kigali-Ruhengeri road at Base. 'By reaching the road,' recalls one senior officer, 'we proved that we were a force to be reckoned with in military terms and capable of taking the capital.' Powersharing was institutionalised under the terms of the final Arusha Agreement signed in August 1993, though this set the stage for the rise of extremist Hutu elements intent instead on a 'final solution'.

'Negotiations were never accepted by the government,' says Patrick Mazimhaka, a lead-negotiator for the RPF,[4] 'since negotiations would expose the ills of the regime and defeat them politically. However, since many European countries were supportive of the Habyarimana government, with the neighbourhood insisting that we negotiate, and given our lack of much material support, we had little option but to go the table at that time.' Under the terms of this agreement, too, the RPA withdrew its forces north of the capital creating a 120 by 20 km demilitarised buffer zone. 'We certainly overestimated what the international community could do to ensure the agreement would stick,' observes Mazimhaka, 'though we could never have expected genocide—even though whenever the regime was weakened and felt threatened, it responded by massacring Tutsis.' The shooting down of President Juvenal Habyarimana's[5] executive jet on the outskirts of Kigali on 6 April 1994 sparked a meticulously planned, 100-day orgy of violence, costing the lives of an estimated 800,000 Tutsis and moderate Hutus. The United Nations Assistance Mission for Rwanda (UNAMIR) deployed under Arusha was powerless to intervene in terms of its mandate, numbers and equipment, though its presence gave false assurance to the international community. Dallaire had said bluntly from the outset that he could do more with the necessary means, but, as he noted, 'There was a void of leadership in New York. We had sent a deluge of paper and received nothing in return; no supplies, no reinforcement, no decisions.'[6]

The genocide worked against the Hutu extremists. It made a swift and total RPA victory imperative. The FAR and *Interahamwe* (lit. 'those who stand together') shifted towards social annihilation, rather than military defence. This served to make an RPA victory easier than it otherwise would have been. There were two lessons from Arusha. Without a political deal in which one includes the most implacable opponent, a counterinsurgency campaign is a lost cause. Worse, if an agreement does not satisfy all constituencies, it can set the stage for greater violence. This second point is a key lesson for international actors: in their rush to ensure peace, they must understand the roots of the conflict and to discern, as accurately as possible, the intent of the parties involved.

Now the boot is on the other foot, what has Kigali under RPF rule learnt from countering insurgencies in Congo and elsewhere?

Countering Insurgency after the Genocide

The three-hour 160 km journey northwest from Kigali along the Ruhengeri Road to the town of Gisenyi on the border with the Congo is a mesmerising overload of colour and activity. Rwanda is Africa's most densely populated country—people line the road at virtually every stage, all going somewhere or carrying something, from sacks of food, ubiquitous yellow plastic water-containers, charcoal, chickens, bananas, sorghum, wood and tin for shelters.

It is along this route that as many as two million Rwandans fled towards Zaire in the aftermath of the Rwanda genocide. Nearly all were Hutu, some fearing retaliation from the RPF, others taken as hostages *en masse* by the perpetrators of the genocide. Having jumped the Rwanda-Zaire border at the Gisenyi crossing on Lake Kivu, they temporarily turned the neighbouring Zairean town of Goma into a seething, cholera- and violence-ridden tented refugee camp.

From then on Rwanda's relations with first Zaire and, since 1997, the Democratic Republic of Congo (DRC) have been strained—with little respite. Two invasions led by Rwanda followed, the first removing Zairean strongman Mobutu from power in May 1997. Both incursions happened ostensibly because Kinshasa was seen to be turning a blind eye to the activities of Hutu extremists on its territory. The same charges are being levelled today at Kabila's son, Joseph, who took over rule following his father's assassination in January 2001 and who, since November 2006, is the first democratically-elected president of the Congo.

The November 1996 operation was not originally designed and planned to remove Mobutu, but developed that way according to several phases.

Phase One: The Rwandans planned to engage ex-FAR/ *Interhamwe* forces at the southern and northern ends of Lake Kivu respectively around Bukavu and Goma at the Kavumu and Mugunga refugee camps, in order to remove the military constraints preventing the refugees from returning to Rwanda. At this time, the Rwandan authorities estimated that there were 300,000 armed and trained Hutu in Zaire, 50,000 in Burundi and Tanzania each, and around 100,000 in Rwanda itself. By taking out the ex-FAR/*Interahamwe* defensive positions, the refugees would, as proved true, be able to return. General James Kabarebe, at the time in charge of the Congo operation, recalls 'The original brief and mission was to try to separate the population from the armed soldiers. This was very difficult to do in the refugee camps where their logistics, food and medicines were being supplied by the Red Cross, UNHCR and other NGOs, and their army by the French[7] and Mobutu.

The NCOs and officer corps of this defeated army were not only more or less intact but they were, because of this support, in better shape and more secure than they were before. Involving

just two Rwandan battalions (3rd Battalion to the North; 101st Battalion to the South), more than a million refugees were able to return.

Phase Two: Following the success of this operation, the *genocidaires* reorganised to move deeper into the DRC, driving with them a smaller part of the refugee population. Mobutu also flew in reinforcements and equipment, including his elite Presidential Guard (Division Spéciale Présidentielle—DSP). 'When they formed a front to attack us, we kept on pushing and defeating them. As a result,' Kabarebe says, 'another dynamic developed.'

Phase Three: Given levels of threat to their own security both from Kinshasa and the presence of increasing numbers of *genocidaires* in their territory, the Rwandans were joined by Tutsis from North and South (the latter known as the Banyamulenge[8]) Kivu provinces. Out of these recruits and the inclusion of other Congolese, including from the Mai-Mai militia 'who had grown tired of Mobutu and the situation but were stuck with what to do', the Alliance of Democratic Forces for the Liberation of Congo-Zaire (AFDL) was formed. The spokesperson for the AFDL was Laurent Kabila, a one-time 'Simba Rebellion' revolutionary colleague of Ché Guevara turned, over three decades, small-time Dar-es-Salaam trader and smuggler. One of Ché's close associates in the Congo in 1965, 'Benigno', said of Laurent Kabila: 'With leaders like that Africa can expect to have long centuries of slavery and colonialism'.[9]

Rudimentary infantry training schools were established at Matere in the north and Remera to the south, with Rwanda providing the command, logistics and leadership, their Congolese allies the bulk of the fighting forces.

Phase Four: As the AFDL advanced on foot across the country, Mobutu's demoralised and poorly (if ever) paid troops also joined the cause. These groups were simply integrated, as there was no need to retrain them. By this time of the war, in March 1997, the AFDL faced the tactical challenge of capturing Kisangani, which had been mined and fortified by Serbian mercenaries recruited by Mobutu. However, there was little alternative for the Rwandans to take the Congolese town since Mobutu had signalled his intent on bombing Kigali by two raids on Bukavu. Kisangani and, to the south, Kindu, were the only likely launching airfield points for such a raid. The Serbs 'who were trying to fight a conventional war against our guerrilla operations' at Kisangani were defeated by an attack on their rear, and fled through the Garamba forest into Sudan. Kindu capitulated shortly thereafter, after a night-crossing of the great Congo River on canoes. The invasion had now changed fundamentally from dealing with the immediate threat of the genocidaires to a Congolese campaign, 'the marrying,' as Kabarebe puts it, 'of our interests of security with the interests of our Congolese partners in power.'

Phase Five: The final phase involved the attack on Kinshasa along two axes, Kikwit on the west and Bandundu on the east, all the time the frontline becoming narrower and narrower. The last big engagement was against Jonas Savimbi's Angolan UNITA forces, long-time allies of Mobutu, at Kenge, about 190 km south of the capital in early May. 'We defeated them,' Kabarebe remembers, 'and marched on Kinshasa from two directions. We treated Kinshasa like the refugee camps at Goma—we did not want to go in fighting and cause mass casualties. So we fought at the airport and went into the city at night for a soft landing. When they discovered we were in town, Mobutu's forces surrendered without a shot being fired.' It was 17 May 1997, just six months after the intervention started.

The bulk of the Rwandan forces walked the entire campaign in their gumboots.

The bulk of the Rwandan forces walked the entire campaign in their gumboots, one battalion (the 101st) moving this way from Cyangugu in the south on the border with Congo and Burundi to the Atlantic Ocean, more than 2,000 km in a straight line. The Rwandans used small aircraft (De-Havilland Twin-Otters and a Britten-Norman Islander) to ferry logistics and commanders. 'We would look for old airfields on our maps, find them, and clear them.' Not only did they have to walk across 'an entire continent', but the biggest menace was 'the sun, heat and mosquitoes—big and hungry enough to bite you through your hair and clothes.'

Acts of such tactical derring-do and making-do aside, the underlying motives for the intervention were strategic and enduring, notably partly to deal with the *genocidaire* forces in the Congo being granted sanctuary by Mobutu and succour by the international humanitarian community, thus improving Rwanda's security and chances of stability and success; partly to dissipate the anti-Tutsi ethnic dimension to regional relations; and partly to build an African alliance against those negative international forces which were seen not only to have sponsored the genocide but were assisting both indirectly through Mobutu and directly with the ex-FAR/*Interahamwe* in the camps, to lay the conditions for a further round of violence.

Onto Kinshasa

'When we captured Kinshasa,' Kabarebe says, 'I called Laurent Kabila on my satphone. He was in Lubumbashi,' in the southern mineral-rich province of Katanga, 'staying in one of Mobutu's villas—he always moved from town to town staying in Mobutu's former houses. I said he should come to Kinshasa. He was surprised. But he quickly called the media in Lubumbashi—he was only the spokesperson of the AFDL—and without consulting the AFDL, proclaimed himself president of the Democratic Republic of Congo.' Zaire was no more.

Yet any hope that Laurent Kabila's rule would lead to a more prosperous and stable period in Congo's history quickly soured as his own regime was characterised by large-scale corruption, human rights abuses and a renewed round of warfare. Kabila soon turned against his Rwandan and Ugandan patrons as he sought to reverse Congolese impressions he was simply a foreign stooge and cement his domestic support base, showing little heart and plenty of darkness as he went easy on the *genocidaires*.

Following his dismissal of Kabarebe as chief of staff and his overtures to new partners, including the various local *Mai*

Mai and foreign militias who had fled Rwanda in the genocide's aftermath in 1994 to set up base in Zaire, Kabila turned his former Rwandan and Ugandan allies against him. As Mazimhaka puts it, 'Kabila resented the fact that his country was great and rich while Rwanda, Kabarebe and others had won the war for him.'

'Kabila II', as it is known in some Kigali circles, began in August 1998 when Rwandan forces again attacked Bukavu and Goma, driving Kabila's forces out, sponsoring a new rebellion. A dramatic attempt to take Kinshasa followed, involving an airlift in chartered Russian aircraft of three battalions of Rwandan and allied Congolese troops coalesced into the Congolese Rally for Democracy (RCD) to Kitona on the Atlantic coast. After swiftly advancing east on the capital, the force was defeated around the N'Djili International Airport 25 km southeast of Kinshasa when the Angolans attacked from the rear and the lightly-armed Rwandan-Congolese fighters were confronted with Zimbabwean armour and helicopters. The Rwandan force made its escape into Angola via the DRC's Bas Congo province before being exfiltrated by air. Until that point the Zimbabweans support for Kabila was wavering given Kinshasa's failure to pay for arms supplied by Zimbabwe Defence Industries.

Nonetheless, this round of conflict was not over, lasting until the negotiation of a peace settlement via the Inter-Congolese Dialogue held at South Africa's Sun City in April 2002, being variously labelled the 'Second Congo War' or 'Africa's First World War', drawing in combatants from virtually all the surrounding countries, including Angola, Zimbabwe, Namibia, Uganda, Rwanda, Chad, Sudan, Central African Republic and Libya along with foreign mercenaries. Further engagements between Zimbabwean and Rwandan forces followed, including in Kasai and at Kabinda near the diamond-rich town of Mbuji-Mayi in the centre of the country as the Zimbabweans sought to secure its riches. However, today the Rwandans maintain respect for the Zimbabwean as 'good soldiers' (a number of Rwandans had been trained in Zimbabwe in the 1994–96 period), though their Angolan allies less so, with some of their generals 'businessmen preferring to be making deals in Kinshasa' and the army 'heavy and slow, heavily mechanised.' Erstwhile allies, Rwanda and Uganda, also famously clashed several times between August 1999 and June 2000 in the town of Kisangani, violent encounters from which bilateral relations have not since fully recovered.

At the heart of the war (and the subsequent peace process) costing an estimated 5.4 million lives (mainly from disease and starvation) was the very future of Congo as a state. At the time of the UN-sponsored Lusaka cease-fire 'putting an end to the mutually-hurting military-stalemate' in mid-1999 which preceded the Sun City political deal, Kinshasa's remit roughly covered 40 per cent of the western sector of the country while foreign troops and guerrilla groups occupied the remainder mostly in the eastern half.

Today Rwanda still faces threats from around a hotchpotch of some 7,000 militia and ex-government forces, grouped into the Democratic Forces for the Liberation of Rwanda (FDLR) based in the eastern Congo, and whose stated aim is to overthrow the government in Kigali. Given a mindset that could not only justify but carry out the genocide, the FDLR—labelled as a 'terrorist' organisation by the United States—believe it is victory or death. The Rwanda government's options are thus to put diplomatic and, failing that, military pressure on their host bases. It also has to allow the political and social space for them to return, even if to face the justice system at home. Such space involves, over time, the depolarisation of society from the perceptions of Tutsis or Hutus, victims or genocidaires, them or us, to one of a Rwandan nation.

Dealing with Domestic Insurgents

General Kabarebe, today chief of the general staff of the RDF, argues that Rwanda was able to deal with those remnants of the ex-FAR/*Interahamwe* inside Rwanda 'in record time' after the genocide 'simply because we employed unconventional means.' Given that an 'insurgency thrives on one thing—the one that has the support of the population wins', it is necessary to 'go deep into what they believe and turn them around.' To achieve this 'one has to be strong and show strength, but this is not enough. One also has to be willing to give in, otherwise one will fight them to the last man.'

In the case of Rwanda, this required 'thinking like an insurgent and their supporters. What are their basic needs and values? Why are they fighting?' There is no point, he argues, in attempting the scorched earth tactics employed by the Ugandans, for example, against the Lord's Resistance Army, destroying food supplies and herding the population into camps. Instead, 'we did not underestimate the power of the peasants whose children were enrolled in the forces of the genocide, and used this to fight the insurgency.' Kabarebe offers one example in the case of an ex-FAR divisional commander whose children and wife, a school teacher, remained in Rwanda. Instead of carrying out reprisals against the family, he went out and identified the wife. Although scared at first, he asked her how she was coping and how her children were. 'She showed me the children. They are Rwandans. I had a responsibility towards them as a Rwandan officer. I gave them money for school fees. I sent the lady for further studies. I provided food for the family.' The news soon reached the husband, and 'broke him as a human being. He was convinced to return home and was integrated into the military.' The individual is now a general officer in the Rwanda Defence Force in the intelligence corps—a 'poacher turned gamekeeper' if ever there was one.

'To defeat them,' Kabarebe maintains, 'we had to convince them that we would not take them to a small Guantanamo Bay. I needed to understand what they were running from. You need to be both a psychologist and a soldier to win this struggle.' And the African peasant has been the centre of gravity of this process. 'They are not complex like Al-Qa'ida. For them the basics like food, clothing and care are important. We used this to win them over as a force for the reconstruction of Rwanda.'

Strenuous efforts the Rwandans argue have been made, through such 'diplomatic channels', to encourage ex-FAR forces to return home to Rwanda. The return of two million Hutu exiles virtually *en masse* from camps around Goma in the Congo from November 1996 has assisted these political efforts, signalling to the insurgents that the returnees had much to gain not only by leaving the Zairean camps but in returning to help rebuild a new Rwanda in which they would have a place and a role. Of course this has not been entirely successful. Those members of the FDLR still operational in north and south Kivu in eastern Congo have continued to wage war against a minority ethnic community and entrench insecurity in that vast territory. Kinshasa's failure to act decisively against this group (and, to the contrary, to work alongside the FDLR in operations against renegade Tutsi general Laurent Nkunda's National Congress for the Defence of the Congolese People) has exacerbated regional fears and suspicions. Until the forces of genocide are seen to have been properly dealt with—disarmed, cantoned and preferably returned to Rwanda—then these insecurities will remain.

But all this, more than anything, as General Kabarebe says, 'takes patience.'

Conclusion: Applying the Lessons

The Rwandan Army is one of the largest contributors to the African Union mission in Sudan (AMIS) and, since 2008, the joint UN-AU peacekeeping mission in Darfur (UNAMID). By April 2008, Rwanda had 3,500 troops in the western region of Sudan where only 7,000 hybrid AU-UN peacekeepers out of the mandated 26,000 had been deployed trying to stop the violence which has so far killed an estimated 200,000 people and displaced 2.5 million others.

Labelled a genocide by the US government and human rights groups, the conflict is driven by a complex combination of factors, none of them easily resolvable and few—if any—under the control of the peacemakers: decades of drought, overpopulation and desertification forcing camel-herding. Whatever its exact cause and label, the conflict and resultant devastation has caused the deaths of upward of 300,000 people since 2003.

President Kagame has likened the mission to his country's genocide. 'Our forces will not stand by and watch innocent civilians being hunted to death like here in 1994,' he said in 2004 as the first Rwandan detachment of 150 troops arrived in Sudan. 'I have no doubt that they will intervene forcefully to protect civilians.'[10] Strategically, the Darfur mission is thus a rallying point for national unity in a post-genocide Rwanda. It also provides a professional challenge to the RDF to again prove its worth, first, to Rwandans and also to the international community, and to exercise leadership in an African context, not as a state but rather on key issues concerning peace, stability and development.

At a tactical level, the lessons from the deployment stress the importance of a clear and viable mandate and the need to equip troops accordingly, the need for troops to be flexible and diplomatic in their responses to local needs, and the importance of good leadership. The personal involvement of the President with the troops before, during and after the mission, is seen as critical to their morale, the relationship of the mission to Rwanda's own circumstances and the mission's success.

But Rwandan commanders are less than sanguine about the prospects for success of the mission. The splintering of the opposition Sudanese Liberation Movement into various smaller entities has fractured their adherence to the May 2006 Abuja peace agreement. The peacekeepers know that these rebels must coalesce as a first step to creating a lasting settlement: a unification which may not, of course, be in Khartoum's best interest.

From Rwanda to Darfur, the overall lesson is clear on both sides of the insurgency coin: without giving the insurgents an attractive option to fighting, a counter-insurgency strategy can at best hold the ring with no victory possible. Divisive—rather than inclusive—politics cannot ultimately win. But the wrong political strategy—based on a misunderstanding of your opponents' strengths and weaknesses—along with the absence of a just cause, will not take you anywhere, only instead, as with Rwanda in 1994, further down a violent path. And never overestimate what the international community can and will do to assist a peace process.

Notes

1. As a Colonel, regarded as one of Kagame's deputies in the RPA, and now Chief of the Cabinet of the Government of Rwanda.

2. See Gerard Prunier, *The Rwanda Crisis: History of a Genocide* (London: Hurst, 1995), p. 96. For details of the RPA's origins and modus operandi, see Prunier's chapter in Christopher Clapham (ed.), *African Guerrillas* (London: James Currey, 1998), pp. 119–133.

3. Romeo Dallaire, *Shake Hands with the Devil: The Failure of Humanity in Rwanda* (London: Arrow, 2004), p. 67.

4. Later Minister of Youth in the RPF government, special envoy to the Great Lakes and until May 2008, Deputy Chairman of the Commission of the African Union.

5. The French-piloted aircraft—a gift from the French government to Rwanda—was returning from a regional meeting at Dar-es-Salaam. Its occupants included Burundi's President Cyprien Ntaryamira who had hitched a ride in preference to taking his older propeller-driven aircraft.

6. Dallaire, op. cit., p. 290. Some 2,538 UNAMIR personnel were on the ground on 7 April 1994. On 21 April, the UN Security Council passed a resolution (912) stating that it was appalled at the large scale of the violence in Rwanda, but at the same meeting voted to reduce UNAMIR to just 270 volunteer

personnel and to limit its mandate. On 17 May, the Security Council (Resolution 918) moved to give UNAMIR a more robust mandate and 5,500 troops, even though, as Dallaire observes (p. 374), it remained vague on the genocide and the role the UN force should play in stopping it.

7. General Kabarebe is the highest-ranking RDF officer among those political and military figures indicted by French and Spanish judges on separate war crimes charges. French Judge Jean Louis Bruguiere issued arrest warrants on 17 November 2006 implicating nine RPF members, including President Kagame and Kabarebe, in the shooting down of the private Falcon 50 jet of President Juvenal Habyarimana on 6 April 1994, the act which sparked the genocide. In February 2008, Spanish Judge Andreu Fernando Merrelles indicted forty officers of the RPA, including Kabarebe and the deputy commander of the UN/AU Darfur force Major-General Emmanuel Karake Karenzi, on genocide related crimes, linking them to the death of nine Spanish nationals during the mayhem before, during and after the genocide in Rwanda and the Congo. The Spanish judge also claims to be in possession of evidence implicating Kagame, but cannot indict him because of his immunity in his status as a head of state.

Comparing the role of the dissidents' and enemies' evidence on which the French and Spanish indictments are based as 'like George Bush being indicted by Al-Qa'ida', Kabarebe believes that this stems from Rwanda's military defeat of the French-sponsored Hutu army and Mobutu, the lack of credibility of the FDLR internationally, and the democratic and economic success of a post-genocide Rwanda. 'The French are humiliated, especially when you look at our progress after liberation from Francophonie influence, compared to those such as Chad, Ivory Coast, Cameroon and others who remain within that armpit. This judicial process is not different to the guerrilla war or to the [French] Zone Turquoise [established as a safehaven for refugees at the end of the genocide, among them many genocidaires]—it is another tool of war, another frontline we must fight'.

8. A minority community of mainly Tutsi Kinyarwanda speakers living in South Kivu, numbering, from recent election statistics, around 300,000.

9. Interview, Documentary Film, El Ché—and Tracing Ché.

10. http://www.telegraph.co.uk/news/main.jhtml?xml=/news/2004/08/16/wsud16.xml.

Dr Greg Mills heads the Johannesburg-based Brenthurst Foundation, is a member of the RUSI Council and in 2008 has been on secondment to the government of Rwanda as strategy adviser to the President. This article is partly based on interviews with serving and retired RPA/RDF officers during 2008, and members of the RPF.

The Boot is Now on the Other Foot, by Greg Mills. From *Royal United Services Institute for Defense and Security Studies*, June 2008, pp. 72–78. Copyright © 2008 by Taylor and Francis Ltd. Reprinted by permission of the publisher. http://www.informaworld.com

UNIT 8

Contemporary Foreign Policy Debates

Unit Selections

Key Points to Consider

- According to Tom H. Johnson and M. Chris Mason, what has to be changed for U.S. engagement in Afghanistan to be successful?

- Why do you agree or disagree with their assessment that such an approach would not require more military troops?

- Do you agree or disagree with Barnett R. Rubin and Ahmed Rashid's position that the current crisis in Afghanistan will only be resolved if treated as a regional conflict that requires a negotiated settlement by all interested parties rather than as a "great game"?

Student Web Site

www.mhcls.com

Internet References

Pajhwok Afghan News
   http://www.pajhwak.com/l
ArabNet
   http://www.arab.net

United States' military progress in Iraq during 2007 occurred at the same time that attacks on U.S. and NATO military personnel increased dramatically in Afghanistan. Currently, there are 67,000 foreign troops stationed in Afghanistan. By the spring of 2008, more international troops had died in Afghanistan than in Iraq. The 40-nation international coalition is much broader in Afghanistan, where only about half of the 65,000 international troops are American. Half of the U.S. forces operate under NATO command and all are struggling to cope with a resurgence of Taliban attacks that are becoming increasingly complex, and deadly. In early November, a Taliban attack on a NATO supply convoy on the Pakistani side temporarily closed traffic through Torkharm and caused NATO forces to seek safer alternate route through the European Caucasus and Central Europe. The increased Taliban attacks in Afghanistan in recent years have shown a remarkable similarity to the same suicide and IED bomb attacks as were used against U.S. troops in Iraq. An important difference between Iraq and Afghanistan today is that the Taliban insurgency operates in every province and controls many districts, including areas surrounding the capital. The Taliban have also formed a parallel government that includes web sites with 24-hour propaganda that rivals many Western organizations.

While Barak Obama campaigned on a pledge to bring most U.S. troops home from Iraq, his position in Afghanistan was less clear during the campaign. Two weeks after winning the election, U.S. President-elect Barack Obama pledged in a telephone conversation with Afghan President Hamid Karzai to increase U.S. aid to Afghanistan. Obama said in the same telephone call that fighting terrorism in the region would be a top priority. The 32,000 American forces in Afghanistan are schedule to be increased by several thousand during 2009. However, it remains highly uncertain whether the current NATO commander, U.S. Gen. David McKiernan, will receive the additional 20,000 troops he has requested.

President Karzai of Afghanistan has been pressing the U.S. government for a long time to address the problem of terrorist bases in Pakistan and alleged cooperation by certain members of the Pakistani government. For years knowledgeable observers and the Afghan government have been pressing the U.S. to address the problem that some members of Pakistan's intelligence service are supporting the Taliban in plotting bombs, attacks in Afghanistan, and advanced warnings about NATO planned operations in the frontier areas of Pakistan where al Qaeda and the Taliban have bases.

Throughout 2008, the U.S. government has sought to increase pressure on the Pakistan government to increase their counter-terrorism operations along the border and pursue rogue elements in their intelligence service. During the fall of 2008, U.S. intelligence agents attempted to increase pressure even more on the most senior officials of Pakistan by providing them

© Department of Defense photo by Tech. Sgt. Cherie A. Thurlby, U.S. Air Force

with new information about ties between the country's powerful spy service and militants operating in Pakistan's tribal areas, according to American military. The U.S. concern is related to evidence that some members of the spy service had deepened their ties with some militant groups that were responsible for a surge of violence in Afghanistan, possibly including a suicide bombing during the fall of 2008 of the Indian Embassy in Kabul, Afghanistan.

The fact that Pakistan is a key ally of the United States in the region with growing opposition to U.S. air strikes in the area greatly complicates the situation for the U.S. While Pakistan denies that any members of their government are supporting the Taliban, the U.S. has grown increasingly frustrated with Pakistan's limited efforts to go after militants in its territory. In the last half of 2008, the U.S. launched several surprise missile strikes and ground operations along the border. The U.S. is also suspected of launching at least 20 missiles from unmanned drones based in Afghanistan that killed scores of suspected extremists and other civilians. These increased attacks are an increasing source of tension between the U.S. and Pakistani governments. Nevertheless, the U.S., Pakistan and NATO forces continue to work together in operations designed to neutralize terrorists operating inside Pakistan. For examples, in September 2008 NATO and Frontier Corps forces on the Afghan side cooperated with Pakistani military forces in a series of complementary operations called Operation Lion Heart.

The ambiguity evidenced by Barak Obama during the campaign about what to do in Afghanistan mirrors debates among U.S. analysts about the most appropriate approach to take in Afghanistan. In "All Counterinsurgency is Local," Thomas H. Johnson and M. Chris Mason argue that the U.S. engagement in Afghanistan is foundering because of the endemic failure to engage and protect rural villages, and to immunize them against insurgency. They argue that the best way to reverse the U.S. fortunes in Afghanistan is for the United States to reconfigure its operations, creating small development and security teams posted at new compounds in every district in the south and east of the country. Johnson and Mason outline why they believe this approach would not necessarily require adding troops but rather 200 district-based teams of 100 people or 20,000 personnel. Their contention is that such teams would be able replace many U.S. troops deployed today.

Current U.S. military planners are estimating that a successful counter-insurgency campaign in Afghanistan will require at many at 30,000 U.S. troops, an extensive civilian component, similar to the one outlined by Johnson and Mason, and a protracted strategy designed to separate civilians from fighters in areas currently controlled by the Taliban. The problem is that the U.S. will not have extra troops to deploy to Afghanistan unless troop levels are reduced in Iraq and elsewhere or the size of the U.S. military is increased. In the meantime, both U.S. and Afghan troops are now training together at a new Counterinsurgency University in Kabul. It remains uncertain whether the American public will support a protracted U.S. presence in Afghanistan.

In contrast to a focus on the military and tactical, Barnett R. Rubin and Ahmed Rashid in "From Great Game to Grand Bargain" present the argument for treating the current chaos in Afghanistan as part of a larger regional conflict that requires a negotiated settlement by all interested settlement by all interested parties rather than as a "great game." Even before the U.S. 2008 election, the Bush administration had approved some preliminary exploratory talks brokered by the Saudis with representatives of the Taliban to discuss possible diplomatic solutions. These exploratory talks are unlikely to lead to wider diplomatic talks between the current government in Kabul, the Taliban and other groups in Afghanistan any time soon. Toward the end of 2008, several military planners and members of the political elite in Pakistan were reported to have accepted as accurate a rumor making the rounds that the United States was collaborating with India and Afghanistan to carve out portions of Pakistan in order to give to India and Afghanistan large tracks of land that are now part of Pakistan. Although the belief is false, the fact that many Pakistani elite members so readily accept it as true suggests that the path to negotiating peace in the region will be a long and difficult one.

All Counterinsurgency Is Local

Prosecuting the war in Afghanistan from provincial capitals has been disastrous; we need to turn our military strategy inside out.

Thomas H. Johnson and M. Chris Mason

June was the deadliest month for the U.S. military in Afghanistan since the invasion in October 2001. July became the second straight month in which casualties exceeded those in Iraq, where four times as many U.S. troops are on the ground. More Americans have been killed in Afghanistan since the invasion began than in the first nine years of the Vietnam War, from 1956 to 1964.

As in Vietnam, the U.S. has never lost a tactical engagement in Afghanistan, and this tactical success is still often conflated with strategic progress. Yet the Taliban insurgency grows more intense and gains more popular traction each year. More and more, the American effort in Afghanistan resembles the Vietnam War—with its emphasis on body counts and air strikes, its cross-border sanctuaries, and its daily tactical victories that never affected the slow and eventually decisive erosion of rural support for the counterinsurgency.

As the Russian ambassador to Afghanistan, Zamir Kabulov, noted in a blunt interview with the BBC in May, the current military engagement is also beginning to look like the Soviets' decade-long Afghan adventure, which ended ignominiously in 1989. That intervention, like the current one, was based on a strategy of administering and securing Afghanistan from urban centers such as Kabul and the provincial capitals. The Soviets held all the provincial capitals, just as we do, and sought to exert influence from there. The mujahideen stoked insurgency in the rural areas of the Pashtun south and east, just as the Taliban do now.

The backbone of the international effort since 2003—extending the reach of the central government—is precisely the wrong strategy.

The U.S. engagement in Afghanistan is foundering because of the endemic failure to engage and protect rural villages, and to immunize them against insurgency. Many analysts have called for more troops inside the country, and for more effort to eliminate Taliban sanctuaries outside it, in neighboring Pakistan. Both developments would be welcome. Yet neither would solve the central problem of our involvement: the paradigm that has formed the backbone of the international effort since 2003—extending the reach of the central government—is in fact precisely the wrong strategy.

National government has never much mattered in Afghanistan. Only once in its troubled history has the country had something like the system of strong central government that's mandated by the current constitution. That was under the "Iron Emir," Abdur Rehman, in the late 19th century, and Rehman famously maintained control by building towers of skulls from the heads of all who opposed him, a tactic unavailable to the current president, Hamid Karzai.

Politically and strategically, the most important level of governance in Afghanistan is neither national nor regional nor provincial. Afghan identity is rooted in the *woleswali:* the districts within each province that are typically home to a single clan or tribe. Historically, unrest has always bubbled up from this stratum—whether against Alexander, the Victorian British, or the Soviet Union. Yet the *woleswali* are last, not first, in U.S. military and political strategy.

Large numbers of U.S. and NATO troops are now heavily concentrated in Kabul, Kandahar, and other major cities. Thousands of U.S. personnel are stationed at Bagram Air Force Base, for instance, which is complete with Burger King, Dairy Queen, and a shopping center, but is hundreds of miles from the heart of the insurgency. Meanwhile, the military's contact with villagers in remote areas where the Taliban operate is rare, typically brief, and almost always limited to daylight hours.

The Taliban are well aware that the center of gravity in Afghanistan is the rural Pashtun district and village, and that Afghan army and coalition forces are seldom seen there. With one hand, the Taliban threaten tribal elders who do not welcome them. With the other, they offer assistance. (As one U.S. officer recently noted, they're "taking a page from the Hezbollah organizations in Lebanon, with their own public works to assist the tribes in villages that are deep in the inaccessible regions of the country. This helps support their cause with the population, making it hard to turn the population in support of the Afghan government and the coalition.")

The rural Pashtun south has its own systems of tribal governance and law, and its people don't want Western styles of either. But nor are they predisposed to support the Taliban, which espouses an alien and intolerant form of Islam, and goes against the grain of traditional respect for elders and decision by consensus. Re-empowering the village councils of elders and restoring their community leadership is the only way to re-create the traditional check against the powerful political network of rural mullahs, who have been radicalized by the Taliban. But the elders won't commit to opposing the Taliban if they and their families are vulnerable to Taliban torture and murder, and they can hardly be blamed for that.

To reverse its fortunes in Afghanistan, the U.S. needs to fundamentally reconfigure its operations, creating small development and security teams posted at new compounds in every district in the south and east of the country. This approach would not necessarily require adding troops, although that would help—200 district-based teams of 100 people each would require 20,000 personnel, one-third of the 60,000 foreign troops currently in the country.

Each new compound would become home to roughly 60 to 70 NATO security personnel, 30 to 40 support staff to manage logistics and supervise local development efforts, and an additional 30 to 40 Afghan National Army soldiers. The troops would provide a steady security presence, strengthen the position of tribal elders, and bolster the district police. Today, Afghan police often run away from the superior firepower of attacking Taliban forces. It's hard to fault them—more than 900 police were killed in such attacks last year alone. But with better daily training and help only minutes away, local police would be far more likely to put up a good fight, and win. Indirectly, the daily presence of embedded police trainers would also prevent much of the police corruption that fuels resentment against the government. And regular contact at the district and village levels would greatly improve the collection and analysis of intelligence.

Perhaps most important, district-based teams would serve as the primary organization for Afghan rural development. Currently, "Provincial Reconstruction Teams," based in each provincial capital, are responsible for the U.S. military's local development efforts. These teams have had no strategic impact on the insurgency, because they are too thin on the ground—the ratio of impoverished Afghan Pashtuns to provincial reconstruction teams is roughly a million to one. Few teams are able to visit every district in their province even once a month; it's no wonder that rural development has been marred by poor design and ineffective execution.

Local teams with on-site development personnel—"District Development Teams," if you will—could change all that, and also serve to support nonmilitary development projects. State Department and USAID personnel, along with medics, veterinarians, engineers, agricultural experts, hydrologists, and so on, could live on the local compounds and work in their districts daily, building trust and confidence.

Deploying relatively small units in numerous forward positions would undoubtedly put more troops in harm's way. But the Taliban have not demonstrated the ability to overrun international elements of this size, and the teams could be mutually reinforcing. (Air support would be critical.) Ultimately, we have to accept a certain amount of risk; you can't beat a rural insurgency without a rural security presence.

As long as the compounds are discreetly sited, house Afghan soldiers to provide the most visible security presence, and fly the Afghan flag, they need not exacerbate fears of foreign occupation. Instead, they would reinforce the country's most important, most neglected political units; strengthen the tribal elders; win local support; and reverse the slow slide into strategic failure.

THOMAS H. JOHNSON directs the Program for Culture and Conflict Studies at the Naval Postgraduate School at Monterey, California. M. CHRIS MASON is a senior fellow at the Center for Advanced Defense Studies, in Washington, D.C. He recently served in the U.S. Foreign Service on the Pakistan-Afghanistan border.

From Great Game to Grand Bargain

Ending Chaos in Afghanistan and Pakistan

BARNETT R. RUBIN AND AHMED RASHID

The Great Game is no fun anymore. The term "Great Game" was used by nineteenth-century British imperialists to describe the British-Russian struggle for position on the chessboard of Afghanistan and Central Asia—a contest with a few players, mostly limited to intelligence forays and short wars fought on horseback with rifles, and with those living on the chessboard largely bystanders or victims. More than a century later, the game continues. But now, the number of players has exploded, those living on the chessboard have become involved, and the intensity of the violence and the threats it produces affect the entire globe. The Great Game can no longer be treated as a sporting event for distant spectators. It is time to agree on some new rules.

Seven years after the U.S.-led coalition and the Afghan commanders it supported pushed the leaderships of the Taliban and al Qaeda out of Afghanistan and into Pakistan, an insurgency that includes these and other groups is gaining ground on both the Afghan and the Pakistani sides of the border. Four years after Afghanistan's first-ever presidential election, the increasingly besieged government of Hamid Karzai is losing credibility at home and abroad. Al Qaeda has established a new safe haven in the tribal agencies of Pakistan, where it is defended by a new organization, the Taliban Movement of Pakistan. The government of Pakistan, beset by one political crisis after another and split between a traditionally autonomous military and assertive but fractious elected leaders, has been unable to retain control of its own territory and population. Its intelligence agency stands accused of supporting terrorism in Afghanistan, which in many ways has replaced Kashmir as the main arena of the still-unresolved struggle between Pakistan and India.

For years, critics of U.S. and NATO strategies have been warning that the region was headed in this direction. Many of the policies such critics have long proposed are now being widely embraced. The Bush administration and both presidential campaigns are proposing to send more troops to Afghanistan and to undertake other policies to sustain the military gains made there. These include accelerating training of the Afghan National Army and the Afghan National Police; disbursing more money, more effectively for reconstruction and development and to support better governance; increasing pressure on and cooperation with Pakistan, and launching cross-border attacks without Pakistani agreement to eliminate cross-border safe havens for insurgents and to uproot al Qaeda; supporting democracy in Pakistan and bringing its Inter-Services Intelligence (ISI) under civilian political control; and implementing more effective policies to curb Afghanistan's drug industry, which produces opiates equal in export value to half of the rest of the Afghan economy.

Cross-border attacks into Pakistan may produce an "October surprise" or provide material for apologists hoping to salvage George W. Bush's legacy, but they will not provide security. Advancing reconstruction, development, good governance, and counternarcotics efforts and building effective police and justice systems in Afghanistan will require many years of relative peace and security. Neither neglecting these tasks, as the Bush administration did initially, nor rushing them on a timetable determined by political objectives, can succeed. Afghanistan requires far larger and more effective security forces, international or national, but support for U.S. and NATO deployments is plummeting in troop-contributing countries, in the wider region, and in Afghanistan itself. Afghanistan, the poorest country in the world but for a handful in Africa and with the weakest government in the world (except Somalia, which has no government), will never be able to sustain national security forces sufficient to confront current—let alone escalating—threats, yet permanent foreign subsidies for Afghanistan's security forces cannot be guaranteed and will have destabilizing consequences. Moreover, measures aimed at Afghanistan will not address the deteriorating situation in Pakistan or the escalation of international conflicts connected to the Afghan-Pakistani war. More aid to Pakistan—military or civilian—will not diminish the perception among Pakistan's national security elite that the country is surrounded by enemies determined to dismember it, especially as cross-border raids into areas long claimed by Afghanistan intensify that perception. Until that sense of siege is gone, it will be difficult to strengthen civilian institutions in Pakistan.

U.S. diplomacy has been paralyzed by the rhetoric of "the war on terror"—a struggle against "evil," in which other actors are "with us or with the terrorists." Such rhetoric thwarts sound strategic thinking by assimilating opponents into a homogenous "terrorist" enemy. Only a political and diplomatic initiative that distinguishes political opponents of the United States—including violent ones—from global terrorists such as al Qaeda can reduce the threat faced by the Afghan and Pakistani states and secure the rest of the international community from the international terrorist groups based there. Such an initiative would have two elements. It would seek a political solution with as much of the Afghan and Pakistani insurgencies as possible, offering political inclusion, the integration of Pakistan's indirectly ruled Federally Administered Tribal Areas (FATA) into the mainstream political and administrative institutions of Pakistan, and an end to hostile action by international troops in return for cooperation against al Qaeda. And it would include a major diplomatic and development initiative addressing the vast array of regional and global issues that have become intertwined with the crisis—and that serve to stimulate, intensify, and prolong conflict in both Afghanistan and Pakistan.

Afghanistan has been at war for three decades—a period longer than the one that started with World War I and ended with the Normandy landings on D-day in World War II—and now that war is spreading to Pakistan and beyond. This war and the attendant terrorism could well continue and spread, even to other continents—as on 9/11—or lead to the collapse of a nuclear-armed state. The regional crisis is of that magnitude, and yet so far there is no international framework to address it other than the underresourced and poorly coordinated operations in Afghanistan and some attacks in the FATA. The next U.S. administration should launch an effort, initially based on a contact group authorized by the UN Security Council, to put an end to the increasingly destructive dynamics of the Great Game in the region. The game has become too deadly and has attracted too many players; it now resembles less a chess match than the Afghan game of *buzkashi*, with Afghanistan playing the role of the goat carcass fought over by innumerable teams. Washington must seize the opportunity now to replace this Great Game with a new grand bargain for the region.

The Security Gap

The Afghan and Pakistani security forces lack the numbers, skills, equipment, and motivation to confront the growing insurgencies in the two countries or to uproot al Qaeda from its new base in the FATA, along the Afghan-Pakistani border. Proposals for improving the security situation focus on sending additional international forces, building larger national security forces in Afghanistan, and training and equipping Pakistan's security forces, which are organized for conflict with India, for domestic counterinsurgency. But none of these proposals is sufficient to meet the current, let alone future, threats.

Some additional troops in Afghanistan could protect local populations while the police and the administration develop. They also might enable U.S. and NATO forces to reduce or eliminate their reliance on the use of air strikes, which cause civilian casualties that recruit fighters and supporters to the insurgency. U.S. General Barry McCaffrey, among others, has therefore supported a "generational commitment" to Afghanistan, such as the United States made to Germany and South Korea. Unfortunately, no government in the region around Afghanistan supports a long-term U.S. or NATO presence there. Pakistan sees even the current deployment as strengthening an India-allied regime in Kabul; Iran is concerned that the United States will use Afghanistan as a base for launching "regime change" in Tehran; and China, India, and Russia all have reservations about a NATO base within their spheres of influence and believe they must balance the threats from al Qaeda and the Taliban against those posed by the United States and NATO. Securing Afghanistan and its region will require an international presence for many years, but only a regional diplomatic initiative that creates a consensus to place stabilizing Afghanistan ahead of other objectives could make a long-term international deployment possible.

Afghanistan needs larger and more effective security forces, but it also needs to be able to sustain those security forces. A decree signed by President Karzai in December 2002 would have capped the Afghan National Army at 70,000 troops (it had reached 66,000 by mid-2008). U.S. Secretary of Defense Robert Gates has since announced a plan to increase that number to 122,000, as well as add 82,000 police, for a total of 204,000 in the Afghan National Security Forces (ANSF). Such increases, however, would require additional international trainers and mentors—which are, quite simply, not available in the foreseeable future—and maintaining such a force would far exceed the means of such a destitute country. Current estimates of the annual cost are around $2.5 billion for the army and $1 billion for the police. Last year, the Afghan government collected about 7 percent of a licit GDP estimated at $9.6 billion in revenue—about $670 million. Thus, even if Afghanistan's economy experienced uninterrupted real growth of 9 percent per year, and if revenue extraction nearly doubled, to 12 percent (both unrealistic forecasts), in ten years the total domestic revenue of the Afghan government would be about $2.5 billion a year. Projected pipelines and mines might add $500 million toward the end of this period. In short, the army and the police alone would cost significantly more than Afghanistan's total revenue.

A long-term foreign troop presence in Afghanistan is simply not tenable.

Many have therefore proposed long-term international financing of the ANSF; after all, even $5 billion a year is much less than the cost of an international force deployment. But sustaining, as opposed to training or equipping, security forces through foreign grants would pose political problems. It would be impossible to build Afghan institutions on the basis of U.S. supplemental appropriations, which is how the training and equipping of the ANSF are mostly funded. Sustaining a national army or national police force requires multiyear planning, impossible without a recurrent appropriation—which would mean integrating ANSF planning into that of the United States' and other NATO members' budgets, even if the funds were disbursed through a single trust fund. And an ANSF funded from those budgets would have to meet international or other national, rather than Afghan, legal requirements. Decisions on funding would be taken by the U.S. Congress and other foreign bodies, not the Afghan National Assembly. The ANSF would take actions that foreign taxpayers might be reluctant to fund. Such long-term international involvement is simply not tenable.

If Afghanistan cannot support its security forces at the currently proposed levels on its own, even under the most optimistic economic scenario, and long-term international support or a long-term international presence is not viable, there is only one way that the ANSF can approach sustainability: the conditions in the region must be changed so that Afghanistan no longer needs such large and expensive security forces. Changing those conditions, however, will require changing the behavior of actors not only inside but also outside of the country—and that has led many observers to embrace putting pressure on, and even launching attacks into, Pakistan as another deus ex machina for the increasingly dire situation within Afghanistan.

Borderline Insecurity Disorder

After the first phase of the war in Afghanistan ended with the overthrow of the Taliban in 2001 (and as the United States prepared to invade Iraq), Washington's limited agenda in the region was to press the Pakistani military to go after al

Qaeda; meanwhile, Washington largely ignored the broader insurgency, which remained marginal until 2005. This suited the Pakistani military's strategy, which was to assist the United States against al Qaeda but to retain the Afghan Taliban as a potential source of pressure on Afghanistan. But the summer of 2006 saw a major escalation of the insurgency, as Pakistan and the Taliban interpreted the United States' decision to transfer command of coalition forces to NATO (plus U.S. Secretary of Defense Donald Rumsfeld's announcement of a troop drawdown, which in fact never took place) as a sign of its intention to withdraw. They also saw non-U.S. troop contributors as more vulnerable to political pressure generated by casualties.

The Pakistani military does not control the insurgency, but it can affect its intensity. Putting pressure on Pakistan to curb the militants will likely remain ineffective, however, without a strategic realignment by the United States. The region is rife with conspiracy theories trying to find a rational explanation for the United States' apparently irrational strategic posture of supporting a "major non-NATO ally" that is doing more to undermine the U.S. position in Afghanistan than any other state. Many Afghans believe that Washington secretly supports the Taliban as a way to keep a war going to justify a troop presence that is actually aimed at securing the energy resources of Central Asia and countering China. Many in Pakistan believe that the United States has deceived Pakistan into conniving with Washington to bring about its own destruction: India and U.S.-supported Afghanistan will form a pincer around Pakistan to dismember the world's only Muslim nuclear power. And some Iranians speculate that in preparation for the coming of the Mahdi, God has blinded the Great Satan to its own interests so that it would eliminate both of Iran's Sunni-ruled regional rivals, Afghanistan and Iraq, thus unwittingly paving the way for the long-awaited Shiite restoration.

The true answer is much simpler: the Bush administration never reevaluated its strategic priorities in the region after September 11. Institutional inertia and ideology jointly assured that Pakistan would be treated as an ally, Iran as an enemy, and Iraq as the main threat, thereby granting Pakistan a monopoly on U.S. logistics and, to a significant extent, on the intelligence the United States has on Afghanistan. Eighty-four percent of the materiel for U.S. forces in Afghanistan goes through Pakistan, and the ISI remains nearly the sole source of intelligence about international terrorist acts prepared by al Qaeda and its affiliates in Pakistan.

More fundamentally, the concept of "pressuring" Pakistan is flawed. No state can be successfully pressured into acts it considers suicidal. The Pakistani security establishment believes that it faces both a U.S.-Indian-Afghan alliance and a separate Iranian-Russian alliance, each aimed at undermining Pakistani influence in Afghanistan and even dismembering the Pakistani state. Some (but not all) in the establishment see armed militants within Pakistan as a threat—but they largely consider it one that is ultimately controllable, and in any case secondary to the threat posed by their nuclear-armed enemies.

Pakistan's military command, which makes and implements the country's national security policies, shares a commitment to a vision of Pakistan as the homeland for South Asian Muslims and therefore to the incorporation of Kashmir into Pakistan. It considers Afghanistan as within Pakistan's security perimeter. Add to this that Pakistan does not have border agreements with either India, into which Islamabad contests the incorporation of Kashmir, or Afghanistan, which has never explicitly recognized the Durand Line, which separates the two countries, as an interstate border.

That border is more than a line. The frontier between Pakistan and Afghanistan was structured as part of the defenses of British India. On the Pakistani side of the Durand Line, the British and their Pakistani successors turned the difficulty of governing the tribes to their advantage by establishing what are now the FATA. Within the FATA, these tribes, not the government, are responsible for security. The area is kept underdeveloped and overarmed as a barrier against invaders. (That is also why any ground intervention there by the United States or NATO will fail.) Now, the Pakistani military has turned the FATA into a staging area for militants who can be used to conduct asymmetric warfare in both Afghanistan and Kashmir, since the region's special status provides for (decreasingly) plausible deniability. This use of the FATA has eroded state control, especially in Pakistan's Northwest Frontier Province, which abuts the FATA. The Swat Valley, where Pakistani Taliban fighters have been battling the government for several years, links Afghanistan and the FATA to Kashmir. Pakistan's strategy for external security has thus undermined its internal security.

On September 19, 2001, when then Pakistani President Pervez Musharraf announced to the nation his decision to support the U.S.-led intervention against the Taliban in Afghanistan, he stated that the overriding reason was to save Pakistan by preventing the United States from allying with India. In return, he wanted concessions to Pakistan on its security interests.

Subsequent events, however, have only exacerbated Pakistan's sense of insecurity. Musharraf asked for time to form a "moderate Taliban" government in Afghanistan but failed to produce one. When that failed, he asked that the United States prevent the Northern Alliance (part of the anti-Taliban resistance in Afghanistan), which had been supported by India, Iran, and Russia, from occupying Kabul; that appeal failed. Now, Pakistan claims that the Northern Alliance is working with India from inside Afghanistan's security services. Meanwhile, India has reestablished its consulates in Afghan cities, including some near the Pakistani border. India has genuine consular interests there (Hindu and Sikh populations, commercial travel, aid programs), but it may also in fact be using the consulates against Pakistan, as Islamabad claims. India has also, in cooperation with Iran, completed a highway linking Afghanistan's ring road (which connects its major cities) to Iranian ports on the Persian Gulf, potentially eliminating Afghanistan's dependence on Pakistan for access to the sea and marginalizing Pakistan's new Arabian Sea port of Gwadar, which was built with hundreds of millions of dollars of Chinese aid. And the new U.S.-Indian nuclear deal effectively recognizes New Delhi's legitimacy as a nuclear power while continuing to treat Islamabad, with its record of proliferation, as a pariah. In this context, pressuring or giving aid to Pakistan, without any effort to address the sources of its insecurity, cannot yield a sustainable positive outcome.

Big Hat, No Cattle

Rethinking U.S. and global objectives in the region will require acknowledging two distinctions: first, between ultimate goals and reasons to fight a war; and, second, among the time frames for different objectives. Preventing al Qaeda from regrouping so that it can organize terrorist attacks is an immediate goal that can justify war, to the extent that such war is proportionate and effective. Strengthening the state and the economy of Afghanistan is a medium- to long-term objective that cannot justify war except insofar as Afghanistan's weakness provides a haven for security threats.

This medium- to long-term objective would require reducing the level of armed conflict, including by seeking a political settlement with current insurgents. In discussions about the terms of such a settlement, leaders linked to both the Taliban and other parts of the insurgency have asked, What are the goals for which the United States and the international community are waging war in Afghanistan? Do they want to guarantee that Afghanistan's territory will not be used to attack them, impose a particular government in Kabul, or use the conflict to establish permanent military bases? These interlocutors oppose many U.S. policies toward the Muslim world, but they acknowledge that the United States and others have a legitimate interest in preventing Afghan territory from being used to launch attacks against them. They claim to be willing to support an Afghan government that would guarantee that its territory would not be used to launch terrorist attacks in the future—in return, they say, for the withdrawal of foreign troops.

The guarantees these interlocutors now envisage are far from those required, and Afghanistan will need international forces for security assistance even if the current war subsides. But such questions can provide a framework for discussion. To make such discussions credible, the United States must redefine its counterterrorist goals. It should seek to separate those Islamist movements with local or national objectives from those that, like al Qaeda, seek to attack the United States or its allies directly—instead of lumping them all together. Two Taliban spokespeople separately told *The New York Times* that their movement had broken with al Qaeda since 9/11. (Others linked to the insurgency have told us the same thing.) Such statements cannot simply be taken at face value, but that does not mean that they should not be explored further. An agreement in principle to prohibit the use of Afghan (or Pakistani) territory for international terrorism, plus an agreement from the United States and NATO that such a guarantee could be sufficient to end their hostile military action, could constitute a framework for negotiation. Any agreement in which the Taliban or other insurgents disavowed al Qaeda would constitute a strategic defeat for al Qaeda.

Political negotiations are the responsibility of the Afghan government, but to make such negotiations possible, the United States would have to alter its detention policy. Senior officials of the Afghan government say that at least through 2004 they repeatedly received overtures from senior Taliban leaders but that they could never guarantee that these leaders would not be captured by U.S. forces and detained at Guantánamo Bay or the U.S. air base at Bagram, in Afghanistan. Talking with Taliban fighters or other insurgents does not mean replacing Afghanistan's constitution with the Taliban's Islamic Emirate of Afghanistan, closing girls' schools, or accepting other retrograde social policies. Whatever weaknesses the Afghan government and security forces may have, Afghan society—which has gone through two Loya Jirgas and two elections, possesses over five million cell phones, and has access to an explosion of new media—is incomparably stronger than it was seven years ago, and the Taliban know it. These potential interlocutors are most concerned with the presence of foreign troops, and some have advocated strengthening the current ANSF as a way to facilitate those troops' departure. In November 2006, one of the Taliban's leading supporters in Pakistan, Maulana Fazlur Rahman, publicly stated in Peshawar that the Taliban could participate as a party in elections in Afghanistan, just as his party did in Pakistan (where it recently lost overwhelmingly), so long as they were not labeled as terrorists.

The End of the Game

There is no more a political solution in Afghanistan alone than there is a military solution in Afghanistan alone. Unless the decision-makers in Pakistan decide to make stabilizing the Afghan government a higher priority than countering the Indian threat, the insurgency conducted from bases in Pakistan will continue. Pakistan's strategic goals in Afghanistan place Pakistan at odds not just with Afghanistan and India, and with U.S. objectives in the region, but with the entire international community. Yet there is no multilateral framework for confronting this challenge, and the U.S.-Afghan bilateral framework has relied excessively on the military-supply relationship. NATO, whose troops in Afghanistan are daily losing their lives to Pakistan-based insurgents, has no Pakistan policy. The UN Security Council has hardly discussed Pakistan's role in Afghanistan, even though three of the permanent members (France, the United Kingdom, and the United States) have troops in Afghanistan, the other two are threatened by movements (in the North Caucasus and in Xinjiang) with links to the FATA, and China, Pakistan's largest investor, is poised to become the largest investor in Afghanistan as well, with a $3.5 billion stake in the Aynak copper mine, south of Kabul.

The alternative is not to place Pakistan in a revised "axis of evil." It is to pursue a high-level diplomatic initiative designed to build a genuine consensus on the goal of achieving Afghan stability by addressing the legitimate sources of Pakistan's insecurity while increasing the opposition to its disruptive actions. China, both an ally of Pakistan and potentially the largest investor in both Afghanistan and Pakistan, could play a particularly significant role, as could Saudi Arabia, a serious investor in and ally of Pakistan, former supporter of the Taliban, and custodian of the two holiest Islamic shrines.

A first step could be the establishment of a contact group on the region authorized by the UN Security Council. This contact group, including the five permanent members and perhaps others (NATO, Saudi Arabia), could promote dialogue between India and Pakistan about their respective interests in Afghanistan and about finding a solution to the Kashmir dispute; seek a long-term political vision for the future of the FATA from the Pakistani government, perhaps one involving integrating the FATA into Pakistan's provinces, as proposed by several Pakistani political parties; move Afghanistan and Pakistan toward discussions on the Durand Line and other frontier issues; involve Moscow in the region's stabilization so that Afghanistan does not become a test of wills between the United States and Russia, as Georgia has become; provide guarantees to Tehran that the U.S.-NATO commitment to Afghanistan is not a threat to Iran; and ensure that China's interests and role are brought to bear in international discussions on Afghanistan. Such a dialogue would have to be backed by the pledge of a multiyear international development aid package for regional economic integration, including aid to the most affected regions in Afghanistan, Pakistan, and Central Asia, particularly the border regions. (At present, the United States is proposing to provide $750 million in aid to the FATA but without having any political framework to deliver the aid.)

A central purpose of the contact group would be to assure Pakistan that the international community is committed to its territorial integrity—and to help resolve the Afghan and Kashmir border issues so as to better define Pakistan's territory. The international community would have to provide transparent reassurances and aid to Pakistan, pledge that no state is interested in its dismemberment, and guarantee open borders between Pakistan and both Afghanistan and India. The United States and the European Union would have to open up their markets to Pakistan's critical exports, especially textiles, and to Afghan products. And the United States would need to offer a road map to Pakistan to achieving the same kind of nuclear deal that was reached with India, once Pakistan has transparent and internationally monitored guarantees about the nonproliferation of its nuclear weapons technology.

Reassurances by the contact group that addressed Pakistan's security concerns might encourage Pakistan to promote, rather than hinder, an internationally and nationally acceptable political settlement in Afghanistan. Backing up the contact group's influence and clout must be the threat that any breaking of agreements or support for terrorism originating in the FATA would be taken to the UN Security Council. Pakistan, the largest troop contributor to UN peacekeeping operations, sees itself as a legitimate international power, rather than a spoiler; confronted with the potential loss of that status, it would compromise.

India would also need to become more transparent about its activities in Afghanistan, especially regarding the role of its intelligence agency, the Research and Analysis Wing. Perhaps the ISI and the RAW could be persuaded to enter a dialogue to explore whether the covert war they have waged against each other for the past 60 years could spare the territory of Afghanistan. The contact group could help establish a permanent Indian-Pakistani body at the intelligence and military levels, where complaints could be lodged and discussed. The World Bank and the Asian Development Bank could also help set up joint reconstruction programs in Afghanistan. A series of regional conferences on economic cooperation for the reconstruction of Afghanistan have already created a partial framework for such programs.

Then there is Iran. The Bush administration responded to Iranian cooperation in Afghanistan in 2001 by placing Tehran in the "axis of evil" and by promising to keep "all options on the table," which is understood as a code for not ruling out a military attack. Iran has reacted in part by aiding insurgents in Afghanistan to signal how much damage it could do in response. Some Iranian officials, however, continue to seek cooperation with the United States against al Qaeda and the Taliban. The next U.S. administration can and should open direct dialogue with Tehran around the two countries' common concerns in Afghanistan. An opening to Iran would show that the United States need not depend solely on Pakistan for access to Afghanistan. And in fact, Washington and Tehran had such a dialogue until around 2004. In May 2005, when the United States and Afghanistan signed a "declaration of strategic partnership," Iran signaled that it would not object as long as the partnership was not directed against Iran. Iran would have to be reassured by the contact group that Afghan territory would not be used as a staging area for activities meant to undermine Iran and that all U.S. covert activities taking place from there would be stopped.

Russia's main concern—that the United States and NATO are seeking a permanent U.S.-NATO military presence in Afghanistan and Central Asia—will also need to be assuaged. Russia should be assured that U.S. and NATO forces can help defend, rather than threaten, legitimate Russian interests in Central Asia, including through cooperation with the Shanghai Cooperation Organization. Russia and the Central Asian states should be informed of the results of legitimate interrogations of militants who came from the former Soviet space and were captured in Afghanistan or Pakistan.

To overcome the zero-sum competition taking place between states, ethnic groups, and factions, the region needs to discover a source of mutual benefit derived from cooperation. China—with its development of mineral resources and access roads in Afghanistan and Pakistan, the financial support it gave to build the port of Gwadar, and its expansion of the Karakoram Highway, which links China to northern Pakistan—may be that source. China is also a major supplier of arms and nuclear equipment to Pakistan. China has a major interest in peace and development in the region because it desires a north-south energy and trade corridor so that its goods can travel from Xinjiang to the Arabian Sea ports of Pakistan and so that oil and gas pipelines can carry energy from the Persian Gulf and Iran to western China. In return for such a corridor, China could help deliver much-needed electricity and even water to both countries. Such a corridor would also help revive the economies of both Afghanistan and Pakistan.

More than Troops

Both U.S. presidential candidates are committed to sending more troops to Afghanistan, but this would be insufficient to reverse the collapse of security there. A major diplomatic initiative involving all the regional stakeholders in problem-solving talks and setting out road maps for local stabilization efforts is more important. Such an initiative would serve to reaffirm that the West is indeed committed to the long-term rehabilitation of Afghanistan and the region. A contact group, meanwhile, would reassure Afghanistan's neighbors that the West is determined to address not just extremism in the region but also economic development, job creation, the drug trade, and border disputes.

Lowering the level of violence in the region and moving the global community toward genuine agreement on the long-term goals there would provide the space for Afghan leaders to create jobs and markets, provide better governance, do more to curb corruption and drug trafficking, and overcome their countries' widening ethnic divisions. Lowering regional tensions would allow the Afghan government to have a more meaningful dialogue with those insurgents who are willing to disavow al Qaeda and take part in the political process. The key to this would be the series of security measures the contact group should offer Pakistan, thereby encouraging the Pakistani army to press—or at least allow—Taliban and other insurgent leaders on their soil to talk to Kabul.

The goal of the next U.S. president must be to put aside the past, Washington's keenness for "victory" as the solution to all problems, and the United States' reluctance to involve competitors, opponents, or enemies in diplomacy. A successful initiative will require exploratory talks and

an evolving road map. Today, such suggestions may seem audacious, naive, or impossible, but without such audacity there is little hope for Afghanistan, for Pakistan, or for the region as a whole.

The next U.S. president must put aside any reluctance to involve competitors in diplomacy.

BARNETT R. RUBIN is Director of Studies and a Senior Fellow at the Center on International Cooperation at New York University and the author of *The Fragmentation of Afghanistan* and *Blood on the Doorstep*. **AHMED RASHID** is a Pakistani journalist and writer, a Fellow at the Pacific Council on International Policy, and the author of *Jihad, Taliban,* and, most recently, *Descent Into Chaos: The United States and the Failure of Nation Building in Pakistan, Afghanistan, and Central Asia*.

Reprinted by permission of *Foreign Affairs,* November/December, 2008, pp. 30–43. Copyright © 2008 by the Council on Foreign Relations, Inc.

UNIT 9

International Organizations, International Law, and Global Governance

Unit Selections

Key Points to Consider

- What administrative reforms would you support to make the United Nations run more efficiently?

- Why is the United Nations such a useful organization for dealing with global problems such as disease, poverty, global crime, and war?

- Do you think the doctrine of the "responsibility to protect" may help prevent future genocides? Why or why not?

- Why have criminal tribunals in such places as Rwanda and former Yugoslavia failed to bring justice to the victims of past atrocities?

Student Web Site
www.mhcls.com

Internet References

"A More Secure World: Our Shared Responsibility"
http://www.un.org/secureworld
Amnesty International
http://www.amnesty.org/
The Digital Library in International Conflict Management
http://www.usip.org/library/diglib.html
Global Policy Forum
http://www.globalpolicy.org
Human Rights Web
http://www.hrweb.org
InterAction
http://www.interaction.org

IRIN
http://www.irinnews.org
International Court of Justice (ICJ)
http://www.icj-cij.org/
International Criminal Court
http://www.icc-cpi.int/home.html&l=en
United Nations
http://untreaty.un.org
United Nations Home Page
http://www.un.org
United Nations Peacekeeping Home Page
http://www.un.org/Depts/dpko/dpko/

International organizations consist of members who are sovereign states or other inter-government organizations, such as the European Union or the World Trade Organization. The most visible international organization throughout the post-World War II era has been the United Nations. Membership grew from the original 50 in 1945 to 185 in 1995. The United Nations, across a variety of fronts, achieved noteworthy results—eradication of disease, immunization, provision of food, and shelter to refugees and victims of natural disasters, and help to dozens of countries that have moved from colonial status to self-rule.

After the first Gulf War in the early 1990s, the United Nations guided enforcement of economic sanctions against Iraq, sent peacekeeping forces to former Yugoslavia and to Somalia, monitored an unprecedented number of elections and cease-fire agreements, and played an active peacekeeping role in almost every region of the world. However, the withdrawal of the U.N. mission in Somalia in the early 1990s, the near-collapse of the U.N. peacekeeping mission in Bosnia prior to the intervention of NATO-sponsored troops, and the delayed U.N. response in sending troops to monitor cease-fire agreements in East Timor and Sierra Leone in 1999, along with recent allegations of sexual abuse of local citizens levied against U.N. peacekeepers in the Democratic Republic of the Congo and the failure of the U.N. Security Council to raise the troops or resources needed for their authorized peacekeeping force in Darfur during 2007 raise serious doubts about the ability of the organization to continue to be involved in peacekeeping worldwide.

Televised photos of U.N. peacekeeping forces standing by and doing nothing in the eastern province of the Democratic Republic of the Congo as thousands of civilians fled advancing rebel forces in 2008 further alienated viewing publics in the West. The fact that the United Nations helped negotiate a cease-fire that permitted civilians to return to their now ruined villages received much less attention. Press stories usually fail to explain that U.N. peacekeeping forces typically operate under detailed mandates that permit them to observe and keep rival forces apart while not getting involved once fight breaks out. Press stories rarely explain that these limited mandates are the only ones that will receive political support by member nations of the United Nations. However, these limited mandates will remain limited and a source of frustration and criticism of U.N. peacekeeping activities until such time that the member states of the United Nations reach a consensus on the need to amend the U.N. Charter or pass resolutions giving U.N. peacekeepers more authority.

The U.N. withdrawal from Iraq in 2003 after a bombing of the U.N. headquarters, subsequent statements by former Secretary General Kofi Annan that the U.S. military intervention in Iraq was a mistake, and the results of an investigation into an illegal kickback scheme in the UN-run Oil-for-Food program that implicated several senior U.N. officials—including Annan's son—greatly increased tensions between the United States

© Photodisc/Getty Images

and the United Nations. Some observers now call for the United Nations to scale back its current level of peacekeeping in order to focus more effectively on global problems that nobody else can or will tackle. Others worry that without U.S. backing, the United Nations will be unable to fulfill an ever growing list of requests in such diverse areas as military, weapons proliferation, economic, social, and the environment.

The policies of the Bush administration proved to be a difficult period for the United Nations. The Bush administration's emphasis on unilateral action and its doctrine of preventive war have posed a profound challenge to the United Nation's founding principle of collective security and threatens the organization's continued relevance. The war in Iraq brought these conflicts to a new height. Washington's rush to invade Iraq split the Security Council in ways that have still not healed. Yet the years since the Iraq invasion showed how much the United States still needs the United Nation's unparalleled ability to confer international legitimacy and its growing experience in nation building. Even after the U.N. presence left Iraq, the United States had to turn to the organization at the end of 2003 in an effort to build legitimacy and support for delaying elections in Iraq.

The United States once again looked toward the United Nations to play an expanded role in Iraqi post-war reconstruction in plans that call for a gradual reduction in the number of U.S. personnel in Iraq. The policy reversal on the part of the Bush administration underscored the fact that the United Nations is a useful body. The United Nations, despite all of its problems, remains the world's best hope against disease, poverty, global crime, and war—and all at a reasonable price. However, few observers doubt that the organization is in a crisis period and requires some major overhauls if it is to function effectively throughout the twenty-first century.

James Traub in "Marching Orders for the United Nations Boss" offers a number of practical suggestions to the new

Secretary General Ban Ki-Moon to make the organizations run more efficiently. Among Traub's suggestions is to chop deadwood and cut red tape within the organization. He also advises the Secretary General to accept that "you can't fix the Human Rights Council—or the Security Council or the General Assembly." However, Traub urges the new Secretary General to appreciate that his speeches really do matter and urges the new Secretary General to take the U.S. Secretary of State to a Redskins game!

The inability of the United Nations Security Council's permanent members to reach a consensus has delayed implementing resolutions that might stop the killing of innocent civilians in places such as Darfur, Sudan, or in the Democratic Republic of the Congo. One idea is described by Gareth Evans, President of the International Crisis Group, in "The Responsibility to Protect: Creating and Implementing a New International Norm." The idea of creating this new international norm was formulated as one way to break the current deadlock in the Security Council over whether the U.N. should be given authority to intervene militarily in conflicts that have or threaten to kill thousands of innocent civilians. The idea was floated years ago by Canada's former Foreign Minister, Lloyd Axworthy. The idea is to use a new doctrine called "responsibility to protect"—a proposal to impose upon the United Nations an obligation to shield people all over the world from genocide and ethnic cleansing. The new doctrine has been picking up support among American neo-conservatives and evangelical Christians alike and is reflected in the wording of a recent U.N. Security Council that recognizes the right of the United Nations to intervene in a sovereign country if the national government fails to protect their own people. For the movement, Western diplomats are focused on trying to reach an agreement with the Sudanese government, the Arab League, Russia, and China on the terms for an expanded international peacekeeping to enter Darfur. However, the new doctrine appears to lay the groundwork for future U.N. military interventions in civil conflicts, including ones that are objected to by the national government.

The lack of a global consensus about what the United Nations should do as violence continues in Darfur reflects a more basic disagreement among world elites about what security should entail and who should be responsible for guaranteeing global security. What should constitute universal human rights remains another core dispute in international relations and law. After the historic election in South Africa, the new government sponsored a Truth and Reconciliation Commission (TRC) that allowed victims to confront their oppressors directly. If accused individuals confessed, expressed remorse, and apologized to their victims, they were not prosecuted through the legal system for their crimes. South Africa's TRC became a model of one approach towards reconciliation that has been used by other war-torn societies. While most outside observers were impressed by the process, many South African victims were disappointed with the meager compensation sums that they received. The pros and cons of a TRC highlight how difficult it can be to structure formal processes for reconciliation after intense and violent conflicts. An approach for dealing with perpetrators of collective violence and crimes against humanity has been to establish special international tribunals. These special courts, established in Rwanda and Yugoslavia, have spent a vast amount of human and monetary resources and resulted in few convictions.

Another approach for dealing with perpetrators of collective violence and crimes against humanities has been to establish special international tribunals under the auspices of the International Criminal Court. The recently established International Criminal Court (ICC) has now sponsored several international war crimes in Rwanda, the former Yugoslavia, and Liberia. The trial of the former Liberian President and war lord, Charles Taylor, was moved to The Hague in The Netherlands as there was concern that holding the trial in West Africa might contribute to additional instability and prove difficult to accomplish from a logistic and resource perspective. To date, none of the criminal tribunals, set up in Rwanda, the former Yugoslavia, or Liberia that were suppose to bring justice to oppressed peoples, have succeeded in directly advancing human rights or implementing the wishes of victims. All of these trials have been lengthy affairs costing billions of dollars. Many important countries, including the United States, continue to refuse to recognize the jurisdiction of the ICC due to sovereignty concerns and an unwillingness to agree to allow U.S. military personnel to be liable for charges that would be tried in under the ICC's jurisdiction. One or more of these reasons are why some have concluded that is would be better to abandon these special courts. In contrast, others argue that such fledgling institutions as the ICC and new norms, such as the Responsibility to Protect—or 'R2P', should be supported as it will take decades to establish new effective international institutions and norms. Another argument in favor of strengthening international law is tied to the fact that international laws and norms operate as one of the few checks that exist to sanction the power of major national states. This longstanding debate has become more salient in recent years as key provisions of the U.S. Patriot Act, passed quickly after the 2001 terrorist attacks and subsequent secret rulings by the U.S. Justice Department authorized the U.S. government to engage in a number of controversial practices. One of the most controversial new practices for many observers has been the secret practice of the CIA to transfer detainees out of the United States, Iraq, Europe, and several other countries to third world countries, including ones with a reputation for torturing prisoners. Revelations that several CIA flights used airports in allied countries without notifying local authorities or gaining the requisite approvals as suspected terrorist prisoners were moved to third world countries created a great deal of outrage among government officials and many members of the public in some European countries starting in 2005. Several European governments complained that the United States had violated their sovereignty and existing treaty agreements. Many legal specialists say the practice contravenes the Geneva Convention. This and other recent U.S. practices justified in terms of the War on Terrorism has caused many legal experts to charge that the United States is undermining fundamental treaties in international law, including the Geneva Convention that outlines long accepted norms on the treatment of prisoners during war.

Running the U.N.

If Ban Ki-Moon is to promote peace around the world, he'll have to get tough at headquarters. He should start by sacking useless employees and shaming the shameful.

JAMES TRAUB

MEMORANDUM:

TO: Ban Ki-Moon

FROM: James Traub

RE: Marching Orders for
         The U.N.'s Boss

I'm sorry to say, Mr. Secretary-General, that you are inheriting a United Nations that's not very happy—and not very healthy, either, despite growing demand for its services. The reservoir of tolerance and good will, both within the staff and among the member states, is perilously low. To be perfectly fair, the organization hasn't really been happy or healthy since 1993, the end of that very brief interval between the first Gulf War and the sudden collapse of peacekeeping missions in Somalia, Bosnia, and Haiti. Brittleness and division is the United Nations' default condition. For your own mental health, it's best not to think that your job is to make the place operate the way things do in highly effective countries like your own, South Korea. Your job is to persuade the members they have something in common, and to make the place work well enough that they continue to resort to it. Here are some tips:

Chop Deadwood and Cut Red Tape

Beijing and Washington—the capitals most responsible for your getting the job—expect you to be more "secretary" than "general." You've been touted as a manager, and you've said forthrightly that the secretary-general needs "greater flexibility matched by greater accountability." Yes, he does; but you can't wait for the members to grant that to you. Start doing what you can do yourself: End the archaic system whereby every document has to slowly circumambulate the upper reaches of the bureaucracy before being signed by your chief of staff; promote talented young people to important jobs, no matter what their civil service grade; take advantage of new buyout provisions to unload a few cords of deadwood in important places like the Department of Political Affairs. You've got to push for the rule changes you need right now, and that will mean publicly harping on the absurdity of a system that deprives you of control over budget and personnel.

Chat with the Chinese

There is a powerful group of countries at the United Nations that you'll quickly find in your way: the bloc of developing countries known as the Group of 77 (G-77). You've got to tell them bluntly that the organization can't work so long as they refuse to grant real autonomy to the secretary-general and the secretariat. You will perhaps be surprised to discover that many of the members don't really care: They view the secretary-general and the secretariat as instruments of the West, and they would rather tangle you in red tape than cede any further authority to the United States and its allies. In the long run, of course, you have to help end this embittered stand-off. In the short run, have a talk with the Chinese. Beijing doesn't want to jeopardize its harmonious relationship with the G-77 countries, but it may be able to loosen the handcuffs that your predecessors have worn. Tell Beijing to tell Egypt, Pakistan, South Africa, and the group's other leading members to cut you some slack.

Flatter, Hector, and Shame

Everything that really matters at the United Nations—even issues of process and administration—comes down to political power and political choices. You've said that the new Human Rights Council has to "meet the heightened expectations of the international community." You're absolutely right; its predecessor, the Human Rights Commission, failed to meet even modest expectations because the worst abusers had no difficulty in gaining a seat, and then they used the position to block resolutions criticizing their behavior. Kofi Annan targeted the commission for reform, and the United States and other industrialized nations joined the campaign. China, Russia, and various authoritarian states in the developing world managed to water down proposed changes, however, and the new body has so far failed to condemn human rights practices in any country—save Israel.

You can't fix the Human Rights Council—or the Security Council or the General Assembly—the way a CEO would fix a company losing market share. You're much less powerful than a CEO, and most of these problems originate in fundamental differences of view among states. Quiet diplomacy, which is the kind you've practiced throughout your career, will get you only so far with problems like these. If you have any influence at all on issues where there are deep, abiding differences of opinion among members, it will be through your ability to shape the climate of debate through public flattery, hectoring, and even the occasional guilt-mongering. Annan challenged African heads of state to stop treating human rights as a Western imposition—and lived to tell the tale. Too much of this, of course, and you'll turn into a self-righteous scold like Boutros Boutros-Ghali, who enjoyed the satisfaction of speaking his mind but accomplished little. The trick is to criticize your own supporters before you turn on others. Also, do it soon. Secretaries-general tend to exhaust their political capital quickly. Even if you feel that the world needs you to serve a second term—and you're bound to feel that way—take on your members while it may still do some good.

Meet and Greet

It's a public job, and you'll have to keep reminding yourself of that. Some of your predecessors, like Javier Perez de Cuelar even Kurt Waldheim, were supremely accomplished diplomats. But they preferred to work indoors. It's evident from the studied blandness of your public remarks that you are of a similar ilk. That won't do. You have said that the United Nations' work in the field must be more firmly grounded in "humanitarian principles" than it now is. The way to cause that to happen is to talk about it passionately and persistently. And not abstractly, either: You have to be willing to single out real failures, both on the part of the United Nations and even, every once in a while, an actual member. (Well, perhaps that's going too far.) Your speeches actually matter; they are minutely parsed around the world. My guess is that you would be your own worst speechwriter. Kofi Annan knew that about himself, and he hired gifted speechwriters. You must do the same (or just keep his).

Your own staff's low morale is less important, and more solvable, than the churlishness of the member-states. You've said that the staff needs "hands-on guidance" and "a clear sense of mission." That's absolutely right. They also need to feel that you're aware of them. Between the imperial Boutros-Ghali and the retiring Annan, secretaries-general have not been very accessible to the troops in recent years. Have lunch in the staff cafeteria every once in a while. Talk to small groups of employees. Don't just deliver pep talks; talk candidly about the organization's faults (but not too candidly, since every syllable you

The Boys in Blue

Kofi Annan [Ghana] 1996–2006
He had quiet charisma, but the Iraq war and the oil-for-food scandal marred his second term.

Boutros Boutros-Ghali [Egypt] 1992–1996
The United States dumped the acerbic and undiplomatic Egyptian after one turbulent term.

Javier Perez de Cuellar [Peru] 1982–1991
He quietly guided the organization out of Cold War paralysis and back into business.

Kurt Waldheim [Austria] 1972–1981
An effective bureaucrat, Waldheim is now remembered mainly for his Nazi past.

U Thant [Burma] 1961–1971
The placid Thant had a low profile but got flak for pulling U.N. peacekeepers from Sinai.

Dag Hammarskjöld [Sweden] 1953–1961
The U.N.'s most effective leader. Hammarskjold died on a peacekeeping mission to Congo.

Trygve Lie [Norway] 1946–1952
The gruff politician helped create the organization but accomplished little in office.

utter will find its way to the press). There is a whole generation of younger officials who have been tested in difficult and dangerous missions; they are the future of the United Nations, and they need to be recognized and promoted and given important things to do.

Find Something for Everyone

But how do you produce "harmony"—your favorite word among the fractious members? Again, bear in mind that this is not, at its root, a problem of ill temper but of different interests. The United Nations means something very different to Kenya than it does to Canada. Other members, such as Cuba or Iran, play the spoiler, while still others, like China, just play defense. The truly noble citizens—the Denmarks—are few and far between. Forget about harmony; it would be achievement enough if you could restore the status quo of June 2002 or so. In the months that followed, the Bush administration drove a wedge straight through the organization with its campaign to win a resolution authorizing war in Iraq. Annan tried to suture the resulting wound with his mighty reform document, which was designed both to persuade the Bush administration that it could do business at Turtle Bay and to create a new ethic of shared responsibility. But while Annan achieved a few real reforms, the acrimonious debate only proved how deep the divisions are between the First and Third Worlds, and between the United States and everyone else.

Your own agenda presupposes that G-77 members come around on management reform, human rights, and peacekeeping. What do you plan on offering them in return? Most of the world's impoverished countries care far more about economic and social development than they do about peacekeeping and nation-building. Kofi Annan gave the United Nations a meaningful role on development issues when he introduced the Millennium Development Goals. You've vowed to bring tangible progress on these measures. It would be excellent if you could persuade the major donors—above all, the United States—to increase foreign assistance (or, for that matter, if you could convince recipient countries to clean up corruption and to spend their own resources more wisely). Use the bully pulpit, if only to show skeptical Third World countries that you're on their side. But understand that the secretary-general has less influence in these matters than does, say, the president of the World Bank.

Deliver Washington

What, then, can you offer the developing world? The answer is simple: influence with the superpower. The United States can, to an extraordinary degree, determine the climate of the United Nations. When the superpower behaves like a bully, the bullied, smarting but helpless, take out their ire at the global body. They loudly belabor Washington and block the American—which is to say, more or less, the Western—agenda. When the United States behaves respectfully, it usually carries the day, even when it's in the minority. Very few countries actually relish being at odds with Washington, and those differences can be overcome easily enough. The Bush administration seems to have belatedly recognized this truth, and it is channeling an increasing fraction of its foreign policy through the Security Council. You have leverage with the White House, at least right now. Use it to encourage this trend in every way possible. It wouldn't be a bad idea to go to a Redskins game with Secretary of State Condoleezza Rice. Ignore whatever criticism comes your way for paying court to President Bush.

Here, then, is the irony of your new job: You get to run one of the world's most prestigious organizations, your face will be on the cover of all the newsweeklies, you and Mrs. Ban will sit at the head table of every event worth caring about—but you're answerable to a board with 192 members, many of whom are not on speaking terms with one another, and almost all of whom are jealous of your authority. You're already talking about a peacemaking trip to North Korea—a no-win situation if ever there was one. Remember: In this job, it's easy to fail, and almost impossible to succeed.

JAMES TRAUB is contributing writer at the *New York Times Magazine* and author of *The Best Intentions: Kofi Annan and the UN in the Era of American World Power* (New York: Farrar, Straus and Giroux, 2006).

The Responsibility to Protect: Meeting the Challenges

GARETH EVANS

Last year, at the height of the Burma/Myanmar regime's bloody suppression of its protesting monks, a well-known Chinese professor from Shanghai was asked by an American newspaper for his reaction. His quoted reply, in two stark sentences, went to the core of the issue I have been asked to talk to you about this evening: *"China has used tanks to kill people on Tiananmen Square. It is Myanmar's sovereign right to kill their own people, too."*

For a great many people in the world, and certainly to Western ears, that is about as chilling and abhorrent a statement as it is possible to imagine, an apparent apologia not only for Tiananmen and the October Crackdown, but the killing fields of Cambodia, the genocide in Rwanda, the bloody massacre of Srebrenica, and the crimes against humanity continuing in Darfur. It seems to embrace the starkest possible interpretation of Westphalian principles—not only that what happens within state borders is nobody else's business, but that sovereignty is a license to kill. It not only challenges head-on those who would argue for the option of coercive external military intervention in at least some of these situations, but seems to ignore all the developments in international human rights law which have occurred since 1945—from the Universal Declaration and the Covenants, to the Genocide Convention and the Rome Statute establishing the International Criminal Court.

For many others, however, particularly in the global South, the Chinese professor's statement, while chilling in its directness and certainly less diplomatically expressed than it might have been, captures a sentiment which has great resonance in the developing world—and which has too often been ignored by enthusiastic human rights campaigners arguing for 'the right to intervene', by coercive military force if necessary, in internal situations where major rights violations were purportedly occurring. While 'the right to intervene' or 'the right of humanitarian intervention' might be seen in most of the global North as a noble and effective rallying cry—and was so seen through most of the 1990s—it had the capacity elsewhere to enrage, and continues to do so, not least among those new states emerging through the whole post World War II period, proud of their identity, conscious in many cases of their fragility, and all too vividly remembering the many occasions in the past when they had been on the receiving end *missions civilisatrices* from the colonial and imperial powers.

There is a third way of reacting to the sentiment expressed in the Chinese professor's statement, and that is not to leap into either attack or defence but to treat it as a *challenge*—to find a solution to the problem of mass atrocity crimes which is neither an absolutist defence of all the worst manifestations of traditional sovereignty, nor an equally absolutist statement of the right to intervene coercively anywhere and any time when people seem to be suffering. At the 2000 Millennium General Assembly Kofi Annan, despairing at the lack of any kind of consensus on this issue throughout the previous decade, put the problem in the clearest of terms: *If humanitarian intervention is indeed an unacceptable assault on sovereignty, how should we respond to a Rwanda, to a Srebrenica—to gross and systematic violations of human rights that offend every precept of our common humanity?*

It was in response to this challenge that the concept of the responsibility to protect was born, in the 2001 report of that name by the Canadian-sponsored International Commission on Intervention and State Sovereignty which I had the privilege of co-chairing with the distinguished Algerian diplomat Mohamed Sahnoun. The core idea of the responsibility to protect (or "R2P" as we are all calling it for short in this age of acronymphomania—a condition not unfamiliar to military audiences!) is very simple. Turn the notion of "right to intervene" upside down. Talk not about the "right" of big states to do anything, but the *responsibility* of *all* states to protect their own people from atrocity crimes, and to help others to do so. Start with the traditional concept of sovereignty, and talk about the primary responsibility being that of individual states themselves, with the role of other states in the first instance being to assist them in that role. But don't stop there: make it absolutely clear that if states do not or cannot meet the responsibility to protect their own people, as a result either of ill-will or incapacity, it then falls to the wider international community to take the appropriate action.

Focus not on the notion of "intervention" but of *protection:* look at the whole issue from the perspective of the victims, the men being killed, the women being raped, the children dying of starvation; and look at the responsibility in question as being above all a responsibility to *prevent,* with the question of reaction—through diplomatic pressure, through sanctions, through international criminal prosecutions, and ultimately through military action—arising only if prevention has failed. And accept coercive military intervention only as an absolute last resort, after a number of clearly defined criteria have been met, and the approval of the Security Council has been obtained.

Well, as many blue-ribbon commissions and panels have discovered over the years, it is one thing to labour mightily and produce what looks like a major new contribution to some policy debate, but quite another to get any policymaker to take any notice of it. But the extraordinary thing is that governments *did* take notice of the R2P idea: within four years—after a series of further high-level reports and a great deal of diplomatic scrambling—it had won unanimous endorsement by the more than 150 heads of state and government meeting as the UN General Assembly at the 2005 World Summit.

The Summit Outcome Document was as explicit as it could have been: in a section headed '*Responsibility to protect populations from genocide, war crimes, ethnic cleansing and crimes against humanity',* there are two substantive paragraphs, the first focusing on the responsibility of sovereign states to protect their own peoples and of other states to assist them in doing so, and the second on the need to take collective action in the case of states 'manifestly failing to protect their populations', including through the Security Council under Chapter VII of the Charter. In just four years, a mere blink of an eye in the history of ideas, a phrase that nobody had heard of had become the central conceptual reference point, accepted as such by the General Assembly, sitting at head of state and government level, without a single dissenting voice.

But it was too early in 2005, and it remains too early now, to break out the champagne. Our Shanghai professor's statement, made two years after the Summit, is clear enough indication in itself that the notion that sovereignty has real limits is not exactly universally accepted. And there are plenty of signs, especially in the UN corridors in New York, where nothing is ever beyond argument, that much more work needs to be done to bed down the new norm. For whatever reason—embrace of the concept but concern about its misuse; ideological association of any intervention with neo-imperialism or neo-colonialism; or in some cases simply embarrassment about their own behaviour—there is an evident willingness by a number of states to deflate or undermine the new norm before it is fully consolidated and operational. The language of "buyers remorse" is in the air. There has been a falling away of overt commitment to the norm in sub-Saharan Africa (although in substance still remaining a significant theme in the doctrine of the AU and some of the sub-regional organizations), and some increased scepticism in the Arab-Islamic and Latin American worlds. And in Asia there was, frankly, never much enthusiasm to start with.

So for those of us who believe that, whatever the compelling attractions of traditional sovereignty, we cannot simply turn a blind eye to mass atrocity crimes, and that the 2005 cannot be

the high water mark from which the tides now recede, there is still a big job ahead. The immediate objective must be to get to the point where, when the next conscience-shocking case of large-scale killing, or ethnic cleansing, or other war crimes or crimes against humanity come along, as they are all too unhappily likely to, the immediate reflex response of the whole international community will be not to ask *whether* action is necessary, but rather *what* action is required, by whom, when, and where.

There have been some encouraging signs—in particular the swift and supportive diplomatic and political response to the crisis in Kenya early in 2008, when responsibility to protect language was much used—that this may be beginning to happen, but there are still three big challenges that need to be addressed if R2P is indeed to have complete reflex international acceptance in principle, and if it is to be given practical operational effect as new cases arise.

The first challenge is essentially *conceptual,* to ensure that the scope and limits of the responsibility to protect are fully and completely understood in a way that is clearly not the case now. In particular, it is to ensure that R2P is seen not as a Trojan horse for bad old imperial, colonial and militarist habits, but rather the best starting point the international community has, and is maybe ever likely to have, in preventing and responding to genocide and other mass atrocity crimes.

The second challenge is *institutional* preparedness, to build the kind of capacity within international institutions, governments, and regional organization that will ensure that, assuming that there is an understanding of the need to act—whether preventively or reactively, and whether through political and diplomatic, or economic, or legal or policing and military measures—there will be the physical capability to do so.

The third challenge, as always, is *political* preparedness, how to generate that indispensable ingredient of will: how to have in place the mechanisms and strategies necessary to generate an effective political response as new R2P situations arise.

The Conceptual Challenge

The conceptual challenge is to address a number of misunderstandings about the scope and limits of R2P—some of them cynically and deliberately fostered by those with other axes to grind, or interests to protect, but the majority the product of quite genuine misapprehension as to what R2P is all about. Let me focus for present purposes on just the two major ones.

The first is to think of R2P too narrowly and to think that it is "just another name for humanitarian intervention." This is absolutely not the case: they are very different concepts. The very core of the traditional meaning of "humanitarian intervention" is coercive military intervention for humanitarian purposes—nothing more or less. But "the responsibility to protect" is about much more than that. Above all, R2P is about taking effective *preventive* action, and at the earliest possible stage. It implies encouragement and support being given to those states struggling with situations that have not yet deteriorated to the point where genocide or other atrocity crimes are a reality, but where it is foreseeable that if effective preventive action is not taken, with or without outside support, they *could* so deteriorate. It recognizes the need to bring to bear every appropriate preventive response: be it political, diplomatic, legal, economic, or in the security sector but falling short of coercive action (e.g. a "preventive deployment" of troops, as in Macedonia in 1995). The responsibility to take preventive action is very much that of the sovereign state itself, quite apart from that of the international community. And when it comes to the international community, a very big part of *its* preventive response should be to help countries to help themselves. A good case study of what R2P means in its preventive dimension is *Burundi,* in Central Africa since 1994, where what could easily have become another Rwanda scale genocide has been staved off by a series of peacemaking, peacekeeping and peacebuilding initiatives by the African and wider international community.

Of course there will be situations when prevention fails, crises and conflicts do break out, and reaction becomes necessary. But reaction does not have to mean *military* reaction: it can involve political, diplomatic, economic and legal pressure, measures which can themselves each cross the spectrum from persuasive to intrusive, and from less coercive (e.g. economic incentives, offers of political mediation or legal arbitration) to more coercive (e.g. economic sanctions, political and diplomatic isolation, threats of referral to the International Criminal Court)—something which is true of military capability as well. Coercive military action is not excluded when it is the only possible way to stop large scale killing and other atrocity crimes, as nobody doubts was the case, for example, in Rwanda or Srebrenica. But it is a travesty of the R2P principle to say that it is about military force and nothing else. That's what 'humanitarian intervention' is about, but it's not R2P.

Even when a situation is very extreme, that still does not mean that coercive military force is necessarily the right course. Quite apart from the legal question of whether force is permitted under the UN Charter—which for nearly all purposes requires Security Council approval—there are a series of prudential criteria, or criteria of legitimacy, which should always have to be satisfied before it is exercised, and all the major reports on R2P leading up to the World Summit have spelled them out in similar terms.

The first of those criteria is certainly the seriousness of the threat: does it involve genocide or other large-scale killing, or ethnic cleansing or other serious violations of international humanitarian law, actual or imminently apprehended? Not ten years or more earlier, as was the case with Iraq at the time of the misguided invasion in 2003, but here and now.

But even if the threshold of seriousness is crossed in one or other of these ways—as was clearly not the case in Iraq in 2003—that still does not mean it is time, under the R2P doctrine, for the invasion to start. There are another four criteria of legitimacy, all more or less equally important, which also have to be satisfied if the case is to be made out for coercive, non-consensual military force to be deployed within another country's sovereign territory: the motivation or primary purpose of the proposed military action (whether it was primarily to halt or

avert the threat in question, or had some other main objective); last resort (whether there were reasonably available peaceful alternatives); the proportionality of the response; and, not least, the balance of consequences (whether overall more good than harm would be done by a military invasion).

In the case of *Darfur,* a great deal of the debate has ignored these considerations, with the choice for the international community too often being characterized as one between the stark options of Doing Nothing and Sending in the Marines, without acknowledging the many way stations in between. There is no doubt that the "seriousness of threat" criterion has been satisfied, with since 2003, in this region of Sudan, more than 200,000 dying from outright violence or war-related disease and malnutrition, well over two million being displaced, peacekeeping efforts proving manifestly inadequate, peace negotiations going nowhere fast, humanitarian relief faltering, the conflict spilling over into neighbouring countries, and the overall situation remaining desolate. But the argument is very strong—and accepted by most governments, and relief organisations on the ground—that a non-consensual military intervention (even assuming that the troops could be found anywhere to sustain it) would almost certainly be disastrously counterproductive, in terms of its impact on current humanitarian relief operations and the very fragile north-south peace process.

Darfur still remains, on any view, an "R2P situation", and one moreover where the responsibility to react has shifted to the international community because of the manifest abdication of its own sovereign responsibility by Khartoum. The inability here to use coercive military measures does not mean that this is a case of "R2P failure": it just means that the international responsibility to protect the people of Darfur against the incapacity or ill-will of the Sudan government has to take other forms, including the application of sustained diplomatic, economic and—as we are seeing now with the prosecution of Bashir—legal pressure to change the cost-benefit balance of the regime's calculations.

The other major conceptual misunderstanding about R2P is at the other end of the spectrum from those which take it that R2P is only about the application of military force. It's the idea that R2P is about every kind of situation in which humans are at risk. Of course one can argue, linguistically and as a matter of good public policy, that the international community has the responsibility to protect people from the ravages of HIV/AIDS worldwide; the proliferation of nuclear weapons and other weapons of mass destruction; the ready availability of small arms, and the use of landmines and cluster bombs; the impact of dramatic climate change, particularly on specific groups like the Inuit of the Arctic circle; and much more besides. But if one is looking for umbrella language to bring these issues and themes together, it is much more appropriate to use a concept like "human security" than to say these are proper applications of the new international norm of "the responsibility to protect".

It is not just a matter here of making the formal point that these cases are clearly not intended to be subsumed under the various descriptions of mass atrocity crimes that appear in the

World Summit outcome document and the relevant lead-up reports. The argument is a more practical one—if R2P is to be about protecting everybody from everything, it will end up protecting nobody from anything. The whole point of embracing the new language of "the responsibility to protect" is that it is capable of generating an effective, consensual response in extreme, conscience shocking cases, in a way that "right to intervene" language simply was not. We need to preserve the focus and bite of "R2P" as a rallying cry in the face of mass atrocities.

Clear thinking in this respect was very much put to the test in the context of Cyclone Nargis in Myanmar recently. French Foreign Minister Bernard Kouchner opened up a hornet's nest when he argued that the initial foot-dragging of the generals—with scores of thousands of lives being thought to be at risk as a result—was itself sufficient to trigger the R2P principle, and to actually justify a coercive intervention, at least in the form of the air dropping or barge landing of relief supplies. Many people, again mainly in the global South, feared that this was the thin edge of the wedge and that R2P would become an excuse for a whole new set of coercive intrusions.

So those of us who were anxious that the whole R2P principle was being put at risk had to scramble quickly to get the debate back on the rails. The way we did it was to go back to the basic core of the concept: R2P is about protecting peoples from mass atrocity crimes, not natural disasters or other ills man-made or otherwise. It was only if the regime's behaviour could reasonably be characterized as constituting a crime against humanity—because of evidence of deliberate intention to harm the surviving delta population, or perhaps because of reckless indifference as to whether they suffered or not—that the threshold application of R2P would be triggered, and even then the multiple prudential criteria would have to be satisfied. In the event, under immense pressure from ASEAN and other neighbours as well as the wider international community, the generals did start to cooperate sufficiently for the feared catastrophe to be avoided. But the case shows how important it is to maintain a clear head about what is, and what is not, an R2P situation if any kind of general consensus is to be maintained.

The Institutional Challenge

When it comes to meeting the institutional challenge of ensuring that R2P is effectively operational, there are a huge range of issues that need to be addressed. For a start, who is actually capable of doing what? There is a large cast of actors potentially available in the international community: the multiple entities that make up the UN system, other global and regional intergovernmental organizations (including the EU, AU and NATO), national governments, and nongovernmental organizations. But who among them can best do whatever job is required, by whatever means are needed—supportive, persuasive, or coercive? And in terms of process, what more needs to be done, in the crucial areas of diplomatic, civilian and military capability, to improve the effectiveness of the response to R2P situations,

again across the whole spectrum from prevention to reaction to rebuilding? I have just written a book of some 350 pages, to be published next month, a large proportion of which is devoted to these issues, and I can't begin to spell out now in the time available what is required.

But it is perhaps worth saying to this audience that when it comes to *military* preparedness, and in particular preparedness not just to mount training or monitoring or showing-the-flag operations but to actually deal with those perpetrating or obviously about to perpetrate atrocity crimes—the situation faced for example by the Dutch peacekeepers in Srebrenica, and by UNAMID forces in Sudan and MONUC forces in the Eastern Congo almost every day—a great deal more needs to be done. Exercising this responsibility poses a number of very difficult problems for military planners because—as this audience will know much better than me—it is not the kind of role in which militaries have been traditionally engaged, where they have well-developed doctrine and for which they can draw on a large body of experience.

What is involved here is neither traditional war fighting (where the object is to defeat an enemy, not just to stop particular kinds of violence and intimidation) nor, at the other extreme, traditional peacekeeping (which assumes that there is a peace to keep and is concerned essentially with monitoring, supervision, and verification). The new task is partly what is now described as "peacekeeping plus" or "complex peacekeeping," where it is assumed from the outset that the mission, while primarily designed to hold together a ceasefire or peace settlement, is likely to run into trouble from spoilers of one kind or another; that military force is quite likely to have to be used at some stage, for civilian protection purposes as well as in self-defense; and where, accordingly, a Chapter VII rather than just Chapter VI mandate is required. New UN peacekeeping missions in recent years have been constructed almost routinely on this basis, but that does not mean that military planners and commanders are yet comfortable with running them.

And that is not the end of the R2P story: the other part of the task is that which may arise in a Rwanda-type case, where there is the sudden eruption of conscience-shocking crimes against humanity, beyond the capacity of any existing peacekeeping mission to deal with, demanding a rapid and forceful "fire brigade" response from a new or extended mission to quash the violence and protect those caught up in it. This is more than just "peacekeeping plus"—dealing with spoilers—but, again, it is not traditional war fighting either.

Together, these "peacekeeping plus" and "fire brigade" operations have been described as "coercive protection missions," which is as useful terminology as any to use in addressing what is needed to create the capability—essentially the same in both cases—to operate them effectively. But getting reasonably clear the overall concept of operations, as this language does, is only the beginning of the story. Operational effectiveness in practice depends on getting a number of other things right: *force configuration* (what kind of force structure, and quantities of personnel and equipment, do militaries have to have to be able to mount these kinds of operations, individually or collectively); *deployability* (how rapidly can the necessary forces get to whatever theater is involved); *preparation* (ensuring that doctrine and training are matched to these operations); *mandates and rules of engagement* (ensuring that they are appropriate for the particular mission proposed); and *military-civilian cooperation* (ensuring that structures and processes are in place to maximize the effectiveness of each). I know that systematic attention is being paid now to all these issues by a number of national forces, and increasingly by those multilateral actors capable of mounting military operations, but still not enough has been done. These problems are going to be around to haunt us for a long time yet to come.

The Political Challenge

The remaining challenge is the age-old one of mobilizing political will. Everything else can be in place, but without the will to make something happen by someone capable of making it happen, the institutional capability to deliver the right kind of response at the right time—whether at the preventive, reactive or rebuilding end of the spectrum—simply won't be there, and even if the capability is there, it will not be used. For almost any spread of options, inertia will have the numbers.

But what I have learned very clearly from four decades of trying to make things happen, nationally and internationally, is that there is no point in simply mourning the absence of political will: this should be the occasion not for lamentation, but mobilization by those both within and outside the decision-making system in question. To explain a failure as the result of lack of political will, or organizational will, is simply to restate the problem, not provide an explanation or any kind of strategy for change. Political will is not a missing ingredient, waiting in each case to be found if we only had the key to the right cupboard or lifted the right stone. It has to be painfully and laboriously constructed, case by case, context by context.

It means ensuring that there is knowledge of the problem; generating concern to do something about it by making the right arguments—not just moral arguments, but national interest arguments, financial arguments, and domestic political arguments; creating a sense of confidence that doing something will actually make a difference; having in place institutional processes capable of translating that knowledge, concern and confident belief into relevant action; and leadership—without which the ticking of all four other boxes will not matter: inertia will win, every time. The discouraging news is that achieving all these things, in both national and international decision-making, is very hard work indeed, and needs a strong measure of luck as well, particularly when it comes to leaders: whether in a situation of fragility and transition a society finds itself with a Mandela, a Milosevic or a Mugabe is not easy to plan. The better news is that at least the arguments and strategies are there, and that there are plenty of civil society actors and public sector actors around—I'm sure some in this room—with the competence, commitment and organizational capacity to advance them.

There is a lot more I could say on all these substantive issues but let me finish on a more personal note. I suspect that for all of us for whom the idea of responsibility to protect really resonates, there will have been some personal experience which has touched us deeply. For many in Europe that will be bound to be scarifying family memories of the Holocaust or Bosnia; for others in Africa and Asia it may be a matter of knowing survivors from Cambodia or Rwanda or Darfur or any of the other mass atrocity scenes of more recent decades; for others still perhaps—and I know this is true of many in the US—it will be the awful sense that they could have done more, in their past official lives, to generate the kind of international response that these situations required.

For me it was my visit to Cambodia in the late 1960s, just before the genocidal slaughter which killed two million of its people. I was a young Australian making my first trip to Europe, to take up a scholarship in Oxford, and I spent six months wending my way by plane and overland through a dozen countries in Asia, and a few more in Africa and the Middle East as well. And in every one of them I spent many hours and days on student campuses and in student hangouts and in hard-class cross-country trains and ramshackle rural buses, getting to know in the process—usually fleetingly, but quite often enduringly, in friendships that have lasted to this day—scores of some of the liveliest and brightest people of that generation.

In the years that followed I have kept running into Indonesians, Singaporeans, Malaysians, Thais, Vietnamese, Indians, Pakistanis and others who I either met on the road on that trip or who were there at the time and had a store of common experiences to exchange. But among all the countries in Asia I visited then, there is just one, Cambodia, from which I never again in later years, saw *any* of those students whom I had met and befriended, or anyone exactly like them. Not one of those kids with whom I drank beer, ate noodles and careered up and down the dusty road from Phnom Penh to Siem Reap in share taxis scattering chickens and pigs and little children in villages all along the way.

The reason, I am sadly certain, is that every last one of them died a few years later under Pol Pot's murderous genocidal regime—either targeted for execution in the killing fields as a middle-class intellectual enemy of the state, or dying, as more than a million did, from starvation and disease following forced displacement to labour in the countryside. The knowledge, and the memory, of what must have happened to those young men and women haunts me to this day.

What this means is that my own attachment to the idea, and ideal, of the responsibility to protect is not just a matter of intellectual persuasion, but of very powerful emotional commitment. I know that will be the case for a great many of you too as it is for people I meet in every walk of life in every part of the world.

You have a role, as senior military personnel, that may well put you, professionally as well as personally, closer to the cutting edge of confronting this problem than most others will ever have a chance to do. So let us work together, in all our different capacities, to ensure that, however many of the world's problems we are unable to solve in the years ahead, we at least make sure that when it comes to mass atrocity crimes we never again—have to look back with anger, comprehension and shame after some new and terrible catastrophe, wondering how we could possibly have let it all happen again—as we've done so often in the past, after the Holocaust, after Cambodia, after Rwanda, after Srebrenica. . . . Let's make sure that when it comes to making the responsibility to protect people from genocide and other mass atrocity crimes, we never again have to say "never again".

Lecture by GARETH EVANS, President of the International Crisis Group, to 10th Asia Pacific Programme for Senior Military Officers, S. Rajaratnam School of International Studies, Singapore, 5 August 2008.

International Crisis Group Web Site, http://www.crisisgroup.org/home/ index.cfm?id=5615&1=1.

From *Speech by President of International Crisis Group to Human Rights Resource Center and Community Legal Centres and Lawyers for Human Rights,* August 13 and 28, 2007. Public Domain.

UNIT 10

The International Economic System

Unit Selections

Key Points to Consider

- How and why may the current global economic slowdown reverse years of prosperity worldwide?

- What are some future perils for the United States in maintaining the current trade relationship with China?

- What are some of the ways in which new technological developments, including the spread of cell phones and cheap computers, are changing the way political and economic actors do business in Africa?

- What are some of the ways in which transnational corruption and black market smuggling can be reduced?

Student Web Site
www.mhcls.com

Internet References

The Earth Institute at Columbia University
http://www.earth.columbia.edu
Graphs Comparing Countries
http://humandevelopment.bu.edu/use_exsisting_index/start_comp_graph.cfm
International Monetary Fund
http://www.imf.org
Kiva
http://www.kiva.org/
Peace Park Foundation
http://www.peaceparks.org/
Transparency International
http://www.transparency.org/
World Bank
http://www.worldbank.org
World Mapper Project
http://www.sasi.group.shef.ac.uk/worldmapper
World Trade Organization
http://www.wto.org/

There had been signs of trouble in the West's strongest economies for several years. However, recent downward trends in Asia or Europe were usually short lived and out of sync with periods of economic slowdowns in the United States. These cycles helped to prevent a widespread global downturn. This compensatory mechanism failed during 2008 as it became apparent that the United States, Europe, and much of Asia, including key sectors in China and other key emerging markets, were all starting to experience the worse economic downturn since the Great Depression of the 1930s. The majority of world citizens, who live in developing countries, never participated in the successful years. Instead, most people in the developing world had already seen their economic standard of living decline in the decades prior to the 2008 downturn.

The global slowdown appeared first as a series of interrelated economic crises in the financial, mortgage, and credit markets in the United States. Each of these crises soon were evident to some degree in many countries in Europe, Asia, and worldwide. As David Cho and Bingyamin Appelbaum describe in "Unfolding Worldwide Turmoil Could Reverse Years of Prosperity," the $700 billion dollar U.S. rescue package, that quickly grew to US$820 billion, failed to stem the growing spread of the various economic crises in the United States or worldwide. As it became clear that the interrelated economic crises were global in scope, more concerns mounted that the crisis may reverse years of prosperity.

Presidents and prime ministers from major countries around the world gathered in Washington in November 2008 for several meetings in attempts to avoid a deepening worldwide recession and to restore confidence in the world markets. However, it proved difficult to agree on specific proposals. Key European allies of the United States pushed for broad new roles for international organizations, empowering them to monitor everything from the global derivatives trade to the way major banks are regulated across borders. But the Bush administration signaled reluctance to go that far fearing that such proposals could potentially co-opt the independence of the U.S. financial system or compromising free markets. Proposals to sharpen existing regulatory tools presented at one of more of the fall conferences appeared to be in conflict with plans to create entirely new ones. While representatives of China shared the call made by European leaders for new international coordination, China, like the United States, was reluctant to cede national control or support the formation of new international organizations. As one senior Chinese official involved in the discussions noted, "It is important to have an agency which can coordinate the global market and policies of different countries . . . but China doesn't like the idea of having a global SEC since no organization should affect the sovereignty of countries."

The positions of major economic powers such as the United States and China are the main reason why few measures came out of a November 15th summit. This economic summit of

© Stockbyte/Getty Images

developed and developing countries had been billed as Bretton Woods II. The first Bretton Woods conference, held after World War II, had created the existing world order led by the World Bank and International Monetary Fund. However, there had been months of preparatory work prior to the first Bretton Woods conference. The conference led by the victors of World War II lasted three weeks. In contrasts, proposals for new international institutions were presented with little or no preparatory work at an annual summit of world leaders. Thus, it is hardly surprising that the only agreement coming out of Bretton Woods II was a general agreement for a new committee of international experts who would review global conditions and regulatory measures and make non-binding recommendations. Many world leaders appeared to be willing to wait for a new round of talks until after President-elect Barak Obama came to power in January 2009. However it was clear to all attendees and observers of the meeting that neither the United States nor the G-7 had the capacity to solve the current economic crises without engaging a much larger set of leaders from emerging economies as well. After World War II, the United States was the sole world economic and political nation-state that had the resources and political clout necessary to shape the postwar economic era. This is not the case today even though most central bankers and elected leaders around the world looked to the United States initially to solve the current crisis. No country yet has a comprehensive strategy to protect one or all countries from the global economic slowdown. As the depth and breath of the economic problems became apparent at the end of 2008, it became clear that the financial system, financial regulation and coordination requires the cooperation and active participation of a broader and more unwieldy group, including emerging economies, many of them loaded with foreign exchange reserves, foreign debts and influence over global financial markets. World leaders and publics are just now beginning to learn that economic interdependence has a dark and uncertain downside.

For years the U.S. trade deficit has been subsidized by foreigners willing to buy U.S. Treasury bills and make substantial investments in the U.S. economy. By the time the economic slowdown of 2008 hit, China owned US$1 dollar out of every $US 10 generated by the U.S. economy. Until recently, China's growing trade with the United States and other developed countries in the West have been credited with providing benefits to all parties involved in the exchanges. While America's economic relationship with China has so far been successful and beneficial for both sides, this relationship in the long run may hold perils for the United States. As the United States continues to experience job losses and increases it's reliance on imports for China for consumer goods and higher end good and services, some politicians and members of the American public are starting to become concerned about future vulnerabilities that the U.S. government and consumer might face. The costs in the short-run of depending so heavily on imports produced in Chinese factories that failed to adhere to U.S. standards of production became much more apparent during 1997 as several U.S. manufacturers had to recall "made in China" products, foods, and even medicines and vaccines that might be harmful to customers. Moreover, the future health of the U.S. economy, including the ability of the U.S. to finance experts increasingly is tied to the willingness of Chinese investors to hold U.S. dollars.

As the United States became more dependent on Chinese investments, the sustained growth of the Chinese economic miracle also became more dependent on sustained demand from U.S. customers to purchase Chinese products. Thus, when U.S. customers boycotted Chinese toys after warnings that they might contain a dangerous chemical recently, more than a quarter of all toy manufacturing factories in China closed. James Fallows explores the growing interdependences between the U.S. and China in "The $1.4 Trillion Dollar Question." In this article, Fallows explains how "the Chinese are subsidizing the America way of life." However, the adverse impacts in China from the economic slowdown in the United States illustrates why Fallows asks in his article whether "We are playing them for suckers—or are they playing us?"

In recent years, there has been a growing sense that some international actions are necessary in order to alleviate the conditions fueling poverty. One approach that has proven to be successful for many is microcredit schemes that lend small amounts of money to very poor individuals to support the startup costs of various types of commercial activities. Microfinance organizations, such as the Grameen Bank that was started in Bangladesh decades ago, have recently received renewed attention since the founder of the Grameen Bank, Muhammad Yunus, was awarded the Nobel Peace Prize in 2006. Others tout the benefits of increasing international trade while still others stress the creative use of new technologies such as cell phones and cheap computers. However, it is probably important to remember that the economic and cultural trends in the modern era of globalization may differ from earlier eras of intense globalization because modern trends are triggering simultaneous integrative and disintegrative changes that are global in scope and are occurring at an unprecedented pace of change. The most significant disintegrative global trends include the rise of cultural extremism in Islamic, Judaic, and Christian cultures; increased economic inequality between and within developed and developing sectors of the world society; and the diffusion of high-technology and weaponry. These trends often spark violent responses that trigger or aggravate international conflicts.

Unfolding Worldwide Turmoil Could Reverse Years of Prosperity

DAVID CHO AND BINYAMIN APPELBAUM

What went wrong?

Last week, the nation's political leaders said the financial system would collapse unless they passed a $700 billion rescue package for Wall Street. On Monday, the first day of trading after the plan passed, the financial system continued to melt down anyway.

Here's why: The plan developed by Treasury Secretary Henry M. Paulson Jr. to buy troubled U.S. mortgage assets might not start for another month. And, despite its huge price tag, it already seems paltry compared with the scale of the rapidly evolving global crisis.

"People are realizing that the Paulson plan is not going to be nearly enough. It's not because the plan is ill-conceived. It looks like it's the right thing to do, but the problem is just growing astronomically," said Martin Evans, a professor of finance and economics at Georgetown University.

The bailout plan is focused on buttressing U.S. financial institutions. But it was global markets that plunged yesterday, as investors sold off commodities in Brazil, currency in Mexico, bank stocks in Russia and the short-term debt of the state of California.

Robert B. Zoellick, president of the World Bank, said the global financial system may have reached a "tipping point"— the moment when a crisis cascades into a full-blown meltdown and becomes extremely difficult for governments to contain.

The mushrooming problems "will trigger business failures and possibly banking emergencies. Some countries will slip toward balance-of-payment crises," he said yesterday, speaking at the Peterson Institute for International Economics.

The crisis threatens to reverse years of prosperity that financed the economic growth in developed and emerging countries through a global financial system that made credit widely available. Banks and governments were able to borrow money on an unprecedented scale by selling debt in new kinds of packages, allowing even the least creditworthy consumers to borrow and spend.

China exported goods and then loaned the money back to the United States by buying those new debt packages. The story was similar for Russia, which exported massive amounts of energy to Europe, and for Brazil, which exported commodities including orange juice and sugar. All used the massive inflows of borrowed money from the developed world to fuel economic expansions and stock market bubbles.

Yesterday, trading on the major stock exchanges in Russia and Brazil was halted after prices crashed. China's major indexes fell about 5 percent. The bubbles appear to be bursting in rapid succession.

Faced with these developments, the markets have not been in a mood to cheer the passage of the Paulson rescue package. At one point yesterday, the Dow Jones industrial average had fallen nearly 800 points, more than 7 percent. It ended the day off 3.6 percent, below 10,000 for the first time since 2004.

"Quite frankly, what the market is looking for is some kind of coordinated action from central banks around the world," said Kathy Lien, director of currency research at GFT Forex. The Paulson plan, she added, is like a "Band-Aid for a problem that stretches way beyond the banking system now."

Treasury officials say that ramping up the rescue package will take time, and that they are working as fast as possible.

Yesterday, the department released the contracting rules for the asset managers they expect to hire to oversee its rescue program, requiring interested parties to apply by tomorrow. The Treasury also named Neel Kashkari as the interim assistant secretary of the Treasury for financial stability to oversee the rescue program until January, when the next administration takes office.

Despite the mammoth bailout, Zoellick and other leaders are now urging central banks from the leading economies to devise a coordinated response.

They don't have a lot of time.

It's been nearly three weeks since Federal Reserve Chairman Ben S. Bernanke warned lawmakers that the nation was at risk of a full-blown meltdown.

Since then, the same problems have afflicted Europe. Governments have bailed out five large financial firms, including two this weekend, triggering fears of additional bank collapses in Europe.

Hypo Real Estate, a German real estate lender, is collapsing under the weight of its own bad loans, forcing the German government and leading banks to announce Sunday that they would lend the company up to $68 billion.

The rescue follows the nationalization of one of England's largest real estate lenders, Bradford & Bingley. Iceland also rescued one of its largest banks, Glitnir. And several European countries were forced to invest billions of dollars in Fortis, one of the largest banks on the Continent, in an ultimately unsuccessful effort to stave off its collapse. Fortis, too, has now been nationalized.

With confidence in banks basically shattered, governments increasingly have been forced to issue explicit guarantees that bank deposits will remain safe.

Ireland last week guaranteed all deposits and liabilities, totaling about $540 billion, at six domestic banks. The pledge included branches of the six banks outside of Ireland, and excluded branches of other banks in Ireland, raising concerns that deposits would now flow from rivals into the coffers of the six government-protected banks as investors flee to safety.

Germany promised Sunday to guarantee all private savings accounts, which hold at least $800 billion. Denmark yesterday announced that it would guarantee all deposits, as well.

The economies of Ireland and Denmark have officially fallen into recession. Investors meanwhile are worried that Pakistan and Argentina might default on their debts. In India, the average interest on loans between banks jumped above 11 percent, reflecting a breakdown of trust.

The bailout has not even thawed critical segments of the U.S. credit markets.

U.S. corporations sold $1.25 billion in bonds last week, marking the sharpest drop in sales volume since 1999, according to Bloomberg. Short-term commercial borrowing fell to $1.6 trillion, down 9 percent in the past two weeks, almost entirely because of a massive decline in borrowing by financial companies that cannot find lenders at any price.

September saw the worst monthly losses in the history of the hedge-fund industry. Investor withdrawals could lead to the collapse of major funds, triggering further sell-offs and exacerbating the financial crisis.

Investors are also increasingly concerned that more U.S. banks will fail before the Treasury can launch the rescue program. Shares of National City, a regional bank based in Cleveland, fell 27 percent yesterday.

Bank of America said its third-quarter profit fell 68 percent, largely because of losses on mortgage loans and credit cards. The company reduced the dividend on its widely held shares by half and said it would try to raise another $10 billion from investors. Its shares were down about 7 percent, to $32.22.

"These are the most difficult times for financial institutions that I have experienced in my 39 years in banking," chief executive Kenneth D. Lewis said in a conference call.

The $1.4 Trillion Question

The Chinese are subsidizing the American way of life. Are we playing them for suckers—or are they playing us?

JAMES FALLOWS

Stephen Schwarzman may think he has image problems in America. He is the co-founder and CEO of the Blackstone Group, and he threw himself a $3 million party for his 60th birthday last spring, shortly before making many hundreds of millions of dollars in his company's IPO and finding clever ways to avoid paying taxes. That's nothing compared with the way he looks in China. Here, he and his company are surprisingly well known, thanks to blogs, newspapers, and talk-show references. In America, Schwarzman's perceived offense is greed—a sin we readily forgive and forget. In China, the suspicion is that he has somehow hoodwinked ordinary Chinese people out of their hard-earned cash.

Last June, China's Blackstone investment was hailed in the American press as a sign of canny sophistication. It seemed just the kind of thing the U.S. government had in mind when it hammered China to use its new wealth as a "responsible stakeholder" among nations. By putting $3 billion of China's national savings into the initial public offering of America's best-known private-equity firm, the Chinese government allied itself with a big-time Western firm without raising political fears by trying to buy operating control (it bought only 8 percent of Blackstone's shares, and nonvoting shares at that). The contrast with the Japanese and Saudis, who in their nouveau-riche phase roused irritation and envy with their showy purchases of Western brand names and landmark properties, was plain.

Six months later, it didn't look so canny, at least not financially. China's Blackstone holdings lost, on paper, about $1 billion, during a time when the composite index of the Shanghai Stock Exchange was soaring. At two different universities where I've spoken recently, students have pointed out that Schwarzman was a major Republican donor. A student at Fudan University knew a detail I didn't: that in 2007 President Bush attended a Republican National Committee fund-raiser at Schwarzman's apartment in Manhattan (think what he would have made of the fact that Schwarzman, who was one year behind Bush at Yale, had been a fellow member of Skull and Bones). Wasn't the whole scheme a way to take money from the Chinese people and give it to the president's crony?

The Blackstone case is titillating in its personal detail, but it is also an unusually clear and personalized symptom of a deeper, less publicized, and potentially much more destructive tension in U.S.–China relations. It's not just Stephen Schwarzman's company that the *laobaixing*, the ordinary Chinese masses, have been subsidizing. It's everyone in the United States.

Through the quarter-century in which China has been opening to world trade, Chinese leaders have deliberately held down living standards for their own people and propped them up in the United States. This is the real meaning of the vast trade surplus—$1.4 trillion and counting, going up by about $1 billion per day—that the Chinese government has mostly parked in U.S. Treasury notes. In effect, every person in the (rich) United States has over the past 10 years or so borrowed about $4,000 from someone in the (poor) People's Republic of China. Like so many imbalances in economics, this one can't go on indefinitely, and therefore won't. But the way it ends—suddenly versus gradually, for predictable reasons versus during a panic—will make an enormous difference to the U.S. and Chinese economies over the next few years, to say nothing of bystanders in Europe and elsewhere.

Any economist will say that Americans have been living better than they should—which is by definition the case when a nation's total consumption is greater than its total production, as America's now is. Economists will also point out that, despite the glitter of China's big cities and the rise of its billionaire class, China's people have been living far worse than they could. That's what it means when a nation consumes only half of what it produces, as China does.

Neither government likes to draw attention to this arrangement, because it has been so convenient on both sides. For China, it has helped the regime guide development in the way it would like—and keep the domestic economy's growth rate from crossing the thin line that separates "unbelievably fast" from "uncontrollably inflationary." For America, it has meant cheaper iPods, lower interest rates, reduced mortgage payments, a lighter tax burden. But because of political tensions in both countries, and because of the huge and growing size of the imbalance, the arrangement now shows signs of cracking apart.

In an article two and a half years ago ("Countdown to a Meltdown," July/August 2005), I described an imagined future in which a real-estate crash and shakiness in the U.S. credit markets led to panic by Chinese and other foreign investors, with unpleasant effects for years to come. The real world has recently had inklings of similar concerns. In the past six months, relative nobodies in China's establishment were able to cause brief panics in the foreign-exchange markets merely by hinting that China might stop supplying so much money to the United States. In August, an economic researcher named He Fan, who works at the Chinese Academy of Social Sciences and did part of his doctoral research at Harvard, suggested in an op-ed piece in *China Daily* that if the U.S. dollar kept collapsing in value, China might move some of its holdings into stronger currencies. This was presented not as a threat but as a statement of the obvious, like saying that during a market panic, lots of people sell. The column quickly provoked alarmist stories in Europe and America suggesting that China was considering the "nuclear option"—unloading its dollars.

A few months later, a veteran Communist Party politician named Cheng Siwei suggested essentially the same thing He Fan had. Cheng, in his mid-70s, was trained as a chemical engineer and has no official role in setting Chinese economic policy. But within hours of his speech, a flurry of trading forced the dollar to what was then its lowest level against the euro and other currencies. The headline in the *South China Morning Post* the next day was: "Officials' Words Shrivel U.S. Dollar." Expressing amazement at the markets' response, Carl Weinberg, chief economist at the High Frequency Economics advisory group, said, "This would be kind of like Congressman Charlie Rangel giving a speech telling the Fed to hike or cut interest rates." (Cheng, like Rangel, is known for colorful comments—but he is less powerful, since Rangel after all chairs the House Ways and Means Committee.) In the following weeks, phrases like "run on the dollar" and "collapse of confidence" showed up more and more frequently in financial newsletters. The nervousness only increased when someone who does have influence, Chinese Premier Wen Jiabao, said last November, "We are worried about how to preserve the value" of China's dollar holdings.

When the dollar is strong, the following (good) things happen: the price of food, fuel, imports, manufactured goods, and just about everything else (vacations in Europe!) goes down. The value of the stock market, real estate, and just about all other American assets goes up. Interest rates go down—for mortgage loans, credit-card debt, and commercial borrowing. Tax rates can be lower, since foreign lenders hold down the cost of financing the national debt. The only problem is that American-made goods become more expensive for foreigners, so the country's exports are hurt.

When the dollar is weak, the following (bad) things happen: the price of food, fuel, imports, and so on (no more vacations in Europe) goes up. The value of the stock market, real estate, and just about all other American assets goes down. Interest rates are higher. Tax rates can be higher, to cover the increased cost of financing the national debt. The only benefit is that American-made goods become cheaper for foreigners, which helps create new jobs and can raise the value of export-oriented American firms (winemakers in California, producers of medical devices in New England).

The dollar's value has been high for many years—unnaturally high, in large part because of the implicit bargain with the Chinese. Living standards in China, while rising rapidly, have by the same logic been unnaturally low. To understand why this situation probably can't go on, and what might replace it—via a dollar crash or some other event—let's consider how this curious balance of power arose and how it works.

Why a Poor Country Has So Much Money

By 1996, China amassed its first $100 billion in foreign assets, mainly held in U.S. dollars. (China considers these holdings a state secret, so all numbers come from analyses by outside experts.) By

2001, that sum doubled to about $200 billion, according to Edwin Truman of the Peterson Institute for International Economics in Washington. Since then, it has increased more than sixfold, by well over a trillion dollars, and China's foreign reserves are now the largest in the world. (In second place is Japan, whose economy is, at official exchange rates, nearly twice as large as China's but which has only two-thirds the foreign assets; the next-largest after that are the United Arab Emirates and Russia.) China's U.S. dollar assets probably account for about 70 percent of its foreign holdings, according to the latest analyses by Brad Setser, a former Treasury Department economist now with the Council on Foreign Relations; the rest are mainly in euros, plus some yen. Most of China's U.S. investments are in conservative, low-yield instruments like Treasury notes and federal-agency bonds, rather than showier Blackstone-style bets. Because notes and bonds backed by the U.S. government are considered the safest investments in the world, they pay lower interest than corporate bonds, and for the past two years their annual interest payments of 4 to 5 percent have barely matched the 5-to-6-percent decline in the U.S. dollar's value versus the RMB.

Americans sometimes debate (though not often) whether in principle it is good to rely so heavily on money controlled by a foreign government. The debate has never been more relevant, because America has never before been so deeply in debt to one country. Meanwhile, the Chinese are having a debate of their own—about whether the deal makes sense for them. Certainly China's officials are aware that their stock purchases prop up 401(k) values, their money-market holdings keep down American interest rates, and their bond purchases do the same thing—plus allow our government to spend money without raising taxes.

"From a distance, this, to say the least, is strange," Lawrence Summers, the former treasury secretary and president of Harvard, told me last year in Shanghai. He was referring to the oddity that a country with so many of its own needs still unmet would let "this $1 trillion go to a mature, old, rich place from a young, dynamic place."

> 'From a distance, this, to say the least, is strange,' said Lawrence Summers—that a country with so many of its own needs still unmet would let 'this $1 trillion go to a mature, old, rich place.'

It's more than strange. Some Chinese people are rich, but China as a whole is unbelievably short on many of the things that qualify countries as fully developed. Shanghai has about the same climate as Washington, D.C.—and its public schools have no heating. (Go to a classroom when it's cold, and you'll see 40 children, all in their winter jackets, their breath forming clouds in the air.) Beijing is more like Boston. On winter nights, thousands of people mass along the curbsides of major thoroughfares, enduring long waits and fighting their way onto hopelessly overcrowded public buses that then spend hours stuck on jammed roads. And these are the showcase cities! In rural Gansu province, I have seen schools where 18 junior-high-school girls share a single dormitory room, sleeping shoulder to shoulder, sardine-style.

Better schools, more-abundant parks, better health care, cleaner air and water, better sewers in the cities—you name it, and if it isn't in some way connected to the factory-export economy, China hasn't got it, or not enough. This is true at the personal level, too. The average cash income for workers in a big factory is about $160 per month. On the farm, it's a small fraction of that. Most people in China feel they are moving up, but from a very low starting point.

So why is China shipping its money to America? An economist would describe the oddity by saying that China has by far the highest national savings in the world. This sounds admirable, but when taken to an extreme—as in China—it indicates an economy out of sync with the rest of the world, and one that is deliberately keeping its own people's living standards lower than they could be. For comparison, India's savings rate is about 25 percent, which in effect means that India's people consume 75 percent of what they collectively produce. (Reminder from Ec 101: The savings rate is the net share of national output either exported or saved and invested for consumption in the future. Effectively, it's what your own people produce but don't use.) For Korea and Japan, the savings rate is typically from the high 20s to the mid-30s. Recently, America's has at times been below zero, which means that it consumes, via imports, more than it makes.

China's savings rate is a staggering 50 percent, which is probably unprecedented in any country in peacetime. This doesn't mean that the average family is saving half of its earnings—though the personal savings rate in China is also very high. Much of China's national income is "saved" almost invisibly and kept in the form of foreign assets. Until now, most Chinese have willingly put up with this, because the economy has been growing so fast that even a suppressed level of consumption makes most people richer year by year.

But saying that China has a high savings rate describes the situation without explaining it. Why should the Communist Party of China countenance a policy that takes so much wealth from the world's poor, in their own country, and gives it to the United States? To add to the mystery, why should China be content to put so many of its holdings into dollars, knowing that the dollar is virtually guaranteed to keep losing value against the RMB? And how long can its people tolerate being denied so much of their earnings, when they and their country need so much? The Chinese government did not explicitly set out to tighten the belt on its population while offering cheap money to American homeowners. But the fact that it does results directly from explicit choices it *has* made—two in particular. Both arise from crucial controls the government maintains over an economy that in many other ways has become wide open. The situation may be easiest to explain by following a U.S. dollar on its journey from a customer's hand in America to a factory in China and back again to the T-note auction in the United States.

The Voyage of a Dollar

Let's say you buy an Oral-B electric toothbrush for $30 at a CVS in the United States. I choose this example because I've seen a factory in China that probably made the toothbrush. Most of that $30 stays in America, with CVS, the distributors, and Oral-B itself. Eventually $3 or so—an average percentage for small consumer goods—makes its way back to southern China.

When the factory originally placed its bid for Oral-B's business, it stated the price in dollars: X million toothbrushes for Y dollars each. But the Chinese manufacturer can't use the dollars

directly. It needs RMB—to pay the workers their 1,200-RMB ($160) monthly salary, to buy supplies from other factories in China, to pay its taxes. So it takes the dollars to the local commercial bank—let's say the Shenzhen Development Bank. After showing receipts or waybills to prove that it earned the dollars in genuine trade, not as speculative inflow, the factory trades them for RMB.

This is where the first controls kick in. In other major countries, the counterparts to the Shenzhen Development Bank can decide for themselves what to do with the dollars they take in. Trade them for euros or yen on the foreign-exchange market? Invest them directly in America? Issue dollar loans? Whatever they think will bring the highest return. But under China's "surrender requirements," Chinese banks can't do those things. They must treat the dollars, in effect, as contraband, and turn most or all of them (instructions vary from time to time) over to China's equivalent of the Federal Reserve Bank, the People's Bank of China, for RMB at whatever is the official rate of exchange.

With thousands of transactions per day, the dollars pile up like crazy at the PBOC. More precisely, by more than a billion dollars per day. They pile up even faster than the trade surplus with America would indicate, because customers in many other countries settle their accounts in dollars, too.

The PBOC must do something with that money, and current Chinese doctrine allows it only one option: to give the dollars to another arm of the central government, the State Administration for Foreign Exchange. It is then SAFE's job to figure out where to park the dollars for the best return: so much in U.S. stocks, so much shifted to euros, and the great majority left in the boring safety of U.S. Treasury notes.

And thus our dollar comes back home. Spent at CVS, passed to Oral-B, paid to the factory in southern China, traded for RMB at the Shenzhen bank, "surrendered" to the PBOC, passed to SAFE for investment, and then bid at auction for Treasury notes, it is ready to be reinjected into the U.S. money supply and spent again—ideally on Chinese-made goods.

Spent at CVS, passed to Oral-B, paid to the factory, "surrendered" to the People's Bank of China, then bid at auction for Treasury notes, our dollar is reinjected into the U.S. money supply and spent again.

At no point did an ordinary Chinese person decide to send so much money to America. In fact, at no point was most of this money at his or her disposal at all. These are in effect enforced savings, which are the result of the two huge and fundamental choices made by the central government.

One is to dictate the RMB's value relative to other currencies, rather than allow it to be set by forces of supply and demand, as are the values of the dollar, euro, pound, etc. The obvious reason for doing this is to keep Chinese-made products cheap, so Chinese factories will stay busy. This is what Americans have in mind when they complain that the Chinese government is rigging the world currency markets. And there are numerous less obvious reasons. The very act of managing a currency's value may be a more important distorting factor than the exact rate at which it is set. As for the rate—the subject of much U.S. lecturing—given the huge difference in living standards between China and the United States, even a big rise in the RMB's value would leave China with a price advantage over manufacturers elsewhere. (If the RMB doubled against the dollar, a factory worker might go from earning $160 per month to $320—not enough to send many jobs back to America, though enough to hurt China's export economy.) Once a government decides to thwart the market-driven exchange rate of its currency, it must control countless other aspects of its financial system, through instruments like surrender requirements and the equally ominous-sounding "sterilization bonds" (a way of keeping foreign-currency swaps from creating inflation, as they otherwise could).

These and similar tools are the way China's government imposes an unbelievably high savings rate on its people. The result, while very complicated, is to keep the buying power earned through China's exports out of the hands of Chinese consumers as a whole. Individual Chinese people have certainly gotten their hands on a lot of buying power, notably the billionaire entrepreneurs who have attracted the world's attention (see "Mr. Zhang Builds His Dream Town," March 2007). But when it comes to amassing international reserves, what matters is that China as a whole spends so little of what it earns, even as some Chinese people spend a lot.

The other major decision is not to use more money to address China's needs directly—by building schools and agricultural research labs, cleaning up toxic waste, what have you. Both decisions stem from the central government's vision of what is necessary to keep China on its unprecedented path of growth. The government doesn't want to let the market set the value of the RMB, because it thinks that would disrupt the constant growth and the course it has carefully and expensively set for the factory-export economy. In the short run, it worries that the RMB's value against the dollar and the euro would soar, pricing some factories in "expensive" places such as Shanghai out of business. In the long run, it views an unstable currency as a nuisance in itself, since currency fluctuation makes everything about business with the outside world more complicated. Companies have a harder time predicting overseas revenues, negotiating contracts, luring foreign investors, or predicting the costs of fuel, component parts, and other imported goods.

And the government doesn't want to increase domestic spending dramatically, because it fears that improving average living conditions could paradoxically intensify the rich-poor tensions that are China's major social problem. The country is already covered with bulldozers, wrecking balls, and construction cranes, all to keep the manufacturing machine steaming ahead. Trying to build anything more at the moment—sewage-treatment plants, for a start, which would mean a better life for its own people, or smokestack scrubbers and related "clean" technology, which would start to address the world pollution for which China is increasingly held responsible—would likely just drive prices up, intensifying inflation and thus reducing the already minimal purchasing power of most workers. Food prices have been rising so fast that they have led to riots. In November, a large Carrefour grocery in Chongqing offered a limited-time sale of vegetable oil, at 20 percent (11 RMB, or $1.48) off the normal price per bottle. Three people were killed and 31 injured in a stampede toward the shelves.

This is the bargain China has made—rather, the one its leaders have imposed on its people. They'll keep creating new factory jobs, and thus reduce China's own social tensions and create opportunities for its rural poor. The Chinese will live better year

by year, though not as well as they could. And they'll be protected from the risk of potentially catastrophic hyperinflation, which might undo what the nation's decades of growth have built. In exchange, the government will hold much of the nation's wealth in paper assets in the United States, thereby preventing a run on the dollar, shoring up relations between China and America, and sluicing enough cash back into Americans' hands to let the spending go on.

What the Chinese Hope Will Happen

The Chinese public is beginning to be aware that its government is sitting on a lot of money—money not being spent to help China directly, money not doing so well in Blackstone-style foreign investments, money invested in the ever-falling U.S. dollar. Chinese bloggers and press commentators have begun making a connection between the billions of dollars the country is sending away and the domestic needs the country has not addressed. There is more and more pressure to show that the return on foreign investments is worth China's sacrifice—and more and more potential backlash against bets that don't pay off. (While the Chinese government need not stand for popular election, it generally tries to reduce sources of popular discontent when it can.) The public is beginning to behave like the demanding client of an investment adviser: it wants better returns, with fewer risks.

This is the challenge facing Lou Jiwei and Gao Xiqing, who will play a larger role in the U.S. economy than Americans are accustomed to from foreigners. Lou, a longtime Communist Party official in his late 50s, is the chairman of the new China Investment Corporation, which is supposed to find creative ways to increase returns on at least $200 billion of China's foreign assets. He is influential within the party but has little international experience. Thus the financial world's attention has turned to Gao Xiqing, who is the CIC's general manager.

Twenty years ago, after graduating from Duke Law School, Gao was the first Chinese citizen to pass the New York State Bar Exam. He returned to China in 1988, after several years as an associate at the New York law firm Mudge, Rose (Richard Nixon's old firm) to teach securities law and help develop China's newly established stock markets. By local standards, he is hip. At an economics conference in Beijing in December, other Chinese speakers wore boxy dark suits. Gao, looking fit in his mid-50s, wore a tweed jacket and black turtleneck, an Ironman-style multifunction sports watch on his wrist.

Under Lou and Gao, the CIC started with a bang with Blackstone—the wrong kind of bang. Now, many people suggest, it may be chastened enough to take a more careful approach. Indeed, that was the message it sent late last year, with news that its next round of investments would be in China's own banks, to shore up some with credit problems. And it looks to be studying aggressive but careful ways to manage huge sums. About the time the CIC was making the Blackstone deal, its leadership and staff undertook a crash course in modern financial markets. They hired the international consulting firm McKinsey to prepare confidential reports about the way they should organize themselves and the investment principles they should apply. They hired Booz Allen Hamilton to prepare similar reports, so they could compare the two. Yet another consulting firm, Towers Perrin, provided advice, especially about staffing and pay. The CIC leaders commissioned studies of other large state-run investment funds—in Norway, Singapore, the Gulf States, Alaska—to see which approaches worked and which didn't. They were fascinated by the way America's richest universities managed their endowments, and ordered multiple copies of *Pioneering Portfolio Management,* by David Swensen, who as Yale's chief investment officer has guided its endowment to sustained and rapid growth. Last summer, teams from the CIC made long study visits to Yale and Duke universities, among others.

Gao Xiqing and other CIC officials have avoided discussing their plans publicly. "If you tell people ahead of time what you're going to do—well, you just can't operate that way in a market system," he said at his Beijing appearance. "What I can say is, we'll play by the international rules, and we'll be responsible investors." Gao emphasized several times how much the CIC had to learn: "We're the new kids on the block. Because of media attention, there is huge pressure on us—we're already under water now." The words "under water" were in natural-sounding English, and clearly referred to Blackstone.

Others familiar with the CIC say that its officials are coming to appreciate the unusual problems they will face. For instance: any investment group needs to be responsible to outside supervisors, and the trick for the CIC will be to make itself accountable to Communist Party leadership without becoming a mere conduit for favored investment choices by party bosses. How can it attract the best talent? Does it want to staff up quickly, to match its quickly mounting assets, by bidding for financial managers on the world market—where many of the candidates are high-priced, not fluent in Chinese, and reluctant to move to Beijing? Or can it afford to take the time to home-grow its own staff?

While the CIC is figuring out its own future, outsiders are trying to figure out the CIC—and also SAFE, which will continue handling many of China's assets. As far as anyone can tell, the starting point for both is risk avoidance. No more Blackstones. No more CNOOC-Unocals. (In 2005, the Chinese state oil firm CNOOC attempted to buy U.S.–based Unocal. It withdrew the offer in the face of intense political opposition to the deal in America.) One person involved with the CIC said that its officials had seen recent Lou Dobbs broadcasts criticizing "Communist China" and were "shellshocked" about the political resentment their investments might encounter in the United States. For all these reasons the Chinese leadership, as another person put it, "has a strong preference to follow someone else's lead, not in an imitative way" but as an unobtrusive minority partner wherever possible. It will follow the lead of others for now, that is, while the CIC takes its first steps as a gigantic international financial investor.

The latest analyses by Brad Setser suggest that despite all the talk about abandoning the dollar, China is still putting about as large a share of its money into dollars as ever, somewhere between 65 and 70 percent of its foreign earnings. "Politically, the last thing they want is to signal a loss of faith in the dollar," Andy Rothman, of the financial firm CLSA, told me; that would lead to a surge in the RMB, which would hurt Chinese exporters, not to mention the damage it would cause to China's vast existing dollar assets.

The problem is that these and other foreign observers must guess at China's aims, rather than knowing for sure. As Rothman put it, "The opaqueness about intentions and goals is always the issue." The mini-panics last year took hold precisely because no one could be sure that SAFE was not about to change course.

It is no exaggeration to say that the stability of the U.S. and Chinese economies over the next few years depends on how today's tensions are resolved.

The uncertainty arises in part from the limited track record of China's new financial leadership. As one American financier pointed out to me: "The man in charge of the whole thing"—Lou Jiwei—"has never bought a share of stock, never bought a car, never bought a house." Another foreign financier said, after meeting some CIC staffers, "By Chinese terms, these are very sophisticated people." But, he went on to say, in a professional sense none of them had lived through the financial crises of the last generation: the U.S. market crash of 1987, the "Asian flu" of the late 1990s, the collapse of the Internet bubble soon afterward. The Chinese economy was affected by all these upheavals, but the likes of Gao Xiqing were not fully exposed to their lessons, sheltered as they were within Chinese institutions.

Foreign observers also suggest that, even after exposure to the Lou Dobbs clips, the Chinese financial leadership may not yet fully grasp how suspicious other countries are likely to be of China's financial intentions, for reasons both fair and unfair. The unfair reason is all-purpose nervousness about any new rising power. "They need to understand, and they don't, that everything they do will be seen as political," a financier with extensive experience in both China and America told me. "Whatever they buy, whatever they say, whatever they do will be seen as China Inc."

The fair reason for concern is, again, the transparency problem. Twice in the past year, China has in nonfinancial ways demonstrated the ripples that a nontransparent policy creates. Last January, its military intentionally shot down one of its own satellites, filling orbital paths with debris. The exercise greatly alarmed the U.S. military, because of what seemed to be an implied threat to America's crucial space sensors. For several days, the Chinese government said nothing at all about the test, and nearly a year later, foreign analysts still debate whether it was a deliberate provocation, the result of a misunderstanding, or a freelance effort by the military. In November, China denied a U.S. Navy aircraft carrier, the *Kitty Hawk,* routine permission to dock in Hong Kong for Thanksgiving, even though many Navy families had gone there for a reunion. In each case, the most ominous aspect is that outsiders could not really be sure what the Chinese leadership had in mind. Were these deliberate taunts or shows of strength? The results of factional feuding within the leadership? Simple miscalculations? In the absence of clear official explanations no one really knew, and many assumed the worst.

So it could be with finance, unless China becomes as transparent as it is rich. Chinese officials say they will move in that direction, but they're in no hurry. Last fall, Edwin Truman prepared a good-governance scorecard for dozens of "sovereign wealth" funds—government-run investment funds like SAFE and the CIC. He compared funds from Singapore, Korea, Norway, and elsewhere, ranking them on governing structure, openness, and similar qualities. China's funds ended up in the lower third of his list—better-run than Iran's, Sudan's, or Algeria's, but worse than Mexico's, Russia's, or Kuwait's. China received no points in the "governance" category and half a point out of a possible 12 for "transparency and accountability."

Foreigners (ordinary Chinese too, for that matter) can't be sure about the mixture of political and strictly economic motives behind future investment decisions the Chinese might make. When China's president, Hu Jintao, visited Seattle two years ago, he announced a large purchase of Boeing aircraft. When France's new president, Nicolas Sarkozy, visited China late last year, Hu announced an even larger purchase of Airbuses. Every Chinese order for an airplane is a political as well as commercial decision. Brad Setser says that the Chinese government probably believed that it would get "credit" for the Blackstone purchase in whatever negotiations came up next with the United States, in the same way it would get credit for choosing Boeing. This is another twist to the Kremlinology of trying to discern China's investment strategy.

Where the money goes, other kinds of power follow. Just ask Mikhail Gorbachev, as he reflects on the role bankruptcy played in bringing down the Soviet empire. While Japan's great wealth has not yet made it a major diplomatic actor, and China has so far shied from, rather than seized, opportunities to influence events outside its immediate realm, time and money could change that. China's military is too weak to challenge the U.S. directly even in the Taiwan Straits, let alone anyplace else. That, too, could change.

A Balance of Terror

Let's take these fears about a rich, strong China to their logical extreme. The U.S. and Chinese governments are always disagreeing—about trade, foreign policy, the environment. Someday the disagreement could be severe. Taiwan, Tibet, North Korea, Iran—the possibilities are many, though Taiwan always heads the list. Perhaps a crackdown within China. Perhaps another accident, like the U.S. bombing of China's embassy in Belgrade nine years ago, which everyone in China still believes was intentional and which no prudent American ever mentions here.

Whatever the provocation, China would consider its levers and weapons and find one stronger than all the rest—one no other country in the world can wield. Without China's billion dollars a day, the United States could not keep its economy stable or spare the dollar from collapse.

Would the Chinese use that weapon? The reasonable answer is no, because they would wound themselves grievously, too. Their years of national savings are held in the same dollars that would be ruined; in a panic, they'd get only a small share out before the value fell. Besides, their factories depend on customers with dollars to spend.

But that "reassuring" answer is actually frightening. Lawrence Summers calls today's arrangement "the balance of financial terror," and says that it is flawed in the same way that the "mutually assured destruction" of the Cold War era was. That doctrine held that neither the United States nor the Soviet Union would dare use its nuclear weapons against the other, since it would be destroyed in return. With allowances for hyperbole, something similar applies to the dollar standoff. China can't afford to stop feeding dollars to Americans, because China's own dollar holdings would be devastated if it did. As long as that logic holds, the system works. As soon as it doesn't, we have a big problem.

What might poke a giant hole in that logic? Not necessarily a titanic struggle over the future of Taiwan. A simple mistake, for one thing. Another speech by Cheng Siwei—perhaps in response to a provocation by Lou Dobbs. A rumor that the oil economies are moving out of dollars for good, setting their prices in euros. Leaked suggestions that the Chinese government is hoping to buy Intel, leading to angry denunciations on the Capitol floor, leading to news that the Chinese will sit out the next Treasury auction. As many world tragedies have been caused by miscalculation as by malice.

Or pent-up political tensions, on all sides. China's lopsided growth—ahead in exports, behind in schooling, the environment, and everything else—makes the country socially less stable as it grows richer. Meanwhile, its expansion disrupts industries and provokes tensions in the rest of the world. The billions of dollars China pumps into the United States each week strangely seem to make it harder rather than easier for Americans to face their own structural problems. One day, something snaps. Suppose the CIC makes another bad bet—not another Blackstone but another World-Com, with billions of dollars of Chinese people's assets irretrievably wiped out. They will need someone to blame, and Americans, for their part, are already primed to blame China back.

So, the shock comes. Does it inevitably cause a cataclysm? No one can know until it's too late. The important question to ask about the U.S.–China relationship, the economist Eswar Prasad, of Cornell, recently wrote in a paper about financial imbalances, is whether it has "enough flexibility to withstand and recover from large shocks, either internal or external." He suggested that the contained tensions were so great that the answer could be no.

Today's American system values upheaval; it's been a while since we've seen too much of it. But Americans who lived through the Depression knew the pain real disruption can bring. Today's Chinese, looking back on their country's last century, know, too. With a lack of tragic imagination, Americans have drifted into an arrangement that is comfortable while it lasts, and could last for a while more. But not much longer.

Years ago, the Chinese might have averted today's pressures by choosing a slower and more balanced approach to growth. If they had it to do over again, I suspect they would in fact choose just the same path—they have gained so much, including the assets they can use to do what they have left undone, whenever the government chooses to spend them. The same is not true, I suspect, for the United States, which might have chosen a very different path: less reliance on China's subsidies, more reliance on paying as we go. But it's a little late for those thoughts now. What's left is to prepare for what we find at the end of the path we have taken.

JAMES FALLOWS is an *Atlantic* national correspondent, his blog is at jamesfallowstheatlantic.com.

How Economics Can Defeat Corruption

What's the dirtiest secret about corruption? Just how little we know about it. Treasuries are plundered and kickbacks are paid, but the nature and scale of the world's shady transactions remain a mystery. Luckily, a little economic detective work is all that's needed to expose the smuggling, cheating, and bribing that is hiding in plain sight.

RAYMOND FISMAN AND EDWARD MIGUEL

It was the odd uniformity of the suitcase's contents that tipped off the baggage inspector: six thick, identical rectangles. They could have been books, but then again, they could have been six bundles of cocaine. And in August 2007, security was tight at the airport in Buenos Aires; the country was in the midst of a presidential election. It was worth taking a closer look. The suitcase's owner, a Venezuelan businessman just in from Caracas, hesitated briefly when asked to open his suspicious luggage. Out tumbled $800,000 in cash. It was, according to U.S. investigators, an illegal campaign contribution from Venezuelan President Hugo Chávez intended for Cristina Fernández de Kirchner, wife of Argentina's former president and a candidate for the presidency herself. What better to grease the countries' friendship, investigators alleged, than a suitcase full of cash?

Such tales of bribery and corruption are as old as politics. Try as we might to rid officialdom of crooks, however, extorting senators, vote-buying presidents, and judges for sale remain all too common. Whether it's the $90,000 in cold cash that turned up a few years ago in a U.S. congressman's freezer, the "Versailles in the jungle" built with the billions embezzled by Zaire's Mobutu Sese Seko, or the bank balances of oil autocrats in Central Asia, venality and excess remain the scourge of modern global politics.

But corruption is not simply a moral concern, warranting a collective finger wagging at political leaders. It's blamed—perhaps rightly—for many of the world's ills. Corruption is widely accused of being an endemic barrier to economic development, responsible for Africa's lasting poverty and Latin America's perennial stagnation. It is, says the conventional wisdom, what makes poor countries poor. It undermines the rule of law, distorts trade, and confers economic advantages on a privileged few. It prevents aid money from reaching disaster victims, topples buildings thanks to shoddy construction, and strangles business with the constant burden of bribes and payoffs.

Yet the truth is that we have very little idea about how corruption works or how pervasive it is. We have anecdotes about rotten individuals—a Ferdinand Marcos, a Robert Mugabe, or a Charles Taylor—but the thievery of a few thuggish rulers tells us almost nothing about the breadth and depth of global corruption. After all, when bribery and embezzlement is done right, it's invisible. Economists haven't even resolved if and when corruption is really a problem: East Asian economies have boomed in recent decades under reputedly corrupt regimes.

What little systematic evidence we do have about corruption comes from surveys administered by groups such as the World Bank and Transparency International. But we economists are skeptical of what people say about corruption (and most everything else, for that matter). It's called "cheap talk" for a reason. And we're especially suspicious of what people say when surveyed on sensitive topics such as bribery and embezzlement. There are obvious reasons to believe that responses to the question, "How much did you receive or pay last year in bribes?" are of questionable accuracy. And if we can't measure something, it's hard to know where it's really thriving, let alone figure out what to do about it.

But all is not lost. The hidden underworld of corruption often reveals itself in unexpected ways—and in situations that allow us not only to measure actual corruption but to test different methods of preventing it. All that's required, it turns out, is a little economics and a dash of ingenuity. To truly understand corruption, we must watch what people do, rather than just listen to what they say. And as we'll see, damning evidence, like cash-filled suitcases, often leaves footprints in the data for those who know where to look.

Damning evidence, like cash-filled suitcases, often leaves footprints in the data for those who know where to look.

Forensic Economics

Economics is fundamentally about how people respond to incentives. So, if we forensic economists want to unearth corruption, we must look for situations where incentives for crooked rewards somehow translate into actions that everyone can see. In other words, by looking in the right places, we can uncover evidence of corruption staring us in the face. Only then can we take up the much more difficult challenge of determining what to do about it.

The Price of Political Connections

Whether through hefty campaign contributions or cushy jobs for former politicians, corporations are constantly accused of trying to profit through political ties. (Just think Halliburton or Russia's Gazprom.) But what's the real value of these companies' connections? If you ask politicians or investors, you're likely to hear a lot of denials. To get the truth, we could ask insiders to put some money where their mouths are, making them bet some of their own cash on whether particular companies are making back-alley deals with politicians to increase their profits. In this political betting pool, raw financial self-interest would lead bettors in the know to reveal their true beliefs about corruption.

This betting pool actually bears a remarkable resemblance to the stock market, where investors (including insiders) place bets on companies based on what they think they're worth. A stock price is a measure of a company's value, which can also include political ties: If connections buy tax breaks, valuable licenses, and advantages in bidding for government contracts, then strengthening political ties should boost profits. These higher profits translate directly into higher stock prices, and conversely, removing those ties should send profits—and stock prices—tumbling.

To illustrate our approach in action, let's take a trip to Indonesia and turn the clock back to 1996. Former President Suharto, who by then had ruled the country with an iron fist for nearly 30 years, would be forced to step down a few years later. However, in 1996, Suharto's government still exercised tight control over the economy: The president decided who could get loans, log for timber, build toll roads, or import rice. In other words, he decided who would make money and how much. If ever there were a time or place where we'd expect the market to place a value on connections, this would be it.

But the aging dictator was in poor health. And because none of his kids or cronies was seen as a capable successor, any leader who followed Suharto would be unlikely to honor (or enforce) the cozy business relationships established under his rule. Any threat to Suharto would translate into threat to the value of connections, and bets would be placed accordingly.

And indeed, Indonesian investors didn't disappoint. On July 4, 1996, the Indonesian government announced that Suharto was traveling to Germany for a health checkup. That may not sound like much, but who travels 10 time zones to get his pulse taken? Investors at the stock exchange were inundated with rumors that Suharto had already suffered a stroke or heart attack. The Jakarta composite index, an indicator of Indonesian stocks' overall performance, much like New York's Dow Jones Industrial Average, fell 2.3 percent on the day of the news.

What was merely bad for Indonesian stocks turned out to be devastating for well-connected companies. One such firm was Bimantara Citra, a media conglomerate run by Suharto's son, Barnbang Trihatmodjo. In the weeks leading up to the July 4th announcement, both the Jakarta exchange and the price of Bimantara Citra bounced around a bit, not gaining or losing very much value. Then, with the market awash with rumors in the first week of July, Bimantara's stock price took a nose dive. The prospect of the company without its connections had shareholders dumping their stock and running for the exits, driving its price down more than 10 percent in just a few days, obliterating about $100 million of its value.

One can just imagine what would have happened to Bimantara shares if the 75-year-old Suharto had died suddenly. In fact, our estimates, based on stock returns during a number of Suharto health scares, suggest that a complete severing of Suharto connections would have resulted in a 25 percent loss for similarly well-connected companies. How much is 25 percent of a company's value? When Apple announced its iPhone to great fanfare in 2007, its shares went up 8 percent; when Pfizer was unexpectedly forced to withdraw its bestselling antibiotic Trovan in 1999, its shares fell 10 percent. So, connections in Indonesia were worth a lot more than a blockbuster new drug or the next big technology gadget—or even both of them combined.

Of course, Suharto's government was considered one of the most corrupt dictatorships of its time, so we should not make generalizations based only on its extreme example. Luckily, researchers have since created market-based measures of political connections in many other countries. Mara Faccio, an economist at Purdue University, has measured the value of political connections for nearly every country with a well-functioning stock market. She has followed the political careers of business tycoons (and the business careers of politicians), traced bloodlines to detect family ties, and read the society columns of local newspapers to track who dines with whom. Her conclusion? Close political-corporate ties exist in nearly every country. In Russia, fully 87 percent of the Moscow stock exchange's value is in companies with close Kremlin connections. Maybe this isn't such a shock in the unruly capitalism of post-Soviet Russia. More surprisingly, nearly 40 percent of the London Stock Exchange is politically connected.

But Faccio found big differences from country to country in the actual value provided by these connections. Although business-government ties are very common in Britain, the stock prices of British companies don't budge when political ties are strengthened. For example, when Rolls-Royce Chairman John Moore was appointed to the House of Lords, there was no detectable effect on Rolls-Royce's stock price. Italy, however, is true to its stereotype; insider connections matter a great deal. When Fiat boss Giovanni Agnelli was appointed to the Italian Senate, his companies' stock prices soared 3.4 percent, adding hundreds of millions of dollars in value overnight.

Sadly, the United States appears to be more like Italy than Britain. Numerous studies have found that the economic fortunes of well-connected U.S. companies mirror the political fortunes of their connections. When U.S. Sen. Jim Jeffords defected from the Republican Party and handed Senate Democrats a slim majority in 2001, Democratically connected companies benefited in the immediate aftermath. Similarly, the stock value of companies with former Republican lawmakers on their boards increased an average of 4 percent when the Supreme Court handed the 2000 election to George W. Bush, while companies with former Democratic politicians on their boards declined.

Sniffing out Smugglers

Well-connected companies may not gain much from being honest about their political ties, but when it comes to bribes, there are a few situations where people or companies do have reason to tell the truth. Before 1999, when the Organisation for Economic Co-operation and Development endorsed a global anticorruption agreement, firms in many nations, including Germany, the Netherlands, and Switzerland, were allowed to pay bribes, just as long as the money went to officials in other countries. Not only was this international bribery permitted by law, it was tax deductible as a business expense. If we could check these corporations' tax returns, their self-reported bribe payments might just be believable. But tax returns aren't the only place that candor on corruption makes an occasional appearance. Truthful reporting of misdeeds by other corporate rogues appears elsewhere in plain sight, thanks to the ready availability of international trade data.

Consider the global trade in antiques. If traders are being honest to customs officials, the value of antiques leaving other countries and bound for the United States should be the same as the value of antiques coming into American ports of entry. But they're not—not by a long shot. A lot more antiques arrive on American shores than the world claims to be sending its way. Leaving aside the rather unlikely possibility of floating

antiques factories, it appears there must be different incentives for antiques importers and exporters to report their dealings truthfully. It turns out there are, and by studying how these different incentives translate into gaps in the trade data, we can get a better handle on the nature of global smuggling.

A short lesson in the laws governing the antiques trade is in order. Most countries ban or severely restrict the export of antique art and other cultural goods. These restrictions include big-time antiquities such as Etruscan chariots and Greek statues that can fetch millions on the market, as well as cheaper trinkets like pre-Columbian pottery shards and old coins. Such objects can only be exported with special government permission, which is rarely forthcoming. So, exporters must either suffer through the bureaucratic hassle of filing for export permits, or simply take their chances with paying off a customs agent at the border. In short, the incentives to lie often outweigh the benefit of telling the truth.

Exporters must suffer through the bureaucratic hassle of filing permits, or take their chances with bribing a customs agent.

Either way, there's no problem on the import side: You're probably free to bring your coins, pottery, statues, and chariots into the United States. The U.S. Department of Homeland Security explains in its handbook for art importers that violating a foreign country's export laws doesn't necessarily mean you're violating U.S. laws. So, while it's OK to bring illegally exported items into the United States, you do have to be honest about what you report to U.S. authorities—or else. The penalties for dishonest reporting include fines and seizure of your merchandise. So on the import side, it pays to tell the truth. The mysterious gap between antiques sent and antiques received—what we'll call the smuggling gap—can be explained by these different reporting incentives. As one might expect, the smuggling gap for antiques is widest for those countries where it's easiest to bribe your way around export restrictions—Nigeria, Russia, and Syria, to name a few. But smugglers of all kinds of products leave similar fingerprints in the data that are visible to economic detectives.

Not surprisingly, smuggling gaps aren't unique to antiques traders. We've looked closely at the prints left by Hong Kong exporters trying to avoid paying Chinese import tariffs. The principle is much the same as with antiques trading, but in reverse: The flee-trading economy of Hong Kong puts few restrictions on exports, so there is no incentive to mislead customs agents about what you are shipping out. But because of high tariffs on certain goods entering China, there is a great deal of deception on the receiving end. For instance, in the late 1990s, Chinese tariffs on perfume were set at 55 percent, and for tobacco products, 70 percent. By contrast, raw steel and aluminum ore, key commodities for China's burgeoning economic machine, came into the country tariff free. You can probably guess where there was a bigger gap: lots of Hong Kong perfume and tobacco went "missing" before it reached China, but not much iron or aluminum.

By looking at the data, we have been able to identify the preferred methods that smugglers use to evade Chinese customs. Think about a smuggler who wants to bring in, say, chickens that face a 20 percent tariff. He could lie about the chicken count in his shipping container, or shave downward the value of each chicken. But what if inspectors counted his chickens by weighing his container or had ready access to the market price for chickens? Our smuggler would be easily caught and punished. But suppose the tariff rate on turkeys is only 10 percent. Our smuggler friend could simply relabel his chickens as turkeys; all the inspector would see if he opened the container is frozen poultry. In the data, this sleight of hand will show up as lots of disappearing chickens on the Chinese side, with turkeys appearing in their place. When we analyzed three years' worth of Hong Kong-China trade data, we found that similar chicken-to-turkey switches—high-tariff wooden seats becoming lower-tariff wooden seat parts, manual drills becoming machine-controlled drills—account for most of the smuggling gap.

Crucially, knowing smugglers' evasive techniques can help policymakers figure out the most effective ways of putting them out of business. Because most of the smuggling we uncovered was of the "chickens-turned-turkeys" variety, a good start would be to equate tariffs on goods that are similar enough to be mislabeled. Of course, Hong Kong smugglers will still surely come up with another way of getting their goods to the mainland. But by plugging up the easiest channel for tariff evasion, the Chinese government—and others—can force a reaction that makes smuggling less profitable and begins to chip away at this gritty underside of economic globalization.

Paving the Road to Corruption

Just as corrupt customs officials might look the other way for a slice of the action, crooked politicians and contractors have been siphoning cash from road-building projects for as long as there have been roads. Road construction requires materials such as sand and stones and lots of manual labor, all purchased locally by contractors. The Tony Sopranos of the world have figured out that there is good money to be made by over-invoicing these contracts: Double the budget for supplies, buy some cheap concrete, and split the leftover cash with your cronies in the roads ministry.

As with all other forms of corruption, we need data before we can investigate potential solutions. Here, we turn to Ben Olken, an economist at the Massachusetts Institute of Technology, who has devised an innovative method of measuring road-building corruption. Olken wanted to figure out how much money was being stolen from a World Bank

construction program in Indonesia. Under the terms of the program, 600 villages received $9,000 each to build a local road. If Olken could determine how much was spent actually building each road, he could find out how much cash had "leaked out," most likely into the pockets of unscrupulous contractors and public officials. So, Olken sent teams of experienced engineers to all 600 villages to assess the quality of each road. The teams dug up road samples, measured pavement depth, and analyzed whether a road had been "watered down" by using cheap sand instead of expensive gravel.

As part of the study, Olken also built in metrics that tried to ensure the money was well spent. Some villages were informed ahead of time that their road project would be audited. Others were ordered to hold "town hall"-style meetings to allow villagers to discuss and monitor construction plans. (Community involvement of this kind has been held up as a cure-all in development in recent years, especially for governance woes like corruption.) There was also a third set of "control" villages, where nothing special was done at all.

In the villages with no special oversight, road funds disappeared at an average of nearly 30 percent, about $2,700. Nearly as much was stolen in the villages with town-hall meetings. In the villages where contractors were forewarned about audits, theft dropped below 20 percent—still a sizeable loss, but a third less than appeared in the other two groups. From just this single innovative study, we can gain insights into the anticorruption efforts that will likely work best in other types of development projects.

The Corruption Cure

So far, we've documented the kingly sums channeled to Suharto's buddies, uncovered the hidden tracks of antiques smugglers, and dug into the contract padding of unscrupulous road contractors. But there is a dizzying array of corrupt practices in the world and an even greater number of plausibly effective anticorruption policies beyond those we've examined. Is there any way to be more systematic in figuring out which policies will work in practice?

Economic principles, together with common sense, can be our most useful guides. We know that economic incentives matter, so a good starting point is to think about the carrots and sticks that motivate potentially corrupt officials. Can greater government financial transparency, perhaps through Web postings of highway contract announcements and more details on the winning bids, help curtail theft in Indonesian road building? Will lowering or linking tariffs on similar products dampen the incentives for bribe-paying traders? Or how about increasing the salaries of government officials to reduce the need to supplement their incomes with kickbacks?

We economists could wait around for the right kind of experiments to take place on their own. But governments tend to make lots of changes simultaneously: Salaries are doubled, enforcement increased, and governments made transparent all at the same time, making it hard to sort out which improvements are really the result of any specific policy. And even if changes are implemented one by one, it's a rare government that sets aside a group of employees or road contracts to serve as a bench mark, like the control villages in the Indonesian road study.

Perhaps the answer is that governments should become more experimental, quite literally, in how they deal with their corruption problems. Officials interested in rooting out corruption must think seriously about evaluating what does and does not work in the real world. Just as medical scientists experiment with different ways of treating human diseases, policymakers can experiment with different solutions to social problems. After all, abstract speculation can take us only so far. At some point, our economic theories must be tested in the chaos of real economies. And once we've understood which anticorruption approaches work—whether higher salaries, government transparency, stricter punishments, or all of the above—policymakers can start to work to end corruption systematically. If they do, they may just find that economics—armed with a little creativity—can make corruption a little less common.

RAYMOND FISMAN is Lambert family professor of social enterprise at Columbia Business School. EDWARD MIGUEL is associate professor of economics at the University of California, Berkeley. They are authors of *Economic Gangsters: Corruption, Violence, and the Poverty of Nations* (Princeton: Princeton University Press, 2008).

UNIT 11

Globalizing Issues

Unit Selections

Key Points to Consider

- What will be the most important global challenges facing the world in the future?

- Do you believe that the world is a better place today than it was 10 . . . 15 . . . 20 years ago?

- Who wins and who looses in a future world characterized by climate change?

- What are the international implications of the cargo that Somali pirates found when they hijacked the frigate called *Faina*?

- Will climate change and dwindling natural resources cause more violent political conflicts in the future?

Student Web Site

www.mhcls.com

Internet References

The UN Millennium Project
http://www.unmillenniumproject.org/
The 11th Hour Action.com
http://www.11thhouraction.com/
CIA Report of the National Intelligence Council's 2020 Project
http://www.cia.gov/nic/NIC_globaltrend2020.html
Commonwealth Forum on Globalization and Health
http://www.ukglobalhealth.org
Commission on Global Governance
http://www.sovereignty.net/p/gov/gganalysis.htm
Global Trends 2005 Project
http://www.csis.org/gt2005/sumreport.html
Greenpeace International
http://www.greenpeace.org/international/
HIV/AIDS
http://www.unaids.org
RealClimate
http://www.realclimate.org/

At the beginning of the twenty-first century, there was a noticeable increase in efforts to predict important changes and to understand new patterns of relationships shaping international relations. For the past ten years, the United Nations sponsored Millennium Project has been assessing the future state of the world by tracking changes in a set of 15 Global Challenges identified and updated by over 2,000 futurists, business planners, scholars, and policy advisers. They provide a framework to assess global and local prospects, and make up an interdependent system: an improvement in one challenge makes it easier to address others; deterioration in one makes it more difficult. The first Millennium Project Human Security Report, published in 2006, found that while the world is plagued with unprecedented economic, ecological and security threats, it is also wealthier, better educated, healthier, and more peaceful than ever.

© Photodisc/Getty Images

One threat to human security that most health experts agree is extremely likely to cause a global pandemic in the future is the bird flu. Since the appearance of a genetically mutated form of bird flu in Turkey at the beginning of 2006 there has been renewed concerns about the prospect of a global flu pandemic. Many experts believe that time is running out to prepare for the next pandemic and that a future bird flu pandemic is the most serious security threat facing the world because nothing else could inflict more death and disruption worldwide. Given the continued spread of HIV/AIDS, including the reoccurrence of increasing infection rates in countries such as Uganda and Thailand, who had previously managed to reduce their HIV/AIDS infection rate, and the heavy toll that the disease has already taken in large parts of the world, the threat of another global pandemic must be taken seriously.

The majority of the world's population is poor and live in regions of the world that will be hit hard by the effects of climate change and rising sea levels. Yet most of the governments in the developing world lack the human and resource capacities needed to manage future catastrophes. These conditions are one set of reasons why many futurists are now predicting that state collapse, civil war, and mass migration will be inevitable in a warming world. While military superiority may aid Americans in struggles over vital resources, it will not be able to protect Americans against the ravages of global climate change. The recent rise of piracy off the East Coast of Africa may be a preview of one type of violent behavior that is likely to increase in the future.

To date, much less agreement has been reached on the extent that global warming and dwindling natural resources are likely to combine to increase violent conflicts over land, water, and energy. However, the evidence is becoming much clearer that certain root causes of violent political conflicts such as environmental degradation and resource scarcities create the preconditions that facilitate future violence among groups. For example, in "The Coming Resource Wars," Michael T. Klare warned that global climate change and dwindling natural resources are combining to increase the likelihood of violent conflict over land, water, and energy. The inadequate capacity of poor and unstable countries to cope with the effects of climate change is likely to result in state collapse, civil war, and mass migration. While military superiority may aid Americans in struggles over vital resources, it cannot protect us against the ravages of global climate change.

Thinking Ahead

Jerome Glenn

W e have the capability to build a better future, but the way we are going about it is terribly inefficient. To improve efficiency, we need to consider the status of the whole and its parts as objectively as possible. One way to do this is to track changes in the set of 15 Global Challenges identified and updated by the Millennium Project over the past 10 years by over 2,000 futurists, business planners, scholars, and policy advisers. They provide a framework to assess global and local prospects, and make up an interdependent system: an improvement in one challenge makes it easier to address others; deterioration in one makes it more difficult.

While the world is plagued by unprecedented economic, ecological and security threats, it is also wealthier, better educated, healthier and more peaceful than ever. The first Human Security Report, published this year, found that the number of armed conflicts declined by more than 40% since the early 1990s; that international crises declined by more than 70% between 1981 and 2001; that the dollar value of major international arms transfers fell by 33% between 1990 and 2003; and that the number of refugees dropped by some 45% between 1992 and 2003. The IMF estimates that the world economy grew 4.8% in 2005, while the population grew 1.15%, increasing annual per capita income by 3.65%.

A Changing Landscape

More than one billion people (16% of the world) are connected to the internet and most may be connected within 15 years, making cyberspace an unprecedented medium for civilisation. This new distribution of the means of production in the knowledge economy is cutting through old hierarchical controls in politics, economics and finance. It is becoming a self-organising mechanism that could lead to dramatic increases in humanity's ability to invent its future.

Meanwhile, water tables are falling on every continent. Forty per cent of humanity gets its water from sources controlled by two or more countries, much agricultural land is becoming brackish, and urbanisation is increasing water demands faster than many systems can supply. Human consumption is now 23% greater than nature's capacity to regenerate or absorb our ecological footprint.

Income gaps are widening within 53 countries, representing 80% of humanity. About 2.5 billion people (40% of the world) live on $2 or less per day. Trade-led economic growth could become a disaster for poorer countries, which will not be able to compete against the growing high-tech, low-wage industrial capacities of China and India. Those countries dependent on commodity exports will fail as their resources are depleted or substitutes are adopted by importers.

Considering all of the above, business as usual will lead to disasters ranging from massive environmental and economic failures to large-scale migrations and increasing rage against what is perceived to be injustice and inequity. There is a growing hunger around the world to do what is right for our common future but, effective leadership and a detailed idea of how to act are lacking.

The Population Spiral

Meanwhile, the world's population of 6.53 billion is expected to grow to about 9 billion by 2050 before it falls rapidly due to falling fertility rates to possibly as low as 5.5 billion by 2100. This assumes no major scientific and technological breakthroughs affecting longevity over the next century—an unlikely assumption. The concepts of ageing, retirement, and health care systems are likely to have to change.

A less predictable factor influencing our future is the changing state of infectious diseases. Although it took 15 years to work out the genetic sequence of HIV, and less than a month to sequence SARS, the strategy of rapidly producing and distributing vaccines may not be able to keep up. An alternative approach is to create medicines that can give a large and fast boost to the immune system irrespective of the disease. These medicines could be stored around the world for faster local distribution, to isolate future infections and stop their spread.

The WHO reports that, after disease and hunger, violence against women is the greatest cause of death among women and notes that one in five women will be a victim of rape or attempted rape in her lifetime. Depending on the country, between 10% and 69% of women report being physically assaulted by an intimate male partner at some point in their lives. The United Nations Development Fund for Women and Amnesty International estimate that one in three women suffer some form of violence in their lifetime. About 80% of the 600,000 to 800,000 individuals trafficked each year are female, making it the "largest slave trade in history."

Just as lines of code were written to create software to do amazing things, genetic code may be written to create life to do even more amazing things, such as producing hydrogen fuel instead of oxygen from photosynthesis. Artificial organs may be constructed by depositing living cells, layer by layer, using ink-matrix printers in a manner similar to 3D prototyping. The factors that are speeding these changes along are themselves accelerating.

The possibility of technology growing beyond human control must now be taken seriously. To better manage the risk, a new internet interface is needed to make the world's scientific and technological knowledge understandable to politicians and the public.

Looking for Leadership

The world also requires a process to focus government, corporate and university scientific, engineering, and medical resources to address the 15 Global Challenges described in 2006 State of the Future. We need transinstitutional management and more serious public education through the media. Former US vice president Al Gore's film, *An Inconvenient Truth* is one example. Imagine having such movies available for all the Global Challenges. What would the world be like if those who work to improve the prospects of humanity were assisted by the many who seem not to care?

Terrorism will continue to get worse as long as the world's systems seem unjust. There is a danger that future desktop molecular and pharmaceutical manufacturing could eventually give individuals the ability to make and use weapons of mass destruction. Creating global partnerships between the rich and poor to make the world work for all, which seemed like an idealistic slogan before 9/11, may prove to be the most pragmatic policy to combat terrorism, as the possibilities increase that individuals may one day have access to formidable weapons technology. To prevent young people from being seduced by the creed of terrorism, we should begin to explore how to connect the systems of education and security in a democratic and effective way.

It has been considered ridiculous to try to achieve health and security for all. Today, it is equally ridiculous to think that an individual acting alone will not one day be able to create and use a weapon of mass destruction. The idealistic maxim that 'the welfare of all is dependent on the welfare of every one' could become a pragmatic long-range approach to countering terrorism, and preventing destructive mass migrations and other potential threats to human security. Ridiculing idealism is short-sighted, but idealism unconstrained by the rigours of realism is misleading.

JEROME GLENN is director of the Millennium Project. He has 35 years' experience in futures research with governments, corporations and international organisations. www.stateofthefuture.org.

Pirates versus Weapons Dealers

Looking for the good guys off the Somali coast.

Clemens Höges, Uwe Klussmann, and Horand Knaup

The pirates that captured the freighter *Faina* didn't know the ship was full of tanks. They also were unaware that by hijacking the vessel, they had ruined an international weapons deal that may have been illegally sending arms to Sudan.

Professionals have their standards, and they stick to their routines, regardless of their nationality or line of business. "As soon as we have entered a ship," says Sugule Ali, a Somali pirate, "we normally do what we call inspection: we search everything." When they boarded the *Faina*, Ali and his men did not have to search long before finding the freighter's valuable cargo. A T-72 combat tank, measuring a full 9.5 meters (31 feet) long, from its stern to the muzzle of its cannon, a 41-ton steel colossus, is hard to miss. There were 33 of the tanks on the two decks of the *Faina*, enough military equipment from Ukraine to fill a medium-sized military parade.

The presence of the tanks made one thing abundantly clear to Ali and his men: By hijacking the ship, they would either be very rich very soon—or dead. The *Faina* was not one of the usual targets—such as tankers, freighters and yachts—that Somali pirates have been hijacking in large numbers in recent months. Tanks are either the property of governments, or of men with a lot of dirty money and few scruples.

But then, human life means just as little to Ali and his fellow pirates—even their own. "Everyone dies only once," says Ali. Speaking via a satellite telephone, Ali told *SPIEGEL* that, before the attack, he had "no information that a ship loaded with weapons was passing through our waters." When he discovered what the ship's cargo was, he was not overly perturbed. "There is no fear" within his gang of roughly 50 men, the pirate claims.

Diplomatic Entanglements

Once they gained control of the freighter, the pirates turned it around and set course for Hobyo, one of several notorious pirate haunts on Somalia's lawless Indian Ocean coast. The first pursuer, the *USS Howard,* an American destroyer under the command of Captain Curtis Goodnight, followed a short time later.

By Friday evening of last week, the *Faina* was anchored off Hobyo and was surrounded by warships and the standoff continues this week. Meanwhile, cabinet ministers, milita officials and intelligent agents around the globe have spent da pondering the vessel's unusual cargo, diplomatic entanglemer and military options. Also on the list of concerns is the crew 21 people on board the *Faina.*

Ali's small-time gangsters, in their sneakers, have climbe up onto a world stage normally reserved for bigger players. the ensuing drama, the boundaries between the good guys ar the villains have become difficult to discern, primarily becau there may not in fact be any good guys. In this production, tl pirates are the equivalent of pickpockets who had the bad luc of stealing a mafia godfather's briefcase.

In reality, the incident is about much more than a hijackir and Ali's demand for $20 million (€ 13.8 million) in ranso money. It is also about anarchy in a failed state like Somalia, ar about the interests of the United States, Russia and the Europea Union, as it gradually takes on a new role on the world stage.

Most of all, it is about Africa's longest-lasting civil war, tl war in Sudan, which is relatively quiet at the moment but cou soon erupt into as bloody a conflict as it was before. And it about the international dealings of arms traders and possib governments that are involved.

The Pirates Spoiled the Deal

Officially, the Ukrainian T-72 tanks were designated for Keny But now there is mounting evidence that the tanks on board tl *Faina* were en route to Sudan via Kenya. If this is true, it wou be embarrassing for Ukraine and devastating for Kenya, whos president likes to portray himself as a peacemaker. At any rat it looks as though pirate Ali and his men spoiled the deal.

The pirates caught sight of the freighter on Thursday, Se 25, at about 4 P.M. It was unarmed, had no escort and was flyin the flag of the Caribbean nation of Belize. Fleeing was not a option for the Ukrainian captain, Vladmir Kolobkov, when h saw the pirates coming. At full steam ahead, the ship's Sulze diesel engine could barely push the *Faina*'s 14,000 tons throug the water at 15 knots—a bicycle's pace. The pirates' open, ligh weight attack boats were easily twice as fast.

Kolobkov also knew that he could not ram and sink th pirates' boats. Professionals bring along the right tools, an

r Somali pirates that means Kalashnikovs and RPG-7 bazoo-
s, which are designed to shoot holes into steel walls. Faced
ith such odds, an experienced captain knows not to play
e hero.

Using cables and grappling hooks, the pirates hoisted them-
lves on board. The crew—17 Ukrainians, three Russians and
e Latvian—surrendered, but not before sending out a distress
gnal, which apparently put the *USS Howard* on the hijacked
ip's trail.

There was, though, someone else who quickly realized
at a hostage crisis unprecedented in the region was taking
ape off the coast: Andrew Mwangura. A former seaman,
wangura sees himself as a social worker of sorts, as some-
e who helps seamen from around the world by providing
formation, contacting relatives and finding doctors. "Seamen
ve no lobby," he says. But in East Africa they have Mwangura
d his "Seafarer's Assistance Programme," headquartered in
ombasa, Kenya.

Ransom for Ships and Crews

the last two-and-a-half years, the offices of his program have
rned into a news center. Since 2006, more and more people
ve been kidnapped, a growing number of ships have been
tacked and higher ransoms have been demanded—and paid—
the Horn of Africa. This year, Somali pirates have attacked
ore than 60 ships in the Gulf of Aden and the Indian Ocean.
t least 10 hijacked freighters and tankers are at anchor off the
ast of Somalia. The pirates are holding their crews, roughly
0 seamen, hostage on board the vessels until their ransom
mands are met.

In this year alone, shipping companies have had to pay $30
illion (€ 20.7 million) in ransom for ships and crews, and
surance premiums have grown tenfold in some cases. The
rate gangs are already making serious inroads into the flow of
obal trade at their bottleneck near the entrance to the Red Sea.
ore than 16,000 ships pass through the area each year. The
oblem is so severe that some shipping companies are already
nsidering ordering their captains to take the long route around
frica.

Hardly anyone knows more about the pirates than Mwangura,
ho maintains a large network of confidantes and informants.
nd because no one else but Mwangura has such good connec-
ons, even in anarchic Somalia and within the pirates' clans,
any are asking for his help, including embassies, shipping
mpanies from around the world, family members of hos-
ges, and insurance companies from the financial centers of
e West.

Where Did the Tanks Come From?

wangura is tense. Many along the coast here are now nervous.
e refuses to meet in his office, because it would mean reveal-
g his address. He prefers a hotel, for reasons that soon become
ear. What Mwangura has to say about the cargo of the *Faina*
ill create problems for dangerous people.

His informants say that the tanks, after being unloaded in
Mombasa, were to be delivered to southern Sudan, where rebels
with the Sudanese People's Liberation Army (SPLA) have been
fighting for independence from the central government in
Khartoum for the last 21 years. The warring parties signed a
makeshift peace treaty three-and-a-half years ago. A referendum for the independence of the south is scheduled to take
place in 2011, but some fear it could trigger a renewed outbreak
of fighting. The southern part of the country has enormous oil
reserves, which have triggered greed. The government and the
SPLA are both using the cease-fire to rearm.

The T-72 is a typical Soviet-era shooting machine, with
unrefined technology, miserable protection for its crew and
enormous firepower. In Sudan, where much of the killing is
done with machine guns, 33 of the tanks would be a huge
factor.

Although Mwangura has no evidence to support his claims
about the clandestine deal, a spokesman for the American Fifth
Fleet, of which the *USS Howard* is a part, backs up his claims,
as do intelligence officials in Washington. Another factor supporting the notion that the tanks were bound for Sudan, not
Kenya, is the way the *Faina* was camouflaged.

Investigating the *Faina*

The trail of this special freighter, which has had various
names—the Marabou, the Loverval and the Matina—can be
found in the databases of the International Maritime Organization (IMO). The Ukrainian ship is registered in Belize, but the
official owner, a company called Waterlux AG, is registered
in Panama. But the IMO lacks even a letterbox address for
Waterlux. All it has is the address of a supposed subsidiary in
Ukraine called Tomex. Tomex does exist, and its offices are in
an elegant building in Odessa, but no one there is willing to
discuss the *Faina*.

All of this secretiveness would be unnecessary if the deal
involving the *Faina* had been normal. However, the exces-
sive caution would make sense if what Nina Karpacheva, the
ombudswoman for the Ukrainian parliament, says is true.
Karpacheva claims that the man behind the deal is Vadim A.,
a businessman from Odessa with an Israeli passport, excellent
contacts within the government bureaucracy and an unsavory
reputation as a juggler of businesses.

Both Karpacheva and Ukrainian Prime Minister Yulia
Tymoshenko are calling for an investigation of the *Faina* affair.
The fact that Tymoshenko has become involved is, perhaps,
not surprising. She has long been engaged in political battle
with President Viktor Yushchenko, whose supporters in the
Ukrainian intelligence service, the SBU, have long lined their
pockets by selling off the remains of the former Soviet arsenal
throughout the world.

The *Faina* case could also prove to be an international
embarrassment for Ukraine in other ways as well. Russia, its
more powerful neighbor, has sent the frigate *Neutrashimy* ("The
Fearless") toward Somalia because Ukraine has no ships suit-
able for such a mission. If the Russians can free the sailors and
restore calm to the Horn of Africa, they will have managed to

polish up their image in the wake of their invasion of Georgia, as well as to demonstrate who is in charge at home, in a realm that was once the Soviet Union.

Unscrupulous Dealmakers

The *Neutrashimy* is likely to face off against thousands of pirates. In addition to Sugule Ali's boats, there are at least four other large groups operating along the Horn of Africa: a band of gangsters called the Somali Marines, a group calling itself the National Volunteer Coastguard, and the Puntland Group and Marka Group.

The pirate gangs can do as they wish along the coast of Somalia, which descended into chaos and civil war after the dictator Siad Barre was overthrown in 1991. Since then, unscrupulous dealmakers from Europe and the rest of the world have taken advantage of the vacuum. Some are dumping toxic waste and possibly even nuclear waste in the ocean off Somalia. Others are illegally exploiting the Somalis' fishing grounds. Ahmedou Ould-Abdallah, the United Nations Special Envoy for Somalia, calls it "a disaster for Somalia's coast, the environment and the population." In the beginning, angry Somali fishermen wielding Kalashnikovs took matters into their own hands and drove away the foreign fishing boats.

In the process, some of them apparently noticed how easy it was to attack ships, and they soon made a business of it. Using the ransom money, they bought themselves mansions, SUV better boats and weapons. But the hijacking and ransacking ships off the Somali coast could soon come to an end.

Spurred to action by the attack on the *Faina,* the defens ministers of the EU agreed last Wednesday to a launch a joi military intervention. Under the plan three EU warships, one them from Germany, will patrol off the coast of Somalia begin ning in December. American and Russian ships will likely jo them. This concerted response will likely deter many pirate The Strait of Malacca off the Malaysian coast, once considere extremely dangerous, became virtually pirate-free after a simil alliance was formed and resolute military intervention began.

Sugule Ali, the pirate, claims that the Somalis have no choi but to take what they can. "An attack on us will not solve tl problems," he says. "There should be a joint discussion of solution to the problems in Somalia." When that happens, l says, "we will return to our old way of life and go fishing again His men, says Ali, are in fact nothing but fishermen, all of the decent people. According to Ali, they treat their prisoners we and "everyone on board is in good shape."

Vladmir Kolobkov, the *Faina*'s captain, died shortly after h ship was invaded, supposedly of heart failure. But instead throwing his body overboard, the Somalis placed the dead ca tain into a cooler so that his family can bury him—if the pow doesn't fail on board, if a solution can be found soon and if tl *Faina* makes it back to Odessa.

The Coming Resource Wars

Michael T. Klare

It's official: the era of resource wars is upon us. In a major London address, British Defense Secretary John Reid warned that global climate change and dwindling natural resources are combining to increase the likelihood of violent conflict over land, water and energy. Climate change, he indicated, "will make scarce resources, clean water, viable agricultural land even scarcer"—and this will "make the emergence of violent conflict more rather than less likely."

Although not unprecedented, Reid's prediction of an upsurge in resource conflict is significant both because of his senior rank and the vehemence of his remarks. "The blunt truth is that the lack of water and agricultural land is a significant contributory factor to the tragic conflict we see unfolding in Darfur," he declared. "We should see this as a warning sign."

Resource conflicts of this type are most likely to arise in the developing world, Reid indicated, but the more advanced and affluent countries are not likely to be spared the damaging and destabilizing effects of global climate change. With sea levels rising, water and energy becoming increasingly scarce and prime agricultural lands turning into deserts, internecine warfare over access to vital resources will become a global phenomenon.

Reid's speech, delivered at the prestigious Chatham House in London (Britain's equivalent of the Council on Foreign Relations), is but the most recent expression of a growing trend in strategic circles to view environmental and resource effects— rather than political orientation and ideology—as the most potent source of armed conflict in the decades to come. With the world population rising, global consumption rates soaring, energy supplies rapidly disappearing and climate change eradicating valuable farmland, the stage is being set for persistent and worldwide struggles over vital resources. Religious and political strife will not disappear in this scenario, but rather will be channeled into contests over valuable sources of water, food and energy.

Prior to Reid's address, the most significant expression of this outlook was a report prepared for the U.S. Department of Defense by a California-based consulting firm in October 2003. Entitled "An Abrupt Climate Change Scenario and Its Implications for United States National Security," the report warned that global climate change is more likely to result in sudden, cataclysmic environmental events than a gradual (and therefore manageable) rise in average temperatures. Such events could include a substantial increase in global sea levels, intense storms and hurricanes and continent-wide "dust bowl" effects. This would trigger pitched battles between the survivors of these effects for access to food, water, habitable land and energy supplies.

"Violence and disruption stemming from the stresses created by abrupt changes in the climate pose a different type of threat to national security than we are accustomed to today," the 2003 report noted. "Military confrontation may be triggered by a desperate need for natural resources such as energy, food and water rather than by conflicts over ideology, religion or national honor."

Until now, this mode of analysis has failed to command the attention of top American and British policymakers. For the most part, they insist that ideological and religious differences—notably, the clash between values of tolerance and democracy on one hand and extremist forms of Islam on the other—remain the main drivers of international conflict. But Reid's speech at Chatham House suggests that a major shift in strategic thinking may be under way. Environmental perils may soon dominate the world security agenda.

This shift is due in part to the growing weight of evidence pointing to a significant human role in altering the planet's basic climate systems. Recent studies showing the rapid shrinkage of the polar ice caps, the accelerated melting of North American glaciers, the increased frequency of severe hurricanes and a number of other such effects all suggest that dramatic and potentially harmful changes to the global climate have begun to occur. More importantly, they conclude that human behavior—most importantly, the burning of fossil fuels in factories, power plants, and motor vehicles—is the most likely cause of these changes. This assessment may not have yet penetrated the White House and other bastions of head-in-the-sand thinking, but it is clearly gaining ground among scientists and thoughtful analysts around the world.

For the most part, public discussion of global climate change has tended to describe its effects as an environmental problem— as a threat to safe water, arable soil, temperate forests, certain species and so on. And, of course, climate change *is* a potent threat to the environment; in fact, the greatest threat imaginable. But viewing climate change as an environmental problem fails to do justice to the magnitude of the peril it poses. As Reid's speech and the 2003 Pentagon study make clear, the greatest danger posed by global climate change is not the degradation of ecosystems *per se*, but rather the disintegration of entire human societies, producing wholesale starvation, mass migrations and recurring conflict over resources.

"As famine, disease, and weather-related disasters strike due to abrupt climate change," the Pentagon report notes, "many countries' needs will exceed their carrying capacity"—that is, their ability to provide the minimum requirements for human survival. This "will create a sense of desperation, which is likely to lead to offensive aggression" against countries with a greater stock of vital resources. "Imagine eastern European countries, struggling to feed their populations with a falling supply of food, water, and energy, eyeing Russia, whose population is already in decline, for access to its grain, minerals, and energy supply."

Similar scenarios will be replicated all across the planet, as those without the means to survivel invade or migrate to those with greater abundance—producing endless struggles between resource "haves" and "have-nots."

It is this prospect, more than anything, that worries John Reid. In particular, he expressed concern over the inadequate capacity of poor and unstable countries to cope with the effects of climate change, and the resulting risk of state collapse, civil war and mass migration. "More than 300 million people in Africa currently lack access to safe water," he observed, and "climate change will worsen this dire situation"—provoking more wars like Darfur. And even if these social disasters will occur primarily in the developing world, the wealthier countries will also be caught up in them, whether by participating in peacekeeping and humanitarian aid operations, by fending off unwanted migrants or by fighting for access to overseas supplies of food, oil, and minerals.

When reading of these nightmarish scenarios, it is easy to conjure up images of desperate, starving people killing one another with knives, staves and clubs—as was certainly often the case in the past, and could easily prove to be so again. But these scenarios also envision the use of more deadly weapons. "In this world of warring states," the 2003 Pentagon report predicted, "nuclear arms proliferation is inevitable." As oil and natural gas disappears, more and more countries will rely on nuclear power to meet their energy needs—and this "will accelerate nuclear proliferation as countries develop enrichment and reprocessing capabilities to ensure their national security."

Although speculative, these reports make one thing clear: when thinking about the calamitous effects of global climate change, we must emphasize its social and political consequences as much as its purely environmental effects. Drought, flooding and storms can kill us, and surely will—but so will wars among the survivors of these catastrophes over what remains of food, water and shelter. As Reid's comments indicate, no society, however affluent, will escape involvement in these forms of conflict.

We can respond to these predictions in one of two ways: by relying on fortifications and military force to provide some degree of advantage in the global struggle over resources, or by taking meaningful steps to reduce the risk of cataclysmic climate change.

No doubt there will be many politicians and pundits—especially in this country—who will tout the superiority of the military option, emphasizing America's preponderance of strength. By fortifying our borders and seashores to keep out unwanted migrants and by fighting around the world for needed oil supplies, it will be argued, we can maintain our privileged standard of living for longer than other countries that are less well endowed with instruments of power. Maybe so. But the grueling, inconclusive war in Iraq and the failed national response to Hurricane Katrina show just how ineffectual such instruments can be when confronted with the harsh realities of an unforgiving world. And as the 2003 Pentagon report reminds us, "constant battles over diminishing resources" will "further reduce [resources] even beyond the climatic effects."

Military superiority may provide an illusion of advantage in the coming struggles over vital resources, but it cannot protect us against the ravages of global climate change. Although we may be somewhat better off than the people in Haiti and Mexico, we, too, will suffer from storms, drought and flooding. As our overseas trading partners descend into chaos, our vital imports of food, raw materials and energy will disappear as well. True, we could establish military outposts in some of these places to ensure the continued flow of critical materials—but the ever-increasing price in blood and treasure required to pay for this will eventually exceed our means and destroy us. Ultimately, our only hope of a safe and secure future lies in substantially reducing our emissions of greenhouse gases and working with the rest of the world to slow the pace of global climate change.

MICHAEL T. KLARE is a professor of peace and world security studies at Hampshire College and the author of *Resource Wars* and *Blood and Oil*, both available in paperback from Owl Books.

Test-Your-Knowledge Form

We encourage you to photocopy and use this page as a tool to assess how the articles in *Annual Editions* expand on the information in your textbook. By reflecting on the articles you will gain enhanced text information. You can also access this useful form on a product's book support Web site at *http://www.mhcls.com*.

NAME:

DATE:

_____

TITLE AND NUMBER OF ARTICLE:

_____

BRIEFLY STATE THE MAIN IDEA OF THIS ARTICLE:

_____

LIST THREE IMPORTANT FACTS THAT THE AUTHOR USES TO SUPPORT THE MAIN IDEA:

_____

WHAT INFORMATION OR IDEAS DISCUSSED IN THIS ARTICLE ARE ALSO DISCUSSED IN YOUR TEXTBOOK OR OTHER READINGS THAT YOU HAVE DONE? LIST THE TEXTBOOK CHAPTERS AND PAGE NUMBERS:

_____

LIST ANY EXAMPLES OF BIAS OR FAULTY REASONING THAT YOU FOUND IN THE ARTICLE:

_____

LIST ANY NEW TERMS/CONCEPTS THAT WERE DISCUSSED IN THE ARTICLE, AND WRITE A SHORT DEFINITION:

We Want Your Advice

ANNUAL EDITIONS revisions depend on two major opinion sources: one is our Advisory Board, listed in the front of this volume, which works with us in scanning the thousands of articles published in the public press each year; the other is you—the person actually using the book. Please help us and the users of the next edition by completing the prepaid article rating form on this page and returning it to us. Thank you for your help!

ANNUAL EDITIONS: World Politics 09/10

ARTICLE RATING FORM

Here is an opportunity for you to have direct input into the next revision of this volume.
We would like you to rate each of the articles listed below, using the following scale:

1. **Excellent: should definitely be retained**
2. **Above average: should probably be retained**
3. **Below average: should probably be deleted**
4. **Poor: should definitely be deleted**

Your ratings will play a vital part in the next revision.
Please mail this prepaid form to us as soon as possible.
Thanks for your help!

RATING	ARTICLE	RATING	ARTICLE
_____	1. The Age of Nonpolarity: What Will Follow U.S. Dominance?	_____	19. After Iraq
_____	2. China Views Globalization: Toward a New Great-Power Politics?	_____	20. Taking Africa Seriously
_____	3. India's Path to Greatness	_____	21. The Fragmentation of Palestine
_____	4. Lulu's Brazil: A Rising Power, but Going Where?	_____	22. Carriers of Conflict
_____	5. The Power of Green	_____	23. Al Qaeda at 20 Dead or Alive?
_____	6. War in Georgia, Jitters All Around	_____	24. Toy Soldiers: The Youth Factor in the War on Terror
_____	7. The Long March to Be a Superpower	_____	25. Al-Qaeda Masters Terrorism on the Cheap
_____	8. Israeli Military Calculations towards Iran	_____	26. Three Pillars of Counterinsurgency
_____	9. Revving up the Cooperative Nonproliferation Engine	_____	27. The Boot Is Now on the Other Foot: Rwanda's Lessons from Both Sides of Insurgency
_____	10. Pakistan: It's Déjà Vu All over Again	_____	28. All Counterinsurgency Is Local
_____	11. Evolving Bioweapon Threats Require New Countermeasures	_____	29. From Great Game to Grand Bargain
_____	12. Strategy and the Search for Peace	_____	30. Running the U.N.
_____	13. In Search of Sustainable Security: Linking National Security, Human Security, and Collective Security Interests to Protect America and Our World	_____	31. The Responsibility to Protect: Meeting the Challenges
_____	14. The Petraeus Doctrine	_____	32. Unfolding Worldwide Turmoil Could Reverse Years of Prosperity
_____	15. The Transatlantic Turnaround	_____	33. The $1.4 Trillion Question
_____	16. Building on Common Ground with Russia	_____	34. How Economics Can Defeat Corruption
_____	17. Lifting the Bamboo Curtain	_____	35. Thinking Ahead
_____	18. A New Path for Latin America?	_____	36. Pirates versus Weapons Dealers
		_____	37. The Coming Resource Wars

ABOUT YOU

Name

Date

Are you a teacher? ☐ A student? ☐
Your school's name

Department

Address

City

State

Zip

School telephone #

YOUR COMMENTS ARE IMPORTANT TO US!

Please fill in the following information:
For which course did you use this book?

Did you use a text with this ANNUAL EDITION? ☐ yes ☐ no
What was the title of the text?

What are your general reactions to the Annual Editions concept?

Have you read any pertinent articles recently that you think should be included in the next edition? Explain.

Are there any articles that you feel should be replaced in the next edition? Why?

Are there any World Wide Web sites that you feel should be included in the next edition? Please annotate.

May we contact you for editorial input? ☐ yes ☐ no
May we quote your comments? ☐ yes ☐ no